COMMUNIST IDEOLOGY, LAW AND CRIME

Also By Maria Łoś

WELFARE AND JUSTICE
MULTI-DIMENSIONAL SOCIOLOGY (*co-author with A. Podgórecki*)
ASPIRATIONS AND MILIEU
ATTITUDES OF POLISH SOCIETY TOWARDS MORALITY AND LAW
(*co-author with A. Podgórecki, J. Kurczewski and J. Kwaśniewski*)

COMMUNIST IDEOLOGY, LAW AND CRIME

Maria Łoś

Associate Professor at the Department of Criminology
University of Ottawa, Canada

St. Martin's Press New York

First published in the United States of America in 1988

Printed in Hong Kong

Library of Congress Cataloging-in-Publication Data
Los, Maria.
Communist ideology, law and crime.
Bibliography: p.
Includes index.
1. Criminal justice, Administration of—Soviet Union. 2. Criminal justice, Administration of—Poland. 3. Law and socialism. I. Title.
KJC9430.L67 1987 364'.947 86-13752
ISBN 0-312-15281-7

To Krystyna Konarska-Łosiowa
a Poet

Contents

Acknowledgements

Writing this book was in many ways a lonely task. I felt at times as if I were in a state of schizophrenia having to cope with my teaching, research and everyday involvement with the problems of North America, while in the evenings returning dutyfully to the world of communist crimes and punishments.

Many people, however, helped to make this project easier. Among them, my colleagues in the Department of Criminology, University of Ottawa, deserve most sincere thanks for their support, friendship and continuing interest in my research. Dr Justin Ciale, who headed the department at that time, helped in many ways; all were appreciated.

This research has been facilitated by research assistantships financed by the Contributions Grant to the Department of Criminology from the Ministry of the Solicitor General of Canada and by a grant from the School of Graduate Studies, University of Ottawa. Ms Rebecca Volk, formerly a graduate student in the department, contributed much to this project. Her help in data collection and in editing the final manuscript was invaluable. I was also assisted by Ms Jadwiga Holenderska who helped to locate and review some Polish materials. Ms Chi Hoang typed the manuscript beautifully and patiently, understanding it so well. She, too, was a refugee, from Vietnam. Mrs Louise Clément-Côté also contributed to the typing of this book and volunteered her free time to finish it on time.

Numerous members of the Polish community in Ottawa showed genuine interest and helped in securing relevant information. Finally, my friends in Warsaw never failed to respond to my inquiries and requests with invariably selfless attitudes, loyalty and readiness to help.

My thanks go also to Mr T. M. Farmiloe of the Macmillan Press for his keen interest in my manuscript, and to Ms Ann Marangos for her contribution as the copy-editor.

While it is always those closest to us who suffer most due to the pressure of a hectic schedule. I prefer to pay my private debts in private.

M. Ł.

Note: This book was submitted to the publishers in 1984. The subsequent 'glastnost' campaign under Mikhail Gorbachev and its revelations on Soviet drug abuse and the severe crime problem have provided a rather timely postscript to this book.

Introduction

The main aim of this book is the exploration and analysis of the nature of relationships between the ideology, state and the economic organization of the USSR and Poland, on the one hand, and various forms of crime and its control, on the other. The choice of these two countries was dictated by several considerations. Since most of the existing English-language literature concentrates on the Soviet Union, I assumed that it would be interesting and illuminating to conduct a comparative analysis which would include the Soviet Union and another less explored European communist country. The comparative study undertaken was expected to result in some, if even tentative, conclusions about the necessary, or universal, consequences of the communist political and economic structure as well as more specific outcomes which may vary from one society to another within the same political camp.

Poland was an obvious choice for me since I have full command of the Polish language, familiarity with Polish criminology and sociology, as well as many years experience living, studying and teaching there. These subjective reasons for the inclusion of Poland into my analysis notwithstanding, there are many theoretical advantages of such a choice. Poland is the largest European country subordinated to the Soviet Union; it is in many ways and especially politically and militarily, a crucial country in the Soviet hemisphere. It is not surprising, then, that Poland is subject to exceptionally strong pressure and that the number of Soviet troops stationed on Polish soil is especially large. On the other hand, this country, with its 1000 years of Christianity, intense patriotic sentiment and well developed civil society rooted in democratic traditions, is historically very different from Russian society and, therefore, its response to the new order is bound to have some very unique dimensions.

I have decided to use the word 'communist' to describe the political and economic organization of the studied countries simply due to the absence of a more suitable term. 'Socialism' has too many meanings and at least some of them appear to be compatible with parliamentary democracy, which Soviet reality definitely is not. Karl Marx's idea of communism was vague and lacked the scientific discipline of some of his other concepts. It must be admitted, however, that after almost 70 years of Soviet attempts to implement Marx's vision, the ideal state of a communist deluge of goods and virtues is not going to emerge from the present dictatorial conditions. Marx's humanistic ideas notwithstanding, the 'real life communism' must be accepted as a valid unit of empirical analysis, and I have decided to use the term 'communism' in this sense with a full awareness of its controversial and imperfect nature.

I have utilized in this project various sources of published information: official criminological literature and statistics, unpublished or '*samizdat*' materials (i.e. printed underground without censorship), press reports, *émigré* publications and western academic and non-academic literature. I have cross-checked and tested every item of information in an attempt to establish its accuracy, both by comparing information coming from various sources and by evaluating the overall consistency of scattered data.

This task of reconstruction and synthesis was very different in relation to each of the studied societies. While the English and French language literature on Soviet criminal justice and crime is relatively extensive, the official Soviet publications are notoriously unreliable. Thus, despite my command of the Russian language, my reliance on Soviet literature was limited. Polish crime and its control, on the other hand, have never attracted much attention from western scholars and publishers, and there is practically no western literature on these matters. My sources, therefore, had to be located in Poland, through both official and unofficial networks of information. The unparalleled period of relaxation of censorship during the legal operation of the Solidarity Union (1980–81) resulted in a multitude of publications, still censored and restrained, but sufficiently candid and revealing to constitute an invaluable source of information. An analysis of press reports in several periodicals of those years has contributed greatly to the construction of as comprehensive a picture as was possible under the circumstances.

My research approach as well as the method of presentation of the results of my analysis is historical to the degree essential for a proper understanding of the present developments. The first part of the book introduces the Soviet and Polish recent history, with special attention being paid to the institutions and forms of control related to the criminal law. Several examples of innovative legal solutions are considered and their meanings and importance in the overall structure of ideological and economic control are illuminated. This analysis is essential to enable the reader to understand the social, political and legal dimensions of the social stratification of crime and its control, which is the subject matter of the second part of the book.

Chapter 1 and 2 give a historical overview of the development of the state and the criminal justice system in both countries. Experts in Soviet and East European studies may find little new in them, but these chapters will be of great help to readers interested in criminology, criminal law or comparative political science who do not specialize in the analysis of communist countries. My goal was to make this book equally accessible to both those readers who know a lot about communist countries and rather little about criminology and those whose interest in criminology is not supplemented by any special expertise in Soviet studies. In addition to a factual overview and a chronological presentation of major developments, the first two chapters contain some analysis of a more theoretical nature. In particular, chapter one attempts to answer some major questions about the nature of the Soviet socio-political reality and its relationship to the capitalist and feudal orders. Chapter 2, on the other hand, includes some comments and insights into the momentous developments begun by the emergence of the Solidarity Union in Poland and followed by the internal military intervention.

Chapter 3 analyses two major forms of 'popular participation' in the dispensation of justice: the inclusion of lay assessors into the adjudicating benches in ordinary courts and the social, or comrades', courts which consist solely of lay members. The historical development of these institutions in both countries, their relationship to the official ideology, as well as their shortcomings and promising aspects are scrutinized. Much attention is paid to their transformations and their changing place within the overall socio-political structure.

Chapter 4 presents the development of and multiple functions played by the laws which penalize idleness and lack of social membership, the so-called anti-parasite laws. The analysis of their history, as well as their uses and abuses is preceded by a discussion of the nature of welfare provisions and other mechanisms which deal with marginal populations. As well, the key ideological concepts of the 'right to work' and the 'duty to work' are analysed in light of the constitutions and economic realities of the Soviet Union and Poland.

Chapter 5 attempts to elucidate the role played by prisons (and to some extent psychiatric hospitals) in the overall system of control. Their utility in securing the state's political and economic goals is scrutinized, as is the use of forced labour and its relationship to the economic cycle governed by the Central Plan. Prison riots and the changing method of their supression are also discussed and interpreted.

Chapter 6 opens Part Two of the book. While the first part attempts to answer the question as to whether the state and law are withering away in these countries, the second part looks at the prospects of the withering away of crime. It begins with an analysis of crimes committed by the top political élite ('red-collar crime'). The structural place and role of this group are scrutinized and its crimes are viewed in conjunction with the nature, sources and limits of its actual power. The analysis is focused on corruption since this is one of the few forms of the abuse of power which is officially criminalized.

Chapter 7 looks at crimes committed by functionaries within the oversized state administration, the criminal justice system and retail trade. These crimes include bribery, extortion and favouritism. An analysis is offered of the socio-political mechanisms which seem to contribute to the occurrence of these types of abuse of office and which determine official reaction to them.

Chapter 8 is devoted to the examination of a variety of crimes committed by managers within the state economy as well as by private entrepreneurs and includes crimes against the Central Plan, against the principles of communist production and against state distribution of goods. In order to offer an interpretation of these offences and their means of control, this chapter also introduces a discussion of the major features and contradictions of the organization of the communist economy and the role of the criminal law in securing its functioning in conformity with ideological principles.

Chapter 9 moves down the ladder of these supposedly classless societies and analyses the nature of crimes committed by workers and peasants. Such criminal activities as employee theft, pilfering and dealing in state property, speculation and 'free unionizing' are explained within the context of the living and working conditions of these groups and their political and economic missions.

Chapter 10 focuses on female crime and its tranformations under communism. Three types of censured behaviour are scrutinized: traditional female deviance (such as prostitution), conventional crime (such as crimes against private property and violent crimes), and non-conventional, economic crime related to the violation of the rules of the new economic order. The growing participation of women in the third category of crime is explained through a reference to the transformations of the position of women within the informal and formal structures of these societies.

Chapter 11 presents a synthesis of what is known about the so-called conventional crime and deviance in the Soviet Union and Poland. Special attention is given to crimes against private property, violent crime, alcohol and drug abuse as well as juvenile delinquency. Throughout this chapter an attempt is made to test the applicability of western criminological theories to the communist reality, and new theoretical propositions are formulated.

Chapter 12 concludes this enquiry into the little known realms of the stratification of communist crime and attempts at its control. This chapter offers a comprehensive comparative analysis of the major findings. The meanings and possible explanations of similarities and differences between the two studied countries are examined, and tentative conclusions are offered as to both the nature of the 'universal' consequences of the Soviet style communist order and the scope and forms of the 'unique' adaptations and solutions generated within this dominant order.

Part One
The Withering Away of the State and Law?

Part One State and Law in ... The Withering away of the State and Law?

1 The State and Law in the Soviet Union

Has crime disappeared in communist countries? The answer is, of course, obvious. It is quite clear that crime has not vanished in Soviet style communist societies, and there are no indications that it is going to. Indeed, the last defenders of this unrealistic thesis can be found not in the East where the reality of crime has been sufficiently forceful to necessitate some shifts even in the official pronouncements, but rather, in the West.[1]

Yet, to answer the above question fully, one has to appreciate the complexity of the implicit assumptions which determine its specific sense. Thus, we have to try to answer such legitimate questions as, whether communist countries are really 'communist' and what that means. Are Marxist predictions about the eventual disappearance of crime applicable to them? What is the status of these predictions within Marxist theory? While these issues could themselves become the subject of a lengthy dissertation, the attempt here to answer them has to be limited in its scope and, therefore, serves simply as a background discussion of crime and criminal policy in the Soviet Union and Poland.

MARX: COMMUNIST PROPHECY

Marx and Engels postulate both in *The Communist Manifesto* and in their other works that law, which is always an expression of the ruling class' interests, will disappear when the victorious proletariat eventually abolishes 'the conditions for the existence of class antagonisms, and of class generally, and will thereby (abolish) its own supremacy as a class' (Marx and Engels, 1973: 30, first published in 1848). As well, crime and conflict, which are seen as resulting from the demoralizing conditions of the class society based on private property, will vanish, thereby making superfluous any permanent apparatus of coercion in the form of the army, police and corrections. Any individual conflicts which may still occur will be easily dealt with informally within the community. These developments, however, will not take place automatically because in the period immediately following the revolution, the proletariat will become a ruling class and will use its political supremacy:

> to wrest, by degrees, all capital from bourgeoisie, to centralize all instruments of production in the hands of the state, i.e., of the proletariat organized as the ruling class; and to increase the total of productive forces as rapidly as possible . . .
>
> (Marx and Engels, 1973: 30, first published in 1848)

> Between capitalist and communist society lies the period of revolutionary transformation of the one into the other. There corresponds to this also a political transformation period in which the state can be nothing but the *revolutionary dictatorship of the proletariat*.
>
> (Marx, *Critique of the Gotha Program*, 1875, reprinted in Bottomore and Rubel (eds), 1963: 261)

The first phase of communism, which emerges from capitalist society and is still 'stamped with its birth-marks' is referred to as a socialist or workers' state. While Marx never develops a full blueprint of its political and economic organization, he often stresses that class struggle will continue at this stage and, therefore, a strong, centralized state will be needed to control and coerce the defeated capitalist class. Workers will enjoy equality, but it will still be based on a bourgeois definition of rights, which ignores individual, physical and mental differences between workers and rather recognizes that 'the right of the producers is *proportional* to the labour they supply' (Marx, 1875, reprinted in Bottomore and Rubel (eds), 1963: 263). In other words, even if it recognizes no class differences, because everybody belongs to the working class, this definition still discriminates against those individuals whose productive capacities are somewhat limited. Yet, according to Marx, the very idea of formalized rights has an inevitable aspect of inequality, since it applies equal standards to unequal individuals. Thus, the ultimate, communist society will not only abolish law and the state apparatus, but it will also do away with the very concept of individual rights. At this stage, the society will no longer need those artificial formulae which impose on people some external standards and rules of discipline and distribution. Rather, members of such a society will spontaneously contribute to the production of common wealth and will share in it in a harmonious way. No external body or idea will be needed to organize their social existence:

> In the higher phase of communist society, when the enslaving subordination of the individual to the division of labour, and with it the antithesis between mental and physical labour, has vanished; when labour is no longer merely a means of life but has become life's principal need; when the productive forces have also increased with the all-round development of the individual, and all the springs of cooperative wealth flow more abundantly – only then will it be possible completely to transcend the narrow outlook of bourgeois right, and only then will society be able to inscribe on its banners: From each according to his ability, to each according to his needs! (Marx, *Critique of the Gotha Program*, 1875, reprinted in Bottomore and Rubel (eds), 1963: 263)

In light of such an idealistic definition of the ultimate stage of communist society, there should be no difficulty in answering the question whether the Soviet Union fulfils the criteria of advanced communism. Quite obviously, it does not. Nevertheless, there remain other important questions which may prove to be much more difficult to answer. For example, has the Soviet Union been engaged at all in building communism during the past 65 years? Is it still at the early stage which calls for a centralized, coercive dictatorship of the proletariat? Or, has it been irrevocably diverted from the path towards communism by Stalin? By Lenin? By international pressure? By a specific conjunction of unique and unpredictable circumstances? Is it, finally, as many new leftist groups would claim, a state capitalism based on the bureaucratic class monopoly over the economy, resulting from a 'betrayal' of the revolution and the regressive development into the highest form of capitalism, namely the absolute monopoly capitalism?

LENIN: REVOLUTIONARY DICTATORSHIP AND REVOLUTIONARY LAW

Any attempt to search for answers to the above questions has to start with a recollection of the early days of the revolutionary period in Russia and specifically the ideas of its chief figure, Vladimir Ilyich Ulianov, better known by his adopted name of Lenin. Lenin's ideological position was formed long before the Soviet revolution. In *What Is To Be Done*, published in 1902, he translates Marx's major ideas into a practical revolutionary programme. He did indeed follow this programme when years later he decided that the sudden outburst of dissatisfaction by the Russian people in 1917 could be transformed into a Marxist revolution. Essentially, Lenin's revolutionary theory rested on the principle of a strong party. He believed that the socialist ideology, developed by Marx and Engels who themselves belonged to the bourgeois intelligentsia, had to be applied faithfully and precisely, without any concessions to the spontaneous tendencies of the working people. For Lenin, '. . . the spontaneous labour movement was pure and simple trade unionism . . . and trade unionism meant the ideological subordination of the workers to the bourgeoisie' (Lenin, 1973c: 58, first published in 1902). The ideology had to come from the educated circles since, as he points out in his influential pamphlet, 'there can be no talk of an independent ideology being developed by the masses of the workers in the process of their movement' (Lenin, 1973c: 57). Under autocracy, the persistent struggle towards a successful revolution could only be carried on by a small, core group of professional revolutionaries, supported, of course, by the organized masses. Effective action by a broad workers' organization would not be feasible because it could not achieve the degree of secrecy and efficiency required in a struggle against the repressive government. It was essential, therefore, 'to concentrate all secret functions in the hands of as small a number of professional revolutionaries as possible' (Lenin, 1973c: 59). Within this core group, strict rules of democracy and mutual confidence would prevail, and the masses of supporters working towards the same cause would have to accept the superiority of such an organization and follow its example of 'true comradeship'. While Lenin was aware of the dangers of such an élitist organization, he strongly believed that the oppressive conditions under which the pre-revolutionary work would have to be conducted justified the extraordinary measures of secrecy and centralization by protecting the movement from constant interference and harassment by gendarmes.

Later, in *State and Revolution*, completed in 1917, Lenin elaborates further the basic scheme of the workers' take-over, warning that strong mechanisms of suppression would be necessary during the transition from capitalism to communism. In Lenin's words:

> The dictatorship of the proletariat will produce a series of restrictions of liberty in the case of the oppressors, exploiters and capitalists. We must crush them in order to free humanity from wage-slavery; their resistance must be broken by force. It is clear that where there is

suppression there must also be violence, and there cannot be liberty or democracy . . . (Lenin, 1973b: 63, first published in 1917)

Nevertheless, Lenin insisted that the suppression of the exploiters could be achieved through 'the simple organization of the armed masses' (Lenin, 1973b: 64), without the special machinery of coercion. Once this period of transition was over, even the reformed, transitional state no longer would be necessary. Rather, without classes to suppress, the state would peacefully wither away. With respect to the future of crime and personal deviations, Lenin's views were equally unambiguous:

> We are not utopians, and we do not in the least deny the possibility and inevitability of excesses by individual persons, and equally the need to suppress such excesses. But in the first place, for this no special machine, no special instrument of repression is needed. This will be done by the armed nation itself. . . . And, secondly, we know that the fundamental social cause of excesses which violate the rules of social life is the exploitation of the masses, their want and the poverty. With the removal of this chief cause, excesses will inevitably begin to 'wither away'. We do not know how quickly and in what stages, but we know that they will be withering away.
> (Lenin, 1973b: 64, first published in 1917)

Despite this confidence, the exact way in which the final ideal of total happiness and social harmony would be achieved was not clear even to Lenin himself: 'By what stages, by means of what practical measures humanity will proceed to this higher aim – this we do not and cannot know' (Lenin, 1973b: 66, first published in 1917).

In short, Lenin tried to preserve the integrity and the fundamental sense of Marxist theory and showed an unqualified confidence in the superiority and practicability of the communist prophecy. However, in his attempt to adjust the theory to the concrete historical conditions, he did introduce some new and controversial elements which may be seen as not fully consistent with the spirit of Marxist philosophy. Primary among these was his belief that the socialist revolutionary ideology and the leadership had to be provided by the bourgeois intelligentsia, suggesting that he rejected the central Marxist thesis which maintains that ideas originate from fundamental class interests and the material conditions of production.

Another distortion of Marxist theory can be found in Lenin's radical belief that the socialist revolution in Russia could follow immediately after the bourgeois revolution despite the absence of such necessary preconditions as a fully developed working class as well as capitalist economic relations and material means of production. While no faithful reader of Marx can accept that the conditions in Russia in 1917 were actually ripe for a proletarian revolution, it must be noted that any practical application of a theory necessitates some compromises, reformulations and adjustments. These Lenin provided with rational explanations for each of his unorthodox changes in his attempt to integrate them into the main body of Marxist ideology. Finally, it must be remembered that:

> the writings of Marx and Engels provided Lenin only scant guidelines to follow in constructing a socialist state. Marx was foremost a social critic, not an architect of the new economic and political order that he predicted. (Smith, 1980: 111)

The February Revolution of 1917, which brought about the collapse of the monarchy, found Lenin in exile in Switzerland and neither he nor the Bolshevik underground committee played any role in these events. It was a spontaneous, and practically non-violent outburst. In addition to the abdication of Tsar Nicholas II, the revolution resulted in the establishment of the Provisional Government as well as the Soviet (People's Council) which represented the workers and soldiers. It was a dual control of power, shared by conservative and moderately leftist elements. Factory committees, elected by the workers, essentially adopted the role of trade unions. 'The program of the new regime, approved by the Soviet, provided for a full amnesty, broad civil liberties, and a complete legal equality of all. Trade unions and strikes were declared legal' (Curtiss, 1973: 88).

The Mensheviks, strongly involved in the creation of the Soviets, supported the dual power arrangement and accepted the legitimacy of the Provisional Government, realizing that the workers were neither ready nor willing to take over the full responsibility for the country. The Bolsheviks (led by Stalin and Kamenev) held basically the same position, but they were weak, and, in contradistinction to the Mensheviks, did not play any role in the developments following the successful insurrection of February 1917. This situation changed, however, when Lenin, who had arrived in Petrograd in April, announced that the bourgeois revolution, which had brought about the shared participation of power by the bourgeoisie, soldiers and workers, had, in fact, created a unique opportunity for an immediate revolution which would establish the absolute rule of the proletariat and peasantry.

(His inclusion of the peasantry in his vision of the socialist state was understandable given the fact that workers constituted a tiny minority in the predominately rural Russia.) Lenin was immediately supported by Lev Trotsky who advocated 'permanent revolution' meaning that 'the socialist and bourgeois revolution should be telescoped into one – with the socialist revolution beginning as soon as the bourgeois revolution had taken place' (Schapiro, 1977: 33).

The Bolsheviks were rapidly gaining strength, due primarily to their superior organization, discipline and own military force – the Red Guard. They had a clear goal and no moral scruples: 'We say that our morality is wholly subordinated to the interests of the class struggle of the proletariat. We deduce our morality from the facts and needs of the class struggle of the proletariat' (Lenin, 1973a: 66, from a speech delivered in 1920).

They amassed considerable funds which they used mainly to provide propaganda to the army. Substantial sums of money came from armed hold-ups and robberies (Chalidze, 1977: 21–4) as well as, most probably, from German sources[2] at a time when Lenin postulated that the masses should not support the national cause in World War I. Lenin defended his position arguing that since wars served the interests of imperialists, the masses should be primarily concerned with the revolution. In August 1917, the Sixth Congress of the Bolshevik Party voted to replace the old slogan 'all power to the Soviets' (i.e. people's councils) with one which called for the seizure of power by the 'armed people' (Schapiro, 1977: 34–5). This new formula was endorsed by the Soviets.

Lenin was pressing for an armed insurrection despite some opposition inside his own party. The protests of those who saw the dangers of such an action were labelled as criminal. Lenin demanded that the dissenters be expelled from the party, maintaining that 'there would be either a dictatorship of the Right or of the Left, and that the Party should not be guided solely by the feelings of the masses, who were inclined to waver from one side to the other' (Curtiss, 1973: 96). The weakness of the Provisional Government coupled with the widespread discontent among the soldiers, workers and peasants ensured a facile victory for the Bolsheviks. The Winter Palace fell quickly and the change of power occurred in the rest of the country.

Despite opposition by the moderate socialists, the Mensheviks, and the Socialist Revolutionaries, the Bolsheviks, with overwhelming support by the army, were able to establish their rule throughout Russia and set up an all-Bolshevik Council of People's Commissars, with Lenin as its president. To cope with 'secret enemies of the regime' and 'disorderly mobs' an All-Russian Extraordinary Commission for Combating Counter-Revolution and Sabotage was established, whose name, abbreviated to *Cheka*, became a symbol of ruthlessness and terror 'dreaded throughout Russia' (Curtiss, 1973: 99; Heller, 1979; Leggett, 1975 and 1981). As a virtually autonomous and extra-legal body, Cheka terrorized the country with its widespread and totally arbitrary application of arrests, torture and executions. In addition to Cheka a network of revolutionary tribunals was introduced to process political cases, while a system of new 'people's courts' was set up to deal with ordinary crimes.

These revolutionary tribunals were to be guided solely by the 'revolutionary consciousness', without any formalized legal codes or procedures. They sentenced to death thousands of politically inconvenient people. Many more executions were carried out directly by Cheka, without reference to the revolutionary tribunals (see, e.g., Juviler, 1976: 24–5). The people's courts, on the other hand, were initially instructed by Lenin to apply pre-revolutionary law, but to interpret it in a way consistent with their socialist consciousness. Yet, in November 1918, a special act banned old legal codes and the people's courts were directed to apply new communist decrees as well as their own socialist judgement:

> The main tendency was to elevate consciousness, loyalty to the Revolution and Bolshevik discipline above any concept of law as such. Revolutionary law was seen as a system of decrees designed to suppress class enemies and to facilitate the construction and initial functioning of socialist institutions. It would wither away once the whole country had become truly Bolshevik. (Kamenka, 1970: 315)

This new legal direction was short-lived, however, and in 1921–22, new codes were drafted which were essentially modelled after the old Russian and West European laws (Hazard, 1978: 637). As well, a new court system was introduced which has been preserved in similar form to this day. Needless to say, these new legislations were not accepted by all. Strong opposition was levelled by a very influential jurist – former judge E. P. Pashukanis – and a group of his followers. The judge claimed that new interpretations of old legal formulae would not alter their bourgeois nature and were thereby inconsistent with Marxist teaching. Pashukanis insisted that a new, flexible law should be devised which would best assist the process of its own gradual withering away. He actually drafted new codes which were consistent with his theory, but they were considered too radical, both by other lawyers and by the political leaders of the day. He claimed that law was an essentially market phenomenon required in order to maintain the maximum stability and continuity of economic relations. The revolution and the radical socio-economic transformations in Russia necessitated in his opinion a transitory system of regulations which would help to administer the new economy and would stress the vertical relations of command and subordination in order to facilitate orderly construction of socialism. Due to his strong position in the party Pashukanis remained very influential until 1937. Even though his theory was never fully accepted and implemented, his theoretical justification of the subordination of the law to the party was politically very convenient, and he did succeed in suppressing criminological studies as well as the teaching of civil law at Moscow University (Kamenka, 1970: 317). Pashukanis was finally ousted when his views could no longer be seen as compatible with Stalin's doctrine of the strong, coercive state. It was resolved that the old form of the law could be radically changed by the very fact that it acquired completely new content under the new social conditions (Hazard, 1978: 641).

While Lenin's legal education made him sensitive to the questions of law and legal order, when faced with the rampant crime and general chaos of the civil war, he clearly preferred more traditional tools of legal control over those vague and flexible legal constructs proposed by Pashukanis. Lenin's main problem, however, stemmed from the fact that he imposed his revolution on a population unwilling to share his enthusiasm for the Marxist prophecy. In short, there was no genuine support for the Bolsheviks throughout the country, a fact which the results of the elections to the Constitutional Assembly on 25 November 1917 aptly proved. In this first, and last, free election in Soviet Russia, the Bolsheviks received less than one-quarter of the 41 million votes recorded. The Assembly was allowed to meet only once under a guard of heavily armed troops before being dissolved by the Bolshevik Central Executive Committee. What followed was a turbulent and exhausting civil war. Despite the firm discipline and the strength of the Red Army, the credibility of the Bolsheviks was dwindling and, with it, the tendency to treat any opposition as counter-revolutionary was intensified. During the period of civil war, the Bolsheviks outlawed all opposition parties, including socialist ones, and strictly banned any factions within the Communist Party itself. Lenin denounced democracy as an interference with the specific logic of a planned economy and the general construction of communism. Numerous members of non-Bolshevik parties were arrested, marking the beginning of an operation which stretched out over many years and which was designed to 'clean out, conscientiously, socialists of every other stripe from Moscow, Petrograd, the ports, the industrial centres, and, later on, the outlying provinces as well' (Solzhenitsyn, 1974: 35):

> There was justice in the priorities of destruction, however: in 1920 they were all offered the chance to renounce in writing their parties and party ideologies. Some declined – and they, naturally, came up first for annihilation. Others signed such renunciations, and thereby added a few years to their lifetimes. But their turn, too, came implacably, and their heads rolled implacably from their shoulders (p. 36). [In 1922 Cheka] was called on to carry out a 'church revolution' – to remove the existing leadership and replace it with one which would have only one ear turned to heaven and the other to the Lublyanka[3] . . . metropolitans and bishops were arrested . . . monks and nuns, whose black habits had been a distinctive feature of Old Russian life, were intensively rounded up on every hand, placed under arrest, and sent into exile. They arrested and sentenced active laymen. The circles kept getting bigger, as they raked in ordinary believers as well. (Solzhenitsyn, 1974: 35–6)

The popular hopes and expectations were thus totally frustrated and 'the bulk of the working class, not to speak of the peasantry, unmistakably turned against the Bolsheviks' (Deutscher, 1973: 105). And so, as Deutscher indicates, the dictatorship of the proletariat came to represent at best the idea of the class, but not the class itself. Trotsky, who relied primarily on the army, went so far as to advocate the political incapacitation of trade unions, charging that they placed the workers' rights to elect representatives above the party, 'as if the party were not entitled to assert its dictatorship even if that dictatorship temporarily clashed with the passing moods of the workers' democracy' (from Trotsky's speech to the Tenth Congress in March 1921, quoted here after Deutscher, 1973: 107).

In the eyes of the leading communists totalitarianism became the only alternative to the loss of power, or, as they called it, the counter-revolution. The working class, exhausted by the revolutionary eruption and pauperized by the years of civil war, was not capable of protesting. The famine of 1920–21, together with the violence of World War I and the civil war, caused the death of 14 million civilians (in addition to the 2 million military deaths) (Lorimer, 1946: 41–3).

Seeing his grandiose plans in ruins, Lenin decided to fight for the support of the peasants 'whose resentment had been aroused by the fact that, while some land had been given to them with one hand, its produce had been forcibly confiscated with the other' (Schapiro, 1977: 47):

> From January 1919 on, food requisitioning was organized and food-collecting detachments were set up. They encountered resistence everywhere in the rural areas, sometimes stubborn and passive, sometimes violent. The suppression of this opposition gave rise to an abundant flood of arrests during the course of the next two years, not counting those who were shot on the spot.
>
> (Solzhenitsyn, 1974: 32)

Lenin's New Economic Policy (NEP), introduced in 1921, was designed to counter the disastrous effects of his rigid policy of total centralization and nationalization of the economy. It created some room for the 'private sector' through the abolition of the forcible requisitioning of agricultural products from the peasantry and the introduction of a fixed rate of taxation of the peasants, accompanied by the political rehabilitation of private farming and commerce, which enabled the peasants to sell their agricultural products. It was an unorthodox move for a follower of Marx, but Lenin realized that it was his last chance to revitalize the devastated agriculture. 'In practice, the desperate need for free exchange of goods was such that, once trade of any kind was legalized, it grew like a snowball and swept away restrictions' (Nove, 1978: 84).

STALIN: POST-REVOLUTIONARY DICTATORSHIP AND LAWLESSNESS

Lenin's new policy was not able to stimulate the sufficient accumulation of capital necessary for the development of heavy industry and the creation of a real industrial proletariat. This problem was to become the major concern of Iosif Vissarionovich Stalin, who essentially ran the party since his appointment to the post of General Secretary of the Central Committee in 1922 and totally dominated the Politburo after Lenin's death in 1924. He responded to the challenge by undertaking the gigantic project of rapid industrialization and the compulsory collectivization of agriculture, aimed at a total elimination of any private enterprise and uncontrolled initiative. The country was terrorized by the utterly unrealistic goals of the Five Year Plan and the bloody hunt for 'kulaks' and other 'class enemies', in which tens of millions of people perished through executions, deportation to concentration camps and remote regions or deprivation of any means of existence. Famine, fear and demoralization reigned throughout the country.

Stalin's main rivals – Trotsky and his followers – were banished early in 1928. Trotsky was eventually murdered by Stalin's agents in 1940. Although Stalin adhered quite faithfully to most of Trotsky's ideas (such as rapid industrialization, the restriction of trade unions and the collectivization of peasants), he did so in a singularly cynical and ruthless way (see, for example, Conquest, 1973).

During these years of repression and terror, Stalin relied heavily on the secret police whose formal structure underwent several transformations. Even before Lenin's death, Cheka was replaced by the State Political Administration (GPU) which became known for its secret trials and its network of Northern Camps of Special Purpose. It was so well hated for its barbaric methods that, in 1934, Stalin decided to abolish the GPU and create a new agency whose powers were to be more limited. This new agency, the People's Commissariat for Internal Affairs (NKVD), extended its power very quickly and resulted in more terror than ever before. It was assisted by three-man boards from the Ministry of Internal Affairs (MVD) which were empowered to sentence people in absentia to labour camps without a hearing, without the right of counsel and without appeal. They also carried out numerous secret executions. These special boards were not guided by criminal law, but by various political enactments and secret decisions, one of the best known being a 1934 statute which introduced a category of 'socially dangerous' persons to the Soviet legal vocabulary. Anyone found to be socially dangerous was 'eligible' for banishment up to five years in a remote area or in the concentration camps of the rapidly expanding empire of the Gulag[4] (see Schapiro, 1977: 146; Hazard, 1968: 68–9). In this way, millions of citizens were transformed into a huge and very economically important prison labour force, organized by and subordinated to the security police, whose political omnipotence was thus reinforced (Smith, 1980: 112; see also Chapter 5 here for more elaborate discussion).

In the area of legal justice, Stalin's initiative was no less authoritarian. The Stalinist legal doctrine, developed by Vyshinski, who was the Procurator (Prosecutor) General and a leading legal theoretician, redefined law as a key element of socialist construction:

> Having once been dismissed as a bourgeois institution, law was converted by Stalin into an instrument of party dictatorship. Its

> function was to create a certain amount of regulation and predictability in routine social affairs and, above all, to invest the decrees of the Soviet state with that magic aura of impartiality and impersonality which the law provides simply by being 'the law'.... Stalin, in line with his coercive interests and inclinations argued by Hegelian dialectic that, before the state and law could wither away, they must reach their greatest peak of development.
>
> (Kamenka, 1970: 313)

It must also be remembered that, in his speech to the Communist Party in 1930, Stalin declared that there were no prospects for the withering away of the state in the foreseeable future but, rather, there existed an urgent need to build a strong and authoritative state. For him the survival of communism in a country surrounded by the hostile capitalist world could only be achieved through the uncurbed development of the centralized and mighty state machinery.

Stalin's unprecedented reign of terror sought to achieve not only the consolidation of his personal rule within the country, but also within the party itself. It culminated in the Great Purge of 1936–38 (see, for example, Conquest, 1973). In the first of the famous public trials, 16 close collaborators of Stalin were charged with treason and executed. This was followed by the Trial of Seventeen charged with plotting the overthrow of the Soviet regime with the aid of foreign powers. Of the accused 13 were executed; 4 received long prison terms. Soon after, 8 prominent generals of the Red Army were executed for espionage. In 1937 Yezhov was appointed head of the NKVD and the terror was escalated even further. As Khrushchev revealed later in his famous 'secret speech' 70 per cent of 139 members and candidates of the party's Central Committee elected at the 17th Congress were arrested and shot (Khrushchev, 1973: 147):

> The purge swept out in ever-widening circles and resulted in wholesale removals and arrests of leading officials in the union republics, secretaries of the Party, Komsomol, and trade-union apparatus, heads of industrial trust and enterprises, Comintern functionaries and foreign communists, and leading writers, scholars, engineers, and scientists. The arrest of an important figure was followed by the seizure of the entourage which surrounded him. The apprehension of members of the entourage led to the imprisonment of their friends and acquaintances. The endless chain of involvements and associations threatened to encompass the entire strata of Soviet society.... Under

the zealous and ruthless ministration of NKVD examiners, millions of innocents were transformed into traitors, terrorists and enemies of the people. (Fainsod, 1973: 142)

The final phase of the Great Purge in the late 1930s involved, predictably, the 'purging of the purgers':

> The prisons began to fill with former NKVD examiners; many prisoners who had been tortured by these same examiners had the welcome experience of greeting their former tormentors as cellmates in prisons and forced labour camps. (Fainsod, 1973: 143)

Nevertheless, even with the tasks of the Great Purge completed, the monster of the Gulag Archipelago continued to grow as did the paranoia of the Dictator. There seems to be much truth in Fainsod's observation that '[t]he ultimate hazard of terror as a system of power is that it ends by terrorizing the master as well as the slave' (Fainsod, 1973: 144). Nobody was safe under Stalin's rule, no ethnic group, no profession, no age category. Indeed, it was the unpredictability and irrationality of the terror which was essential for its efficiency:

> The entire operation was designed to strike fear into the hearts of those who remained and thus to silence them, lest they will be next. Some of the effectiveness of the system would be lost if it were not arbitrary, that is, if one could predict where its hand would fall. Apparently, it is in popular insecurity that the regime's security has been thought to lie. (Hazard, 1968: 69)

Stalin's first Five Year Plan, which began in 1929, brought a visible deterioration of the working and living conditions of the workers due to the soaring inflation, overcrowded housing conditions in unprepared cities, and the abolition of the autonomy of trade unions. The functions of the trade unions became very narrowly defined, strikes and all other forms of collective bargaining were forbidden, and the Central Committee declared that 'there could be no antagonism between state managers and the workmen because the manager was representative of the state, and the state was the creature of the workmen' (Hazard, 1968: 60). The whole social structure was forcibly reconstructed to serve the aims of the gigantic industrial expansion, the collectivization of agriculture, and the development of the totalitarian machinery of control and discipline.

AFTER STALIN: BUREAUCRATIZED PARTY DICTATORSHIP AND 'SOCIALIST LEGALITY'

Upon Stalin's death in 1953, after a short period of 'collective leadership', Nikita Sergeevich Khrushchev took over the office of General Secretary of the Communist Party, and in 1958 he acquired the post of Prime Minister as well, in a fashion similar to Stalin before him. Khrushchev denounced Stalin's 'cult of personality' and the terror and abuses of Stalin's era. Beria, Stalin's close associate and the head of the secret police and national security, was shot along with other high security officials within a few months after Stalin's death.

Khrushchev's reforms aimed at advancing the power of the party which had been weakened by Stalin's dictatorial style. Moreover, he substantially curtailed security measures, the arbitrary powers of the secret police and other security organizations. His act of amnesty brought home large numbers of individuals who were languishing in concentration camps; many of those who had died in the camps or had been executed were publicly rehabilitated.

With respect to agriculture, Khrushchev publicly revealed that Stalin's policies had completely devastated its expansion. As a result, he introduced new measures and incentives, while imposing on the kolkhozes production objectives which were totally unrealistic under the conditions created by his predecessor. 'Khrushchev pressed campaigns upon the farms using for this purpose the party machine, which interfered with little or no regard for local conditions, and did great damage' (Nove, 1978: 363).

Despite the rather mixed results of his economic policies and the increased use of the party apparatus to suppress and control the society, Khrushchev announced, at the Twenty-Second Party Congress in 1961, that the Soviet Union had finally entered the stage of building communism, where the class struggle was no longer present, and where the transitory form of the state, i.e. the dictatorship of the proletariat, was no longer needed. He did not, however, intend to do away with the state; quite the contrary, he supported the idea of a strong state, but re-labelled it a 'state of all the people'. Analogically, the party was to change in nature from the 'vanguard of the proletariat' to the 'vanguard of the Soviet people'. The governmental functions were to be gradually transferred to 'public organizations' which, in turn, would represent the communist society as a whole. Naturally, the Communist Party would be the most important among them, in its role of organizer and controller of all areas of social and economic life. As a result, 'during the early 1960s, the party assumed closer control of industry and agriculture and the trend seem[ed] to be for the party to become everything that the government used to be' (Daniels, 1973: 160–1).

With respect to the legal order, Khrushchev propagated the notion of 'socialist legality' by emphasizing due process and the protection of citizens' rights. He fervently condemned secret trials, trials *in absentia*, principles of collective responsibility, and other extreme abuses of legality which had been part of both legal theory and practice under Stalin. The NKVD and the Special Boards were abolished, and military courts previously extensively used against political 'offenders', were deprived of jurisdiction over civilians (except in espionage cases). A new secret police agency was launched by Khrushchev, formally called the Committee of State Security and commonly known as the KGB (see Barron 1974, 1983). It was, in theory, subordinated to the Council of Ministers and, in practice, to the party; it was also submitted to some forms of control by the Procuracy (Prosecutor General). In the area of conventional crime, strong attempts were made to depoliticize and de-Stalinize the criminal justice system and to limit its arbitrariness and repressiveness:

> Between 1953 and 1956 several less serious offences ceased to be considered crimes, and were treated as lesser infractions or not punished at all. Parole again became possible. Penalties for petty pilfering of state and public property fell from draconian seven to ten years to more reasonable penalties from six months' 'correctional labor' without confinement to three months' confinement for first offences. (Juviler, 1976: 71; see also Juviler, 1974: 23–4)

This was, however, a short-lived trend, and the process of liberalization was sharply reversed in the late 1950s. For example, antiparasite laws were passed, which did not require any special legal procedure for condemning people for 2 to 5 years of compulsory labour in exile. They were officially designed to strengthen the socialist work ethic and discipline and to allow communities to participate in the dispensation of justice (the development of anti-parasite laws will be discussed later in Chapter 4). They were part of the 'popularization of justice' package which Khrushchev attempted to implement despite some opposition on the part of legal experts and political hard-liners. (It is interesting to note that the 'popularization' policy also included visiting court sessions, comrades' courts and voluntary para-police detachments. For more detail see Juviler, 1976: 70–82; Juviler, 1974: 24–35; and Chapter 3 here). This resurgence of 'legal utopianism', consistent with Marxist ideology, can be partially explained by Khrushchev's personality and social background:

> Khrushchev, a poorly educated, blustery man from a small farming and mining village in the Ukraine, never fully mastered the controls of the complex bureaucracies that dominated the Soviet system. He distrusted bureaucracies and bureaucrats and turned to the people for support. In order to stem crime, he urged housing units, factories and shops to resuscitate comrades' courts and other informal tribunals. Voluntary citizens' brigades patrolled the streets to maintain law and order. As if to symbolize the decentralization of legal administration, Khrushchev abolished the All-Union Ministry of Justice, leaving only the 15 republic ministries. (Smith, 1980: 113–14)

Despite the fact that this 'popularization' campaign was in clear contradiction to his endorsement of due process and legality, Khrushchev could not comprehend why so much disorder and confusion were caused by his progressive approach. Eventually, he responded to his critics by introducing a totally new policy of stern measures and punishments. This party programme, passed in 1961, 'placed in the distant future the cultural and material development that would permit the regime to replace criminal punishment with measures of public influence and education' (Juviler, 1974: 35). Under the major revision of Soviet criminal law, many new offences were formulated, such as the failure to report any preparation or commission of serious crimes against the state, criminal negligence, causing damage to farm machinery, or false reporting on plan fulfilment. Conditions for parole were made stricter and a category of 'especially dangerous recidivists' was created (Juviler, 1976: 83). Penalties were increased for numerous offences and the use of capital punishment was drastically extended. According to Juviler, in the early 1960s, some 700 to 1000 offenders were shot every year on various criminal charges (Juviler, 1976: 84):

> Death by shooting for ten other newly listed crimes and six listed ones, and other more severe penalties, were prescribed to protect law enforcers, camp authorities, and cooperative inmates from violence or resistance, females from rape, and the state from such economic crimes as large scale theft, currency violations and bribery.
> (Juviler, 1974: 37)

It was not until Khrushchev's fall in 1964 that another attempt at a collective leadership was undertaken with Brezhnev and Kosygin as the top representatives of the party and government. When, however, Brezhnev was given the additional post of State President in 1977, it was quite clear that he not only attempted, but in fact acquired a virtual monopoly of power in the Soviet Union. Brezhnev carefully preserved the totalitarian power of the Communist Party as well as the dictatorial power of its General Secretary. Writing in 1977, Schapiro expressed this view of the Soviet political system, then still under Brezhnev's rule:

> In two respects the formulation of the policy of the party and the enforcement of that policy on the state machine has remained unchanged since the early years of Soviet power. In the first place, all initiative comes from above, from the leaders, and in the last resort from one leader, the General Secretary. . . . Secondly and for the same reason, the influence which party opinion can exercise on policy is strictly limited. . . . The apparatus can silence unwelcome criticism, it can curtail debate, and it can sidestep responsible opinion, because in the last resort the livelihood and position of every critic and of everyone who voices his opinion depends on it.
>
> (Schapiro, 1977: 78)

Brezhnev undertook the task of modernizing the Soviet administration, industry, and above all, its military strength. He emphasized the need for realism, rationality and the participation of experts in policy making in general, and in the area of criminal justice in particular. 'It was a system run by cautious and conservative men who rose through various massive bureaucratic organizations and felt most comfortable administering policy through them' (Smith, 1980: 114). The task of fighting crime became a very important function of the state, the fulfilment of which required well-developed bureaucratic organization, expertise and strong management. Brezhnev gradually neutralized the 'popular' institutions introduced by his predecessor by co-opting them from above and integrating them into the state's struggle against crime (Sharlet, 1978: 323). In Sharlet's opinion:

> . . . gone is the Khrushchevian spontaneity and enthusiasm, the publicly proclaimed significance of peer pressure, and the ideological rhetoric on the gradual devolution of certain state functions to organizations of 'social state government' which would serve as classrooms in the education of the 'new Soviet man'.
>
> (Sharlet, 1978: 223)

Both, Brezhnev' successor Yuri Andropov, the former head of the KGB for fifteen years, and Konstantin Chernenko who succeeded Andropov in 1984 have upheld this reliance on the centralized control apparatus to maintain at least appearances of order. Despite the absence of the physical terror of the intensity practised by Stalin, to this day terror has continued to be an effective means of securing the obedience of the Soviet people. It is, however, a more sophisticated, quiet form of terror, backed by a totalitarian system of ideological, cultural, educational and economic institutions, all of which skillfully use political criteria in their routine application of rewards and punishments. Nevertheless, some remnants of overt terror remain, the best examples of which are the vast network of labour camps (see, Chapter 5 here) and the pervasive presence of the world's most powerful secret police force. In short, there is no doubt that fear continues to reign throughout the Soviet Union; it seems unlikely that it will subside in the near future.

STATE CAPITALISM? INDUSTRIAL FEUDALISM? COMMUNISM?

In keeping with Lenin's early efforts to concentrate total power in the hands of a small, selected group of the professional revolutionaries, the Soviet political system remains completely centralized. The idea of a centrally planned, fully nationalized economy, complements perfectly the principle of the centralized hierarchical party structure. Institutions such as the Supreme Soviet, which is the highest legislative authority, serve a purely symbolic function, being in reality completely subordinate to the party through special administrative arrangements and the party discipline. Accordingly, the Supreme Soviet 'has never on a single occasion, since it first met in 1937, been recorded as voting otherwise than by complete unanimity' (Schapiro, 1977: 93). Moreover, it meets in full session only about 48 hours a year.

It seems quite obvious, therefore, that the state is not likely to wither away, since any process of disintegration would threaten such pillars of Soviet communism as the bureaucratized party rule, state ownership of the economy and the principle of central planning. All these key elements of the Soviet system require highly developed apparatus and hierarchical bureaucratic structures to secure their operations. Moreover, since their operation is bound to interfere with individual freedoms and wishes, they have to be accompanied by a fair measure of coercion and repression which can never be suspended or even significantly relaxed.

The question to be considered here is: can one individual be held responsible for the present realities in the Soviet Union? Was it, for example, Lenin's fault? History shows that he interpreted the little guidance from Marx and Engels in the best way he could. He adjusted their ideals to the concrete conditions in his country, a phenomenon which is inevitable in all cases where theories are applied to real life situations. In order to maintain the radical direction of political developments, he had to suppress spontaneity, democracy, trade-unionism and dissent within the ranks of socialists themselves. His actions can be seen to follow logically his mission to secure the communist rule in the country. If they were often ruthless and morally repugnant, this was the price to pay for their effectiveness. Without them, there could be no socialist revolution and no communism in Russia. Lenin was of the opinion that one could use any means necessary to bring about a superior social order to a world tormented by hostility, exploitation and misery. He realized that such an ideal order could not be generated voluntarily and spontaneously by people whose common sense rejected the fantasy of utopia. Perhaps Lenin's main fault was that he believed Marx, that he interpreted literally the tenacious dream of this nineteenth-century prophet, and that after Marx, he believed that an initial strengthening of the post-revolutionary state would lead eventually, by curious, dialectical processes, to its natural dissolution.

Or, was Stalin to blame? Was Stalinism an aberration or was it a logical continuation of Lenin's ambitious project? Stalin rejected Lenin's relaxed policy of the NEP as inconsistent with Marxist theory, which indeed it was. The reasonableness of the NEP, with its tolerance for capitalist habits (private property and private market), was quite alien to the spirit of Marx's model. While Lenin reversed the direction of revolution by responding to the needs of the people as well as the economy, Stalin introduced a harsh manoeuvre, which he himself described as a revolution from above. Yet, he inherited, not invented, the dictatorship of a minority party, the mechanisms of suppression of democractic institutions, and the policy of forcible elimination of opponents of the newly established regime. There can be no doubt that it was Lenin who laid the foundations for a totalitarian political system, which were further developed and strengthened by Stalin. Nevertheless, it would be incorrect to claim that Stalin's personal despotism and his unprecedented reign of terror and savagery was a logical or inevitable consequence of the situation he inherited.

What about Khrushchev? While he condemned and rejected the Stalinist methods of massive terror, his critique and analysis did not reach beyond the 'negative characteristics' of Stalin himself, whom he described in his speech during the 20th Party Congress (1956) as 'demoralized', lacking of 'even elementary modesty, demanding 'absolute submission to his opinion', 'a distrustful man, sickly suspicious', 'suffering of persecution mania', 'capricious, irritable and brutal' (Khrushchev, 1973). Khrushchev, however, never attempted to examine the nature of the post-revolutionary Soviet structural arrangements, which had made possible the uncontrolled tyranny of the megalomaniac who had preceded him. He did not analyse the logic and continuity in the political organization of the Soviet Union. He never questioned the main dogmas of Marxist ideology, never scrutinized their implications and never worried seriously about the lack of genuine support for the party among the Soviet people. A continuation of coercion and suppression has thus been inevitable, since no real structural changes have ever been introduced to alter the rigid, centralized and intolerant one-party system, originally introduced by Lenin and developed by his successors. Changes initiated not only by Khrushchev but by Brezhnev as well amounted to nothing more than palace revolutions, which, significant as they were, did not touch the core of the system of power.

Some Leftist critics of the Soviet Union argue that 'its increasing totalitarianism can only be the result of profound class antagonism and not the victory of socialism' (Cliff, 1974: 123). They maintain that capitalism has not been abolished in Russia. Rather, due to the early nationalization of industry, it jumped directly into the most advanced state of capitalism – the stage of perfect monopolization of capital. Indeed, the state capitalism in Russia is characterized by the state monopoly over the economy made possible by the bureaucracy's virtual control of the economy. The bureaucracy, in turn, as 'a partial negation of the traditional capitalist class, is at the same time the truest personification of the historical mission of this class' (Cliff, 1974: 170). The separation between the function of ownership and that of management is treated as spurious and, indeed, ideologically manipulated to create a false impression that the Russian economy has nothing in common with the capitalist relationships of production.

> The state appears to stand above people, as personified ownership, while the bureaucrats who direct the process of production and are therefore historically the personification of capital in essence, appear as labourers, and as such, producers of values by their labour itself. (Cliff, 1974: 171)

Similar criticism has been levelled by Milovan Djilas, a Yugoslavian communist and Vice-President under Tito. After his fall from power in 1954, Djilas accused Soviet-style communism of being a direct reversal of the verbalized intentions and predictions of Marx as well as those of the leaders of the Soviet revolution. He, too, argued that the greatest illusion was that industrialization, collectivization and the destruction of capitalist ownership would automatically result in a classless society. Djilas maintained that while the old classes had indeed been abolished, a new class had emerged from the Bolshevik party which organized itself according to the Leninist idea of the professional revolutionary élite. These, then, were the roots of the new oligarchy which eventually transformed the Communist Party into a vehicle of its own reproduction and expansion of power. This new 'party bureaucracy' class established a monopoly over the whole society, and above all, over the working class which it exploited, subjugated and kept in poverty. Djilas argued that this new class had all the privileges inherent in ownership since it 'used, enjoyed and disposed of' nationalized property.[5] Members of the new class had much larger incomes and more extensive privileges than was necessary to recompense them for the functions they fulfilled in the bureaucracy. Moreover, the new class had an exclusive right to distribute the national funds, to set wages, to plan and manage production, and so forth (Djilas, 1957).

While Djilas initially saw this new class in the context of the state capitalism, he has since radically revised his interpretation. In a recent interview, he used the label 'industrial feudalism' as the most accurate description of the Soviet system, where social relations are similar to those between vassals and their superiors. Djilas explained the situation thus:

> What we have there is an enormous chain of privilege-dispensing and privilege-consuming relationships. . . . Your place and advancement in this chain are not a function of your work or talent but of your usefulness and loyalty to the barons immediately in command of you, and ultimately of *their* use and loyalty to the centre.
>
> (from an interview conducted by Urban, 1979: 36)

The thesis which describes the Soviet reality as a bureaucratic state capitalism does have some appealing ingredients. There is no doubt that there exists a contradiction between the interests of the bureaucratic élite and the rest of society, and that this élite virtually possesses the economy and the institutional infrastructure. The label attributed to this group, be it 'class' or 'élite', is of secondary importance. What does matter, however, is whether Soviet communism is treated as modified capitalism, modified feudalism or as a totally new formation.

Soviet communism relies heavily on industrialization as a means of progress towards the fulfilment of the prophetic vision of full production and freedom from material pressures. Since industrialization has both stimulated the development of capitalism and been effectively moulded by it, it is not surprising that the most fundamental features of industrialization seem to be inseparably linked to capitalist institutions and relationships. Essentially, those features include: the need to accumulate capital, the existence of a large working class selling its labour for wages, the presence of a group which owns or at least controls the industrial base and which profits from the work of direct producers, and finally, the existence of an extensive market of commodities produced by the workers but controlled by and profitable to those who do not work productively. While these basic elements of industrial organization can be easily recognized in Soviet society, there are, however, other features of capitalism which seem to be antithetic to the basic logic of Soviet communism. The most obvious among them are: principles of competition, economic rationality, profit orientation and the supremacy of economic criteria in economy-related matters. A direct interest in profits and in economic growth induces the capitalist owners and controllers of industry to apply the most cost-effective approach to production. The Soviet reality, however, is based on ideological principles, which explicitly contradict the rules of economic rationality and efficiency. Potentially profitable solutions, especially those practised in capitalist countries, can be easily discredited as ideologically unacceptable. The rigidity of planning, the overcentralization of the economy, and the political criteria of promotion and selection for managerial positions counteract any effort to increase productivity and reduce waste. As well, the élite does not have a direct interest in profits; its economic gains, albeit immense, are not directly linked to the production output in any given enterprise or company.

As is argued elsewhere (Łoś 1979a: 131–2), it is the ideology in Soviet-style societies which provides the ultimate criterion of progress. The ideology, in turn, is fulfilled when its demands (for example, the Plan) are fulfilled on paper. Real production is of secondary importance. The ideology, unlike the economy, is able to reduce its inner tensions and contradictions solely by ideological means. The Communist ideology does not serve the interests of any class distinguished by its relationship to production. It predominantly serves the interests of the ruling élite which is distinguished by its relationship to the ideology (i.e. position in the party power structure). The subordinate 'class' (society at large) is not only forced to sell its labour for wages, but also to give up human rights connected with other areas of expression and activity. The core of oppression is found, above all, in that latter fact. It does not mean, of course, that low economic living standards are irrelevant. The economic hardship is acute and oppressive, but it cannot be seen simply as exploitation. The workers realize that their potential is being wasted, rather than directly appropriated by the rulers. They are not given the opportunity to work efficiently and competently and their effort is measured by arbitrary and irrational political criteria. The basic contradiction within the economy is exemplified by the fact that workers' labour contributes to the greater and better-equipped political oppression and control. Its contribution to the growing wealth and economic domination of the ruling class, although real, seems to be of lesser importance.

The party bureaucracy, together with the secret police, dominate the whole political and economic scene. The basic contradiction within the party consists in the incompatibility of the rational demands of bureaucratic organization and the irrational requirements of the ideology. This major contradiction produces the constant growth of bureaucracy, its ever-increasing ambiguity (for instance, widespread double recording of information – fictitious and more realistic items separately), and the intensification of the repressive apparatus within it. The bureaucratized ideology substitutes a fiction for reality. When the contradictions within the fiction are negated, they produce even a grander fiction, which must reinforce itself in ever more inclusive domains. The essential role of the economy seems to exist in its ability to produce sufficient economic, military and security bases, to inspire the ideology with the necessary confidence (coercive power).

In sum, while the labels 'industrial feudalism' and 'state capitalism' both adequately describe some aspects of the Soviet situation (the former perhaps somewhat better than the latter), it may be more appropriate to regard Soviet communism as a completely new formation which constitutes the logical outcome of an attempt to impose the Marxist utopia on an existing society. Since no mechanisms are proposed by Marx or his followers to prevent authoritarian development, to forestall economic decline or to preclude the accumulation of power and privilege in the hands of the victorious vanguard, 'real life' communism, as with any other socio-economic formation, creates inevitably its own élite and vested interests. These, in turn, need to be protected, and with them privileges need to be defended and opposition needs to be appeased. So far, no mechanisms have been developed to remove the reality of greed, privilege and power struggle from the socio- political reality of complex societies. Some devices have emerged, however, to regulate and mitigate their impact. The parliamentary democracy of western capitalist societies seems to be designed to play exactly such a role. Yet, its explicit rejection by Marx and his followers has not been accompanied by any realistic response to these perennial problems of human societies. This is why Marxist ideology, as indeed any other ideology which claims to guarantee the elimination of human vices and which denies any need for legal safeguards and mediating mechanisms, should be treated with great caution and why its actual practical application has led to such an uncontrollable escalation of terror and repression.

2 The State and Law in Poland

THE GENESIS OF THE COMMUNIST STATE IN POLAND

The history of the communist rule in Poland is, of course, shorter than that of the Soviet state. Moreover, there never was a communist revolution in Poland. Rather, the Marxist ideology was simply imported from the Soviet Union and imposed on the Polish people against their wishes and political preferences. Despite its different origins, therefore, the communist state in Poland, as well as its legal instruments, closely resemble those prevailing in the USSR.

The Soviet subjugation of Poland in the 1940s was fully consistent with Lenin's plans and hopes, even if it could not be accomplished during his lifetime. His unsuccessful efforts were eventually carried through by Stalin as a result of his strengthened international position following the spectacular victory over the Germans. Stalin's actions were, however, facilitated by the political groundwork started by Lenin. He had gathered around himself a number of Polish radical socialists who were expected to help him export the revolution to their homeland. One of these socialists, F. Dzierzyński, was even nominated as the first chairman of the Soviet secret police, Cheka. This group was given wide ranging assistance in its efforts to organize political work among the Polish workers and peasants in the attempt to divert them from the patriotic cause of national defence and direct them to join in the proletarian mission of the Soviet state. These Polish revolutionaries were also expected to spread propaganda among the estimated 2.5 million Poles who were stranded within the Soviet borders after the revolution.

With the onset of the German revolution, Poland became an even more desirable and strategically important target. Lenin's Polish advisers, however, were no longer familiar with the situation in their homeland and clearly underestimated the intensity of the opposition and hostility against the Soviet-style revolution. As well, many Polish exiles, who joined the Polish Division of the Red Army, did it clearly in the hopes of returning to Poland and with no intention of helping the revolutionaries in their plans of conquering it (Zenczykowski, 1983: 11).

Lenin's scheme suffered the ultimate blow when the progress of the Red Army into Polish territory was halted by a victorious Polish counter-offensive in 1920. The Soviet-sponsored Temporary Revolutionary Committee established in eastern Poland had to face the reality that it was unwanted there and fled hastily back to Moscow.

When the acute economic crisis in the 1930s brought a wave of strikes and demonstrations by workers and peasants, radical ideas were gaining more popularity among workers and intellectuals. The Communist Party could not, however, play any significant role because its leadership in the Soviet Union had been undermined by the Stalinist purges. Numerous communists were arrested or shot, and the Communist Party of Poland was eventually dissolved in 1938.

In September 1939, when German troops marched into Poland and smashed the heroic resistance of the unprepared Polish forces, Stalin seized the opportunity to attack Poland and annex its eastern territories. Mass deportations of Polish citizens into the USSR followed, including some 15 000 officers taken as prisoners of war and executed in 1940 by the NKVD (the Soviet secret police).[1]

At the same time, a genuine exodus to the Soviet Union occurred, involving some 3000 Polish communists (Zenczykowski, 1983: 53). Their idealistic expectations were soon confronted with the realities of the Stalinist police state. Their welcome was cool and full of suspicion; they were not allowed to join the Communist Party of the USSR and many were forcibly exiled to remote areas of the country.

In 1941, however, Stalin decided to start more energetic communist activity in Poland and initiated, through his Polish emissaries, the creation of a pro-Soviet workers' party. Another organization was established simultaneously in the Soviet Union with the purpose of directing and controlling this party's functioning. Ironically, it was called the Union of Polish Patriots. Many activists who had taken part in the communist exodus from Poland became now involved in the Union.

The Teheran conference of October 1943, which involved the ministers of foreign affairs of the United States, Great Britain and the Soviet Union, made it clear to Stalin that the Soviet interests in Poland were relatively secure. Indeed, shortly thereafter, the Union of Polish Patriots was instructed by the Soviet leader to undertake steps towards the preparation of a future communist government for Poland despite the existence of the legitimate Polish government in exile in London. As a result, the National Home Council was created in Poland at the beginning of 1944 and was soon united with the Union of Polish Patriots in the USSR. In July of the same year, the Polish Committee of National

Liberation (PKWN) was founded in Moscow and was designed to play the crucial role in the introduction of the Soviet rule in Poland (see Kersten, 1981 for relevant documents).

This committee prepared the Manifesto to the Nation and waited for an opportunity to move its headquarters into Poland.[2] And indeed, as soon as eastern Poland was occupied by the Red Army, the PKWN relocated there and declared itself the sole authority. On 1 August 1944 the Home Army, loyal to the Polish government in exile, began an uprising in Warsaw against the German occupancy in the hopes of taking over the city before the Red Army could occupy it. The Germans were able to quell the uprising after 63 heroic days however, and Warsaw was virtually levelled to the ground, while the Soviet troops waited at the outskirts of the city, apparently pleased to see the Home Army's defeat. Soon after, the PKWN was transformed into a provisional government.

Such was the status quo at the time of the Yalta conference in February 1945, when Churchill, Roosevelt and Stalin decided that a 'Polish Provisional Government of the National Unity' should be formed on the basis of the newly created one. Its Soviet origins were concealed from the Western leaders, who were not particularly inclined to question Stalin's version which presented the provisional government as a genuine Polish creation. The Yalta agreement did stipulate, however, free democratic elections to the Polish parliament. It is worthy of note that this condition has yet to be fulfilled some 40 years after the Yalta conference.

A new government, totally dominated by communists, was created soon after the conference and Boleslaw Bierut was nominated as president. He eventually also became the General Secretary of the Polish United Workers' Party, which acquired the status of the dominant, monopolistic party in 1948. The government in London was declared illegal, as was the Home Army and all other organizations which the new rulers perceived as threatening. Sixteen leaders of the outlawed parties were arrested by the NKVD and brought to trial before the Soviet Military Tribunal. Most of them were imprisoned and eventually died in the Soviet Union. In 1945 and 1947, decrees of amnesty were issued for all members of those military and political ogranizations deemed illegal. While approximately 100 000 people took advantage of these amnesties, most of them suffered harassment, long prison terms or secret executions (Karpiński, 1982: 8–9; *Encyclopaedia Britannica*, 1972, vol. 18: 139). Many groups continued their underground struggle against the new order. Even though they were portrayed to the public as bandits and murderers, their goals have never lost the respect and admiration of the society. Even when, in a series of trials, many Home Army veterans were falsely accused of collaboration with the Germans, the public silent support remained on their side (see e.g. Steinsbergowa, 1977).

Arrests and harassments were not limited to members of the banned organizations. Churchmen were subjected to vicious persecution, and the new rulers went even so far as to arrest the primate of Poland in 1953. Peasants were forcibly collectivized despite their total opposition and adamant resistance to the communist methods in agriculture. The Six Year Plan introduced in 1950 was so strongly focused on heavy industrialization that it almost totally neglected the basic needs of the population. The 'iron' discipline was imposed on workers, with harsh penalties handed down for absenteeism or any other infringement of work regulations. The oppression and random prosecution intensified considerably in 1949 with the onset of the so-called Stalinist period and included as well communists suspected of party deviations. The Secret Police, led by the newcomers from Moscow, were as dreaded as their Soviet counterparts who were also active on Polish territory. In addition, the courts lacked any prestige, as total political control over judges was justified by the legal theory of A. Y. Vyshinskii, the omnipotent chairman of the Soviet Procuracy under Stalin (Szerer, 1979, 1981).

The new leaders were clearly more concerned with the effectiveness of their actions than their legality. Nonetheless, they did pass some new laws which included the 1944 decree on the Protection of the State and its second, more developed, version issued in 1946, known as the Small Criminal Code. Although it was intended as a provisional law, it remained in force until 1969. Due to their 'revolutionary' nature as well as their vague legal terminology, both these decrees provided ample possibilities for arrests and the imprisonment of inconvenient individuals (Karpiński, 1982: 15; Falandysz, 1981a: 30).

Thus, the society, decimated and ravaged by the long war and occupation, continued to suffer and lived in increasing terror. As Bethell put it: 'Poland was the only country that fought the Germans from the first to the last day. It was also the only country unable in any way to enjoy the fruits of victory' (Bethell, 1969: 164).

THE POST-STALINIST YEARS

Essentially, lawlessness and fear prevailed in Poland during the whole period of Bierut's reign. He died suddenly during a visit to Moscow early in 1956, just at the time when Khruschev had decided to close the Stalinist chapter in the communist block, thereby making Bierut's rule no longer viable. It must be noted, however, that some important changes were taking place even before Bierut's death, as a direct result of the post-Stalin reforms carried out by Khrushchev in the USSR. For example, many political prisoners were released and rehabilitated and party authorities admitted to having gone too far in their attempts to secure the new order. As early as January 1955, Bierut used the word 'mistakes' and explained that they had resulted from:

> the tendency to widen the field of activity of the security forces, from attempts to extend their functions, or from their interference in various aspects of state and social activity under conditions which did not justify such interference. (Quoted in Karpiński, 1982: 34)

Another party official published an article in February 1955 in which he openly stated that:

> [t]here were cases when innocent people were arrested and illegally detained and cases in which, instead of attempting to establish the objective truth, the evidence was stretched to conform with pre-determined false accusations. There were cases when scandalously inadmissible methods were used during investigations . . . In the course of the past several months, the Politburo has taken a series of steps to remove these deviations and restore healthy relations in the security forces.
>
> (From J. Morawski's article in *Nowe Drogi*, quoted here after Karpiński, 1982: 35)

Khrushchev's anti-Stalinist speech at the 20th Congress of the Communist Party of the USSR early in 1956 brought some hope to the suppressed people of Poland. They demanded reforms and the termination of the police terror. In June of the same year, a general strike was staged in the industrial city of Poznań. Workers who took to the streets were met by armed troops who, in turn, were ordered to fire into the crowd. Even though many people were killed or wounded and many others were arrested,[3] the party remained in a state of crisis due to the changing political and social climate. Some personnel changes were necessary and eventually Wladyslaw Gomulka, a one-time General Secretary of the Polish Workers' Party (i.e. the communist party), was proposed as the new party leader. Although never charged, Gomulka spent the Stalinist years in prison for his relatively moderate views and especially for his opposition to the forced collectivization of agriculture and the total subordination of Poland to the Soviet Union (for more details see Bethell, 1969: ch. IX). It was not surprising, therefore, that he gained some credibility in the eyes of the frustrated nation.

Yet, the removal of most of the Stalinist hardliners from the Politburo, political liberalization and the rising hopes in Poland were met with apprehension by the Soviet rulers, who feared that the Polish 'thaw' might go too far. Khrushchev, along with a number of other top Soviet officials, arrived unexpectedly in Warsaw, and Soviet divisions stationed in other parts of Poland and in western parts of the USSR were moved nearer to the capital. Khrushchev accused the Polish Communist Party leaders of 'treachery and of selling their country to American imperialism' (Bethell, 1969: 214). While the tension increased within the city, the Poles, and especially workers and students, once again prepared themselves to defend their country despite the overwhelming military superiority of the Soviet army. Finally, however, the Soviet delegation reached some agreement with the Polish communists and the candidacy of Gomulka as the General Secretary was accepted. Nevertheless, conditions were set in order to restrict the press and tighten general control over the society, which, in the preceding months, had freed itself from the Stalinist dictatorship. As well, Soviet troops remained stationed in Poland and any negotiations concerning the return of the Polish eastern territories annexed by the Soviet Union were thereby dismissed.

Three days after the agreement, however, mass demonstrations broke out in Budapest. They began as a manifestation of solidarity with the Polish struggle for liberalization, but grew into a national movement for self-determination. The Polish people openly sympathized with the Hungarians and collection boxes were placed in the streets of Polish towns in order to send supplies of food and medical articles. Gomulka openly supported the liberal communist leader in Hungary, premier Imre Nagy, and maintained this support even when the latter renounced the Warsaw Pact[4] and proclaimed the return to a multi-party system. On 4 November 1956, however, the Soviet Army attacked Budapest, Nagy was arrested, and many lives were lost.[5] It was a bitter lesson for both Gomulka and the Polish society in general and it was decided not to risk further what had already been gained.

The relaxed policies of the early years of the Gomulka rule were particularly apparent in the areas of culture and science as well as in state–church relations. While there were also some significant changes in the organization of the economy, its basic structure remained unaltered. Agriculture was decollectivized, but the state control over peasants remained rather tight. Workers' councils, established in November 1956 in response to workers' demands, were gradually phased out, and within two years they lost even the legal basis of their existence when a new law on 'self-government' replaced the initial legislation.

General elections to the Diet were held in 1957 and followed the well-established Soviet pattern of a no-choice ballot. Thus, even if the most flagrant and brutal abuses of human rights had been curtailed, the nature of the political and economic organization, based on the Communist Party's monopoly, remained unchanged. As well, the subordination of the Polish ruling party to the Soviet Communist Party was not and, clearly, could not be limited by the events of October 1956. If these principles had been rejected by Gomulka, they would undoubtedly have been enforced in a way already demonstrated in Hungary, namely through Soviet military intervention.

Gradually, however, the political, economic and cultural situation in Poland deteriorated to such a point that the Polish people seemed unable to tolerate it any longer and several social rebellions took place. In March 1968, students organized mass protests against censorship, the lack of basic freedoms and police interference in cultural life. Their demonstrations and rallies were crushed by the police, the student leaders were arrested and some 1600 students were expelled from the university (even though most of them were eventually readmitted). Among the new repressive measures imposed on intellectuals was a bill which legalized party intervention in academic life and abolished the elective nature of the more important university positions. As well, as a result of the political trials which followed the student revolt, at least 15 people received prison sentences ranging from 1.5 to 3.5 years (Karpiński, 1982: 137). It was also about this time that a change in the Soviet policy towards Israel took place and the Polish authorities followed suit. A vigorous anti-Semitic campaign was initiated which, in turn, triggered the dismissal and harassment of numerous individuals of Jewish descent. The already suppressed society was subjected to new restrictions and to intensified ideological controls. The Warsaw Pact invasion of Czechoslovakia in August 1968 served as an additional reminder that any attempt at the liberalization of the political system was bound to be forcibly suppressed. Nevertheless, 2 years later, the Poles rose again.

On 15 December 1970, workers of the Gdańsk shipyards went on strike to protest against the sharp price increases and the generally oppressive economic and political situation. They organized rallies and demonstrations. Before long, workers in several other coastal cities followed their example. A large protest was staged in front of the Regional Party Headquarters. Police and special army units were brought to the scene, issued with live ammunition and instructed to use it in order to suppress the revolt swiftly. Soldiers, ordered to fire into the crowd, were falsely informed that the uprising was an attack organized both by pro-German native elements in the northern part of Poland as well as underground para-military organizations directed from London by the enemies of Poland (Jerzewski, 1982: 4). While many soldiers and officers eventually refused to obey the orders, most were misled or at least confused by the official interpretation of the events and were completely cut off from any outside information or influence. The words of one participant of the army offensive testify to this prevailing lack of awareness among army troops:

> . . . It was my first contact with the crowd for which I was waiting. I wanted to prove to myself, to other soldiers and to this crowd that the army is an instrument which can pacify anything and prevent any uprising . . . I was simply deceived, fooled. I realized this after the first attack, when the first emotional arousal subsided. . . . This emphasis on the struggle, on the soldier's honour was quite intentional.
>
> (Jerzewski, 1982: 10; this author's translation from Polish).

The workers, however, were not intimidated by the bullets and violence, and continued their protests. Strikes spread to other parts of the country and there was a danger of a general revolt. Eventually, party officials met at an emergency plenary meeting hoping for some changes or remedies to the growing threat of 'counter-revolution'. Such a remedy was found in the person of Edward Gierek, who replaced Gomulka as the General Secretary of the party while Gomulka and several of his close associates were removed from the Politburo. Once again, personnel changes at the top of the party were presented as a way out of severe crises caused by the injustice and inadequacy of the prevailing order. At a subsequent meeting of the party, a text was circulated in which Gomulka was criticized for his faulty economic policies and improper approach towards the unrest on the coast. The document tried to present the workers' dissatisfaction as being directed against Gomulka himself and not the party in general and to blame him personally for the social tension.

Gierek offered workers words of encouragement and promised economic reforms. As well, he announced a number of specific concessions in the areas of food prices, minimum wage levels and social security benefits. He also made a solemn commitment to initiate an investigation of the massacres in Gdańsk and other cities. Eventually, he succeeded in persuading the workers' strike committees to cease their protests and go back to work. Indeed, his new rhetoric and his 'working class style' achieved even more; it spurred some enthusiasm and genuine hope for economic improvements, increased opportunities for non-party members and greater religious tolerance.

Broad economic reforms did indeed take place, but they were not designed to increase workers' participation in decision-making or to reduce existing inequities. Quite to the contrary, new policies of investment and financial support for modern, export-oriented industries resulted in a sharper differentiation within the society at large, and within the working class specifically. More traditional industries were neglected and allowed to deteriorate while huge foreign loans were poured into new 'futuristic' projects. Although the principles of management were changed in a technical sense, their essence remained unaltered. Clearly, the dogma of the total subjugation of production to the party could not be challenged. The importance of the so-called nomenklatura (i.e. the party's exclusive right to nominate managers and officials on all levels of economic and political administration) increased to the point where it encompassed practically all and even the most marginal, positions of responsibility. The society experienced the suffocating pressure of a steadily increasing monopoly of the party over all spheres of citizens' lives. Moreover, the initial improvements in the artificially revitalized economy proved to be short-lived and the increased expectations of consumers were left unmet.

In 1976, strikes and protests erupted once again in Poland, this time, in the large industrial plants in Warsaw and the nearby city of Radom. Similar to the previous strikes, these too were suppressed by special police detachments. Many participants as well as passers-by were injured, some of them fatally. The number of fatal casualties is not known, but the case of one death of a 28-year-old man, J. Brożyna, beaten by police long after the demonstrations in the streets were over, exemplifies well the lawlessness of the forces of order. All three witnesses of the brutal event, willing to testify in court against the police, were promptly arrested. One died during the investigation while the other 2 were sentenced to 8 and 6 years in prison (see *Prologue*, 1980: 52–6). Research into the June events and their aftermath, conducted by J. J. Lipski, indicates clearly that this was not an unusual occurrence.

> What happened then is the rule in the People's Republic of Poland; . . . Whoever lodges a complaint to the procuracy about being beaten

by the police will himself be accused of beating them. Similar fate awaits the witnesses of police brutality or a witness who may testify to the innocence of someone who has been singled out by the police for conviction.

(Lipski, 1983: 85; this author's translation from Polish)

Thousands of workers were arrested and dismissed from work. Their speedy trials before both special petty crime boards and the courts were a parody of justice. Judges received detailed instructions as to the sentences to be meted out and the only witnesses admitted to the courts were policemen. Arrested workers were routinely beaten and tortured. Their legal rights were drastically curtailed and trials were often conducted 'in camera' or before a specially selected audience.

The brutality and the lawlessness of the aftermath of the June 1976 strikes initiated a strong reaction among intellectuals and students. The Workers' Defence Committee (KOR) was created by a group of concerned intellectuals (see Lipski, 1983; Raina, 1978). The committee and its supporters organized financial, legal and medical assistance for victims and their families. They also started collecting information regarding the illegalities and violence perpetrated by the police and other agencies. Special bulletins were issued almost daily, thousands of copies of which were typed by volunteers[6] and distributed, mainly through networks of friends.[7] Eventually, more sophisticated underground publishing houses sprung up and a loosely organized movement of dissent and opposition grew quietly into a powerful network. Arrests and constant harassment[8] appeared to have little effect on the determination and commitment of those involved and new volunteers were constantly recruited. The awareness of the inherent injustice of the Marxist–Leninist model was growing proportionally to the increased availability of uncensored reading material and alternative educational opportunities.[9]

The stage was thus prepared for the emergence of the Solidarity Union. As in 1970, again in 1980, the shipyard workers of Gdańsk stopped working and requested that the authorities recognized their demands. Once again, the workers made it very clear that they were on one side while the party was on another. They realistically acknowledged the implications of Poland's subordination to the USSR and the impossibility of abolishing communism in one 'satellite' country. They knew, of course, that to challenge Poland's foreign relations or the political domination of the party would inevitably bring an invasion by the Red Army. Reluctantly, they accepted these limits and negotiated for less radical reforms, which would give them some control over the economy and their own lives. Their demands included social control over the mass media, the limitation of censorship, the equality of all citizens before the law, judicial independence, the release of political prisoners and the reform of welfare policies. Most important of all, they won the registration of the Free and Independent Trade Union 'Solidarity', which was followed by the registration of its rural counterpart. One of the most significant demands was the workers' claim that they should have the right to choose their plants' directors and to request their dismissals. This proved, however, to be an unacceptable threat to the system of 'nomenklatura', which enabled the party to exercise full control over production and the workers themselves.

In the endless negotiations and bilateral talks, with the workers on one side of the table and party officials on the other, the irreconcilable gap between the working class and the élite was exposed and broadcasted to the world. The party's all-pervading corruption and ideological bankruptcy were revealed; the very foundations of the Marxist ideology were proclaimed lacking and contradictory to the interests of the society at large and the working class in particular. Thousands of party members left the party, embarrassed by the public exposure of the totalitarian mechanisms of which they were a part. Many others were expelled in frantic purges and usual scapegoating tactics.[10] These could not, however, restore the party's credibility as it became clear that it never had any. This truth, once publicly proclaimed, could no longer be suppressed by demagogical tricks and the routine exercise of control. Instead, such tactics had to be replaced by extraordinary measures which would shake and shock the society and firmly reinstate the communist order, and would clearly have to involve the use of force. Yet, it was Solidarity's noble commitment to non-violence and negotiation which gave the Soviet and Polish authorities the confidence that immediate Soviet military intervention could be avoided since they had enough time to work on their innovative model of invasion from within. Apparently, as early as the spring of 1981, plans had been made to prepare such an internal military operation.

The authorities continued to use their stalling tactics in carrying out the signed agreements, pretending that they were acting in good faith and that the delays resulted from numerous genuine bureaucratic difficulties. In the meantime, various policies were employed to divide workers and farmers and to increase acceptable forms of military presence within civilian life through assistance to older farmers and flood victims, through their participation in the campaign against corruption and black-marketeering, and so forth. Moreover, the post of the General Secretary was given to the minister of defence, General Wojciech Jaruzelski, and many other important positions were taken over by high army officials. The deadlines for the implementation of many hard-won reforms and new legislations were set for 1 January 1982. Yet, given that plans had already been contrived to crush the Solidarity movement in the last weeks of 1981, these deadlines were clearly never meant to be met (see Łoś, 1983d).

The developments of 1981 placed the Solidarity leaders in an impossible position. On the one hand, the geo-political situation of Poland dictated that they should limit themselves to purely reformist demands, while on the other, the political reality and popular expectations pushed them towards a more radical stance. Given the lack of any legal opposition parties, it seemed virtually impossible for Solidarity to limit itself to a role of a trade union and to shy away from representing and protecting the political interests of its members. It was these political interests, however, which clearly clashed with the key principles of the organization of the communist state. The Polish citizens' overwhelming desire for parliamentary democracy had eventually led Solidarity to its bold demand for free elections in Poland, a demand which has been interpreted by many as Solidarity's major political mistake and the one which eventually brought about its destruction. And yet, the destruction of a mass movement which constituted a clear alternative to the controlled state institutions was a logical and necessary step for the totalitarian regime to take. Any specific resolutions and demands by Solidarity were not and, indeed, could not be responsible for its eventual suppression.

Independent public opinion surveys conducted in 1980–81 indicate clearly the prevailing political sentiments. For instance, a study of a representative, nation-wide sample of the Solidarity members[11] carried out in October 1981 provides interesting insight into the public attitudes towards the key organizations in Poland. According to the obtained results, 95 per cent of the respondents expressed their trust in Solidarity, 94 per cent in the Church, 50 per cent in the police and 7 per cent declared that they trusted the Communist Party ('Opracowania . . .', 1981: 404).

The long period of fruitless negotiations and stalling techniques used by the government put on trial the credibility of the Solidarity Union and its commitment to non-violence. A provisional economic reform announced by the Council of Ministers in November 1981 disregarded completely Solidarity's recommendations and the substance of the historical agreements signed by the authorities in Gdańsk in August 1980. Indeed, all the government's solemn undertakings remained on paper while, in reality, it continued to ignore the 10 million strong workers' movement. Solidarity was left with a choice between confrontation or political annihilation. Numerous independent surveys of Solidarity members' attitudes carried out in the fall of 1981 indicated an overwhelming support for the adoption of a more radical line (see e.g. *AS*, 1981: 201–2). There was a clear danger of either strife within the ranks of Solidarity or a sharp radicalization and a suicidal challenge to the binding totalitarian principles. Before it was ready to make its final policy choices, however, Solidarity and the whole nation was faced with the new reality of the internal military invasion led by the combined military and security forces subordinated to the Communist Party.

THE STATE OF WAR: CHANGE OR CONTINUITY?

The announcement of the imposition of the state of war was made on 13 December 1981 (for the text of the announcement see Ruane, 1982: 307–15). Given the terms of the Polish Constitution and several international conventions signed by Poland, this state of war was an illegal act. In the absence of any provisions in the Polish Constitution allowing for the introduction of martial law, the only option left to the ruling group intent upon crushing Solidarity by force, was the imposition of the state of war as regulated by s. 33(1). This section stipulates that:

> A decision regarding a state of war may be made only in the case of military aggression on the Polish People's Republic or when international agreements imply the necessity of a joined defence against aggression. Such a decision is made by the Diet, and when the Diet is not in session, by the State Council.
> (*Konstytucja* . . ., 1952, s. 33; this author's translation from Polish)

Subsection 2 of the same article affirms that a state of war can be introduced by the State Council only when it is clearly required for reasons of security and national defence. That there was no military aggression from outside Poland directed against the country's security and national defence or that of her allies is an established historical fact. Moreover, on 13 December 1981, the Diet was still in session and yet the decision to introduce the state of war was made by the State Council. By unilaterally introducing the decision without submission to the Diet, the

Council assured the element of surprise, which was deemed essential for the success of the 'coup'.

In Poland, as elsewhere, a law becomes binding only if it is published in the official gazette that announces current legislation. With respect to the state of war, however, although the decree was not published until 14 December 1981, the State Council declared that it would come into effect immediately after its passage, that is, on 12 December at midnight. Scores of people were arrested under the new 'war laws', as yet unpublished and presented to the public only through television announcements and street posters. Hundreds of people were eventually sentenced to long prison terms on the basis of these laws, doubly illegal, because of their unconstitutionality and because they had not been formally proclaimed at the time of these arrests. It must be stressed that the actions for which these individuals were arrested and imprisoned had been legal prior to the decree published on 14 December.

The army and the police performed the major role in the imposition of the 'war measures'. According to popular opinion at the time, the Communist Party, weakened by its inability to lead the country in the days of Solidarity, was incapable of playing any role in the 'coup'. While there is some truth to this view, it should be also noted that it was clearly in the interests of the party to maintain a low profile in this highly militarized attempt to subjugate physically the Polish society.

There can be no doubt that, in the long run, the party was expected by the Soviet leaders to continue to exercise its rule, irrespective of its social rejection and disapproval. Its overt association with the military suppression of the popular trade union movement would clearly be against the long-term interests of the Soviet bloc in general and the Polish Communist Party in particular. The highly visible uniforms of General Jaruzelski and his associates in the National Salvation Council (including 16 generals, 1 admiral and 5 colonels) were quite effective in moulding the image of a temporarily paralyzed party unable to prevent the internal military invasion. While this image did not serve to increase the credibility of the party, at least it spared it the moral odium of the armed suppression of a genuine workers' movement. Contrary to the belief of numerous Western commentators, the party has never relied on the Polish workers and has never had any support from them. The party élite has always consisted of the professional 'apparatchiks', while the rank and file members are generally recruited from the state bureaucracy and those professions and agencies where party membership is either obligatory or highly 'recommended', such as the police, the security forces, the army, the judiciary, the mass media, the scientific and educational establishments and the agencies of the state-run trade unions. The Polish workers, on the other hand, could never be relied upon to adhere to the communist ideology and practice and their membership in the party has always been very low.

What must be borne in mind, however, is the fact that the party is not an agency separate from the army and the police, but rather it encompasses them in accordance with the general principles of the political organization, and the specifics of the obligatory party membership of all their full-time members. Of course, these agencies have been subordinated, in some measure, directly by their Soviet counterparts; the army, for example, through the Warsaw Pact and the security forces through the presence of Soviet officials within the Polish Ministry of the Interior. Their Soviet supervisors, in turn, are themselves subject to the Communist Party of the USSR as is the Polish Communist Party itself. It seems that the circle of power begins and ends in the Politburo in Moscow and, despite the inevitable disagreement, hostility and strain among these major arms of its power, they cannot be seen as independent of or in substantial conflict with each other.

The security forces participating in the assault on the Polish society in December 1981 belonged in part to the military sector and in part to the police forces controlled by the Ministry of the Interior and included special military police as well as ZOMO, ROMO and MO. Created in 1973 following the 1970 workers' protests, ZOMO is a professional, anti-riot police force which is extremely well paid, trained and equipped, and numbers about 25 000. Trained in special camps, many of which are in Czechoslovakia, members of ZOMO live in isolation in special quarters, where they undergo continuous brain-washing. They are usually selected from among army draftees who are given the option of serving their 2-year obligatory military duty with ZOMO in place of the usual army service. The incentives are purely material and include good pay, good food and good accommodation. Thus, while ZOMO is truly a type of military force, it is presented to the public as a police formation in order to protect the reputation of the army. As well, notorious violent criminals are often recruited to this special force in lieu of a prison sentence ('Mala Encyklopedia . . .', 1983: 9–10).

ROMO are special detachments created during the state of war. Their members are recruited from among the voluntary police force (ORMO), military border guards, and those who can be forced or blackmailed into joining them. MO is the regular police force which has been experiencing an acute crisis since 1980, when the Solidarity Union appeared to exert considerable influence on many of its members to the extent that efforts were undertaken to create free trade unions within the police force itself.

In 1981–82, the numbers of those willing to work in MO has decreased by some 25–40 per cent, and this despite the generally tighter job market ('Mala Encyklopedia . . .', 1983: 10).

ZOMO is the major mobile anti-riot force, used to control strikes and street demonstrations. Unlike ROMOs, they are always issued firearms which they are authorized to use as a last resort. They are also equipped with truncheons made of metal and covered with rubber. In addition to these, other devices frequently used during the state of war included: water cannons, tear gas, special smoke candles with asphyxiating gas, bullets with paralyzing gas, and deafening grenades ('Nasi okupanci', 1982: 13). ROMO is a more 'static' force, on the other hand, which was, during the state of war, relied upon to keep general peace and to enforce the martial law.

The security forces which participated in the imposition of the state of war were told stories about alleged underground organizations and plots directed against them and their families. Special leaflets were printed informing some party and security functionaries of the alleged plans of the Solidarity unionists to set fire to their homes, kidnap their children and kill their wives. These were designed to increase their feelings of insecurity and isolation from society which, in turn, alienated them from Solidarity supporters (e.g. 'Różne', 1983: 22). These and similar 'morale building' techniques were important instruments used to intensify their hostility against the social movement which first threatened their vested interests in the status quo, and then, additionally, appared to threaten them personally.

The well-staged show of force on 13 December 1981 and in the following months was expected to terrorize the society, to break the new sense of solidarity among the people and to instill anew that fear which had helped the party to exercise its control since the days of Stalin, but which had been dangerously undermined by the moral victory of the free trade union movement. In order to reinstate this fear, the state needed not only the real means of repression, but also highly visible intimidating displays such as the armed police on each corner, the armoured vehicles parked in conspicuous places, the tens of thousands of arrests and internments, the military commissars in each factory, office and school, the false rumours, the intimidations, the martial courts and exemplary penalties. The colossal cost of such an operation and the maintenance of the gigantic security forces in a country with a totally devastated economy, seemed to remain unnoticed by leaders preoccupied with their never-ending struggle against societal dreams of political plurality and democracy.

The examples and descriptions of terror and intimidation following

13 December 1981 are numerous: letters smuggled from prisons and camps, eyewitness accounts of strikes and demonstrations crushed by the police and endless lists of victims of violence and abuse. The horror of the early ZOMO efforts to suppress the workers' opposition against the state of war is well illustrated by the following eyewitness account of the events in the mining district of Poland on 16 December 1981:

> [ZOMO first attacked] the women and children, who had gathered around the mines. Streams of water from water cannons were directed at the crowd even though the temperature was well below –10°C. Tanks rolled in, firing blank bullets, and after them, ZOMO, police and soldiers. They were hitting [with their truncheons] without looking. They fired real bullets into the crowd. There are dead. The women and children throw themselves on tanks. . . . They are swept away by water. . . . They try to stop the tanks with their own hands. The pandemonium of gun shots, cries and shouting, explosions of tear gas grenades, the wild screams of ZOMOs, the rattle of broken windows, the groans of the wounded, and the sirens of ambulances increases. . . . Ambulances are not allowed into the area, even when doctors and nurses insist on getting there, they are attacked by ZOMO, police and soldiers. The battle to get the wounded brings more victims. Near the Wujek mine, during the rescue operation, nine members of medical teams were beaten up and taken to hospital in serious condition. The attackers damage ambulances, they drag out injured miners, they beat them . . . and drag them to the military vehicles. . . . They beat and kick an unconscious miner with a lung wound and they drag him to a nearby canal and push him into the water . . .
> ('Teraz dopiero . . .', 1982: 18; this author's translation from Polish)

The New York Committee in Support of Solidarity summarized some of the excesses of the first weeks of the state of war in this way:

1. In several instances in Gdańsk, Katowice and elsewhere, the authorities fired on striking workers.
2. In those instances *plastic* bullets were used. They can be as deadly as the lead ones and deadlier if they stay in the body. No X-Ray can detect plastic; at least two miners died on the operating table while surgeons looked in vain for the bullets.
3. In several instances, nerve gas and other unidentified gas inducing coma and violent vomiting were used by the riot police.

4. In several instances, these gases were released from helicopters attacking peaceful civilian crowds surrounding the striking factories.
5. Police brutally beat, and sometimes crippled, wounded workers in ambulances and in hospitals, as well as doctors and nurses treating them.
6. In –20°C temperatures, water cannons were used against the striking workers, against their families gathered at factory gates, and against peaceful gatherings in front of monuments and churches.
7. Arrested people were dragged out of their homes – often only in their underwear – to detention camps.
8. Arrested people have been held, sometimes drenched in water, in sub-zero temperatures in tents, barracks and stadiums ('We accuse', 1982: 1).

There exists a verified list of approximately 60 names of those who had been killed between December 1981 and December 1982 as a result of beatings, torture, and the use of force against peaceful demonstrators. What remains unknown are the numbers of deaths indirectly caused by the war measures through heart attacks, lack of necessary medication in prisons and camps, inaccessibility to doctors because of disconnected telephones and other disruptions, suicides, secret murders, executions of mutinous soldiers and so forth ('Victims of war', 1983: 13). The numbers of those physically and psychologically crippled are impossible to establish but, judging from numerous reports, they appear to be extremely high.

The brutality and unpredictability of the security forces are well illustrated by the following account of an onlooker's experience in a small Polish town on 31 August 1982, the second anniversary of the birth of Solidarity:

> I walked by the post office, passing a patrol which marched calmly by; nobody attacked it. When shots sounded, I was convinced they were blanks, even when I heard the scream, and saw his shirt turn red. . . . After the crowd in the Market Square was dispersed, I found myself in a small group of people in the square behind the Small Church. With horror I saw a police van driving full speed straight at us. We scattered looking for shelter. When I turned around, I saw the van chasing in circles after a young man who was trying to get away. Suddenly a hand appeared in the van's window and a shot was heard. The boy threw his hands up and fell. The van ran over him, stopped and ran over him once again in reverse. A moment passed before I realized I

was screaming 'murderers' . . . [Next day] on 1 September, our children went to school. They saw, they heard, they know. This knowledge is forever. ('It was premeditated murder . . .', 1982: 3)

The underground publications were full of first-hand accounts of beatings and torture in prisons, camps, and in the course of arrests and cross-examinations. Much of this violence was directed against very young people, including high school students. Clearly, these young people, who could not remember the terrors of the Stalinist years, were perceived by the authorities as the most important target group for their real and simulated scare techniques. They realized that Solidarity emerged only because they had overlooked the 'dangerous' moment of the dissipation of fear and the unprecedented rise of hope. And they knew that the young generation would find it most difficult to give up this hope. The following reports illustrate well these violent attempts to suppress the Polish youth:

> On 3 April [1982], 17-year old Emil Barchański, a lst grade student of M. Rey High School in Warsaw died tragically. Arrested as a result of the detection of the clandestine press, he had been cruelly beaten during cross-examination, a fact which he disclosed during his trial. He has been afraid for his life ever since. As it appears – his fear was justified.
>
> (Mietkowski, 1982: 32; this author's translation from Polish)

> Tomasz Sokolewicz, the chairman of the Federation of School Youth [an independent youth organization] has been arrested in Warsaw. He was accused of possession of printing machines. A witness for the defence testified that he had proof that the equipment had been planted at Sokolewicz's place. After a few days, the witness was found dead in one of the rivers near Warsaw. He was wearing swimming trunks, but the police investigation protocol implied that his body was drifting against the current. The victim suffered from asthma . . . and never swam.
>
> (Mietkowski, 1982: 31; this author's translation from Polish)

The Minister of the Internal Affairs stated in his speech in the Diet in March 1983 that, between December 1981 and March 1983, 2580 people had been sentenced for anti-state activities and 1462 for offences under the state of war decree (*Rzeczpospolita*, 1983). Typical crimes involved the possession of underground leaflets, the display of Solidarity pins or other banned symbols, the organization of meetings, marches or demonstrations, and the refusal to either work in militarized enterprises or to obey any other orders of the military authorities. Many such cases were decided in martial courts, where accused persons were often deprived of their basic legal rights including the rights to counsel and appeal. Many judges were forced to preside in these martial courts under the threat of losing their jobs or even freedom. In addition to these courts, thousands of cases were dealt with in summary trials by petty offence boards (a quasi- court agency with very lax legal safeguards).

The judges themselves were subjected to enormous political pressure and intimidation. For example, five days after the introduction of the 'war measures' in December 1981, a military commissar instructed the chairmen of the Warsaw district courts to submit the names of those judges who were politically unreliable and who, therefore, should be dismissed in light of the new, urgent need to 'streamline' the justice system. The commissar indicated in his speech that the frontline of the war was right in the courts and that 'of utmost importance was now the political attitude of the judges, not just their qualifications or abilities'. He suggested that all judges who actively supported Solidarity or other independent unions should be removed immediately from the bench ('Instrukcje', 1982: 36). In the early days of state of war, many judges were forced to sign a 'loyalty oath' and subsequently, a number of judges who either refused to sign or to try Solidarity activists were dismissed ('Sedziowie . . .', 1982: 37).

This political subjugation of judges is not recent; indeed, since the imposition of communist rule, the judiciary have never been an independent body in Poland. The courts have always been submitted to party guidance and control, party membership has been virtually compulsory and individual judges have been evaluated and remunerated according to political criteria. The blatant exercise of control by the military commissars, assigned to all courts all over Poland under the provisions of the state of war decree, once more made this fact obvious to all Polish citizens. It must be emphasized, however, that this return to the Stalinist style of revolutionary justice was made possible only through the preservation throughout the post-war period of the principle of ideological control over justice.

Despite the suspension of the state of war on 18 December 1982, the courts, both martial and civilian, continued to be useful tools of the rulers; however, they tended to be utilized in a more selective way. There was a clear shift away from the wave of mass arrests and summary trials and towards careful preparations for a series of show trials of chosen groups from among the leading opposition activists. They included the Solidarity Union leadership,[12] the founders of the KOR (Workers'

Defence Committee created in 1976)[13] and the workers of the underground radio station 'Solidarity'.[14]

There also emerged alternative ways of punishing and isolating insubordinate individuals without the involvement of the courts or the penal boards. Among them, compulsory army conscription and internment in military penal camps were probably the most widely used. Unlike the well-publicized campaign of arrests and the mass internment of Solidarity activists, this project of removing inconvenient individuals was done quietly in order not to disturb the Western world's sanguine hopes that the suspension of the state of war was a reassuring sign of 'normalization' in Poland. In reality, at this point in time, when the 'show of force' stage was over, the terror became subtle and disguised and was replaced by precise and regularized repression.

There is ample evidence that it was possible to suspend and then to repeal the state of war and yet to continue repression and military control over the society, a phenomenon which is not difficult to explain. It must be remembered that repression and tight controls have always been present in Poland under communism and, therefore, any attempted explanation should focus on their intensity and specific forms rather than on the general mechanisms of carrying them out. For example, the Polish criminal law and its enforcement are uncommonly harsh and the legal changes which took place after the imposition of the state of war simply broadened the possibilities for even more extensive punitive use of the law. Most of them became permanent laws. They include hundreds of bills passed in 1982–83, among them the law on trade unions, the bill on censorship (which abolished a more civilized law passed in 1980 as a result of the Gdańsk Accords), the bill regarding persons who avoid employment (so-called 'parasites'), the new juvenile law (which dangerously broadened the rights of the police to deal with insubordinate youths), the new Teachers' Charter (punitive and political in nature) ('Normalizacja', 1982: 2–4) as well as a new bill concerning the Ministry of Internal Affairs. The latter introduced a clear division between the security forces (SB) and the ordinary police (MO) and legalized most of the extraordinary powers enjoyed by them under the state of war. The new bill indicates that various forms of intervention into the lives of citizens (such as detention for 48 hours, searches, the installation of listening devices in their homes, cars, etc.) may be undertaken, not only in connection with suspected crimes, but also in cases of other activities which interfere with public order and security (ss. 4, 6 and 7). Moreover, section 9 introduces 11 rather vague types of situations which justify the use of firearms by the functionaries of the SB and MO. They include situations (e.g. demonstrations or strikes) which are dangerous to property, public buildings or economically important works ('Analiza prawna . . .', 1983: 51–2).

Two other important bills, passed on 18 December 1982 and on 28 July 1983, introduced several amendments to the Polish Penal Code and the Code of Criminal Procedure which were aimed explicitly at political nonconformists. They include a new section in the Criminal Code, (s. 282a), according to which anyone who undertakes any actions in order to incite either a riot or public unrest is liable to the penalty of deprivation of liberty for up to three years. The same penalty applies to anyone who organizes or leads a protest action which violates legal regulations. Moreover, the existing section 278, which penalizes membership in a secret union, has been revised to include specifically membership in any union which has been dissolved or whose registration has been refused. The penalties range from up to 3 year's imprisonment for ordinary members to up to 5 years for the funders and leaders of such associations ('Analiza prawna', 1983: 53–4). Finally, when the martial law was eventually lifted in July 1983, the Diet empowered the government to declare a state of emergency, making possible a civil crackdown on any future unrest. As a result of all these additions to the existing body of the law, the martial law became, despite its formal withdrawal, a permanent feature of the 'law and order' reality in Poland. The amnesty for political prisoners detained under the state of war decrees was only partial and the authorities received special powers to re-imprison them if the need arises in the future. In his comments regarding the amnesty, General Jaruzelski clearly stated that:

> Organizers of counter-revolution should harbor no illusions whatsoever. The lifting of martial law is not tantamount to the cessation of struggling with evil and crime. Law enforcement organs should hit hard at this dangerous fringe. ('Amnesty . . .', 1983: 1)

> Any attempts at antistate activity will be curbed no less unswervingly than during martial law. ('Charades . . .', 1983: 16)

THE CRIMINAL LAW AND THE STATE

Most of the findings presented in Chapter 1 on the State and Law in the Soviet Union are directly applicable to the situation in Poland. Although the origins of communism were rather different in the USSR and in Poland, the underlying principles and the mechanisms of its development are the same. Any differences which can be detected stem from the distinctive cultural traditions, the unique geographical, ethnic and demographical features of these countries, as well as the many specific historical events and circumstances.[15]

The direct control and subjugation of Poland to the Soviet Union does imply, however, the basic similarity of their political institutions and laws. It is interesting to note that, until 1976, there was no clause in the Polish Constitution which could entrust the Communist Party with the monopoly of power. In the Constitution of 1952 there was simply no mention of the party at all. The 1976 amendment to the Constitution introduced a vague, but ominous section which stipulated that the Polish United Workers' Party (i.e. the Communist Party) is the leading political force in the construction of socialism.[16] Nevertheless, its functioning and relations with other institutions remained completely undefined. For example:

> [n]one of the agencies of the party are authorized to be organs of the state, nor do any party agencies have any constitutional right to act in the name, or on behalf, of the Polish People's Republic.
>
> (Gidyński, 1976: 44)

According to the Constitution, the Diet is the supreme organ of the state's authority. Yet, the majority of members of the Diet are, in fact, nominated by the party, with the 'no-choice' elections functioning as a rubber stamp for the party's selection of candidates. Moreover, the Diet can deliberate only when in session. These sessions, in turn, are normally limited to approximately 10 days per year, during which the Diet approves an average of 20 statutes. As in the USSR, in Poland there is no seperation of power into legislative, executive and judicial branches. The Supreme Court is, in fact, subordinate to the supreme organs of the state power, which are, in turn, totally dominated by the party. Although the Constitution stipulates that common court judges be elected, the Statute on Organization of Common Courts clearly states that they are appointed and can be recalled by the State Council on a motion by the minister of justice. Supreme Court justicies are appointed by the State Council for 5 years only and can be recalled even before the expiration of their term. The term may or may not be renewed depending on the political evaluation given the judge. These realities clearly suggest the lack of any guarantees of judicial independence.

There were many discussions and critiques published during the Solidarity period concerning the unacceptable level of political control over judges (Strzelecka, 1981a; Falkowska, 1981a; Ambroziak, 1981; Rudnicki, 1981). One of them maintains, for example, that:

> [t]here are many institutional limitations on the judges' independence, for example the binding guidelines of the justice system, the supervisory role of the Ministry of Justice which influences the judicial policy through various statistical indicators and criteria of evaluation of judges' performance (e.g. the dependence of the judge's income on the total value of the adjudicated fines), . . . political statements by powerful officials before the court decision has been reached, or the creation of a specific political atmosphere around some cases.
>
> (Soltysiński, 1981: 3; this author's translation from Polish)

According to the Constitution, courts are called upon to protect the political system of Poland, the accomplishments of the working people, the socialized property and citizen's rights. As well, they are expected to punish criminals. To this end, a special role within the criminal justice system is played by the Procurator (Prosecutor) General, whose tasks include criminal investigation, prosecution in criminal cases, the supervision of prisons and the regulation of the lawful functioning of the state administration. The Procurator General is subordinate to the State Council which consists mainly of high party officials and serves to represent the party's interests.

The present Penal Code of the Polish People's Republic was enacted in 1969 when the old pre-war code and all its subsequent revisions had been repealed. The code was the long awaited result of many years of legislative and ideological work and was announced and praised by party officials as a truly socialist and most progressive piece of legislation. Needless to say, its content, as well as practical implementation, have been moulded by the concrete political conditions of post-war Poland and the direct influence of the USSR. Following the example of the penal codes enacted under Khrushchev, the Polish Codification Commission, which is attached to the Ministry of Justice, has:

> pulled together and rather mechanically combined the remnants of the pre-war way of thinking and techniques of codification with the revolutionary law of the People's Republic. Furthermore, it has exhibited exceptional ardour in its efforts to restrict judges, to broaden the rights of the state prosecutor and to ensure stern punishment for criminals.
>
> (Falandysz, 1981a: 31–32; this author's translation from Polish)

The Polish Penal Code of 1969, which has earned the reputation of being the most punitive in all Europe, has been attacked in recent years by a number of critically minded experts on Poland's criminal law (e.g. Jasiński, 1978). In the relatively liberal era of the free operation of the Solidarity Union, many such critiques were published in the officially printed press and scientific periodicals (e.g. Falandysz, 1981a, c, d; Podemski, 1981a, b, c; Memorial, 1981). Moreover, energetic steps were undertaken to initiate work on new legislation. The difficulty with the Polish Penal Code as well as the accompanying legal texts (e.g. Andrejew, 1975) stems from the fact that their strongly repressive character is hidden under a liberal and progressive rhetoric, which emphasizes decriminalization, decarceration and rehabilitation. A careful examination of the actual application of the law is necessary, therefore, to uncover and properly assess the mechanisms of increased punitiveness enhanced by the new 'scientific' solutions introduced in the Bill of 1969. The most notorious and evident among these are:

1. The raising of the mandatory minimum period of deprivation of liberty from one week to three months.
2. The extended option of imposing fines or confiscating all or part of the offender's property.
3. The broadening of the scope of the definition of recidivism and the increase in sanctions for chronic offenders well beyond the statutory maximum sentence for the given offence.
4. The introduction of a sentence of incarceration in social readaptation centres on top of regular prison sentences (while these new incarceration terms are for at least two and no more than five years, no advance decision is made as to the specific length of the term).
5. The introduction of exceptionally stiff sentences for offences of 'hooligan character' (and especially for repeated offences of this nature) despite the strong opposition of lawyers to such a vague legal category which can be applied arbitrarily to a broad spectrum of offences including political ones.

Many other provisions of the Penal Code, although seemingly progressive, in reality offer considerable opportunities for abuse and the intensification of punitiveness. These opportunities have been dutifully seized by judges who have had little choice but to follow the sentencing guidelines issued by the party. For example, although the number of capital offences has been reduced in the 1969 Code from 94 to twelve and their exceptional character stressed, the actual application of capital punishment by hanging has increased considerably.[17] During the 10 years preceding the introduction of the new law, the death penalty had been adjudicated in 72 cases, yet in the 10-year period following 1969, 131 such sentences were handed down (see Zadrzyńska and Juńczyk, 1981; Kubiak, 1981: 13; Grajewski and Lammich, 1981: 414; Łyczywek, 1981: 9).[18] Among the factors which contributed to this increase in the judicial utilization of capital punishment has been the basically humane decision to abolish life imprisonment and to replace it with a 25-year term. According to Grajewski and Lammich (1981: 415), 'this assumption is strengthened by the fact that the number of offences punishable by death has not increased since 1969'.[19]

Contrary to its declared intentions, this change has produced a clear increase in judicial punitiveness. For example, during the last 5 years before the introduction of the present Code, 159 offenders had been sentenced to life in prison, whereas in the 5 years following its enactment, 233 convicted individuals received 25-year sentences, while in the subsequent 5-year period their number exceeded 300 (Grajewski and Lammich, 1981: 414).

Various forms of pre-trial diversion and alternative noncarceral penalties have been introduced into the Code, which concur with the current trends in modern penology. These, however, have resulted in the more frequent application of supplementary penalties (fines, confiscation of property, deprivation of parental rights, and so forth) not instead of but in addition to prison sentences. Moreover, even if the proportion of sentences involving unconditional deprivation of freedom had not increased in the 1970s, the length of the average prison sentence became much longer (for example, while the average prison sentence totalled 13 months in 1965, by 1979 it had virtually doubled to 24.5 months – see 'Sprawa Patronatu', 1981: 42). Consequently, short sentences became relatively less frequent and the proportion of sentences involving at least three years' incarceration has increased considerably. Moreover, many sentences which had involved fines were being replaced eventually by a prison term as a result of the marked tendency to adjudicate very high fines irrespective of the offender's ability to pay (Jasiński, 1978; Grajewski and Lammich, 1981).

THE COMMUNIST STATE AND LEGAL CONSCIOUSNESS IN POLAND

The analysis of some of the major aspects of the state and law in Poland presented in this chapter demonstrates clearly that neither shows the tendency towards gradual atrophy forecasted by Lenin. While the revolutionary laws passed under Bierut were harsh, they were marked by inconsistencies and gaps, and most of the repressions and police terror of these years were not backed by the laws of the time. Rather than being guided by the letter of the law, the legal practice was left to the 'revolutionary consciousness' of the law enforcers and their interpretation of the need to defend the new order by all means available.

Stalin's death brought about a wave of protests and demands for change in all institutionalized areas of life. The lawlessness of the Stalinist era was officially condemned and pressure was exerted to curb the powers of the secret police and the Procuracy, and to limit political control over judges. Just as in Khrushchev's Russia, the new emphasis in Poland was on legality, due process and the protection of citizens' rights. Thus, the content of the law was not really challenged or perceived as a problem since the urgency of procedural reforms and guarantees overshadowed the shortcomings of the law itself (for more detailed analysis see Falandysz, 1981a: 30). The new bills enacted after the 'thaw' of 1956 continued to be extremely harsh. The most notorious among them were: the bill regarding the protection of socialized property of 1958–59 and the anti-hooligan law of 1958 which introduced summary proceedings for people charged with hooliganism. The Penal Code of 1969 followed the same line as Khrushchev's penal legislations and was marked by unusually stern penalties and general repressiveness. Hundreds of new bills, hastily passed during the state of war when public opinion was suppressed and terrorized, went even further. They extended considerably the scope and degree of harshness in both the substance of the law and the legal procedure. Far from being reduced and weakened, the law emerged from the various crises of the communist state in Poland visibly strengthened, at least in the formal sense.

On the other hand, however, the gap between the society at large and the authorities continued to widen and the political alienation of the masses, who are supposed to 'rule' the country, reached a magnitude reminiscent of the Stalinist years or even that of the German occupation during World War II. The law lost its preponderance and authority, the common legal concepts and rules assumed double meanings and legal consciousness evolved towards a new, unpredictable state, as attested to in the following passages:

> At first I was ashamed that my dad was in prison, because in our family no one has ever been jailed, and I remembered that when the father of one of the boys was locked up for theft, other boys laughed at

him and shouted: 'thief's son'. At school, the teacher gave me money and sausage and said that the money was for us and the sausage for my father. But I told her that he was not in prison, that he had just gone away. And I burst into tears. She told me not to be ashamed, because it was not my father's fault, but that of those villains who put him behind bars.
(Marek, 10, son of a worker arrested in 1982 for his union activities, in 'Stan wojenny . . .', 1983: 28; this author's translation from Polish).

On 18 and 19 November [1982] the trial of Wladyslaw Frasyniuk [the chairman of the Wroclaw Region of Solidarity] took place in the Regional Court. When Frasyniuk was brought into the courtroom everyone present stood up. ('Frasyniuk . . .', 1983: 14)

The political prisoner does not assume an attitude of superiority towards criminal prisoners, remembering that they are, to a great extent, victims of the prevailing order.
(From the Code of the Political Prisoner[19] published by the underground Solidarity press, reprinted in 'Więźniowie polityczni', 1982: 48; this author's translation from Polish)

At 9.00 a.m. the ZOMOs enter the factory. There are around 500 of them. They are armed with truncheons, shields and helmets with visors. We tighten our circle, holding hands. Women cry. We pray for the ZOMOs, for their wives and children. One of them takes his helmet off . . . I saw tears in his eyes; immediately other ZOMOs took him away . . . (A participant's account of a strike in Lenin's steel-works in Cracow in December 1981, crushed by ZOMO)

As these examples indicate, 'law and order' is not a straightforward matter in contemporary Poland. Both prisoners and guards are actors in a complex political drama, while the legal and moral consciousness of the society undergoes profound transformations. The criminal and the hero may share much more than just prison space in their uneven struggle against the repressiveness of the 'forces of order', and yet they may also be poised against each other in numerous confrontations staged by the ruling alliance of the political, military and police forces. For, the criminal is left to the mercy of his jailers and may, if duly rewarded or blackmailed, follow their orders and join the forces of repression.[20]

The society loathes its criminals, but it also abhors the prisons which house them, and it revolts against the suffering they share with the society's heros in the numerous penal institutions notorious for their barbarism. The pressure and uncertainties of the historically unique configuration of political relations in recent years in Poland have shaken and sharpened social consciousness. While some moral sentiments may have become humanized and elevated to an unusual level of refinement, some others may have degenerated into the dangerous state of apathy, hatred or vengeance, or may have been drifting and pulsating, pushed and torn by contradictory forces of order and disorder, reason and madness, freedom and repression.

The whole society is on trial when conventional moral judgements can no longer be taken for granted and when all the traditional categories and stereotypes break under the pressure of a massive, alien assault on the society's cultural substance. In many ways, one can compare the present moral and legal experiences of the Poles to those of inmates of concentration camps or peoples in occupied territories; there, too, moral categories must be re-evaluated and subordinated to the dominant interpretation of the extraordinary situation and of its ultimate political significance. Questions are thus asked: what is the purpose of the law, which laws are to be obeyed, who are the 'real' criminals, whose interests are served or threatened by the law-abiding mentality and what are the primary moral obligations and loyalties of the members of the suppressed group? These new attitudes are among the significant, although not sufficiently explored, consequences of the political developments in Poland before and after 13 December 1981, the day of the imposition of the state of war.

It can be assumed that whenever the official law is void of moral legitimacy, informal group ethics and individual moral maturity become of the utmost importance. Pawelczyńska, a Polish sociologist, sums up her memories of Auschwitz's moral subculture in the following words:

> Prisoners at Auschwitz had to be capable of creativity in the sphere of moral standards. . . . Only the person who fully understood weakness could survive and salvage his values; one needed an intelligence that was nondogmatic, that reacted flexibly to the environment, drawing the most apt conclusions from a concrete situation over which one had no control. Only such an attitude and skill enabled one to make a relevant moral choice. (Pawelczyńska, 1979: 140)

Gross, in his study of Poland under German occupation during World War II, presents a subtle analysis of the complex relationship between the declining moral authority of the law and the increased recognition for the importance of individual moral sophistication:

> Never are *all* laws, even those enforced by an illegitimate authority, considered by the public to be abuses of justice. There are always some laws that can be called regulatory. Such laws, and the normative obligation to respect them, seem to the public to be a natural and necessary component of orderly social intercourse, no matter who is charged with their enforcement. Thus in any system the guardians are perceived also as executors of laws that do not necessarily violate the ordinary citizen's sense of personal dignity and justice. As a result, some degree of ambiguity is introduced into the citizen's understanding of the limits of legitimacy in the rule of his oppressors, and the necessity of recognizing which acts are outside and which within these limits makes strong demands on the subject's sense of discrimination. (Gross, 1979: 20)

Thus, the imposed law is rarely seen as unacceptable in its totality, but rather is met by ambivalent attitudes which recognize the pragmatic functionality or even moral virtue of some legal norms, while rejecting those parts which are more directly related to the ideological and repressive aims of the rulers. This ambivalence is even more conspicuous in the attitudes towards law enforcement and penal institutions. Since the majority of citizens accepts the necessity of policing, maintaining order and protecting society from dangerous individuals, the agencies charged with these tasks automatically acquire some legitimacy, and yet they are simultaneously dreaded as representatives of the political tyranny.

While Polish legal consciousness seems to have come back to that state of apprehension and disapproval of the official law which prevailed in the Stalinist era, it has now acquired new moral sophistication learned through the experience of Solidarity and the revival of Christian values. The ambivalence of legal consciousness has recently shifted from an attitude of selective scepticism about the neutrality and utility of the law which was characteristic of the 1960s and 1970s (Podgórecki, 1966, 1971, 1973, 1974), to an overwhelming distrust of all aspects of the law and its enforcement after December 1981. The military rule has undoubtedly contributed to that present prominence of an antagonistic vision of the law held by the majority of the citizens. It seems that, in the 1960s and 1970s, the society supported the criminal law insofar as people were in favour of rather stern measures for conventional criminals (Podgórecki *et al.*, 1971). Nevertheless, at the same time, there prevailed attitudes of cynicism about the legitimacy of many laws regulating everyday relations between citizens and the authorities. As a report prepared by a Polish discussion group known as 'Experience and the Future' correctly observes, this scepticism was shared, at least to some degree, by the officials themselves, for the malfunctioning of both the legal and political systems produced 'a situation in which both public opinion and the authorities themselves [came] to consider abuse of and disregard for the law justified' (*Poland Today*, 1981: 39). It seems that, in the 1980s, this public scepticism has been transformed into an attitude of profound hostility and rejection of the official legal system.

3 The State and Popular Justice in the Soviet Union and Poland

POPULAR JUSTICE AND COMMUNIST IDEOLOGY

The law and its enforcement is strongly institutionalized and professionalized in both the Soviet Union and Poland. Following the period of ruthless lawlessness during Stalin's reign, considerable efforts have been made to increase the level of legality in the functioning of the criminal justice system. As a result, new codes, new and better defined procedures and new categories of criminals have been introduced into the formal body of the law. Nevertheless, while such a trend aims at enhancing the legitimacy and 'respectability' of the legal system, it also presents several ideological problems. Paramount among these is the fact that objections can be raised as to the principle entrusting a specialized group of professional experts with the exclusive right to pass judgements on others and to enforce the laws of the country. There is something distinctly 'uncommunistic' about a situation in which a manual worker is subject to a trial conducted by highly educated members of the professional élite. There have been various steps undertaken, therefore, to reduce this obvious discrepancy between the ideology and the practice.

Another ideologically troubling aspect of the legal system in communist countries is its current reliance on rigidly codified sets of norms. Quite contrary to the early directives formulated by E. B. Pashukanis (see 1978 and 1980 English editions) which suggested a flexible and open-ended approach to the law, the present solutions tend to favour those basic legal structures closely resembling the disapproved 'bourgeois law'. While they are differently employed, interpreted and enforced, they nevertheless retain the appearances of the 'old type of law' (see Hazard, 1978; David, 1954: 157–85) and, therefore, are subject to ideological criticism. Such law is believed to have at least two kinds of biases. First, its content is determined by legal experts and the impact of the legal consciousness of the masses appears to be dangerously limited. Secondly, the existence of such fixed sets of laws suggests that society is basically static in nature. Such an assumption, however, is contrary to the Marxist view of society which gives much importance to the constant change and dialectic transformations of socio-economic life. Given the dynamic nature of society, the law has to be able to respond quickly to change by assuming the form of the versatile elements of the evolving social reality. According to this view, defended strongly by many Soviet law professors in the 1950s, 'law must be "dialectically" applied as circumstances require' (Lapenna, 1975: 76).

The level of importance attached to such ideological issues has fluctuated significantly, since the early days of revolutionary Russia. As well, the remedies adopted by Soviet leaders and their Polish counterparts have varied significantly, and range from verbal ideological pronouncements to the establishment of special lay courts for workers. The doctrine of 'socialist legality', so important for an adequate understanding of the prevailing political conception of the law, has also undergone frequent modifications.

As mentioned in Chapter 1, it was under Khrushchev that the most conspicuous shift towards the 'popularization' of justice took place. It was coupled, however, with an ardent emphasis on socialist legality, which implied greater reliance on due process, formalized procedures and uniformity of the law. How this new faith in legality could coexist with the spontaneous and arbitrary dispensation of justice by lay collectives and community volunteers was not at all clear. Consequently, as indicated by Eugene Kamenka:

> [in] these circumstances, the attempts of Soviet jurists to systematize a post-Stalinist Marxist philosophy of law have completely lost their theoretical unity and thrust and have become little more than barometric indications of the relative strengths of competing pressures within Soviet society. (Kamenka, 1970: 320)

Khrushchev's modified theory of the withering away of the state and law, which postulated a gradual replacement of the state coercive apparatus with citizen's assemblies, was bound to be disliked by both lawyers and legal bureaucrats as well as by hard-line doctrinaires who favoured a more centralized model. Nevertheless, Khushchev was successful in his attempts to introduce at least some forms of popular participation into the justice system. They were subsequently curbed, however, as a result of the shift in his own approach as well as the more bureaucratic orientation of his successor. Yet, some of these popular legal bodies have persisted to date and have been eventually transplanted into other communist countries. Some of them, such as the voluntary militia detachments or the petty crime penal boards have acquired unequivocally bad reputations as repressive and arbitrary extensions of the state coercive apparatus. Others, notably the comrades' courts and the people's assessors have earned a far less unanimously derogatory image, which suggests both that they may have some merits and that the problems in their functioning may be at least partially explained by the inherent flaws of the overall legal and political context. These two institutions will be discussed below in more detail.

PEOPLE'S ASSESSORS

The role of the people's assessors is significantly different from the jury system within the Anglo-American common law tradition in that they are expected to give their opinion concerning both the fact and the proposed sentence. Those suggestions, made by some Soviet legal experts in the mid-1950s regarding the introduction of some sort of a jury system to strengthen the legality of criminal justice, were promptly rejected as too reminiscent of the Tsarist era when the jury was in fact employed in the Russian courts. The form which was finally found acceptable both to the authorities and to the legal profession was one modelled on the German institution of lay judges. Indeed, it was used in the early, post-revolutionary period when the revolutionary tribunals consisted of a judge and six people's assessors. At that time, however, the professional legal expertise was of little use since the old law was itself treated with suspicion and the new decrees were vague and ideological in nature. This unusual proportion of professional and lay judges, therefore, had a strong ideological justification.

Subsequently, in the period 1922–24, during which many key pieces of legislation were passed and the new Soviet court system emerged, this proportion was revised so that each court was thereafter expected to sit one judge and two people's assessors. This principle was soon undermined, however, by Stalin's dictatorial reforms in the 1930s at which time an extensive judicial power was given to special benches of three judges without lay assessors. As well, many cases were tried in special summary proceedings and did not even require the presence of the defendant or his representative.

In the late 1950s the mixed bench regained its importance, a move which was portrayed as the ultimate expression of the democratization of justice. According to this arrangement, benches of one professional judge and two lay judges were to adjudicate most civil and criminal cases in all courts whenever they functioned as courts of original jurisdiction. The lay judges for the bottom level courts were supposed to be elected at general meetings by employees or, in rural areas, by residents. The lay judges for the upper level courts were to be chosen by local Soviets (councils) in a manner similar to that of the professional judges (Hazard, 1968: 176). It is this system which remains in place to this day.

The people's assessors are not expected to have any knowledge of the law itself and continue to work full time elsewhere during their two-year term of service in the courts. They must receive paid leave for all court sessions they are obliged to attend, which, in turn, must not exceed 10 days each year. They have virtually all the same rights and duties as the professional judge and can, theoretically, outvote him or her, if they so choose. While they sit at trials together with the judge, they may not preside during the court sessions. Unlike the jury system where the professional judge cannot participate in the juror's conference, all three members of the bench deliberate cases together 'in camera'.

The rejection of the jury system and the introduction of lay assessors into the Polish courts in the 1940s was a direct result of Soviet pressure to pattern the Polish legal system after that of the USSR. Thus, the scope of lay participation was gradually increased from the initial narrow range of criminal cases to the final extension of its participation, in the 1950s, to the majority of criminal and civil cases. In cases which involve capital offences, the court may sit in extended benches consisting of two judges and three lay assessors. In summary proceedings and in trials held 'in camera', however, lay judges are normally excluded (Resich, 1973: 54–5). Polish lay assessors serve three-year terms and are nominated by local councils (the counterparts of the Soviets in the USSR) from lists provided by meetings of employees, residents or members of various organizations. The procedures involved in the selection of candidates are not specified in the Polish Constitution. The people's assessors may be repealed by the appropriate council before the expiration of their terms if they neglect their obligations, defame the court or are unable to carry on their duties (Resich, 1973: 57).

Most of the evidence from the Soviet Union shows that the people's assessors, unlike professional judges, are very passive during the trials and do not seem to have much influence on the outcome (e.g. Juviler, 1976: 75; Hazard, 1968: 176; Smith, 1980: 117). As one of the commentators puts it:

> . . . observation of court proceedings indicates that the judge's professional knowledge gives him sufficient leverage over the people's

> assessors so that they seldom challenge his view of the merits of the case before the court. (Barry and Barner-Barry, 1982: 157)

This tendency is even more pronounced in case of political trials. A recent study by Amnesty International found that the people's assessors set silently throughout the proceedings and played virtually no role in these trials (*URSS. Les prisonniers* . . ., 1980: 118).

The same impression has been conveyed by observers of court sessions in Poland. While the lack of interest or active participation by lay judges has been noted by many commentators, the real significance of their presence was the subject of a penetrating investigation undertaken by a research team of lawyers and sociologists in 1964. The researchers assumed that, according to the declared intentions of the legislators, lay assessors were expected to become *a sui generis* factor of the societal control over the courts of law (Podgórecki, 1971: 265; 1974: 128; Zawadzki and Kubicki, 1972: 33–4) and, as a result, they undertook to assess the lay judges' performance from this perspective.

The project employed a variety of techniques to study the extent to which these expectations were fulfilled and the exact nature of the role played by the assessors. They included questionnaires addressed to the lay judges themselves, the professional judges, lawyers and prosecutors; in-depth interviews with randomly selected assessors; observations of the assessors' elections and court sessions, as well as secret observations of the actual behaviour of the lay judges during the 'in camera' deliberations. The latter technique was slightly controversial but was executed with the utmost care to secure the full anonimity of the observed individuals (for a more detailed description, see Podgórecki, 1971: 267; 1974: 129; Zawadzki and Kubicki, 1972: 35–6).

The study established that most lay assessors tended to be white collar employees while the second largest group was comprised of skilled workers. On average, most had acquired high school education and were between the ages of 25 and 40. The ratio of men to women was quite high.[1] While the lay judges' court attendance record was very good, as a rule they were not interested enough in the cases they were expected to participate in to study the files before the day of the trial. This low active interest in cases was especially pronounced in women.[2] As far as the behaviour of professional judges during trials and deliberations was concerned:

> [t]hey rarely [gave] the lay judges any information about the cases. . . . It [was] also only on rare occasions that a professional judge explain[ed] to the lay judges the legal aspects of the case. He [was] not

> likely to give them any directives aimed at stimulating their active participation in the trial. (Podgórecki, 1974: 131)

Accordingly, '[t]he lay judges interfered very little with the course of the proceedings. Rarely if at all, did they ask questions. When they did, however, it was usually to the point' (Podgórecki, 1974: 132). The secret observations of the 'in camera' conferences showed that in about half of the cases, there was no sign of disagreement between the judge and assessors; in roughly one-quarter of the cases, some controversy arose but the final decision was imposed by the judge; and in the remaining quarter, some type of compromise was reached. More educated people, younger people, and men tended to have more influence over the course of the trial and its deliberations. Whatever little influence they were able to exercise over the final verdicts, it was clearly documented that they favoured less stringent punishment and pressed for moderation. Finally, the analysis of the questionnaire and interview data suggested that the people's assessors' subjective perception of their role was in clear contrast to their actual limited impact. They saw themselves or, perhaps, wanted to see themselves, as fully active participants in the court proceedings.

In his final evaluation of the role of lay assessors in criminal trials, Adam Podgórecki introduces the concept of the 'control reference group'. Unlike the normative reference group to which one aspires or the comparative reference group whose norms and standards one employs as criteria with which to evaluate one's status or behaviour,[3] the control reference group comprises more of a watchdog role than an active influence. According to Podgórecki:

> [t]he lay judges, even though they may remain passive, carefully observe the course of the court proceedings in all its phases. . . . The judge cannot be unaware of the vigilant attention of his two monitors and must be quite conscious of the limitations imposed upon him by their very presence. (Podgórecki, 1974: 135)

It appears, therefore, that lay judges do perform the control role for which they are designed, even if they do it in a distinctly subdued manner. A question, however, arises as to what kind of social values they represent and to what degree they may be influenced or manipulated by the political centres. Clearly, their selection does not guarantee that they represent a random cross-section of the society. Rather, the proceedings at the general meetings in the work places and villages are apt to be almost totally dominated by the party and party-run trade unions. Hazard's observations of the Soviet lay assessors confirm this suspicion and he states that '[t]he Communist Party shares in the selection by these institutions, and the nominations are unopposed' (Hazard, 1968: 177). The Polish study found that the majority of lay assessors were indeed members of the Communist Party (Podgórecki, 1974: 130) despite the fact that party membership within the total population amounted to only 2 or 3 per cent. As well, a more recent article, published in 1981 in the official weekly of the Solidarity Union, criticizes the overwhelming political influence upon the selection of assessors. The author, a well-known legal scholar, stresses the need for change and states that in the pre-Solidarity period:

> the political authorities secured for themselves full control over the selection of the 'appropriate' people. This was easily done since the activities of many social organizations, and especially the trade unions, lacked authenticity and were totally subordinated to the authorities.
>
> (Falandysz, 1981b: 11; this author's translation from Polish)

Characteristically, numerous individuals, including many entire work crews, after the imposition of the state of war boycotted the lay assessors' selection meetings thereby refusing to give any legitimacy to the process which they found lacking in authenticity. There has emerged a clear understanding that both the process of selection and the actual role of the people's assessors in the courts are being manipulated by the party. Moreover, the growing awareness of the totalitarian nature of the law has led many people to reject all its aspects and to refuse to play any part in its official administration.

There are two major aspects of the principle of lay participation in the administration which are emphasized by the communist defenders of this institution. One, already discussed, is the ability of laymen to bring common law values and judgements to the legal process and to forestall the potential danger of the domination of the administration of justice by élitist, professional groups. The second assumed contribution is related to the lay assessors' role as knowledgeable disseminators of the law within their communities. It is presumed that they are able to convey to other people the lessons they have learned from their own first hand experiences in court. There is, however, no research on the extent and ramifications of the actual fulfilment of this function by the people's assessors. These two aspects, while logically almost contradictory, are clearly consistent with those orthodox Leninist principles which favour the rotation of roles within society in order to prevent narrow specialization and maintain the contact between the professions and the realities of common life.

A comprehensive evaluation of the fulfilment of these two major aims is a difficult task. The first one is easier to assess, however, than the second. As mentioned above, while lay judges are very passive and their presumed common people's values are rarely aired in court, they nevertheless seem to play the role of watchdog. There are several important reasons, however, why this may not be sufficient to prevent most of the abuses which take place in the courts and especially during political cases. First of all, as a rule, the people's assessors are nominated by the party or by party-run organizations and the election procedures at the general meetings are not democratic.

Secondly, those lay judges who are not bound by the party discipline and are willing to exercise their own judgements may still be intimidated by the fear that their rebellious behaviour in court might be disclosed at their work places. Clearly, to oppose a judge or to accuse her or him of a lax attitude towards the law is a potentially dangerous step to take.

Thirdly, even though there are many lay judges whose integrity cannot be questioned, they can be easily deferred from the more sensitive cases and assigned only to the routine non-political ones.

And, finally, even if they exercise some moderating or restraining influence over judges, the lay assessors cannot change the law itself or the legal structures in which they are participating. It must be remembered that, despite the considerable reforms of the legal procedures which took place under Khrushchev and Gomulka, legal safeguards are still rather tentative and lax. For example, even the principle of the presumption of innocence, met with strong opposition by hardliner doctrinaires, could never be incorporated explicitly into the laws of these countries. Nor has the right to counsel from the moment of arrest ever been guaranteed in their constitutions. Moreover, the very nature of the communist law, which itself is a tool of a monopolistic party, seems to necessitate totalitarian means of enforcement. A law which tries to regulate every aspect of an individual's life and to subordinate it to an ideologically accepted model, undoubtedly needs extensive coercive machinery to implement it.

It is fair to conclude, therefore, that, while the presence of lay judges in communist courts does not appear to increase the level of repressiveness and lawlessness and may, in fact, even reduce it, it can neither prevent party interference with the administration of justice nor alleviate the inherent defects of communist legal systems.

COMRADES' COURTS

The comrades' courts are an excellent example of the emphasis on the social and collective enforcement of moral and legal norms. They were introduced by Lenin in the early days of the Soviet rule to deal with the problems of discipline during the period of civil war. At that time, the comrades' courts were set up in the Red Army (in 1917) to help tighten military discipline, and in the trade unions (in 1919) to cope with work-related infractions (Yin, 1982: 7–8). Even though they had virtually ceased to exist by 1922, they were later revived in the late 1920s as a supplement to the new court system and were especially useful in the rural areas. Eventually, the intensification of police terror and the dictatorial tendency towards centralization within the administration of justice resulted in their total eclipse by the late 1930s (Boiter, 1973: 145–6; Solomon, 1981–82: 27–37). Their second revival came after Khrushchev's announcement in 1959 that the time was ripe for a gradual transfer of power from the state to the various social organizations and collective bodies. Shortly thereafter, a model draft statute regarding comrades' courts was published which set the general pattern for all the republics (Boiter, 1973: 146).

The comrades' courts operate under the immediate supervision of the local trade unions and housing administrations and are subject to general supervision and guidance by the party committees and local Soviets (Juviler, 1974: 33). They may be set up in enterprises, institutions and plants as well as in residential and rural areas. Judges are elected for two years by open ballot at special meetings from among the work crews or residents and do not have to possess any legal skills or knowledge. The bench consists of three lay judges and defendants may not be represented by lawyers (they may, however, be represented by co-workers or neighbours). Court sessions are informal with no fixed rules or procedures and are supposed to involve the defendant's colleagues or neighbours both as a means of exercising social pressure upon him and simultaneously strengthening the community's awareness of the importance of certain norms. Indeed, during the trial, everyone present may, with the permission of the chairman, put questions to the defendant or witnesses.

The comrades' courts may not impose sentences of deprivation of freedom; their sanctions are regarded as educational measures rather than punishments. They typically include: a public apology to the victim, a warning, social censure, a reprimand, a small fine, compensation to the victim, a recommendation to the management to transfer the offender to a lower paid, manual or less responsible job or to fire him, or a recommendation to the housing administration to evict him (Juviler, 1974: 33; Yin, 1982: 9–). Since 1977 they have also the power to suggest depriving a 'guilty person' of bonuses due to annual production results and they can refer an alcoholic to a compulsory treatment (Butler, 1977: 329). The comrades' courts may also turn over cases to common courts or other state agencies. Moreover, they may, if needed, request legal assistance from the judiciary and prosecutors. There is no possibility of appealing the sentence to any independent legal body; the only avenue of appeal is a complaint to the trade unions commissions or the executive committees of the Soviets. Cases may be brought before comrades' courts by various bodies and individuals, including, for example, people's militia detachments, trade union committees, local Soviets, plant managements, public prosecutors, public organizations, housing committees, work collectives, individual citizens and finally, the comrades' courts themselves (Barghoorn, 1972: 299; Yin, 1982: 9).

There are three broad categories of cases dealt with by the comrades' courts:

1. cases in which the courts have exclusive jurisdiction because the charges refer to violations of moral standards and communal rules rather than legal norms;
2. first-time petty offences which, according to the law, may be diverted from the courts by discretional decisions of the law-enforcement agents; and
3. cases transferred from common courts as a result of the presiding judge's decision that such a move would be beneficial and appropriate (Boiter, 1973: 147).

The nature of cases considered by the comrades' courts in work places and in housing areas differ considerably. The former handle mainly violations of labour discipline and other on-the-job infractions and especially the unauthorized use of tools, equipment or vehicles and theft of state property as well as private property belonging to fellow workers (Boiter, 1973: 147). Residential courts, on the other hand, deal with violations of dwelling regulations, cases of damage to buildings and premises, quarrels over the use of shared or subsidiary facilities, disputes over cost of repairs, family disagreements, wife or child beatings, negligence in the rearing of children, foul language, slander, unruly behaviour, and so forth (Boiter, 1973: 147; Yin, 1982: 14). In addition, both types of courts may handle petty, first-time offences which involve small scale speculation, the distillation of moonshine liquor, alcoholism and hooliganism. In short, the range of behaviour within the jurisdiction of the Soviet comrades' courts is extremely broad. Indeed, according to the official regulations, any case of anti-social conduct or style of life not consistent with a given community's values may be brought before such a quasi-judicial forum.

The structure and jurisdiction of the Polish 'social courts' (described by Krakowski, 1970) is practically identical to those of the comrades' courts in the USSR. There are two types of social courts both of which were established by the Law on Social Courts of 30 March 1965: (1) the workers' courts at state companies and (2) the social conciliatory commissions in residential areas. The workers' courts are created at state companies, ostensibly upon the initiative of the workers' councils by means of a decision taken at a general meeting of employees. They must then be accepted by the regional councils of trade unions. While they are formally independent of the justice system and are guided by the trade unions, the common courts are supposed to assist in case of need (Circular letter, 1967: item 66).

Each workers' court votes on its own regulations, defining in detail its rules and procedures. Master regulations are proposed by the Central Council of Trade Unions while the regional councils of trade unions assure the conformity of the individual regulations with the master by-laws. Similar to the Soviet comrades' courts, the workers' courts deal with disputes between workers and with petty offences against the disciplinary rules of the company or against the nationalized property. They do not adjudicate labour disputes or cases which are already subject to criminal or civil proceedings, nor do they consider cases involving executives and deputy executives. The jurisdiction of conciliatory commissions is basically the same as that of their Soviet counterparts. As well, the sanctions available to the Polish social courts seem to be identical to the measures employed by the comrades' courts in the USSR (Kurczewski and Frieske, 1978: 153–427; Łoś, 1978: 811–815; Krakowski, 1970; Rybicki, 1972; Kos-Rabcewicz-Zubkowski, 1976).

Given the shortage of reliable, current empirical evaluations, the assessment of the performance of the Soviet comrades' courts and Polish social courts is, of course, very difficult. There is, however, a number of scattered sources which provide some insight into the real working of these institutions. While, nevertheless, the Polish data are of a more systematic and scientific nature,[4] the Soviet information comes mainly from journalistic enunciations in the Soviet press and observations by Western researchers.

Early experiences in the USSR indicate that there were some

traditions prevalent within the Russian countryside[5] which promoted the relatively easy acceptance of the village social courts established in 1929. According to Solomon, these village courts took root so easily because, 'as peasant courts, [they] provided a setting for peasants to resolve disputes and to police themselves, according to custom and common sense if not to law' (Solomon, 1981–82: 29).

The kolkhoz and factory comrades' courts, however, were far less successful since they attempted to impose new labour discipline on the peasant workforce which, in turn, resented the coercive rules and ruthlessness of the collectivization and intensive industrialization under Stalin. As well, neither the management nor the trade unions supported these lay bodies as they preferred to reserve for themselves the right to control and discipline their work crews. Indeed, the directors of both the kolkhozes and factories were authorized to levy penalties on workers unilaterally, without any hearings or formal procedures. Solomon indicates that managements frequently used comrades' courts to do the 'dirty work' for them and especially in cases of unpopular firings and so forth (Solomon, 1981–82: 33). The courts seemed to have little integrity, independence or sense of tradition and thereby tended to abuse their power. Solomon quotes an example of a sentence meted out to two workers found guilty of absenteeism, which illustrates well the sense of power exhibited by some comrades' courts judges. The decision in this particular case was to sentence the defendants to:

> five years' strict isolation (i.e. incarceration), but taking into account twenty years' continuous working record, to replace this with six months of corrective work, and taking into account the victory of the proletariat on all fronts, to consider the sentence conditional.
> (Solomon, 1981–82: 33–4; the sentence quoted by Solomon was presented in Shliapochnikov, 1934)

Currently, Soviet comrades' courts, and especially those in work places, appear to be rather dormant and are not taken very seriously either by the authorities or by the public. Although there are probably more than 300 000 formally constituted comrades' courts (Boiter, 1973: 145; Juviler, 1976: 81), they tend, in Juviler's words, to 'operate infrequently, lapsing into inactivity until prodded to meet in one of the periodic local campaigns of the party for grass roots prevention' (Juviler, 1976: 82). Attempts to revive comrades' courts which include a revised statute enacted by Presidium of the RSFSR Supreme Soviet in 1977 (see Feldbrugge, 1977: 349) do not appear to have had much impact on their functioning.

Similar views are expressed from time to time in the daily Soviet press as the following excerpts from two articles in *Pravda* illustrate:

> [H]ooligans still have their own way in the streets of most of the province's communities, committing outrages without any fear whatsoever. . . . You can't count on volunteer police aides. . . . Or, take the comrades' courts. There are hundreds of them in the city and province, but barely half of them function.
>
> (Starukhin and Khalin, 1979: 11–12)

> [T]he magic of figures is insidious . . . [T]he annual report of the plant's council on courts states that 90 more cases were heard in 1978 than in 1977. And the trend is continuing this year. . . . One's suspicions are aroused by the fact that such statements and conclusions remain almost completely identical from one year to another. . . . After turning a case over to a comrades' court, the representatives of management or of shop trade union committees consider that their duty has been done. They rarely attend court sessions, which substantially reduces the authority and effectiveness of collective condemnation . . . Infractions are often examined hastily, without the sort of complete, comprehensive and objective investigation of circumstances that would rule out unjust condemnation and punishment. (Tairova, 1979: 4)

Another type of criticism raised in *Pravda* deals with the fact that:

> [r]epresentations from management concerning violations of production discipline are virtually the chief source feeding the courts' activity. Thus, the role of the public organizations and the labour collective itself is reduced to naught. (Tairova, 1979: 4)

In sum, the impression one gains is that the Soviet comrades' courts are rather inactive, and when they do act they are inefficient, they enjoy little prestige and tend to serve as an auxiliary punitive arm for management. Their low prestige has been confirmed by at least one Soviet public opinion survey (Targonsky, 1977: 78). It seems, however, that this description is more applicable to the courts in the work places rather than those in the residential areas. There is some evidence which shows that the latter do play a part in solving the daily problems facing Soviet citizens whose inadequate living conditions generate tension and discord among neighbours. As Yin has explained, the overcrowded living quarters and shared kitchens, bathrooms and other facilities, occasion many unavoidable altercations. The pains of collective living seem to necessitate the existence of some easily accessible mechanisms of collective conflict resolution:

> Given the material scarcity, collective ownership and joint facilities . . . and the resulting physical contacts, how can the Soviets do without the readily accessible comradely court? In a true sense, this body is administering justice of the peace between individuals, households, apartment-sharers and acquaintances constantly running into each other. . . . The reason for the comradely court lies mainly in the compact style of life. As long as the Soviet economy continues its present course by placing priorities on heavy industry, the need for the court is real. It is called upon to police the rudimentary behaviour in collectives. (Yin, 1982: 15–16)

These findings on the Soviet comrades' courts are, by and large, consistent with the picture emerging from the Polish studies on social courts. At present the workers' courts seem to be practically non-existent and where they do exist, they do not show much life. The conciliatory commissions, on the other hand, are relatively active in certain areas and do perform some limited but needed functions, not unlike their Soviet counterparts.

The most thorough study of the workers' courts were conducted in 1960 in a region of Poland where these courts were introduced on an experimental basis before the appropriate legislation was passed by the Diet. A wide range of techniques was employed including interviews, document analysis (especially of the minutes of trials held in these courts), content analysis of press materials, and participant observation. Interviews were conducted with employees, party and union activists, workers' court judges and secretaries (Podgórecki, 1974: 151–2). The results of this study, however, are not necessarily representative of the present situation. It must be remembered that the courts were functioning on an experimental basis at the time of the study. Even more importantly, it was a period of post-Stalinist liberalization in Poland when many people still believed in Gomulka's promises of democratization of social life.

The study showed that the employees' reaction to the social courts was, at that time, rather favourable, even if they did have reservations about some specific aspects of their operation. While the defendants who were interviewed in this study expressed a general acceptance of the outcome, the majority felt that they were singled out unjustly for prosecution or that there was a gross disproportion between the offence and the shame of having to face the entire staff of the company (Podgórecki, 1974: 153). The analysis of documents showed that, indeed, the criteria for the selection of cases were not clear. Moreover, cases involving administrative and managerial personnel, which generally tend to be more complex, were never submitted to workers' courts:

> A further finding was that mobilization of public opinion was by no means always easy or possible. In those companies in which there was a peculiar negative sub-culture in the form of a 'sentiment' for theft, it was difficult to evoke strong collective condemnation against it. Therefore, [the ability to influence] public opinion depends on whether it is possible to mobilize sufficiently active nuclei of such opinion in the given environment. (Podgórecki, 1974: 157)

Additionally, it was found that workers felt entitled to use factory tools for their own purposes and that, consequently:

> [a]ttempts to punish workers for using the nationalized means of production for their individual, non-income needs [were] inconsistent with this legal sentiment, and thus, it [was] impossible to consolidate collective opinion to condemn such behaviour.
> (Podgórecki, 1974: 157)

On the positive side, it was noted that, in several companies, the social courts actually contributed towards improving some aspects of the organization of production in order to prevent infractions. These recommendations were mainly related to the methods of storage, catalogueing and the dispensation of expensive materials or tools (Podgórecki, 1974: 155).

In its final report the research team stressed, among other things, the need for a more careful definition of the courts' jurisdiction and the range of sanctions, the inclusion of managerial cases and the exclusion of offences related to the non-profit use of factory equipment by the workers. While the bill which was eventually passed in 1965 was compatible with several of the recommendations resulting from the 1960 research and its subsequent follow-up enquiries, the legislation was in clear conflict with some of the other recommendations. In particular, the jurisdiction of workers' courts remained rather broadly defined and the illegitimate use of factory equipment was included as one of the relevant offences. The bill permitted the inclusion of persons in managerial positions, but excepted company directors and their deputies. In typical fashion, however, none of the official documents and publications accompanying the new legislation ever referred to the illuminating and methodologically sound study. As interpreted by A. Podgórecki, '[t]his [meant] that the legislators [did] not consider science as an institutionalized partner to which they should turn for opinion in those instances where scientific researches might shed light upon the problems of interest to them' (Podgórecki, 1974: 160).

Another important Polish study focused on the social conciliatory commissions (Kurczewski and Frieske, 1978; 1979). Conducted in 1974–75, it utilized a number of research techniques, including the analysis of available statistical data and legal documents, a public opinion survey of a representative sample of 972 persons from within the Polish adult population, questionnaires administered to a random sample of the inhabitants of two small towns, observations of actual sessions and interviews with the clients. It appears from this study that the range of cases considered by the commissions is similar to that of the Soviet residential courts. The authors of the project contended that the most peculiar feature of the social conciliatory commissions was their active promotion of harmony and neighbourly cooperation without access to the means of state coercion. As a result, their activities were focused on conciliatory efforts, their procedure was flexible and any steps undertaken during the session had to be voluntarily accepted by the interested parties (Kurczewski and Frieske, 1979: 37).

Since the commissions do not have any means of coercion at their disposal, their main aim is to guide the parties toward some form of agreement or compromise. The members of the panel conduct the proceedings in a very informal way allowing the parties to exchange their opinions and insults, but all the while, urging them gently to see the other participant's perspectives. The sessions are, in principle, open to the public, however, if one of the parties or the judges prefer to keep it closed, they are always free to do so. While there are no court fees, the parties are asked to donate some money for various community purposes.

What is worthy of note is the researchers' observation of an increased tendency by the common courts to transfer case of private accusation to the commissions so that they might conduct the initial conciliatory sessions legally required for these types of cases. By 1971, 40 per cent of all cases handled by the commissions fell into this category. The authors of the study considered this fact an undesirable development since it could eventually lead to the transformation of the commissions into extensions of the common court system.

The nation-wide opinion survey showed that 79 per cent of the respondents tended to favour those methods of conflict resolution based on mediation and compromise. In their response to another question, 59 per cent thought that it would be better to have a solution acceptable to both parties even if it were not fully consistent with the law, and only 28 per cent expressed the view that a strictly legal solution would be most desirable. Moreover, 46 per cent of the respondents had read or heard about the social conciliatory commissions, 20 per cent were familiar with some cases presided over by the commissions, and 2 per cent had first-hand experience as parties in such cases. Thirty-four per cent had never heard about the commissions. Most of the respondents were of the opinion that the best method of dealing with conflict is private mediation. The second most preferred option was the commission, while the common court appeared to be the least popular. It was also found that the degree of acceptance indicated in the evaluation varied directly with the level of knowledge and understanding of the functioning of the conciliatory commissions.

A detailed study of two selected towns, one with a common court and another without a court, indicated significant differences between them. The inhabitants of the latter believed, rather unrealistically, that the commissions would perform the role of both a court and an informal neighbourly body. Even though the commission enjoyed some prestige, there was resentment towards specific decisions and the lack of means of enforcement of the applied sanctions. In the larger town, there existed a greater indifference towards the local commission and, therefore more realistic expectations and generally more favourable opinions about its performance in specific cases. In sum, while the study provided a mixed picture of the functioning of the commissions, it confirmed that the need for such a body did in fact exist and postulated that much would depend upon the future relationship between the common courts and the commissions as well as upon the proper information about the nature and the aims of these social tribunals.

While the Polish conciliatory commissions seem to be reasonably active, in some localities at least, the period following the formal legalizations of the workers' courts in 1965 witnessed a rather rapid process of decline of these social courts (Rybicki, 1972: 26–7). There may be many reasons for this deterioration. One probable factor is the gradual suppression of most of the gains and limited liberties won by the Polish working people in the short period of the political 'thaw' initiated by the October events of 1956. The climate of hope and guarded faith in the new institutions quickly disappeared and was replaced within the disillusioned society once again by mistrust, fear and the refusal to cooperate. This may explain the lack of popularity given the court sessions and the workers' reluctance to either attend them or to serve as social judges. Another explanation, however, may help to elucidate the marked decline in the authorities' enthusiasm for these new vehicles of popular justice. It is important to note that it was at this time when, with the ousting of Khrushchev, the 'utopian model' came under strong attack from the new breed of Soviet party bureaucrats and legal scholars (see, for example, Sharlet, 1978).

The much-delayed Polish legislation, although faithfully modelled after that of the Soviet Union simply came too late to serve its initial ideological and political purpose. The new Soviet line was strongly in favour of legal professionalism; a major article in the leading legal journal went so far as to portray public opinion as an illegal interference in criminal cases. It further claimed that the opinion of a given collective does not always conform to the legal consciousness of the Soviet people (quoted in Smith, 1980: 136). It was an unmistakable sign that popular participation in the dispensation of justice was no longer deemed useful. However, as Smith indicates, 'rather than abolish the courts, the party leadership chose to restrict their jurisdiction, reduce their prestige, increase their supervision, and transfer the majority of their functions to established judicial institutions' (Smith, 1980: 136).

Any evaluation of the potential usefulness of social courts must include the context in which they operate. The obvious danger in any totalitarian state is the reality that such social bodies become mere extensions of the coercive state power, capable of penetrating in deeper and more deceitful ways into the social fabrique than the more conventional tools of state control. While this applies to those cases concerned with work discipline, it must be remembered, however, that the more clearly political cases of dissent and opposition are dealt with by professional bodies, and social courts are not generally relied upon to enforce correct political views. Nonetheless, both in the USSR and in Poland, the selection of social judges takes place under considerable pressure from the party and party-controlled trade unions. This is supported by the fact that in the early 1960s (the period of these courts' most vigorous operation) one out of every three judges of the Soviet comrades' courts was a party member. As well, at present, the party is clearly expected to review the comrades' court cases during the local party meetings and thereby provide these social tribunals with the right 'direction in the struggle for discipline and the legal order' (Sharlet, 1979: 351).

Nowhere in the statutes of the Soviet comrades' courts or the Polish social courts is there any clause concerning judicial independence. Furthermore, the Polish follow-up study on workers' courts conducted in 1963 showed that most of the courts were called into being through the initiative of the party or trade unions; only half of the judges were blue collar workers while almost 90 per cent of the defendants were from that class. The majority of cases were instituted by the company's administration, the prosecutor or the petty crime penal board (for more detail see Łoś, 1978: 814). In short, the social courts tend not only to reflect the authoritarian relations prevailing in the communist economy, but also serve to perpetuate them. In view of these findings one has to accept the opinion expressed by a legal scholar who contended in an article in 1972 in Poland, that 'further development of the social courts in the work places depends above all on the strengthening of self-management and democracy inside the enterprises themselves' (Rybicki, 1972: 28; this author's translation from French).

Another frequently cited danger involved in the use of these popular justice bodies is the arbitrary attitude towards the law which may serve to confuse the general public and lower their general respect for the law. This has been confirmed to some extent by the available data. The courts' performance is rather erratic and unpredictable and there exist no legal safeguards. Errors and inexcusable blunders are not infrequent (Rybicki, 1972: 28). The previously quoted Polish study on the workers' courts found, for example, that, in two cases, persons not belonging to the panel participated in the secret conferences during which the final decisions on individual cases were made. In still another instance, a case which was tried and concluded in a workers' court was subsequently sent to a common court of law. According to the study, this incident was followed by a sudden decrease in the number of people present at the subsequent trial and gave rise to generally negative attitudes towards social courts (Podgórecki, 1974: 155).

Yet another problem results from the very nature of any 'peer justice' institution. Such structure involves enormous exposure to public scrutiny and condemnation by peers; for some people, the psychological trauma of being publically shamed may have devastating consequences. All those familiar with the descriptions of the impact of 'degradation ceremonies' and informal labelling tend to be aware of the psychological and moral damage which they may occasion (Garfinkel, 1956; Goffman, 1963).

Finally, as indicated by a number of authors, lay courts may create conflicts and animosity among people thereby weakening their solidarity. It is a reality that almost everybody in the work places is involved in some form of theft of state property and that many male residents of the overcrowded housing developments are drunk virtually every night. It is inevitable, therefore, that those singled out and castigated by their peers for such behaviour must feel strong resentment. Those who participate in or even passively witness the questioning and lecturing which occurs in the courts must also feel uncomfortable. They know, however, that they cannot change the conditions around them and, as a result, their frustrations are often channelled into some form of collective scapegoating.

Yet, to balance this bleak picture, it must be remembered that social courts do have some positive role to play in these countries. As mentioned earlier, residential courts help to ease problems resulting from harsh conditions of collective living. By the same token they may relieve common courts of some potential cases of petty crime, although it is doubtful whether many of them would be tried in any court of law if lay tribunals were not available. In addition, their accessibility makes social courts potentially attractive; they are easy to approach, they do not usually involve any fees, they take place in familiar settings, they use simple language, and they do not normally involve long delays. Theoretically, they are a perfect incorporation of Nils Christie's provocative idea of 'returning conflicts to the people'. For him:

> conflicts represent a potential for activity, for participation. Modern criminal control systems represent one of the many cases of lost opportunities for involving citizens in tasks that are of immediate importance to them. . . . This loss is first and foremost a loss in opportunities for norm-clarification. . . . Maybe decisions on relevance and on the weight of what is found relevant ought to be taken away from legal scholars, the chief ideologists of crime control systems, and brought back for free decisions in the courtrooms. . . . Specialization in conflict solution is the major enemy . . .
>
> (Christie, 1976; excerpts from pp. 13, 14, 20)

Thus, while condemning the shortcomings of the lay tribunals, it should not be unwittingly taken for granted that professional justice is the ultimate, or at least, the superior response to the problems of crime and conflict. Christie argues that it is not, and there may be even more reasons to believe that he is correct when the combination of professional and political aspects of the communist dispensation of justice are considered. In communist countries, conflicts are not simply 'taken away' from people and translated into some hermetic legal concepts, but are also screened, interpreted and censured by the monopolistic political party. After all, it was seen as one of Khrushchev's great achievements that he restored 'party control over the security agencies, the courts and the Procuracy after years of Stalinist abuses and arbitrariness' (Sharlet, 1979: 328).

It seems clear that progress in the civil institutions of any society can only go as far as the limits of its political and economic organization allow, and therefore, any social experiments executed under the restrictive conditions of a one-party state are fated to be either co-opted or thwarted.

4 Law, Ideology and Economy: The Case of Anti-Parasite Laws*

IDEOLOGY, ECONOMY AND SOCIAL INSURANCE RIGHTS

The Western economy is regulated by market laws and protected by a safety net of social insurance and welfare provisions. The Soviet-style economy, on the other hand, is regulated by the central plan and buttressed by the criminal law. This is not to suggest that the criminal law never acts on behalf of capitalist economic interests or that there are no social benefits under communism. It is, however, important to understand how all-pervasive the presence of the criminal law is in the Soviet economy and how restrictive the ideological bounds of the system of social welfare are.

The ideology of modern capitalism accepts the necessity of some measures which mitigate unfair consequences of the market economy and the technological revolution. Social insurance and welfare provisions are presented as examples of such measures which are meant to contribute to the equalization of opportunities and the elimination of poverty and are thereby linked to humanitarian values and the ideology of equal opportunities. While their interpretation varies according to the nature of the political parties involved, none of the major Western parties propose, for example, to dismantle the unemployment insurance system based on the claim that capitalism does not produce unemployment.

The communist ideology, on the other hand, sees welfare as an integral part of the economy, which is, in turn, inherently fair, and free of the problems produced by capitalism. Indeed, the only function of income supplementation through any sort of special benefits is the recognition and rewarding of proper attitudes towards work and the reinforcement of the ideological model of the centrally planned economy, and not the compensation for its possible detrimental impact on the individual citizen. Given the ideological denial of the existence under communism of such undesirable phenomena as unemployment,

*The first two sections of this chapter incorporate extensive exerpts from M. Łoś, 1983c.

for example, it is understandable that no official argument can be made in favour of the introduction of unemployment insurance (for more detailed discussion, see Łoś, 1982b; 1983c).

Welfare rights, like any other rights of the people in communist countries, have to be analysed within ideological and economic contexts of these countries. Since the rights are meant to constitute an integral part of the economic relations (see Jaśkiewicz *et al.*, 1970; Zieliński, 1978), they should not be seen as human or civil rights of the citizens. Thus, they are not rigid and universal, but depend fully on the level of cooperation of various groups with the so-called progressive forces of history (see, e.g. Hazard, 1978; Markovits, 1978). Indeed, it is very clear that the idea of equality of social status for all citizens has not been promoted by the political doctrine of the communist countries. It has rather emphasized the functional differentiation of income and privilege according to the needs of industrial development and political stability and has paid lip service to the privileged position of the working class. The notions of justice and equality are treated with suspicion as being too abstract to have any material meaning. They are sometimes used as the language of popular propaganda which is not meant to have any real meaning, and is merely expected to appeal to the traditional social values in order to build up the citizens' morale and their faith in a better society.

Egalitarianism in wages was denounced during the Stalinist years as 'bourgeois' and economically inappropriate. Instead, material incentives were called for and a highly differentiated wage-scale along with an elaborate system of privileges and perks were introduced. The post-Stalin years brought significant changes in the income and tax policies, which, in turn, produced some reductions in the inequalities of economic status and some increase in the minimum wage level. These modifications, however, were typically not presented as moves towards a more egalitarian society, but rather as economically desirable and socially profitable developments of a truly socialist nature. It was probably assumed that the rehabilitation of the egalitarian principles would neither be consistent with Marxist ideology, nor help the programme of the 'socialist reconstruction' which relied on deep divisions and the destruction of solidarity among various classes (see, e.g. Nove, 1978).

The ideological decision about the necessity of the rapid industrialization of the Soviet Union made at the XVth Congress of the Communist Party in 1927 has had a long-lasting impact on the nature of the social security measures in communist countries. Indeed, they have been completely subordinated to both the demands of the economy and to superior economic and political objectives.

The demands of the job market called for the use of incentives for the full mobilization of all able-bodied members of the society. As a result, in 1930, all relief payments to the unemployed in the Soviet Union were stopped and workers were forced by law to accept any job, and even those outside or much below their qualifications.

The political demands of the construction of a new, socialist, society were as pressing as the economic ones. The class ideology had to be constantly reinforced, not only through the verbal glorification of the workers, but also through the practical confirmation of their privileged status and discrimination against other groups. Despite this overt show of support, the workers were not really trusted and their political indoctrination and full subordination to the party had to be effectively carried out. This could be done only through mass membership in the state-run trade unions. It follows, then, that the delegation to the trade unions of the welfare tasks constituted a convenient policy and provided the unions with both some measure of legitimacy as well as significant coercive and controlling powers. In this way, the importance of union membership was strongly increased, and the right of the trade unions to refuse membership to 'uncooperative' workers became more threatening. In 1933, the entire administration of social insurance in the Soviet Union was turned over to the trade unions, which, by that time, had already been completely subordinated to the party (see, e.g. Rimlinger, 1971).

The new Soviet State's desperate need for the support of the workers led to the portrayal of the state as a dispenser of gifts to the workers and, therefore, to the abandonment of any idea of a contractual model of insurance based on contributions paid by workers. Obviously, the extremely low wages in the nationalized economy were expected to compensate the expenditure borne by the state in connection with the state employees' pension programme, while also being conducive to the growing dependence of the workers on the 'gifts' from the state and, thereby, their increased vulnerability to political pressures and control. In the absence of any essential changes in the position of those workers who retained their status of hired labourers and did not have any share in the factory management, the programme of welfare hand-outs claimed to constitute the most obvious practical difference between the situation of the working classes under socialism and capitalism. Naturally, the propagation of such a belief within communist countries was only possible when information about the developments in the area of welfare in Western countries was fully suppressed. As well, ideologically crucial visibility of the privileged position of the workers was strengthened by the contrast between their situation and the lack of any insurance or social security provisions for the peasant class.

The cult of the proletariat and industrialization contributed to the official policy of discrimination against peasants who represented the 'ideologically backward' elements within the society. It was not until 1964 that Khrushchev finally announced a form of social insurance programme for the collective peasants. The country's agricultural base was completely devastated and he saw in the social insurance provisions a convenient tool with which to stimulate productivity within collectivized farming. Nevertheless, the inferior status of the farmers was carefully preserved and was best represented by the amount of benefits available. The pensions of the most hard working peasants could not significantly exceed the minimum level of pensions for industrial workers and employees (see, for example, Rimlinger, 1971; Madison, 1968).

An even more drastic discrimination was exercised against the farmers in Poland where all official attempts at collectivization have failed and farms continue to be privately owned. Until the late 1970s, the condition for receiving an old-age pension was the surrender of the family farm to the state upon the owner's retirement. Such an arrangement was expected to lead to the gradual nationalization of the farms, but instead, the peasants' resentment against the attempted collectivization resulted in widespread massive resistance towards the scheme. Even the new pension scheme for farmers introduced in the late 1970s has been given a hostile reception by farmers, who resent being expected to pay unreasonably high insurance contributions towards subsistence level benefits. In general, the structure of the Polish social insurance system is very similar to that of the USSR. The rapid industrialization of the 1950s required the full mobilization of all men and women and the duty to work was very rigoristically enforced. The well-known Soviet principle 'no work, no eat' was followed faithfully by the Polish authorities. And, as in the Soviet Union, the state-run trade unions were given the power to control work-related benefits and, in turn, to use them as a system of rewards and punishments for workers.

In sum, the Soviet-style social insurance programmes have been based on the clearly defined ideological premises which give privileged status to the employees of the nationalized economy, impose the obligation to work upon the adult members of society and penalize the unemployed. As far as the nature of these programmes is concerned, social insurance is neither seen as a contract nor a citizen's right, but as a gesture of good will and as proof of the benevolence of the state and the party.

The social functions of the national insurance programmes are, in essence, reduced to the roles of regulating the labour market and encouraging the increase in productivity, as well as the facilitation of social and political control. The low wages make workers and their families economically dependent on social benefits and on the various price reduced services and provisions, which include, for example, holidays, factory and school meals, nurseries, coal and potatoes. Workers' wages are paid 'according to their work' and not 'according to their needs' and are not designed to provide for the worker's family since both spouses are expected to work and not all workers have families. It is believed that higher wages would mean considerable waste in the cases of either a single person or a childless couple. The various forms of subsidizing families coupled with their direct dependence on the political attitudes of the employees increase the workers' reliance on the state and its political organizations – the party and the trade unions. Such an extended dependence on the state is easily achieved by the centralized communist system, where collective wage negotiations are banned, where the state-run trade unions do not represent the workers, and where the party determines both wages and benefits.

POVERTY, UNEMPLOYMENT AND THE RIGHT TO WORK

The communist state has no legal obligation to provide supplementary assistance to anyone, no matter how desperate their needs. As a result, there is no appeal machinery available to unsatisfied claimants. Administered by the local councils, public assistance in these countries is means-tested, but it does not recognize any consistent principles of eligibility and its scope is extremely limited.

It is officially emphasized that there is no poverty within communist society and, therefore, any formalized system of poverty relief is not ideologically acceptable. The notion of the unconditional right of every citizen to the minimum acceptable standard of life is equally incompatible with the dominant ideology. The constitutions of most of the communist countries were altered in the 1970s to make it even clearer that all the rights of the citizens are inseparably linked with the fulfilment of the basic citizen's duties which, in turn, consist mainly of participation in productive work and loyalty towards the party line and its political alliances.

Since, based on the Marxist ideology, unemployment is inconsistent with the rules of the organization of communist society, neither the

Soviet Union nor Poland have established anything similar to the unemployment benefits existing in Western countries. Not only do the unemployed not receive any financial support, they also lose their rights to free health services, price-reduced medicines, and the use of nurseries and child-care centres for their children (whose fees may be too high for them in any event). During the acute economic crisis in the early 1980s in Poland, the unemployed people were also excluded from the food rationing programme which aimed to alleviate the extreme shortages. In essence, this meant that they were denied access to the official food distribution system. In addition, as a rule, there is no distinction made between various groups of unemployed. It does not matter whether they are out of work because suitable jobs are unavailable or because they have been dismissed for their political views, or because they are widows who were supported by their husbands, or because they have alcohol or drug addiction problems, or simply because they are genuine procrastinators.

Since there is a general understanding that there is no acceptable way of obtaining any assistance from the state, there exists a tendency to hide one's poverty rather than announcing it in any way. Since there is no officially accepted concept of poverty, many people suffer destitution without developing the awareness of being members of a socially distinct category, namely the poor. The political slogan which maintains that there is no poverty in communist countries has (and of course is meant to have) a magic quality. There are no poor when nobody is labelled as poor; there are no unemployed when nobody can claim the unemployment benefits. In fact, the average person suffers such acute forms of deprivation that there is no sharp contrast between the standard of living maintained by the majority of the citizens and those who are actually below the poverty line. While this reality makes the poverty less visible, it probably renders it more threatening and real.

Unfortunately, although not surprisingly, the statistical data on poverty and unemployment in communist countries are not published and any estimates must be treated with caution. One such estimate prepared by McAuley was concerned with the situation in the Soviet Union in the late 1960s. He arrived at the conclusion that, at that time, over two-fifths of the population were living in poverty, with the state farm workers suffering a much more acute degree of deprivation than the rest of the population (McAuley, 1977; see also Timofeev, 1982). It seems that, since then, the standard of living in the USSR not only has failed to improve, but most probably has greatly deteriorated due to protracted economic crisis.

During the Solidarity period in Poland considerable efforts were made to break through the façade of the deceptive ideological propaganda. Many previously unpublished findings were made available to the public and new studies were initiated. Some estimates of the extent of the problem of poverty were reported in the weekly magazine of the Solidarity Union in 1981. These studies defined poverty by biological rather than social criteria, that is, in terms of conditions where the satisfaction of elementary human needs becomes problematic. According to this published study, 6 million Poles (out of a population of 34.4 million) lived below the so-defined poverty line. Half of them resided in rural areas. One out of three children lived in families experiencing extreme hardship. These children were likely to drop out of school very early and, despite the requirement of compulsory primary education, 11 per cent did not attend school at all (Woycicka, 1981: 11).

Other published reports corroborate these findings. They indicate, for example, that the rate of infant mortality is very high among poor families, children suffer frequently from ear and eye ailments, tuberculosis and neurological disorders (Czabański, 1981a; Milotworska, 1982). Only 40 per cent of the elderly receive pensions or any other type of benefits (Czabański, 1981a; Woycicka, 1981; Nowakowska, 1982). From among those who do receive pensions as many as 65 per cent have incomes below the poverty level (Nowakowska, 1982: 4). Moreover, 300 000 disabled people do not receive disability benefits either because they never worked or because their work record was too short to make them eligible (Czabański, 1981a). The overwhelming majority of those who live under the poverty line do not receive any social assistance or receive it only from the Church. Some may occasionally receive used cloth, coal or potatoes from the state but very few are extended any financial help (in fact, only about 0.2 per cent of the Polish population receive long term welfare benefits, Nowakowska, 1982: 6). A 1973 study of 1719 recipients of social assistance found that 30 per cent did not possess any of the following items: a light coat, a winter coat, a warm sweater and more than one pair of of shoes. Forty-four per cent of the claimants were practically homeless and lived in totally uninhabitable dwellings (Nowakowska, 1982: 4).

The generally accepted claim that there is no unemployment in Soviet-style communist countries is clearly erroneous. While there was no structural unemployment during the intensive industrialization, in the 1930s in the Soviet Union and 1950s in Poland, subsequent periods of economic stabilization and eventual decline have produced both unemployment and under-employment which, in turn, have contributed to many social problems. While a planned economy allows the state to adjust the number of jobs according to the current demand, this can only be done up to a point. Both the financial costs involved in the creation of jobs and the human costs connected with shifting the manpower to those areas with new job opportunities, pose difficult problems. As Katsenelinboigen correctly observes:

> one should not forget that workers are not robots. They are human beings. If an enterprise needs fewer labourers, it does not mean that dismissed workers easily agree to move to an enterprise located in another region. They have families who like the area where they live. For humanitarian reasons they may be allowed to look for work in the region of their domicile. It is for these reasons that unemployment also exists in a planned economy.
> (Katsenelinboigen, 1978a: 15; this author's translation from French)

The rapid economic decline in the late 1970s and the obvious failure of the Stalinist model of intensive industrialization have significantly reduced employment opportunities, and especially the demand for unskilled labour in both the USSR and Poland. Moreover, grossly inadequate wages coupled with unsafe, depressing working conditions do not always provide sufficient incentives for workers either to remain at their jobs or look for others. As well, some people who lose their jobs because of their political views or activities cannot find alternative employment since jobs are virtually monopolized by the state, the body which dismissed them in the first place. Neither they nor any other unemployed, yet able-bodied (or at least diagnosed as such), people can count on any financial assistance from the state. Raina describes the typical fate of a Polish dissident in the 1970s in the following manner:

> The characteristic tactic of the Gierek regime has been to starve out the dissidents. Once an academic dissident is forced out of his job, no other scholarly institution in Poland would dare employ him. The state bureaucracy is also closed to him. He is surely not a skilled manual worker, unskilled jobs are not often available. And even if he succeeds in finding a manual job, the security service would doubtless intervene. Unemployment benefits are not provided in communist countries, for 'unemployment' does not officially exist. The dissident thus has no source of income. How does he then bear up against this ill fortune? A vast circle of silent sympathizers keeps him alive. Friends

and colleagues pool their limited resources to help their helpless friend. (Raina, 1978: 345)

In the Soviet Union as well, many political non-conformists, religious and ethnic activists, and applicants for emigration find themselves inevitably among the ranks of the officially non-existent category of the unemployed. This method of persecution is by no means limited to intellectuals and artists however. Numerous workers share the same fate. In 1977, some of these workers launched a desperate attempt to create the Free Trade Union Association in the Soviet Union:

> They [were] ordinary people, who were taught in school, in the Komsomol, and in the army, that the Soviet system was the best in the world. For the most part they believed what they were told. Their problems began at work. They saw managers furthering their careers by bribery, swindling, stealing 'socialist property', concealing industrial accidents, paying illegally low wages, and so on. As 'honest labourers' they stood up to defend socialist property, to demand proper implementation of the Labour Code and the Constitution. Their reward for their loyalty was the sack. They discovered the truth behind the official propaganda about 'the right to work' – it is granted by the ruling bureaucrats to those who behave. . . . The members of the Free Trade Union Association say, 'We are the great army of Soviet unemployed, thrown outside the factory gates for exercising our right to complain, our right to criticize and our right to free speech'. (Haynes and Semyonova, 1979: 17)

Predictably, most of the members of this union ended up in prisons or psychiatric institutions. Western trade unions and international labour organizations debated whether or not to support the union and, more often than not, found some suitable rationalizations to remain uninvolved (see Haynes and Semyonova, 1979: 20–2; Levin, 1982: 12). In Poland, the protests and strikes of 1968, 1970 and 1976 were followed by waves of dismissals and, in 1981, the delegalization of the Free and Independent Trade Union 'Solidarity' resulted in the firing of its more outspoken members (*Les droits* . . ., 1983: 248–56). Moreover, legal amendments introduced during the state of war made it extremely easy to fire employees for their convictions.

Even during the Solidarity period, when political dismissals were not so frequent, very bleak predictions were published indicating the extent of unemployment in the years to follow. Enormous foreign debts and the lack of funds to import materials necessary for production were among the most prominent reasons for concern. *Polityka*, the official weekly magazine, stated for example, that 'the work crews dependent on the foreign imports [were] the most threatened by the work stoppages (to avoid the prejudiced word 'unemployment')' (Wróblewski, A. K., 1981: 1; this author's translation from Polish). It estimated that 'between one half million and one million people [were] threatened with unemployment' (Wróblewski, A. K., 1981: 4). According to the same source, the Labour and Wages Department prepared a draft of a resolution which aimed to alleviate the consequences of unemployment. The draft encouraged the industrial and administrative workers to go back to the countryside, to try to get employment in the area of services or mining, or to retire early (Wróblewski, A. K., 1981: 4).

An official woman's magazine claimed in 1981 that:

> approximately one million people employed in clerical jobs in Poland [mostly women] could be made redundant without any harm to the functioning of the economy. . . . More than a million people needlessly employed in the huge bureaucracy impedes the modernization of the economy.
>
> (Zukowska, 1981: 4; this author's translation from Polish)

Subsequently, this threat of massive unemployment was quelled by introduction of an early retirement scheme and other similar measures.

The well hidden, political and structural unemployment is only one of the side effects of the communist organization of the economy. Another, better known, phenomenon caused directly by the centrally planned employment policies is the prevailing pattern of under-employment, or the reality that the number of employees is, as a rule, greater than would be justified by rational economic considerations. While under-employment has some merits as a means of limiting unemployment, it also has some clearly undesirable side-effects. '[It] gives people greater job security, but it makes them less responsible for their activities, which, in turn, results in negative consequences, such as absenteeism, alcoholism, low productivity, etc.' (Katsenelinboigen, 1978a: 16; this author's translation from French).

It seems that both the Soviet ideology and practice represent an attempt to achieve an impossible fusion of two principles which are described in the Soviet Constitution as, on the one hand, the right to work, and on the other, the duty to work. Section 40 of the Constitution of the USSR states that citizens of the USSR have the right to work. It explains that:

> this right is ensured by the socialist economic system, steady growth of the productive forces, free vocational and professional training, improvement of skills, training in new trades or professions, and development of the systems of vocational guidance and job placements. (*Constitution* . . ., 1977: s. 40)

This right, as indeed all other rights guaranteed by the Constitution, is conditional and not absolute. It is clearly stated in section 59 that 'the exercise of rights and freedoms is inseparable from the performance by the citizens of duties'. As stressed by Hazard, the 'socialist' rights are not abstract and universal, but rather they are exercised only in so far as their enforcement conforms to the economic and ideological role they are designed to play (Hazard, 1978). They are generally understood as the moral and political duty of the state to provide that which the citizens are entitled to, and only in some rare cases are they also interpreted as the individual's specific rights, the enforcement of which the individual can actively seek. It is argued that there is no need to legally safeguard citizen's rights since the party and government do everything that is objectively possible under the given economic conditions to implement the best policies of needs satisfaction. Under such circumstances, there is no room for any real conflict between an individual and the state. Thus, both the Soviet and the Polish Constitutions guarantee the right to employment, yet there exist no other legal regulations nor legal appeal machinery which would secure the enforcement of this right. Indeed, the official legal interpretation in Poland says that 'the constitutional right to work [which is expressed in section 68] does not entitle citizens to obtain employment, but merely imposes upon the state an obligation to conduct a policy of full employment' (Jaśkiewicz *et al.*, 1970: 139; this author's translation from Polish). There are no legal guarantees, of course, which would ensure that such a policy would in fact be executed.

Not only are the citizens of communist countries constitutionally entitled to obtain employment, but they are also obliged to keep it. Section 60 of the Soviet Constitution states that:

> [i]t is the duty of, and a matter of honour for, every able-bodied citizen of the USSR to work conscientiously in his chosen, socially useful occupation and strictly to observe labor discipline. Evasion of socially useful work is incompatible with the principles of socialist society. (*Constitution* . . ., 1977)

The Polish Constitution expresses similar ideological concerns when it maintains that 'work is a right, a duty and a matter of honour for every citizen' (*Konstytucja* . . ., 1952: s. 19).

In contradistinction to the right to work, which is not backed up by any concrete legal provisions, the enforcement of the duty to work has been made possible by the 'criminalization' of the unemployment and establishment of special penal procedures to deal with it.

THE DUTY TO WORK AND THE CRIMINAL LAW IN THE SOVIET UNION

The first attempts to penalize idleness, absenteeism and labour turnover were undertaken in the early period of intensive industrialization. Stalin's ambitious plans to create overnight a true proletarian class which did not exist at the time of the October Revolution (despite the fact that the revolution was carried out in its name), were bound to encounter enormous problems. Alec Nove summed up the atmosphere of the period very well in the following passage:

> The peasant-workers, bewildered by their new surroundings, often short of food and adequate lodging, rootless and unsettled, wandered about in search of better things. Not for them the 'pathos' of the great construction of socialism. (Nove, 1978: 197)

The great need for manpower for the construction of industries coupled with the problems of discipline among the new unskilled and unurbanized work force led to the introduction, in 1930, of various administrative penalties for those who attempted to leave their jobs (Juviler, 1976: 49). Criminal sanctions for violations of labour discipline were introduced in 1940 whereby, quitting a job without permission, was penalized by 2 to 4 months imprisonment, and absenteeism was punished by up to 6 months of correctional labour (Juviler, 1976: 60; Hutchings, 1971: 116). When most of the industrial production was militarized in 1941 the punishment for leaving a job without authorization was increased to 5 to 8 years in prison (Juviler, 1976: 61). By 1951, however, these sanctions were quietly dropped (Berman, 1957: 1202) and eventually, with the death of Stalin, both absenteeism and leaving one's job were formally decriminalized (Stead and Sterling, 1982: 5). What followed, however, was a sequence of anti-parasite decrees which later became an obligatory model for other communist countries.

At first, this new anti-parasite crusade had clear ethnic overtones. A 1956 decree directed against Gypsy rootlessness and idleness was a prime example of this orientation. It provided that Gypsies, who wilfully avoided useful labour and indulged in vagrancy, be sentenced to up to five years of corrective labour (Armstrong, 1967: 165). Soon after, in 1957, special anti-parasite 'laws were enacted in Central Asian republics according to which able-bodied adult citizens who [led] an anti-social, parasitic mode of life, maliciously avoiding socially useful work, and likewise living on income not earned by labour' could be sentenced to two to five years of exile in labour colonies (Beermann, 1957: 214). This original legislation was very much in tune with Khrushchev's early fascination with 'popular justice'. The sentence was pronounced by a general assembly of the offender's 'collective' which consisted of his 'peers' in the factory, kolkhoz, village, housing development, etc. (Feldbrugge, 1973: 484; Beermann, 1957: 214). The decision was made in open voting by a simple majority of participants at the meetings. No legal safeguards or avenues for appeal were provided. It is quite apparent that these laws were aimed at breaking up the traditional values and moral codes of the Moslem culture in order to impose Russian and 'socialist' attitudes upon the Asiatic minorities (see Pomorski, 1981: 25; also Massel, 1968, on earlier efforts to break the Moslem culture). The procedure was clearly adjusted to the local traditions to secure its greater effectiveness. As indicated by Beermann:

> [given] the still existent influence of meetings of elders, the parasite law with its notion of popular justice was more acceptable to the public mind, while it also greatly strengthened the hand of those groups which were supporting the law as an additional tool in eradicating those remnants of Shamanism and other undesirable phenomena. (Beermann, 1962: 198)

In 1961, the Russian Republic (RSFSR) passed its own version of an anti-parasite bill which was subsequently copied by all other republics regardless of whether or not they already had their own laws on parasites. The former penalties were maintained and supplemented by a provision for the confiscation of property acquired by non-labour means. The decree gave the jurisdiction over parasite cases to the criminal courts and prohibited general meetings of neighbours (Smith, 1980: 129–30; Armstrong, 1967: 173). Those people who were employed but were suspected of having a job purely for the sake of appearance and obtaining income not earned by labour were to be dealt with by their labour collectives whose decisions had to be approved by the executive committees of the local Soviets. Some such cases could also be handled by the regular courts (Lipson, 1970: 327; Berman, 1973: 206–7).

Eventually, in 1965, the local Soviets took over all the parasite cases, with the exception of those which involved inhabitants of the Moscow and Leningrad areas, these remained within the jurisdiction of the criminal courts. Punishment by deportation to remote labour colonies continued to be meted out to these 'big city parasites', while other offenders were assigned compulsory work within the area of their domicile. It seems quite probable that this distinction was actually aimed at political dissidents whose removal from larger cities was deemed politically desirable. It should not be overlooked, however, that this policy was also fully consistent with the party's attempts to prevent any increases in the crime rates of the larger cities, a phenomenon which was always portrayed as a typical consequence of capitalist-style urbanization. To achieve this goal, the authorities introduced very strict controls over the urban population. For example, offenders who were incarcerated for the minimum five years were (and still are) forbidden to return to their homes in major cities. As well, citizens with criminal records, and especially those convicted for violent crimes or classified as recidivists, were strictly prohibited to settle in these cities. The system of internal passports and permits and of compulsory registration further helped to alleviate the crime-related problems in big cities by displacing them into smaller towns and suburbs (for more details, see Shelley, 1981: 145).

The distinction between the two kinds of parasites based on their place of residence was overhauled by a 1970 decree of the RSFSR Supreme Soviet. The decree gave full jurisdiction over the parasite cases to the executive committees of the local Soviets, the decisions of which were binding and could not be appealed. The parasites who failed to start 'honest work' within 15 days after receiving an official police warning were to be assigned compulsory work within their province, territory or autonomous republics. The failure to carry out the compulsory tasks was defined as a criminal offence under section 209–1 of the RSFSR Criminal Code (Feldbrugge, 1973: 484). This section, introduced at the beginning of 1970, stipulated that:

> [t]he malicious evasion, by a person leading an antisocial, parasitic way of life, of the implementation of a decision of the executive committee of a *rayon* (or city) Soviet of Workers' Deputies on employment and the termination of a parasitic existence is punishable by deprivation of freedom for a term of up to one year or by coercive

labour for the same term. The same act committed by a person previously convicted in accordance with the first part of this article is punishable by deprivation of freedom of up to two years.

(Decree . . ., 1970)

In 1975, section 209–1 was repealed and replaced by the new section 209 which provided the same punishment as the former section, but defined the offence involved in a more general fashion as 'systematically engaging in vagrancy or in begging, and also over a long period of time leading another parasitic form of life' (Edict . . ., 1975). Simultaneously, a new procedure was introduced to deal with the 'parasitic style of life'. The suspects were to be summoned to the internal affairs boards and warned about their lack of employment. If they failed to find a job within one month another warning would be issued and, upon the expiration of another one month period, a criminal prosecution would be initiated under section 209 (Resolution . . ., 1975). Subsequently, in October 1982, an amendment to the Russian Republic Criminal Code was passed which doubled the penalties for crimes under section 209. The previous penalty of up to one year of deprivation of freedom or of corrective labour was changed to one to two years of similar measures. The penalty for recidivists was raised from the previous term of up to two years' deprivation of liberty to a term of one to three years. The same decree introduced a possibility of committing convicted parasites to special 'upbringing-and-labour rehabilitation centres' for similar terms (Decree . . ., 1982; 'Social parasites . . .', 1983). Moreover, the decree makes it compulsory for chronic alcoholics who engage in a parasitic way of life to undergo compulsory treatment and labour reeducation (Decree . . ., 1982).

The introduction of stiffer penalties and the shift from the administrative to strictly criminal definition and handling of parasites might have been influenced by the sharp decline in Soviet economic growth and the increasing realization that Soviet society, plagued by alcoholism, crime and corruption, is morally distintegrating. These attempts by Brezhnev administration to build up the decaying morale of the work force and symbolically cleanse the society of its incorrigible elements were continued with a special zeal by Andropov during his short term in office (see e.g. Burns, 1983a; 'Social parasites . . .', 1983; Kulagin, 1983).

There are numerous legal problems with the Soviet anti-parasite legislation, some of which have been identified and challenged by Soviet jurists. At the early stage, the utilization of social meetings was one of the obvious targets of the legal critics. As well, the definition of punishment as a social or administrative sanction was attacked by those who saw it as a clearly punitive measure belonging within the realm of the criminal law. (Some opinions of the Soviet jurists are summarized in Armstrong, 1967; Beermann, 1957, 1960b; Berman, 1973; Juviler, 1974: 28). With the subsequent changes in the law, the ambiguous combination of administrative and criminal procedures and shifting jurisdiction over parasite cases raised justified objections. Another controversial area, for example, involved the persistent attempts to achieved through legislation the dual aims of punishing and educating the parasites, a purpose which some western as well as Soviet critics considered misleading and impractical (e.g. Smith, 1980: 129). The early anti-parasite laws were also challenged on constitutional grounds as the Constitution of the USSR and the Basic Principles of Criminal Procedure clearly stated that no individual may be deemed guilty of an offence or subjected to criminal punishment without a proper conviction and sentence by a criminal court (Beermann, 1966: 388). Indeed, the current legislation is not immune from such criticism either:

> A peculiarity of the realm of legislation under discussion is that punishment is prescribed by way of repression against a person with a peculiar way of life and not against a person guilty of committing any acts. (Tverdokhlebov, 1972: 117)

Furthermore, the anti-parasite laws have been attacked for their clear violation of international conventions signed by the Soviet Union. Two conventions of the International Labour Organization are among the most often quoted: convention 29, ratified by the USSR in 1956 which condemns the use of forced or compulsory labour in all its forms, and convention 122, ratified in 1967, which stipulates freedom of choice of employment (Tverdokhlebov, 1972: 125).

The most obvious criticism, however, concerns the vagueness of the definition of social parasitism itself. It appears that this label has been applied to a great variety of behaviour, and its meaning has shifted considerably over time. In the initial legislation of 1957 parasites were identified as able bodied adult citizens who led an anti-social, parasitic mode of life, maliciously avoiding socially useful work, and likewise living on income not earned through labour (Beermann, 1957: 214). This was a general, moralistic definition, based on the ideological belief in the superior value of work and on the political desire to impose the 'socialist morality' on the culturally most distant minorities.

The 1961 anti-parasite law introduced many new elements into this definition, a fact which testified clearly to Khrushchev's preoccupation with the remnants of the capitalist mentality and private profit orientation. Ideological purity of the economic model seemed to be the prevailing factor in the wording of the law at this stage:

> Such people frequently hold jobs for appearance's sake while in actual fact living on unearned income and enriching themselves at the expense of the state and the working people or, although able-bodied, hold no job at all but engage in forbidden businesses, private enterprise, speculation and begging, derive unearned income from the exploitation of personal automobiles, employ hired labour and obtain unearned income from dacha and land plots, build houses and dachas with funds obtained by non-labour means, using for this purpose illegally acquired building materials, and commit other antisocial acts. (Edict . . ., 1961)

In 1965, however, the definition was once again simplified and focused on two basic elements: the avoidance of useful labour and the engagement in a parasitic way of life. Such a definition was general enough to cover all kinds of nonconformist behaviour or attitudes and was probably prompted by the increase in dissident activities and the intensified efforts by the state to suppress them. The best known early instances of the application of anti-parasite laws to prosecute non-conforming intellectuals occurred when Yosif Brodsky, the poet, was sentenced in 1964 and Andrei Amalrik, the historian, in 1965. Moreover, the forms of 'capitalist' economic activities described in the 1961 legislation were covered by exceptionally harsh laws on economic crime passed in the early 1960s which effectively removed the need for retaining them in the anti-parasite section of the Criminal Code. Finally, the changes of 1975 expanded the 1970 definition by adding vagrancy and begging, which had previously been treated as separate offences. It appears that the focus shifted in mid-1970s from a more economic orientation towards a moralistic one, while carefully preserving the general scope of the label in order to render it applicable to cases of political, religious or ethnic opposition.

The application of the anti-parasite law to punish people for their views or beliefs is not an infrequent occurrence. A report on Soviet prisoners of conscience published in 1980 by Amnesty International quotes several recent instances of prison sentences for parasitism. These include Alexander Ogorodnikov, the spokesman for a discussion group of Russian Orthodox believers (sentenced in 1978), Valentyn Poplavsky, a member of a group of unemployed workers which attempted to establish a free trade union (1978), Grigory Kostynchenko (1977) and Ivan Antonov (1978), both Baptist pastors, and Joseph Begun, a mathematician sentenced in 1977 for campaigning for Jewish emigration rights (*Prisoners* . . ., 1980: 21, 22, 59). According to the report:

> [w]hat makes this legislation particularly dangerous for dissenters is that it is common for Soviet citizens to be dismissed from their jobs directly because of their nonconformist behaviour. . . . In numerous cases dismissed scientists and other professional employees have been unable to find even low-paid, menial work, since the authorities not only have not helped them to find work suited to their particular skills but have put obstacles in the way of their finding any work at all. Thus the threat of being charged with 'parasitism' has hung over people who have seriously tried to find employment.
>
> (*Prisoners* . . ., 1980: 59)

Nevertheless, it would be incorrect to assume that political dissidents are the main target of the anti-parasite legislation. Rather, the legislation appears to aim at a variety of socially, politically and economically inconvenient groups, such as undisciplined workers, alcoholics and drug addicts, small-time hooligans and criminals, playboys and snobs sporting Western clothes, private entrepreneurs and people living on the fringe economy of prostitution, begging, vagrancy and speculation (see e.g. Lipson, 1970: 328–9; Juviler, 1974: 28; Smith, 1980: 129).

There is a recurring theme in the Soviet press and criminological literature which links crime to parasitism and crime prevention to the effective application of the anti-parasite laws. It appears that it is officially believed that, while the parasitic style of life leads almost inevitably to criminal involvement and deviance, it is also frequently caused by them. Despite the inconsistencies in the interpretation of the direction of any such causal relationships, there seems to exist a consensus that the fight against parasites contributes significantly to the general cause of crime prevention. Frequent examples of this belief can be found in the current Soviet press:

> It's alarming that a large percentage of identified drug addicts have no jobs and lead the life of parasites . . . [S]tepping up the struggle against parasitism can be an effective prevention measure against drug addiction and other crimes. (Antelava, 1982: 15)

> One troublesome factor is property crimes, such as larceny and robbery. Many of the people who commit these crimes are not engaged in socially useful labour. This indicates that our internal affairs agencies have still not fully mobilized their potential for fighting crime. ('Public Opinion . . .', 1980: 16)

> The experience of public life dictates the need to step up the struggle against all sorts of parasitic elements, drunkards and hooligans, whose antisocial behaviour is at variance with our way of life and with the norms of Soviet law. However, we have still not been able to achieve a situation in which these norms are applied vigorously and consistently everywhere. (Rekunkov, 1982: 3)

The naïve faith that the struggle against parasites will produce a crime and deviance free society is not, however, shared by all experts. A more realistic attitude is very clear in the following citation from *Pravda*:

> Chronic drunkenness – the chief cause of a parasitic lifestyle – is not a sudden affliction. The All-Union Institute for the Study of the Causes of Crime did research on a group of parasites who had committed crimes. As it turned out, more than half of them had begun working at a very young age. They were not drunkards then, much less chronic alcoholics. Sociologists have established that most drinking is done not after work, but during the latter half of the workday. Apparently, indignation over drinking and parasitism in certain collectives goes hand in hand with tolerance from those who stray from the straight and narrow . . . (Anashkin, 1982: 20)

Some press reports do admit that the problem of parasitism results partially from the careless dismissals of employees which in turn lead to the existence of a sizable category of 'temporarily unemployed' workers. For example, a report on Western Siberia, a region known for its labour shortages, states that in Omsk alone approximately three thousand employees are dismissed by enterprise managers every year. According to the police there is a close relationship between the number of employees dismissed from work and the overall crime level (Serov, 1980: 2). Nonetheless, there is no serious analysis of the reasons for these dismissals and of the fate of the unemployed. As a result, the identification of the link between unemployment and criminal involvement inevitably leads to punitive policies against parasites. In some republics, the parasitic style of life is treated as an aggravating circumstance in cases where the offender is charged with some other offence or offences. In the Kirgiz Republic, for example, in the past:

> a person was sentenced to up to six years' deprivation of freedom only for repeated theft of state or public property or for such theft by prearranged conspiracy. Now this punitive measure . . . also applies to theft committed . . . by a person who avoids socially useful labour. (Demichev, 1982: 14)

Empirical research is scarce and it is strongly coloured by ideological assumptions. A typical example is a study conducted in the early 1970s which focused on crime committed against person and property as well as on parasitism (Djekebaer, 1975). The author explains the persistence of such crimes in terms of the retarded psychological development among individuals who have not understood the nature of the socialist changes within society. Socialist society does not encourage consumerism and personal gain orientation, and therefore, crimes such as vagrancy and parasitism are dangerous because they directly undermine the moral fabric of the new social order. They are unfortunate leftovers from the capitalist era when asocial attitudes towards work and feelings of alienation were justified. The author insists that crimes of parasitism and idleness must be dealt with strictly because they foster other crime. He claims that, in 1971, approximately 20 per cent of all crimes were committed by able-bodied parasites, a clear increase over the 11 per cent in 1964 and the 12 per cent in 1962. According to his findings, among those convicted for parasitism, 80 per cent were men and 20 per cent were women; 45 per cent of the offenders were over 35 years of age and only 3.5 per cent were under 20 years of age; 62 per cent had not completed full primary education, 27 per cent had primary education and 1.9 per cent had some college or university education (Djekebaer, 1975: 73–4).

Djekebaer goes on to list the reasons for the parasitic existence, among which the most important are such factors as health, loss of documents, lack of a desire to work, lack of appropriate jobs, drinking problem, and finally dissatisfaction with wages offered (Djekebaer, 1975: 79). The admission of the exceptional importance of poor health as one of the major factors responsible for an individual's parasitism must necessarily be seen as a powerful indicator of the failure of such crucial support systems as health care, social insurance and rehabilitation programs. Indeed, punitive measures seem to be the only response available to the Soviet authorities in their struggle to 'sanitize' their society.

In short, the parasite laws are useful in suppressing dissent, covering up structural unemployment and the failure of the health system, removing from the streets alcoholics, drug addicts, misfits, petty offenders and other people seen for various reasons as a nuisance or threat. It is worthy of note that the criminal labels of parasitism and hooliganism are sufficiently general and flexible to eliminate the need for the infamous 'analogy rule' used under Stalin to prosecute any kind of behaviour on the basis of its alleged affinity to specific criminal offences actually contained in the Penal Code.

THE DUTY TO WORK AND THE CRIMINAL LAW IN POLAND

The history of the anti-parasite legislation in Poland is much shorter than that of its Soviet counterpart. The first Polish anti-parasite law was passed in October 1982 when the society was paralysed by the terror of the state of war. While there were several attempts to introduce such laws in the 1960s and 1970s they were successfully opposed by the joint forces of lawyers, social scientists and other groups aware of the dangerousness of the possible uses and abuses of a criminal law of this kind. Although practically all other communist countries introduced laws patterned on the Soviet model, the Polish lawyers' opposition was for years remarkably firm and effective. As a result, numerous drafts of the law ended up in the waste baskets of the Ministry of Justice.

The first serious attempt to pass an anti-parasite legislation was undertaken in the late 1960s and energetically promoted by Gierek upon his nomination as the General Secretary of the party in 1970. It was exactly the time when a new anti-parasite law was passed in the Soviet Union, and Gierek was probably under considerable pressure to follow suit. What was perhaps even more important, however, was the fact that the economy was virtually ruined and Gierek desperately needed some tangible scapegoats to help dissipate the widespread feelings of frustration and anger. While his predecessor, Wladyslaw Gomulka, was an obvious choice as a convenient scapegoat at one end of the social hierarchy, Gierek tried to balance his attacks on the former General Secretary with a well orchestrated campaign against those at the other end of social spectrum, namely idlers, drunkards and parasites who had seemingly hindered economic progress and were responsible for the social, economic and political problems of the late 1960s. The mass-media presented numerous exaggerated accounts of the dangerousness, maliciousness, and corruption of those social drifters who got drunk daily without ever having to go to work.The label 'parasite' became a familiar word in Poland, and the desperate public, looking for a panacea in a time of deep economic crisis did not seem to object to the idea of the application of some clearly punitive measures against those who lived at the expense of the 'honest working people'.

The proposed draft met, however, strong opposition from intellectuals who were more aware of the pitfalls of such a law and of its actual application against dissidents in the Soviet Union. Several meetings were organized at the universities and spontaneous working groups prepared briefs and memoranda, all of which attempted to demonstrate that the shortcomings of the proposed law outweighted any advantages. They quoted international conventions ratified by Poland, the Polish Constitution, the vagueness of the key legal terms, the immorality of the coercion to work and, finally, the reality of underemployment and the growing threat of unemployment. Eventually, the enactment of the law was postponed, most probably as a result of the opposition by an influential faction within the party itself, with one of the reasons being the cost involved in setting up the labour colonies proposed in the bill. Another draft was proposed in 1977 following the workers' protests and the rapid growth of the organized opposition. Once more legal, moral and political arguments were used to demonstrate its shortcomings. Similar arguments reemerged again in the early 1980s when a new version of an anti-parasite law was hastily prepared by the authorities alarmed by the growing power of the Solidarity movement (Skupiński, 1982, 3; Podemski, 1982a: 6; Jarecki, 1982: 37).

In a critical article in the weekly *Polityka*, Jan Skupiński identified eight groups of people who would most likely be dealt with under the proposed law:

1. criminal offenders (who should be charged anyway under the Penal Code);
2. individuals with illegal earnings (who should be dealt with under the administrative and fiscal laws);
3. seasonal workers (who are not in conflict with any moral or legal norms);
4. alcoholics (who should be offered treatment and assistance);
5. maladjusted juveniles (who should be offered counselling and assistance in finding work or completing education);
6. mentally disturbed people (who should be offered medical treatment);
7. prostitutes (who should not be dealt with by any punitive measures since prostitution is legal in Poland);
8. individuals without work due to sheer idleness or other socially

disapproved motives (who should be subject to purely social and not penal measures since their behaviour does not violate the criminal law).

Skupiński argued, therefore, that there was really no need for such a law and that it would not serve any useful purpose. He went even further, moreover, to warn that its introduction would be followed by the development of new criminal subcultures into which the above-mentioned potentially threatened groups would try to assimilate in order to satisfy their needs (Skupiński, 1982: 3). As well, other authors stressed that the potential target population of anti-parasite laws consisted of alcoholics and drop-outs, who had neither the qualifications nor the psychological qualities expected from employees. No employer would want to hire them and, even if the local administrations imposed on the managements the obligation to employ parasites, the economic and educational results of such arrangements would likely be disastrous (Podemski, 1982a: 6; Kedzierska, 1982: 7).

Despite the massive opposition of the 1980s which extended far beyond the elitist intellectual circles, the draft was submitted to the Diet in 1982. Both the Catholic Church and the Solidarity Union prepared special statements condemning the draft (Jarecki, 1982: 37). The Solidarity's declaration expressed the belief that 'the bill aimed in reality at the creation of legal bases for constant repression of those people dismissed from work for their union activities, political oppositional involvement, or inconvenience to the management or authorities for any other reason' (Jarecki, 1982: 38; this author's translation from Polish).

The discussion of the proposed bill by the members of the Diet was, as always, rather limited and dogmatic. Nevertheless, several speakers used harsh words to express their opposition despite possible repressions for doing so. One of the speakers, Mr Malcużyński, who was not a member of the party, criticized the attempts to pass such a socially important bill during the state of war when public opinion was completely suppressed. He openly asked about the fate of thousands of workers, intellectuals and members of the Solidarity, who were dismissed from work. As well, he stressed the futility and danger of dealing with social and medical problems through the mechanical application of penal measures. He indicated that all experts and even officially appointed consultants and special task commissions found the draft unsatisfactory ('Echa ulicy . . .', 1982: 14–15). This unusually daring speech ended with the openly political remark:

> The passing of a law which only creates the appearances of a solution to an acute social problem, without reaching to its sources and without searching for appropriate, nonpenal remedies is, in my opinion, politically harmful and socially demagogical.
> ('Echa ulicy . . .', 1982: 15; this author's translation from Polish)

Another member of the Diet, Mr Auleytner, a Catholic representative, argued that not all moral norms should be enforced by coercion, and he regarded the moral duty to work as one such norm. Moreover, he insisted, that any notion of compulsory work should be rejected as unconstitutional especially since the Constitution describes work above all as an honour, and, as such, he argued, it cannot be imposed on people under the threat of penal sanctions. His criticism was also directed at the vagueness of the definition of parasitism and the lack of any rational basis or need for such legislation. Finally, Auleytner expressed the fear that 'the bill against people who avoid employment [might] become a fictitious law, which in reality [would] not solve anything' ('Echa ulicy . . .', 1982: 13–14; this author's translation from Polish).

Eventually, 12 members of the Diet voted against the bill while 22 abstained, a remarkable manifestation of opposition in an institution routinely making unanimous decisions. Yet, the overwhelming majority of members voted, out of habit and fear, to support the enactment of the bill and it was passed on 8 October 1982.

The law carefully omits the compromised term 'parasite' and, instead, refers to 'persons who avoid employment'. This change of legal terminology was duly explained by the Deputy Minister of Justice:

> if the law is to achieve its objective, any pejorative labels, even only in the title, are not recommended. We have also avoided this label, because of the resolutions of the international law.
> ('Z Sejmu . . .', 1982: 2; this author's translation from Polish)

The change of terminology has not, however, had any impact on the letter of the law which is very closely patterned after the respective Soviet legislation, with the only exception being its exclusion of women. Persons who avoid employment are defined as able-bodied men, 18 to 45 years of age, who have been out of work for three months and are not registered in an employment agency. The new law demands that they report to a local government office and give a full explanation of their behaviour. They are then registered as 'people persistently avoiding employment' and are obliged to report whenever called. In the meantime, their sources of income are investigated. In the absence of criminal irregularities, their behaviour is treated as an administrative offence and they may be assigned to public works for a maximum of two months per year when situations warrant. Failure to participate in public works entails either the limitation of freedom for up to one year or a fine. Failure to visit the office when called or to give required information is punishable by either the limitation of freedom for up to three months, or a fine ('Plenarne obrady . . .', 1982: 3; 'Echa ulicy . . .', 1982: 13–14; 'The Institutionalization . . .', 1982: 61–2).

It was officially announced in April 1983 that, between January and April of that year, 104 people were placed in the registers of the 'people persistently avoiding employment' ('Obraz Tygodnia, 1983:1). Yet, subsequently, the number of those potentially threatened with this label has increased considerably as a result of political dismissals and the deteriorating economy. It can be argued, therefore, that even if the law is not going to be applied to all those who fit the label, its mere existence fulfils an important control function. The danger of this law cannot be overestimated, for, even if the penalties are not as stiff as was initially feared, the law itself gives the authorities the legal right to harass, question and control those people who are dismissed from work for political reasons, those who are involved with social or religious groups[1] which are willing to sponsor their activities or those who need help and medical treatment, but cannot get it because of the evident failure of the welfare and health systems.

THE INTRICATE OBJECTIVES OF ANTI-PARASITE LAWS

The existence and utility of anti-parasite laws cannot be explained in terms of a single aim or function they serve, for they may be applied to serve various purposes depending on the circumstances and the prevailing ideological, political and economic needs. Their very nature indicates that they are designed to play versatile roles and, while their effectiveness in any specific area may be limited, their overall impression on the functioning of communist societies is far from negligible.

It is often argued that the Soviet anti-parasite laws were meant to secure the highest possible level of the mobilization of manpower in the face of serious labour shortages. Yet, similar laws were enacted in 1982 in Poland in the period of the most pronounced labour surplus since the war. Even in the Soviet Union, many cities, regions and branches of the economy experience similar difficulties with absorbing all the surplus labour which is mobilized by the existing pressures. Of course, the anti-parasite statutes play an important role in ensuring that even the most unpleasant, dangerous or degrading jobs are taken and that manpower is shifted to those regions or industries which experience labour shortages. Clearly, however, the persistent and conspicuous emphasis on the duty to work cannot be fully explained by the needs of the economy. It appears that work has another prominent aspect. At work, people can be disciplined, controlled and contained for eight hours a day, six days a week. Their movements are known, their deviations are spotted immediately, their social contacts are easier to locate and, above all, they can be constantly reminded of the dominant political dogmas and taboos and of the nature of conformity expected from every citizen.

While the anti-parasite law urges people to seek employment and remain in their jobs, it also offers a supplementary system of control for those who do not want, cannot or may not work. The participation of the agencies of local administration in the enforcement of the anti-parasite laws and their broad powers to question, monitor and restrict suspected individuals assure a comprehensive control system over the lives of all citizens, whether employed or not. The penal measures themselves tend to be treated as the last resort and not the main objective of the current Soviet and Polish anti-parasite laws. A system of warnings and checks is orientated more towards surveillance and subordination than towards punishment for its own sake.

The simple truth that full employment facilitates full control in a one-party (one-employer) state has not, however, been the only consideration of the anti-parasite legislation. The early Soviet enactments under Khrushchev clearly aimed at demonstrating that ordinary citizens can assume some disciplinary functions within society. This was hoped to have both ideological and educational significance, by signalling the beginning of the process of the 'withering away' of the state administration, and by employing informal means of mutual control with the purpose of inculcating socialist work ethics. The target groups were initially chosen almost exclusively from among the Asian minorities which were perceived as the most difficult to reach and educate through purely formal means. Their ideological reeducation and socialization into the dominant Russian culture were perceived as a necessary step towards their successful subjugation on the political, cultural and economic levels. Soon, however, the Soviet officials' loss of confidence in the people's willingness to spontaneously enforce the socialist moral and ideological standards led to the total abandonment of the popular participation model in their efforts to implement the rules against procrastination.

Subsequently, when the memories of the Stalinist terror subsided and new forms of opposition began to emerge, the 'parasite' label was extended to include all those nonconformist individuals who violated the rules of a totalitarian monolith by their refusal to cooperate fully and to follow mechanically the directives. While acts of political opposition have usually been punished under special sections on political crimes, in some cases of religious or intellectual dissent, charges of parasitism have been found more convenient since they can be dealt with swiftly in summary trials and do not allow for any appeal procedures.

In addition, the increasingly evident deficiency of the health care system coupled with the inability and ideological reluctance of the party to establish a comprehensive system of social assistance and social insurance, have led to the persistent and conspicuous perpetuation of an army of social dropouts and rejects. And yet, their presence has to be denied in order to protect the myth of the caring communist state. Destitution, unemployment, alcoholism, beggary, homelessness and deprivation of medical treatment must be negated and the streets must be kept free of the sight of misery and unhappiness of those forgotten and abandoned and in need of support systems which are not available. Punitive measures appear to be the Soviet-style governments' preponderant response to this dilemma. An important and often underestimated function of the anti-parasite procedures is, therefore, their role in concealing the drastic deficiencies in both the human services and individualized care in these highly collectivized and bureaucratized societies.

5 Prisons, Politics and the Economy: the Ultimate Relationship

SOVIET PRISONS, POLITICS AND ECONOMY

There seems to exist a very intimate relationship between the Soviet economy and ideology on the one hand and the network of penitentiary institutions, on the other. As mentioned in the preceding chapter, penal law has been employed as a powerful instrument in the state's attempts to discipline the labour force and to assure its full mobilization. Moreover, penal institutions are themselves production-oriented organizations which fulfil extremely important economic function, not only by forcing inmates to work, but primarily by making them work in locations, in occupations and under conditions which could never attract any free labourers. The forced labour of inmates, probationers, and convicted 'parasites' is, therefore, a convenient solution to a problem of labour shortages in inhospitable, but economically important regions or in industries which are notorious for their exceptionally harsh or unsafe conditions. In short, the labour of the '*zeks*' (convicts) is 'needed for degrading and particularly heavy work which no one, under socialism, would wish to perform' (Solzhenitsyn, 1976: 560). Thus, it appears that slavery has been successfully reintroduced into Russia in the aftermath of the victorious Bolshevik revolution (see e.g. Sellin, 1976: 113–27 for a description of penal slavery in Tsarist Russia).

The first concentration camps for the class enemies of the new Soviet state were established by a decree of 5 September 1918 (Conquest, 1968: 77). In 1919, the number of forced labour camps, located primarily in the Arctic zone of Siberia, rapidly increased to accommodate tens of thousands of real and imaginary counterrevolutionaries. It was, however, the inauguration of the First Five Year Plan in 1929 and the beginning of the intensive industrialization under Stalin which were accompanied by an unprecedented increase in the numbers of prisoners in the hard labour camps of SLON (the Russian abbreviation for the secret police camp empire – the Northern Camps of Special Purpose –

administered after 1930 by GULAG, the Chief Camp Administration). While in 1928 apparently only 30 000 inmates were detained in such camps[1] (a figure roughly comparable to the number of prisoners sentenced to hard labour in Tsarist Russia), their numbers grew more than 20 times during the first 2 years of the Plan. The rapid rate of increase of the inmate population continued in the following years, reaching nearly 2 million by 1931 and a staggering 5 million by 1933–35 (Cliff, 1974: 30; Juviler, 1976: 56). While these numbers were most probably surpassed in the late 1930s during the period of the Great Purge and the Second Five Year Plan, the published estimates vary greatly, from the most conservative figure of 5 million (Wheatcroft, 1983: 224) to the highest estimates of eight to 15 million (e.g. Dallin and Nicolaevsky, 1947: 54–62; Cliff, 1974: 31; Conquest, 1982: 438).

The use of slave labour was particularly advantageous economically at the earliest stage of industrialization when 'labour-intensive endeavors operating at high human but low capital cost created an insatiable demand for new inmates to work where no available inducements would muster enough free labour' (Juviler, 1976: 56). In the 1920s, peasants forced out of their villages during the compulsory collectivization constituted some 70 per cent of these convicts. About 15 per cent were political prisoners while another 12 to 15 per cent were ordinary criminals (Juviler, 1976: 57). The peasant labour force was perceived by the authorities as inexperienced, unreliable and unstable, and the strictly controlled camp labour was seen as a viable means of disciplining and subjugating them. The NKVD had clear instructions as to the numbers of slave labourers required for various grandiose projects romanticized in the Soviet media (including, for example, the White Sea Canal, the Moscow-Volga Canal, the Volga-Don Canal, the Trans-Siberian Railway or the Magnitogorsk Complex). This quota system, based on totally unrealistic production targets, contributed greatly to the terror of random arrests and long sentences, which were carried out in order to secure the required supply of convict labour and to compensate for the high death and morbidity rates in the camps.[2] Political terror was thus reinforced by the purely economic demands of the 'new socialist industry', so eulogized in numerous songs, poems, and political speeches.

Slave labour projects were duly included into the Central Economic Plan and were expected to be completely self-sufficient. It is doubtful, however, whether they were actually turning a profit for, despite all the efforts to force prisoners to work conscientiously and enthusiastically, their labour was nothing more than what it was: the forced labour of slaves who could not be expected to have respect for either the work projects or for their masters. While sabotage, waste and faulty production were common place, the supervisors seemed to care only about the fulfilment of the quantitative production quotas imposed on them by the central planners (Solzhenitsyn, 1976: 565–71). As well, the mass imprisonment of engineers, technicians and managers in the concentration camps had an adverse effect on the economy by acutely worsening the already existing shortages of qualified personnel (Nove, 1978: 236–7, 256, 377; Solzhenitsyn, 1974: 44–5, 48). And yet, despite all these drawbacks, the GULAG's economic contribution was enormous and indispensable: it was able to force people to toil all days and every day on meager rations of bread and water in inhuman conditions, as the following excerpts exemplify:

> Who, except prisoners, would have worked at logging ten hours a day, in addition to marching four miles through the woods in predawn darkness and the same distance back at night, in a temperature of minus 20, and knowing in a year no other rest days than May 1 and November 7? (Solzhenitsyn, 1976: 561)

> And who would be sent down into the Dzhezkazgan mines for a twelve-hour workday of dry drilling? The silicate dust from the ore there floated about in clouds, and there were no masks, and in four months they were sent off to die of irreversible silicosis. (Solzhenitsyn, 1976: 562)

And who else would venture to 'the savage tundra where human foot had never trod, [and where] the ant-like prisoners . . . laid down rails. . . . They slept five hours a day on the bare ground, surrounded by signboards saying, 'CAMP COMPOUND'' (Solzhenitsyn, 1976: 562).

There are, however, some limits to the utility of slave labour and the capacity of the state to organize and control such a gigantic and yet socially invisible workforce. Apparently, by 1938, the camps were so overcrowded that some means of reducing the number of prisoners was imperative. And, indeed, orders to this effect were issued by the NKVD. The reduction was to be achieved not through the release of the surplus inmates, but rather by their mass extermination. 'This was when the chiefs of convoy began to test the accuracy of machine-gunfire by shooting at the stumbling zeks. And this was when every morning the orderlies hauled the corpses to the gatehouse, stacking them there' (Solzhenitsyn, 1976: 112). Death became a common punishment for the non-fulfilment of the production quota, the infraction of discipline or mere physical weakness. It assumed many forms. In one of the camps, for example, the death carriages awaited those who worked too slowly:

> a frame of sixteen by ten by six feet on a tractor sledge, made of rough beams, fastened together with construction staples. A small door, no windows, and inside nothing at all, not even any bed boards. In the evening those to be punished . . . were taken from the penalty isolator and packed into the carriage, locked in there with an enormous lock, and hauled off by tractor to a vale two to three miles from the camp. . . . After a day it was unlocked and the corpses were tossed out. The winter storms would bury them. (Solzhenitsyn, 1976: 113–14)

Daily executions were carried out in all camps. In one camp, 'they used to shoot from thirty to fifty men every day' (Solzhenitsyn, 1976: 115). In another, 'they led them up to a deep shaft blindfolded and shot them in the ear or the back of the head' (Solzhenitsyn, 1976: 115) and in yet another 'for many months . . . day and night, at the morning and the evening checks, innumerable execution orders were read out' (Solzhenitsyn, 1976: 115). While the executions of inmates were clearly common-place, millions of others died of hunger, exposure and disease.

The existing documentation indicates that the collectivization of agriculture and heavy industrialization, both totally justified by the dominant ideology, led directly to the creation of the prison empire of a magnitude unprecedented in Russian history.[3] Nevertheless, prisoners were not the only Soviet citizens given compulsory work assignments and submitted to the 'iron' discipline. Free labourers as well were subject to extraordinary constraints and repressions and were threatened with criminal sanctions for leaving their jobs without permission, absenteeism or any other manifestation of an incorrect attitude towards work. Peasants were coerced into a new form of serfdom through the collectivized farms and were thereby submitted to the absolute tyranny of the farm directors and the local party activists. The prisons clearly served an additional, 'educational' function for those citizens at large, by reminding them of the necessity of obedience and submission.

With Stalin's death, Khrushchev denounced the existence of the labour camp network and solemnly undertook its dismantlement. While his announcement might have been prompted by the widespread strikes and revolts initiated by the inmates in numerous camps (Sellin, 1976: 131), it was, nonetheless, basically consistent with Khrushchev's general political line at the outset of his reign. Although it is difficult now to judge the sincerity of Khrushchev's promises, it is clear that the reality of the labour vacuum left by the complete removal of the inmates' manpower would have been, in any event, economically unacceptable. A compromised solution was implemented therefore which appeared, at the time, to be most advantageous both politically and economically and which actually led to a considerable reduction of the prison population. There were at least two important economic factors which made it possible to release a substantial number of inmates in agreement with Khrushchev's declared policy of liberalization and reinstatement of 'socialist legality'. First of all, the need for forced labour was more or less diminished with the completion of the major construction projects. Secondly, 'more and more of the labour formerly done in the camps was being performed by discharged convicts forced by law or poverty to settle and accept jobs within the camp zones' (Sellin, 1976: 132).[4]

Substantial numbers of inmates, however, remained in the camps and labour colonies, which were slightly remodelled and submitted to various new legal controls. Colonies for juveniles and adults were separated and some formal statements concerning the protection of prisoners' rights were made, including the Fundamentals of Corrective Labour Legislation of the USSR and the Union Republics. While, however, the Fundamentals state that 'the execution of a sentence shall not aim at inflicting physical suffering or degrading human dignity' (*Prisoners* . . ., 1980: 90), they do not explicitly ban such measures if they are treated as means to some other ends. According to the stated purpose of the legislation in question, criminals are to be punished as well as corrected and reformed 'in the spirit of a conscientious attitude to labour and exact observance of the laws and respect for the rules of the socialist community' (*Prisoners* . . ., 1980: 80).

The 1969 legislation entrusted the execution of the deprivation of freedom to the Ministry of the Interior of the USSR and to the corresponding ministries in the republics. According to the Fundamentals, only those convicts who have committed less serious offences must serve their sentences within the republic where they were sentenced. Those convicted of more serious offences or repeated offences, on the other hand, must serve their sentences in labour colonies located in other republics. As observed by Feldbrugge, '[t]his system allows the authorities to place serious offenders, particularly political prisoners, from the smaller union republics thousands of miles away from their homeland in Russian and Siberian camp populations' (Feldbrugge, 1975: 128). In this way, this policy plays an important role in facilitating the process of political and cultural subjugation of non-Russian nationalities. Although the use of native language is not formally forbidden, prisoners are often reprimanded or even punished for speaking languages other than Russian in colonies in the Russian Republic. These sanctions are especially vigorously applied to political prisoners from such republics as the Ukraine and Lithuania, many of whom were sentenced for resistance to the policies of Russification in their republics (*Prisoners* . . ., 1980: 100–1).

In accordance with the Fundamentals, only a minority of convicts are incarcerated in prisons. The majority serve their sentences in four types of camps: general, strict, hard and special. The RSFSR Corrective Labour Code explains that:

> the more serious the crime committed and the greater the social danger of the criminal act and the personality of the convicted person, the more hard and severe must be the convicted person's conditions of imprisonment in the aim of strengthening the punitive influence exercised on him. (*Prisoners* . . ., 1980: 91)

In 1977, a special amendment to the Fundamentals added a fifth type of labour camp: the colony-settlement, to which prisoners who make progress towards correction can be reassigned. This reassignment applies only to first-time offenders convicted for less serious offences. Another amendment of 1977 strengthened the importance of conditional release with mandatory employment. Such release is conditional based on the inmate's acceptance of an assigned job in a designated place, where he is housed in a communal dwelling with other convicts, kept under police supervision and deprived of basic freedoms. According to a report by Amnesty International, Soviet officials often refer to this type of labour as 'work for the economy' (*Prisoners* . . ., 1980: 86). Thus, despite the liberal rhetoric of rehabilitation and decarceration espoused by these legislations, it is very clear that they do produce 'a permanent and reliable supply of easily deployable labour' (Feldbrugge, 1977: 350), and their economic function might well have been one of the major considerations in their enactment.

The size of the forced labour army, reduced in the early years of Khrushchev, has increased steadily ever since. *The First Guidebook to Prisons and Concentration Camps of the Soviet Union* (Shifrin, 1982) lists 1976 camps, 273 prisons and 85 psychiatric prisons. A recent report issued by the US Department of State asserts that there are some 1000 forced labour camps in the Soviet Union (*Report to the Congress* . . ., 1983). The estimates of the total average number of inmates in Soviet prisons and labour camps vary considerably, but it is possible at least to establish the probable range within which the actual number should be located. The most frequently quoted estimates for the 1970s range from around one million (Reddaway, 1973: 3–6; Zeldes, 1981: xiii), to 1.5–2 million (Sakharov, 1975: 43; Chalidze, 1977: 200; Neznansky, 1979: 6), to 2.5–3 million prisoners (Shtromas, 1977: 298). It may be reasonable to assume after Juviler (1976: 106) therefore, that the Soviet prison population in all penal facilities is probably not less than 1–1.5 million, which, in turn, indicates a rate of 400–600 prisoners per 100 000 inhabitants. It is worth noting that this rate is considerably higher than the rates of imprisonment per 100 000 in Western countries. In 1979, for example, the respective figure for the United States was 212, Canada 95, England and Wales 85, France 70, Australia 65, and The Netherlands 25 (*Basic Facts . . .*, 1982: 6).

This estimate does not include parolees working in mandatory job placements and other convicts sentenced to forced labour without incarceration. The earlier quoted report by the US Department of State and a concurrent report by the Central Intelligence Agency estimate that about 4 million people in the Soviet Union are being compelled to partake in some kind of forced labour (*Report to the Congress . . .*, 1983: 19; 'C.I.A. Says . . .,' 1982: 2). The C.I.A. report maintains that approximately 2 million people are actually incarcerated (85 per cent in some 1100 forced labour camps and 15 per cent in prisons). Another 1.5 million convicts have been given probation with compulsory work assignments (normally away from their homes), and half a million have been parolled from penal institutions to perform forced labour for the remainder of their terms. Forced labourers are believed to be employed in a wide variety of economic activities, including manufacturing, construction, logging and wood processing, mining, the production of building materials and agriculture. The C.I.A. based its report on satellite photos, which helped locate labour camps and estimate their size, and on interviews with former inmates. It stressed the Soviet ideological commitment to the rehabilitative role of labour, but did not overlook the more direct economic utility of this huge army of penal labour. Thus, it postulated that:

> [g]iven the worsening labour shortage in parts of the Soviet Union, this relatively efficient, flexible method of deriving some economic benefit from an increasing crime rate is likely to continue to rise.
>
> ('C.I.A. Says . . .', 1982: 3)

In addition to internment in a prison or corrective labour colony, the list of penalties also includes exile for a maximum of five years to a specified locality within the USSR.[5] This sentence may be imposed either as the only punishment or as a supplementary punishment to be served after a term of imprisonment. Yet another sanction, banishment for a maximum of five years, prohibits the convicted individual from residing both in his place of residence and, sometimes, in other specified localities. Corrective work without imprisonment for up to one year is yet another form of punishment. Finally, the death penalty. While it is the type of punishment least frequently mentioned in the Soviet media, nevertheless it is one which may be imposed in peace time for 18 different offences. These range from violent crimes (not necessarily involving the taking of life)[6] through economic crimes (aimed against state property) to hijacking, sabotage and political crimes. It is extremely difficult to establish any reliable estimates regarding the actual frequency of the application of the death penalty. It has been established by Amnesty International that:

> virtually all death penalty cases are shrouded in official secrecy to such an extent that it is not possible to learn from official sources the nature of the proceedings or evidence against convicted people or their subsequent fates. (*Prisoners* . . ., 1980: 87)

Nevertheless, some estimates are possible and Van den Berg has recently concluded, based on an exhaustive review of various available sources, that 'at a conservative estimate, 2000 death sentences have been handed down annually during the 1960s and 1970s' (Van den Berg, 1983: 162). Not all of these sentences, however, were carried out. It has been estimated that the number of actual executions is probably about three times lower than the number of death sentences (Simis, 1981). Yet, some other authors claim that there are as many as 1750 executions yearly, i.e. five executions daily (Zeldes, 1981: xiii). Still, it must be noted that, in some cases, a prison sentence may, in fact, mean death or permanent disability. First of all, 'disrupting the work of a corrective labour institution' is one of the eighteen offences for which death can be imposed (*Prisoners* . . ., 1980: 86). Secondly, inmates are routinely mistreated and exposed to the cold and hunger. Thirdly, they do not receive necessary medical assistance and fourthly, many are serving their sentences in the so-called extermination camps. According to the documentation gathered by Shifrin, there are approximately 40 such camps in the Soviet Union. For example, there exist about 33 camps where prisoners are assigned to the mining and enrichment of uranium ore (Shifrin, 1982: 32–5, 178). Needless to add, little effort is made to provide protective clothing and other safety precautions for the prisoners. The plight of inmates who do fall ill is unmerciful, as Shifrin describes:

> These are death camps. Prisoners contaminated by radiation are removed from these camps and brought to facilities for invalids to die. This is not done for philanthropic reasons, but to prevent those still healthy prisoners unaware of the hazards of their work from becoming demoralized. (Shifrin, 1982: 178)

Tens of thousands of other inmates of usually strict regime labour colonies are employed in highly toxic work environments in either the arms industry or the military services. The prisoners perform normally high-risk duties in military nuclear plants and clean the nozzles of atomic-powered submarines. As well, they operate glass-polishing machines, cleave mica and work with lacque enamels, all without ventilation (Shifrin, 1982: 31–5). It is very clear that the use of inmate labour affords generous and desperately needed savings to the Soviet military budget, and, as a result, this practice is not likely to be abandoned.

Theoretically, there is no life sentence; 15 years is the maximum length of imprisonment which can be imposed by a court. Offenders convicted of a crime committed while serving a term of imprisonment, however, may be required to serve their second term after the completion of the first one. The Russian Penal Code was amended in 1983 to provide for up to 5 years' further imprisonment for 'wilful disobedience' by inmates of corrective labour institutions. The offence is very vaguely defined and the trial may take place within the institution itself ('Wilful . . .', 1984: 18). According to several authors, the majority of those sentenced to deprivation of freedom spend about three years in penal institutions (Zeldes, 1981: 67; also Shtromas, 1977: 298; Chalidze estimates that an average prison sentence is 3.4 years – 1977: 200). Zeldes claims that approximately fifty per cent of all male inmates are recidivists, i.e. those convicted two times or more (Zeldes, 1981: 83). It has been estimated that the average number of political and religious prisoners is at least 10 000 (*Prisoners of Conscience* . . ., 1975: 53; Neznansky, 1979: Report to the Congress . . ., 1983: 1). It has to be remembered, however, that dissenters are often charged under 'non-political' articles of the Criminal Code that is, articles that do not deal with political offences (e.g. *Prisoners* . . ., 1980: 56–60; Feldbrugge, 1974).

In addition to the adult male institutions, there also exist prisons and labour colonies for women, for women with infant children, and for juveniles. While Shifrin was able to establish the location of 119 such facilities, he stated in his guidebook to Soviet prisons (1982) that the list is far from complete. According to his findings, the conditions in these prisons and camps are extremely harsh and compulsory labour is often similar to that assigned to adult male prisoners. He cites examples of inmates in the intensified regime children's camp in Gornyi (Novosibirsk Region) who are 'assigned backbreaking duties, despite the prevalence of hunger in the camp. Those who fall in and request [a] transfer to a hospital are beaten' (Shifrin, 1982: 18). In another Novosibirsk camp, 1500 women, including nursing mothers, 'are given physically exhausting duties in a plant in which reinforced concrete plates are manufactured' (Shifrin, 1982: 18). It is also reported that many infants brought to the camps with female prisoners fall ill and die for lack of care and medical attention (Shifrin, 1982: 18).

It is estimated that approximately 60 to 70 per cent of all tried juveniles are sentenced to a term in a juvenile labour colony. These colonies are classified into three types: standard-regime colonies for males, standard-regime colonies for females and intensified-regime colonies for male recidivists. All inmates are required to work. Family visits and parcels are strictly limited and letters are subject to censorship. The emphasis on security is made very apparent in all these colonies through the presence of fences, armed guards and watchtowers (Barry and Barner-Barry, 1982: 301). They are certainly very different from the idealized version of juvenile rehabilitation centres based on the Makarenko model and publicized by the Soviet Union.

It is impossible to describe the extent of human suffering and exploitation taking place within the camps and prisons of the gigantic penal network of the Soviet Union. The guidebook prepared by Shifrin (1982), the reports on prisoners of conscience published by Amnesty International (*Prisoners* . . ., 1975, 1980), the report to the Congress prepared by the US State Department (1983) and numerous memoirs and eye witness accounts help to define the major dimensions of the prison reality. The most commonly mentioned and very well documented realities include such persistent features of the conditions in penal institutions as the following:

Extremely Harsh Conditions of Transport to and from the Camps

Prisoners may remain in transit for a month or more. They are often transported over long distances in overcrowded trains with very limited sanitary facilities, inadequate supplies of food, water and fresh air (windows are locked and cannot be opened and there is no ventilation).

A frightening account of one such transportation describes the conditions as follows:

> Fifteen people in a sleeping compartement. Everybody bathed in sweat. Food spoiled. For two days they did not take prisoners to the lavatory. People had to use the corridors. . . . Dirt. Stink. Suffocation. One man died during the deportation. It was a terrible torture.
>
> (*Prisoners* . . ., 1980: 107–8)

While in transit, prisoners are subject to very strict security measures and are at the mercy of the guards. Women are often abused by male guards. Children are abused by adults. Amnesty International quotes, for example, a case where:

> the guards had tormented the [female] prisoners by making their shower water alternatively boiling hot and cold, and had then driven them naked down a corridor in front of male guards and prisoners. The girls were subsequently made to run a gauntlet of guards who beat them with fists, keys and a hosepipe. They were then crowded into tiny 'box' cells and ill-treated in other ways.
>
> (*Prisoners* . . ., 1980: 109–10)

In another account of the suffering experienced by transported prisoners, a Jewish would-be emigrant sentenced to six years imprisonment in 1975, relates:

> The streams of blood spilled, the violence that I witnessed during that trip, both in the transit prisons and in the trains, was incredible. In Odessa and Kharkov we were beaten with wooden hammers for our complaints about the lack of sanitary conditions and poor quality food. . . . In Ulyanovsk a group of juvenile delinquents were placed in our train carriage (they were being transferred to the regular camps) and half of them were raped. They were children who were starting to live and so many of their lives were already broken.
>
> (*Prisoners* . . ., 1980: 166)

Inadequate Accommodation

Overcrowded cells, cement floors, dampness, filth, very primitive sanitary facilities, lack of ventilation and inadequate heating are characteristic of the majority of Soviet prisons and camps (see e.g. *Prisoners* . . ., 1980: 110–12; Shifrin, 1982: 59).

Hunger

According to all reports, hunger is a permanent feature of prisons and colonies in the Soviet Union. The legally prescribed diet is defined in terms of the bare biological minimum. Prisoners are, however, often deprived of their meagre rations by the prison administration. Food may be stolen from them or taken away as a form of punishment. Article 56 of the RSFSR Corrective Labour Code states that people who are put in a punishment or discipline–isolation cell or in any other punishment facility within the labour colonies shall receive reduced food rations (*Prisoners* . . ., 1980: 113). Moreover, prisoners who systematically fail to fulfil their work quota may also be put on reduced food rations. The smuggling or acquisitioning of food in violation of the established proceedings is a serious offence. The food rations and number of parcels allowed per year vary according to the severity of the regime. For example, inmates in ordinary regime colonies are allowed three parcels while prison inmates are denied the right to receive any at all (for a more detailed description of prison and camp diets see *Prisoners* . . ., 1980: 112–22 and Feldbrugge, 1975: 135). According to Juviler, there is 'more than probable cause to believe that Soviet codes and regulations institutionalize hunger as the main way to pressure, control, and punish prisoners' (Juviler, 1976: 107).

Inadequate Medical Care

Amnesty International is not alone in its opinion that the 'combination of low grade, badly cooked and hastily eaten food with heavy labour in unhealthy conditions and a harsh climate causes some prisoners to emerge as chronic invalids' (*Prisoners* . . ., 1980: 122). Moreover, as indicated by Juviler, there are many reports of 'permanent physical damage, loss of limbs and deaths needlessly inflicted by indifference and neglect or even flashes of cruel hostility on the part of some MVD [Ministry of the Interior] medical staff' (Juviler, 1976: 108). The prison medical staff consists solely of employees of MVD against whom prisoners cannot lay charges of negligence. Amnesty International indicates that there have been persistent reports of prisoners dying as a result of medical neglect (for more information on medical care see *Prisoners* . . ., 1980: 122–32; Shifrin, 1982: 136; Feldbrugge, 1975: 135). The fate of the terminally ill inmates is especially tragic. According to Shifrin's documentation (1982: 77) there exist special camps where they are eventually brought to await their death without being offered any medical care.

Hard Labour and Unhealthy Working Conditions

As indicated earlier, prisoners are under obligation to work and hard labour is officially described as both a rehabilitative measure and a punishment. That work is treated as punishment is clearly demonstrated by the fact that the nature of the work is differentiated according to the severity of the correctional regime. Not only the refusal to work, but also the failure to fulfil the output norms are among the most serious offences. Severe punishments, most commonly involving the deprivation of food, are meted out regardless of the reasons for the non-fulfilment of the work quota including illness, disability, old age, or the lack of implements, parts or materials necessary to carry out the assigned tasks. The sanction for a repeated failure to fulfil the production norms is confinement in a punishment cell with a reduction of rations to the starvation level and the deprivation of the right to purchase food or receive parcels (e.g. Shifrin, 1982: 136). An electronics engineer released from a labour camp in 1976 recounts:

> Some placed a leg under a falling log, others chopped off a finger. Some even deliberately allowed a hand to become frost-bitten so that it would have to be amputated. An atmosphere of hopelessness and despair reigned in the camps. . . . In the summer, swarms of midges, tiny gnat-like insects, plagued and literally devoured the prisoners. . . . Yet the quotas had to be met and the prisoners had to continue working – swollen from illness, bloodstained, and hungry.
>
> (Shifrin, 1982: 167–8)

Another ex-prisoner of a tundra camp reports his experience of the mid-1970s:

> We worked under all frost conditions, even at well under —40 degrees. The prisoners, as a result, were coming down with pneumonia the whole time. It was almost impossible, however, to get permission from the medical assistant to be relieved from work.
>
> (Shifrin, 1982: 181)

While all correctional colonies are cloaked in secrecy, those camps which provide forced labour for the construction of military installations are, of course, treated as top secret. There are, however, some reports on such camps, where prisoners:

> live under the most primitive conditions in tents both summer and winter (with temperatures falling to —50C) and are assigned to build roads to the military installations in the area as well as dig pits for

> missile silos or construct underground airfields. The prisoners live a long way from population centers, which explains the irregular delivery of food and water and the resulting chronic hunger that prevails in camps. (Shifrin, 1982: 296)

As discussed earlier, prisoners are often employed to perform extremely dangerous types of work and are routinely forced to labour in unhealthy conditions (for more details see *Prisoners* . . ., 1980: 135–45; Shifrin, 1982: 31–5, 178, 182).

Brutality and Physical Ill-treatment of Prisoners

The beating of prisoners (and especially non-political inmates) is routine. There are numerous accounts of brutality, torture and beatings applied by both prison guards and those inmates employed by them to beat their fellow prisoners. The latter method is frequently used against political prisoners. In many known cases, such abuses resulted in the death of the prisoners involved (*Prisoners* . . ., 1980: 165–7). Handcuffs are often applied to prisoners in a manner which causes great pain. A conscientious objector described this kind of torture:

> The handcuffs were attached to a chain that, fastened around the knees, had applied such a painful squeezing pressure on the handbones that I lost consciousness. I felt as if my hands had been sawed into two. I was brought to again when the supervisor struck me in the back with his bunch of keys and kicked me in the stomach. (Shifrin, 1982: 314–15)

Another prisoner reported:

> It was a nightmare. The personnel at the facilities beat the prisoners constantly. We had no energy to resist as we were kept in a state of constant undernourishment . . . [T]hey waited . . . for a prisoner to come out of his cell . . . then they beat him savagely and threw him into the isolation cell. Prisoners returned from the lockup all covered with bruises. (Shifrin, 1982: 149)

In brief, Soviet prisons and labour camps are notorious for their cruelty and brutalization of inmates. It appears from the existing documentation that beatings, rapes and torture are the reality which most Soviet prisoners experience, witness, or are involved in with the approval of the prison authorities.

Restrictions, Punishments and the Predominance of Secret Regulations

The types of punishment which may be applied to prisoners are so numerous that space restrictions prevent their listing here (reliable accounts are provided by e.g. Feldbrugge, 1975; *Prisoners . . .*, 1980: 157–65). One of the most dreaded, however, is the punishment cell. According to the law, prisoners may not be placed in a punishment cell for a period exceeding fifteen days, but they can always be held longer on the grounds that they committed some new breach of discipline during the initial period of their isolation. Thus, the Amnesty International report maintains that, in effect, 'there is no upper limit on the period a prisoner can be held in a punishment cell' (*Prisoners . . .*, 1980: 159). During his internment in a punishment cell the prisoner is prohibited from receiving visitors, sending letters, receiving parcels, purchasing food, or smoking. The prisoner spends all his time in the cell. The cells are unfurnished and are usually damp, cold and airless, with rough walls and floors. A wooden box with iron cross-pieces without bedding is issued in the evenings and serves as bed for the punished convict. He is fed differently on alternate days: one day he receives a piece of bread, hot water and some salt, the next day he is allotted a ration consisting of approximately 1300–1400 calories which often consists of inedible or spoiled products (*Prisoners . . .*, 1980: 160).

The actual operation of the penitentiary system is regulated in conjunction with the Rules of Internal Order decreed in 1972 and revised in 1978 by the USSR Ministry of the Interior, but never published. These rules, which are very restrictive and oppressive in nature, violate some of the provisions of the Corrective Labour Codes of the republics which, in turn, are often inconsistent with the general principles of penitentiary law (for details see Feldbrugge, 1975: 132–5; Juviler, 1976: 108–9). As a result, it is very difficult to differentiate between legal and illegal practices and punishments.

Lack of Social Control Over Prisons

In theory, prisoners are entitled to lodge complaints and requests to the superior officials within the prison services or to the General Prosecutor. The effectiveness of such complaints is, however, extremely limited and inmates who complain frequently are punished by the prison authorities for making 'unfounded' or 'slanderous' allegations.

Many political prisoners try to appeal to organizations outside the Soviet Union hoping, in this way, to initiate either protests or public campaigns on behalf of Soviet prisoners. And, indeed, 'there is ample evidence of the fact that the active interference of public figures in the West and of world public opinion has sometimes had a favourable effect on the position of political prisoners in the USSR' (Feldbrugge, 1975: 136). As well, samizdad publications (i.e. uncensored, underground materials circulated in the Soviet Union without formal authorization) made available many prisoners' memoirs, diaries, reports and open letters to the Soviet authorities in order to alert public awareness within the Soviet Union to the abuses and degradation to which prisoners, exiles and other convicts are exposed. Nevertheless, the prison reform movement remains very loose and fragmented since it is most diligently persecuted and threatened with annihilation by the omnipotent KGB.

Strikes and rebellions staged by prisoners themselves are the least known expressions of opposition against prison abuses. While it is difficult to estimate their frequency, there are several reports which show convincingly that they are normally resolved through the use of firearms and not by means of peaceful negotiation. Shifrin cites, for example, a 1953 rebellion in a mining camp whose exhausted, starving prisoners demanded better working conditions and more food. At first, the authorities negotiated since 'they needed the nickel, molybdenum, and chrome mined by the prisoners for the arms industry' (Shifrin, 1982: 183). Soon, however, they changed their tactics and bombed the prison from airplanes. Another uprising took place in 1968 in the *Shepetovka* prison in protest against systematic beatings. 'The guards shot into the crowds of prisoners, who, in their protests, demanded justice. Ten people were killed, others saw their sentences extended and were sent to the uranium mines' (Shifrin, 1982: 77). Similarly, the desperate *Darievka* prisoners went on strike in 1971, 'only to be fired on by the guards from their watchtowers. There were casualties. More than 50 prisoners were tried and despatched to unknown destinations' (Shifrin, 1982: 77).

* * *

While the preceding characteristics provide a good description of life within the Soviet prison network and the opposition against it, the picture would not be complete without a description of the unique penal alternative provided by psychiatric prison hospitals. This form of punishment is normally reserved for 'nonconformists' who have not violated the criminal law and, therefore, whose prosecution is not conveniently attained by the authorities.

Juviler describes this alternative thus:

> Any defiance of authority might bring commitment as insane. The offending behaviour did not have to be religious, cultural, or political dissent. Nondissidents could be committed psychiatrically for confronting authority by refusing an investigator's demand to corroborate a murder charge against his friend by false testimony, or by making a fuss when petitioning at government or party reception offices. Dissidents, however, provided most of the tens of hundreds of recruits for psychiatric hospitals. (Juviler, 1976: 111–12)

A citizen may be forcibly committed through civil procedure, criminal procedure or a transfer from a correctional institution, to a prison-like psychiatric institution, run by the Ministry of the Interior (for details, see excellent documentation in *Prisoners* . . ., 1980: 172–204 as well as in Juviler, 1976: 112–16; Boukovsky, 1971; Van Voren, 1983). The essence of this practice is well described by the American psychiatrist Walter Reich:

> the KGB – especially after it was taken over in 1967 by Yuri V. Adropov . . . – had regularly referred dissidents to psychiatrists for such diagnoses in order to avoid embarrassing public trials and to discredit dissent as the product of sick minds. Once in psychiatric hospitals, usually special institutions for the criminally insane, the dissidents were said to be treated with particular cruelty – for example, given injections that causes abscesses, convulsions and torpor, or wrapped in wet canvas that shrank tightly upon drying. (Reich, 1983: 21–2)

It appears that the definition of mental illness has been considerably revised by Soviet scholars to accommodate deviations from the political norm. Dr Andrei Snezhnevsky, head of Moscow's Institute of Psychiatry, devised a theory which introduced a new type of mental illness known as 'sluggish schizophrenia', which could be diagnosed on the basis of very mild, non-psychotic characteristics of behaviour. He conducted extensive studies which, he claimed, proved the hereditary nature of sluggish schizophrenia. Needless to say, these studies have been dismissed by Western scholars as inadequate (Reich, 1983: 23). Striving for scientific precision, psychiatrists in the Serbsky Institute of Forensic Psychiatry claim to have ascertained that 'ideas of truth and justice most frequently arise in personalities with a paranoid structure' (quoted after Juviler, 1976: 115). This explicit politicization of the definition of schizophrenia makes the application of this essentially vague and subjective label considerably more dangerous in the Soviet Union than in Western democracies. Amnesty International published a sample of excerpts from psychiatric diagnoses conducted by officially appointed doctors. Among them were such types of mental illness as 'nervous exhaustion brought on by the patient's search for justice', 'schizophrenia with religious delirium', 'reformist delusions', 'psychopathy with tendency to litigation', 'delusional ideas of reformism and struggle with the existing socio-political system in the USSR' and a 'mania for reconstructing society' (*Prisoners* . . ., 1980: 184).

The movement against the abuses of psychiatry for political purposes has a dramatic history and dates from the 1950s. The abuses of the Stalin era, although intensified in 1930s, were relatively infrequent in those years in comparison to the extent to which they are presently carried out. Clearly, in the days of the Great Purge, Stalin preferred open terror over the more subtle measures favoured by his successors. Near the end of his reign, however, the use of psychiatry in order to isolate 'troublemakers' increased considerably and special facilities were developed for this purpose. In 1955, a commission appointed by the Central Committee to investigate the alleged abuses of psychiatry found that they did, in fact, take place. Yet, no action was ever initiated on the basis of the commission's findings. The Special Psychiatric Hospitals remained under the control of the MVD and were not transferred to the Ministry of Health as demanded by their critics. Apparently, Khrushchev strongly supported the political abuses of psychiatry (Van Voren, 1983: 6).

In 1969, the Action Group for the Defence of Human Rights was founded and an appeal concerning the political uses of psychiatry was submitted to the United Nations Commission on Human Rights. The Commission did not, however, take any action on behalf of the victims of such abuses. In 1971, the Canadian Psychiatric Association was the first and for some time the only body which elected to condemn the Soviet policies publicly (Van Voren, 1983: 10). Shortly after the Canadian condemnation, the already impressive documentation available in the West was supplemented by a 150-page document prepared by Vladimir Bukovsky, himself a victim of Soviet psychiatry. The matter was debated during the Congress of the World Psychiatric Association held in Mexico in November 1971. No resolution, however, was passed and Professor Vartanyan, a Soviet psychiatrist and one of the most outspoken defenders and practitioners of 'political psychiatry', was elected as an associate secretary and a member of the Executive Committee. Soon after, Bukovsky was put on trial, accused of anti-

Soviet agitation and propaganda and sentenced to the maximum penalty of 12 years: 2 in prison, 5 in a camp and another 5 in exile (Van Voren, 1983: 11; Boukovsky, 1971). In 1973, the British Royal College of Psychiatrists passed a resolution against the Soviet abuses of psychiatry and has since remained very active in organizing support for the anti-political-psychiatry movement inside the USSR. The American Psychiatric Association also issued a statement, but failed to mention the Soviet Union by name (Van Voren, 1983: 12).

As a result of the growing international pressure in the mid-1970s, Soviet authorities stopped using psychiatric confinement for well-known dissidents while quietly increasing the numbers of internments of less famous nonconformists. In 1976, vigorous Western campaigns on behalf of several dissidents led to the release of Leonid Plyushch and his forced expulsion from the Soviet Union. Shortly thereafter, Bukovsky was released as well, in exchange for the Chilean communist Luis Corvalan. Plyushch's account of his experiences in psychiatric confinement was circulated among Western specialists. It stands as a powerful commentary on the state of Soviet psychiatry:

> I saw in my own case that the first days are meant to break a person morally straight away, break down his will to fight. Then begins the 'treatment' with neuroleptics. I was horrified to see how I deteriorated intellectually, morally and emotionally from day to day. . . . I did not have a thought in my head. The only thoughts that remained were: the lavatory, smoking and the bribes you had to give to the orderlies to get an extra visit to the lavatory. (Van Voren, 1983: 15–16)

In 1977, a group of Moscow intellectuals founded the Working Commission to Investigate the Use of Psychiatry for Political Purposes. It undertook to collect documentation on the political use of psychiatry and to help the victims of such practices. In the same year, the Congress of the World Psychiatric Association in Honolulu passed three resolutions condemning these Soviet abuses. Shortly after, it became known that 'prisoners of Soviet labour camps had prepared to stage a series of mass hunger-strikes if the resolution [was] not passed' (Van Voren, 1983: 19). The Moscow Commission demanded the subordination of the Special Psychiatric Hospitals to the Ministry of Health and the eradication of abuses by orderlies and doctors, including the beating of patients and the use of painful treatments as punishment. The Commission published an Information Bulletin in which such abuses were noted. Gradually, however, all the members of this group were arrested, tried, and sentenced to long terms in prisons, camps or exile.

Characteristically, the most severe sentence was meted out to a psychiatrist who was frequently called upon by the Commission to examine the forcibly interned patients. His sentence of seven years in a strict regime camp and five years in exile was meant to deter other psychiatrists from following in his footsteps. The trials were conducted before selected audiences and violated numerous procedural rules. As is common in such political trials, the accused activists could not choose their lawyers and most of them declined the services of the court appointed defence attorneys (for more information see Van Voren, 1983: 26–49; Burns, 1981; Bloch and Reddaway, 1977; Fireside, 1979; Bukovsky and Gluzman, 1975; Chorover, 1973).

Early in 1983, the year of the Seventh Congress of the World Psychiatric Association, two resolutions were forwarded to the Association's headquarters which called for the expulsion, or at least suspension, of the Soviet member association. The Soviets did not want to take chances, however, and the Soviet All-Union Society of Neurologists and Psychiatrists announced its withdrawal from the World Psychiatric Association. While there were some indications that leading Soviet psychiatrists wanted to continue the membership, the withdrawal was apparently ordered by the new leader of the Soviet Union, Yuri V. Andropov, as both an indication of his rejection of foreign pressure for human rights and as a warning to Soviet psychiatrists to desist from concessions and conciliation (Biddle and Slade, 1983).

There are some Western observers, however, who wonder whether it is not, in fact, natural to question the sanity of those individuals who show dissent, especially since their nonconformity means almost inevitable repression and confinement within the frightening penal institutions. Given this, the questions remain: could not Soviet dissenters be exhibiting a pathological lack of a sense of self-preservation? Could they not, despite all the rationality of their criticism of the Soviet system, be nothing more than a collection of desperate Don Quixotes who long ago lost touch with the reality of the police state? Could it be that Soviet doctors, socialized in Soviet society, really perceive these individuals as severely disturbed? A prominent psychiatrist from Washington postulates on this matter thus:

> If I am right – if the tragedy of Soviet psychiatry is part of the tragedy of Soviet society, a tragedy that has caused distortions of the ways in which Soviet people perceive each other – then at least some of those healthy dissidents are sincerely seen to be mentally ill, not only by the

psychiatrists and the KGB but by much of the population of that historically wounded land. (Reich, 1983: 50)

These are intriguing thoughts. The discussion of Reich's statement along with various other aspects of the material contained in this section, however, will be postponed until the final section of this chapter in order to include first an analysis of the available information on the Polish correctional network.

POLISH PRISONS, POLITICS AND ECONOMY

As indicated in Chapter 2, the Polish penal law and criminal justice system have been extremely punitive. It is not surprising, therefore, that the number of prisoners interned in Poland has been alarmingly high for years. In addition to long sentences involving the absolute deprivation of liberty, there is also a pronounced trend to detain those awaiting trial for long periods of time. As well, the noble idea of rehabilitation has been translated by the Penal Code into two options, frequently used by the courts. These alternatives involve either protective supervision or detention in centers of social rehabilitation and can be applied only to persistent recidivists. Both these measures are adjudicated for a period of anywhere from three to five years commencing after the completion of the offender's term in prison (ss. 60–5). Protective supervision imposes many obligations and restrictions on the sentenced person, e.g. his place of residence, type of work, remuneration, and freedom of movement. Social readaptation centres do not differ significantly from prisons and their main 'educational' feature is hard labour. The duration of retention in such centres is not determined in advance, but rather is theoretically dependent on the progress made by the inmate towards his social reintegration. Both sanctions are generally perceived by prisoners and many legal experts as extremely unfair. They serve no educational function, but rather further isolate and economically exploit chronic, and often petty, offenders (Balandynowicz and Porowski, 1980). These measures may also be utilized to incapacitate political activists whose frequent clashes with the law are often classified as hooligan excesses, thereby qualifying them for terms in readaptation centres.

An accurate estimate of the prison population in the late 1970s is difficult to ascertain since all information relating to penal institutions is classified. There exist, however, fairly reliable estimates published during the Solidarity period (1980–81) which are confirmed by many legal experts and criminologists. They quote figures ranging from 120 to 200 thousand prisoners,[7] with some reaching as high as 400 000 when all forms of imprisonment, detention or 'rehabilitative' incarceration are taken into consideration (this latter figure was quoted during the defence lawyers' convention in 1981 – see Jotecka, 1981: 40). These estimates seem to be fully consistent with earlier leaks and secretly circulated data which many specialists were aware of, even if they could not include them in their published works. In an official interview in 1981 (prior to the imposition of the state of war), the Deputy Director of the Central Board of Penal Establishments stated that there were 76 076 convicted prisoners and 20 000 detainees awaiting trial (Jotecka, 1981: 10). These numbers were criticized and rejected as unrealistic by all authorities in the field who dared to pronounce their views on this highly sensitive matter. An article in the official weekly *Polityka* maintained, for example, that there were more than 100 000 prisoners at the end of 1980 (Podemski, 1982b: 5), and a representative of the Institute for the Study of Court Law at the Ministry of Justice estimated, during a conference at the University of Warsaw, that there were 130 000 convicted prisoners in Poland (Jotecka, 1981: 10). While this latter figure has been accepted by some experts, others still reject it as much too conservative. If it is accepted, however, that the true number of prisoners before the imposition of the state of war was in fact somewhere between 120 000 and 200 000 (the latter estimate was quoted by the 'Patronat' association among others; the association will be discussed later in this chapter; see 'Sprawa Patronatu', 1981: 44), then the rate of imprisonment per 100 000 population amounts to an extraordinary figure of 350–580. These rates are 1.5 to almost 3 times higher than the corresponding rate in the USA, 4 to 6 times higher than the Canadian rate, and 14 to 23 times higher than The Netherlands's imprisonment rate (these estimates are based on the Western imprisonment rates published in *Basic Facts*, 1982: 6). The Polish rate is, on the other hand, lower than the rate of 400–600 per 100 000 in the Soviet Union. Naturally, the Polish prison population was much higher during the Stalinist period than it is at the present time.

While the numbers of inmates in Polish penal institutions seem to testify to extremely punitive sentencing policies, the conditions to which these prisoners are subjected indicate an unusual degree of repressiveness and cruelty on the part of the correctional system. Until 1980, there was practically no information available to either the society at large or interested researchers regarding the conditions and daily routines within the penitentiaries. This degree of secrecy has been partially alleviated due to the efforts of the journalists encouraged by the changed political atmosphere in 1980–81. Some of this information has been disclosed and even published in the censored media. Also, a group of concerned citizens was formed and demanded its official registration as a Society to Assist Imprisoned Persons and their Families ('Patronat'). The Society was intended as a non-political, charitable organization, similar to one which had existed in Poland (under the same name) from 1909 until 1949 when it was abolished amidst the Stalinist terror. Attempts to re-establish Patronat during the period of relative liberalization in the late 1950s were not successful since the idea of letting representatives of the society gain insight into the prison regime was politically unacceptable. Such authorization would imply certain external controls over a crucial part of the coercive apparatus and an unthinkable demand for accountability in the area most critical for the orderly functioning of an authoritarian, one-party state. Indeed, the repressive roots of the seemingly peaceful post-Stalinist 'reconstruction' era had to remain hidden despite all the new rhetoric of the 'political thaw' and 'socialist democracy'.

Similarly, the petition to re-establish Patronat lodged in November 1980 immediately after the legalization of Solidarity, was promptly rejected by the authorities. Yet, in response to considerable pressure by Solidarity and the growing unrest inside the prisons, this decision was eventually reversed. Patronat was finally registered on 21 July 1981 as a charitable association entitled to provide moral, legal, financial and medical assistance to prisoners and their families, regardless of the nature of their crimes. In the aftermath of this decision, the censor's ban on media or public discussion of even the idea of such an organization was partially lifted (T.O., 1981: 21–2). On 18 December 1982, however, Patronat was once again dissolved. The official explanation for this decision claimed that:

> Its main objectives appeared to be the negation of structures and the undermining of the activities of the agencies of authority and state administration as well as interference in the functioning of penal institutions.
> ('Rozwiazanie Patronatu', 1983: 9; this author's translation from Polish)

Despite its short legal existence, however, Patronat's activities, coupled with the relaxation of censorship regulations, contributed to an unprecedented increase in the public's knowledge of the abuses and horrors of the Polish prison network, which many people had believed to be commonplace in the Soviet Union but foreign to their own country. Moreover, the changed political atmosphere of the early 1980s released the long suppressed anger of the inmates themselves, and a wave of prison strikes and riots swept the whole country (see for example Falkowska, 1981b: 5, 15; 'Jeszcze raz . . .', 1981: 2; Strzelecka, 1981b: 13; Jotecka, 1981: 10; 'Bunt Wieźniów . . .', 1981: 2; Soroka, 1981: 5, 14). The Deputy Minister of Justice admitted in a televised interview, at the end of 1981, that 109 out of the 146 prisons in Poland had experienced riots after August 1980 in which, according to him, two prisoners had been killed by special security (Zalega, 1981: 10). The press reports on these prison disturbances, and especially those published by the weekly *Solidarność* (before its closure in December 1981) and some scientific journals, provide valuable insights into the prisoners' plight and the nature of their grievances. (It is important to note that since these reports were published in the censored media they cannot fairly be accused of exaggeration or defamation as underground or *émigré* accounts often are.) On the basis of this material, then, it can be concluded that the most persistent and best documented deficiencies of the prison system include the following areas:

Inadequate Living Conditions

Due to the prevailing sentencing patterns and general correctional policies, prisoners live in overcrowded cells, have no adequate sanitary or recreational facilities, and usually no or very limited access to any forms of treatment, counselling, medical care, or educational opportunities. On average, a prisoner has 2 square meters (21 square feet) of space in a communal cell. The cell itself usually has very little light, often an insufficient number of beds ('surplus' prisoners sleep on the floor) and sanitary conveniences located directly in the cell, not separated in any way from the living space. Normally, prisoners are not allowed to keep their personal belongings or clothing (Wróblewski W., 1981: 29–30; 'Sprawa Patronatu', 1981: 42; Zmarzlik, 1981: 8–9; Porowski, 1980: 75).

Hunger and the Poor Quality of Food

Hunger seems to be a permanent feature of Polish penitentiaries. Food deficiencies in prisons and juvenile correctional institutions are planned to the extent that the officially approved food norms are drastically inadequate and are worsened by the fact that members of the staff regularly steal foodstuffs from the prison kitchens. Moreover, because of the general shortage of food, prison employees buy up most of the supplies from the canteen, making it impossible for inmates to supplement their rations with whatever limited purchases they are authorized to make (e.g. 'Listy . . .,' 1981: 8, 9; Zalega, 1981: 10; Soroka, 1981: 5, 14; Jakubiec, 1981: 13).[8] Moreover, misbehaving prisoners may be forbidden to make such purchases for up to 3 months. Parcels from home are also very restricted. Finally, the reduction of prison food rations by as much as half for up to 14 days was applied until 1981 as one of the principal penalties. Despite its violation of international conventions signed by Poland, this sanction was in full agreement with the prison regulations drawn up in 1974 ('Zarzadzenie . . .', 1974: 8, s. 85.1.9). These regulations were revised during the Solidarity period as a result of a pressure by both Solidarity experts and prisoners ('Zarzadzenie . . .', 1981: 4).

Inadequate Medical Care

Access to medical care is extremely limited in prisons. For obvious reasons, health problems resulting from the physical abuse of prisoners are very rarely brought to the attention of the prison medics. Even if they are, they are seldom acted upon. 'The medic happens to be the wife of the director of security, who, in turn, is responsible for the prison's internal order and legality and the work done by his men. She would not turn against her husband' (Pelc, 1981: 9; this author's translation from Polish). Even if the medic has no family ties with the prison administrators, she or he is considered a member of a team which has to work together to assure the smooth functioning of the prison. The following account was offered by a prisoner in a letter of his published in the weekly *Solidarność*:

> The medical staff, led by the medic, play the role of 'God and the Tsar' here. When someone really needs medical attention and asks for basic medicines, the medic's face changes instantly and he accuses the patient of simulating an illness in order to obtain medicines. Despite complaints sent by patients to the Ministry of Health, no answer has been yet received. Perhaps the complaints have never been forwarded by this Penal Institution.
>
> (Wiezień, 1981: 9; this author's translation from Polish)

Another prisoner wrote that inmates who go to see a doctor are often sent back with a written report stating that they have simulated illness, an act which is considered an offence (Wiezień X, 1981: 9). In general, it appears that the medical staff is unwilling to risk any active involvement in the treatment of prisoners for a number of reasons, with the possibility of excusing them from work as a major one. As well, scant medical supplies preclude any serious treatment and, as a result, drugs prescribed to inmates are often totally inappropriate. Cases of serious surgery performed on inmates without the use of anaesthetics, be they out of parsimony or sheer callousness, are not uncommon (Wróblewski W., 1982: 33–4). This alarming neglect of prisoners' health problems is well documented through numerous accounts of political internees and prisoners of the state of war period which repeatedly cite cases of the serious deterioration of health, or even death, of internees caused by lack of medical attention. Indeed, given the existing data, it is possible to conclude that while health care in Poland is totally inadequate in general, it appears to be virtually non-existent in that country's penal institutions.

Hard Labour, Inadequate, Dangerous Working Conditions

The main means of rehabilitation in both the Polish penal institutions and the juvenile correctional institutions is hard labour. The work duty is treated by the penal authorities in such a rigorous manner that there can be no doubt about the importance of the prisons' economic function to the rulers of the country. Even sick and disabled inmates are routinely forced to work. According to prison regulations, refusal to work is the most serious offence and is punishable by one month of solitary confinement or one to six months in a special isolation unit. Until recently, guilty offenders have also had their food rations drastically reduced (the 'hunger penalty') and their heads shaved (Zarzadzenie . . ., 1974: 8–9, s. 85.1 and s. 92.2). Contrary to the provisions of international conventions, work is also used as a punishment and the type of labour is related to the type of regime in the given prison; i.e. the stricter the regime, the heavier and more dangerous the work performed.

While convicts receive 20 to 30 per cent of their earnings, they do not earn the right to a retirement pension. This is seen by many of them as a serious problem especially given the protracted duration of their stays in penal establishments. Long working hours, harsh working conditions and the total neglect of safety standards frequently lead to accidents and the contraction of chronic diseases by both adult prisoners and juveniles as well. Such victims, however, are not eligible for disability benefits or proper compensation. In the case of a very severe disability, the victim may at best receive a symbolic lump sum of money, which is in no way comparable to the work accident compensation which all working people are entitled to in principle (Jotecka, 1981: 10–11; Falkowska, 1981b: 5, 15; Jakubiec, 1981: 13). In addition, both adult and juvenile inmates are often ordered by prison staff to work, usually at night and without remuneration, on the construction of private houses or other private ventures for them. (This kind of exploitation, which is also very common in the Soviet Union, is one of the most often stressed by protesting inmates – see, for example, Zalega, 1981: 10; Jakubiec, 1981: 13).

Brutality Towards Prisoners

The constant beating of inmates in both adult and juvenile institutions is another common feature of Polish penal institutions. While there are many techniques of beating and torturing prisoners which do not leave any permanent marks (for a detailed description see Pelc, 1981: 8), not infrequently, however, inmates suffer concussions, fractured bones, crushed kidneys, and many other injuries. These are normally diagnosed by doctors as the result of either fights with other prisoners or innocent accidents, such as slipping on the stairs, etc. (see 'Listy . . .', 1981: 8, 9; Zalega, 1981: 10). Injured prisoners cannot hope for a disability pension or even reasonable medical treatment. Indeed, in most cases they are not allowed to see a doctor and are often 'stored' in solitary confinement for a period of 'recovery'. A typical list of prisoners' grievances verbalized during their recent protests included demands similar to those formulated by inmates of the Suwalki prison: 'Investigate and call to account prison functionaries guilty of the maltreatment of inmates, by hanging them on bars, beating them, and applying other forms of repression' (Zalega, 1981: 10; this author's translation from Polish). Further documentation cites more sophisticated tortures as well. A representative of Solidarity reports in *Solidarność*, for example, that:

> In conversation with prisoners, the issue of the so-called 'belt-chamber' (*pasownia*) is raised again and again. This device is used to torture insubordinate prisoners. What I saw went beyond my worst suspicions. . . . The room is around 7 to 8 m^2 (75–85 square feet) in

> size. It has a double door and a thick, plexiglas window. Thick walls and a vestibule are designed to absorb sound. There is a large pedestal the size of a large bed in the center. It has six metal handles to which belts can be attached. According to prisoner's accounts, the convict is put on the pedestal, and his legs, arms and chest are tied in such a way that his shoulder blades meet. The torturer presses the victim's chest with his knees to squeeze out all the air and then tightens the belt as much as he can. He puts a matchbox or a bar of soap under his spine. This causes pain. . . . The victim stays in such a position for 6, 12 or even 24 hours. After only six hours, he is not able to hold anything in his hands for two weeks. . . . The decision to use the 'belt-chamber' is made by the director of the prison, while the prison doctor gives his opinion as to whether the prisoner's health allows its application. . . . Another, frequent form of torture consists of squeezing the prisoner's testicles.
>
> ('Jeszcze raz . . .', 1982: 2; this author's translation from Polish; see also Falkowska, 1981b: 5, 15; 'Dziekuje . . .', 1981)

Less sophisticated forms of violence including daily beatings, setting dogs on prisoners, burning their skin, and so forth, are systematically undertaken without any formal authorization from the director. They take place most frequently when the guards get drunk in the evening and 'entertain' themselves by abusing prisoners (Pelc, 1981: 8; Jotecka, 1981: 11; Wróblewski, W., 1981: 30; Kaźmierczak, 1981: 12–14; Jakubiec, 1981: 13).

Two reports published in Poland in 1981 describe the horrifying tortures to which male juveniles are submitted in correctional institutions. They include the most brutal forms of beating, setting fire to the boys' hair, burning their skin and genitals, hitting the soles of their feet with sticks, putting rolled newspapers between their toes and igniting them, attaching strings to the boys' genitals and pulling them and trampling on boys laying on the floor so to crush and bruise them to the point of losing consciousness (Jakubiec, 1981: 13; Kaźmierczak, 1981: 12–14). The author of one of these articles explains that there is a clear negative selection made when filling the positions of instructors in juvenile institutions. Those chosen are frequently immoral people with criminal records and no professional or personal qualifications for such work. They tend to drink heavily while on duty and not infrequently coerce inmates into committing crimes (Jakubiec, 1981: 13) or abusing weaker prisoners (for an analysis of peer subcultures in Polish correctional institutions see Łoś and Anderson, 1981).

Restrictions, Punishments and the Predominance of Secret Regulations

The lawlessness of the prison reality intensified in the 1970s by the arbitrary nature of the prison regulations introduced by the Minister of Justice in 1974 as temporary by-laws to be shortly replaced by a new code (Zarzadzenie, 1974). The regulations emphasized the duty to work and greatly expanded the range of previously existing penalties. The recommended penalties included the 'hunger penalty', the 'hard bed' (a bed with no mattress or pillow), solitary confinement for up to half a year, head shaving and the deprivation of visits and correspondence. (They were extremely restricted even without the application of such punishment.) The regulations gave the guards enormous discretion and power over prisoners thereby making a mockery of any claims that prisons attempt to rehabilitate offenders. Indeed, in the case of several prison rebellions, the demand to abolish the unlawful by-laws was among the highest priorities of the dissatisfied prisoners (Falkowska, 1981b: 5, 15; Porowski, 1980: 57–58; Strzelecka, 1981b: 13, Jotecka, 1981: 10, 11; Wróblewski, W., 1981: 29). It was as a result of these uprisings that the Minister of Justice declared in 1981 that the use of the hunger penalty and the head shaving be discontinued and the prison regulations be revised accordingly (Zarzadzenie, 1981: 4).

Lack of Social Control Over Prisons

As previously mentioned, the public is not allowed to know or judge what is happening 'behind the bars' of the prisons. There is no external body to which convicts can appeal decisions made by prison authorities or complain about conditions, maltreatment and penalties. Prisoners are only entitled to lodge complaints to the superior levels of the correctional administration, and penalties are threatened for 'false representations'. As well, and despite the prohibition of the censorship of complaints explicitly stated in the Code of Penal Procedure, binding prison regulations authorize prison directors to censor all complaints and to append them with their own comments. The said regulations also prohibit collective statements of complaints by groups of inmates (Porowski, 1980: 74–5). Any attempts to organize groups outside the prisons sympathetic to the prisoners' cause are strictly prohibited, as exemplified by the short legal existence of the association Patronat and the suspension in 1982 of the Polish Penitentiary Society. In sum, convicts are totally separated from society, left to the mercy of prison guards and correctional authorities, exploited economically, abused physically and deprived of basic civil and human rights guaranteed by the Code of Penal Procedure.

* * *

Given this description of the realities of the Polish penal system, it is apparent that while there are significant affinities between the Soviet prison system and its Polish counterpart, it is worthy of note that the Soviet-style political abuses of psychiatry are relatively infrequent in Poland. Some incidents of this type, however, did take place in Poland during the Stalinist period. It has largely been through the integrity and professional traditions of the Polish psychiatric community that the repeated attempts by the Ministry of the Interior to 'politicize' this practice have remained ineffective for the most part. Despite this virtual ineffectiveness, however, intensive attempts at 'politicization' were introduced again during the state of war. In April 1982, for example, on the eve of the anticipated pro-Solidarity marches, the Warsaw police requested that a selected Warsaw mental hospital admit a large number of potential 'troublemakers'. The director of the hospital was able to refuse this request, however, on the basis of the existing law which precluded compulsory confinement on a simple motion by the police (Wróblewski, W. 1982: 23).

Later, the same year, four political internees were forcibly placed in a psychiatric institution when they asked for medical assistance in connection with their purely physical ailments. They were, however, eventually transferred back to an internment camp. Finally, prolonged psychiatric observation in a prison hospital was ordered in the case of Anna Walentynowicz, an extremely popular worker from a Gdańsk shipyard and one of the most celebrated heros of the 1980 Gdańsk strikes (Wróblewski, W., 1982: 33–4). While some other cases of forcible confinement of Solidarity activists and supporters in psychiatric institutions have been reported (e.g. 'Nowa forma . . .', 1983: 64), there is still no systematic inventory of all the verified cases. Unlike other such cases, though, whether or not these individuals have been released from the psychiatric institutions is unknown.

Nevertheless, despite these troubling occurrences, the extent and nature of the police abuses of psychiatry continues to be far less serious than these taking place routinely in the Soviet Union.

DISCUSSION

This chapter is meant to provide some general insight into the structure and problems of the penal policies in the USSR and Poland. Naturally, prisons are among those aspects of the functioning of the state which can be easily attacked and criticized in any country, since they are, by definition, repressive, coercive and always to some degree arbitrary. The purpose of the above discussion is not to compete with the bleak descriptions of those ultimate forms of coercion in any of the Western countries, but rather to gather and present the now accessible and even in some cases officially published information about their particular forms, features and roles in these two selected communist countries.

To anyone familiar with Poland's unique humanitarian traditions and progressive legal culture, this account makes clear the overwhelming implications of that country's subordination to communist rule. Most of the penal solutions and policies have been directly transplanted from the Soviet Union. As well, the nature of the Polish prison network, although by necessity adjusted to the different geographical and social conditions of Poland, bears a striking resemblance to the notorious Soviet penal archipelago. Even more significant than the importation of specific legal solutions or regulations is the impact of the economic and political context which has been moulded according to the Soviet ideology. It is the latter which determines the purpose and major functions of the criminal justice system. Any serious analysis of the nature of the legislation and the judiciary in Poland and in the Soviet Union demonstrates their objective subordination to the monopolistic Communist Party. For, it is the party which allocates and defines the political and economic roles they are expected to play in any given period of time and which can easily bring about any politically desirable alterations in these roles through the subjection of the legislative and judicial functionaries to direct party discipline.

The economic role of penal system is a good example of such synchronization of the legal system with the political will of the party. In the Soviet Union, for example, chronic shortages of manpower, especially in the harsh conditions of Siberia, make it logical for the Communist Party to seek the economic employment of convicts and thereby to encourage the growth of the prison population. Convicts may be sent to areas where natural resources or industrial or military development needs require a large supply of workers, but where the inhospitable climate or drastically unsafe conditions deter free labourers from constituting this work force. In addition, prisoners can be forced to work overtime, in the most disciplined fashion, without much regard for safety requirements, labour regulations or the cost of social insurance benefits and compensations in the event of the worker's loss of health or limbs.

This highly economic means of employing a large army of slave labourers which has been successfully developed and applied in the Soviet Union, has no doubt contributed to both the large prison population and the specific structure of the Polish penitentiary system as well. The ideological programme of economic expansion and heavy industrialization of Poland introduced during the Stalinist era entailed the massive mobilization of all able-bodied males and females and was accompanied by an unprecedented growth in the rate of incarceration. In addition to the clearly political functions of these repressive policies, the large inmate population provided the badly needed supply of cheap, deployable and disciplined labourers. Even though Poland's economy began to experience a problem of surplus labour in the early 1980s, the advantages of prison employment seemed to outweigh any disadvantages related to the changing needs of the labour market. Either that or the patterns tested and found functional in the communist superpower cannot be easily rejected as inapplicable in this 'satellite' country despite the diminishing economic usefulness of such solutions.

Several interesting historical studies, involving a number of European countries, have identified and traced a clear relationship between the labour market and the penal system (above all Rusche and Kirchheimer, 1968; Chambliss, 1964, 1971; Sellin, 1976). A perusal of these studies indicates that the development of the Soviet penal system provides one of the best illustrations of this thesis. While the Soviet model provides the clearest example, the pervasive Soviet influence on the Polish political, economic and penal institutions renders the main thrusts of the following analysis equally applicable to Poland. While, however, labour shortages certainly help to explain the nature of the relationship between the economy and the penal system, they should not be seen as an isolated and static factor. Many dimensions, including the ideological, political, economic and even geographical, have to be considered in any analysis of the unique Soviet prison archipelago.

Geographical Conditions

The severe climatic conditions in huge areas of the Soviet territory offer a possible explanation for the relationship between economy and penal policy. Essentially, prisoners have been viewed as the only viable labour force employable in the mines and industries of these rich but inhospitable regions. It is worthy of note that, by the eighteenth century in Russia, the exploitation of mines in the Urals and Siberia was heavily dependent on penal slave labour. Indeed, Sellin's account of that period seems strikingly akin to the reality of the contemporary Soviet labour colonies and forced settlements in Siberia, with the only difference being that the heaviest punishments are reserved now for the political rather than the criminal offenders:

> In addition to political and religious dissidents exiled there to fend for themselves, and other obnoxious persons – vagrants, petty offenders, serfs expelled by their masters of village communes – to colonize the land under police surveillance, common criminals of the worst kinds were sent to slave in the mines. (Sellin, 1976: 116)

Yet, the 'geographical explanation' is not fully satisfactory. Certainly, there are other countries with inhospitable regions which, nevertheless, do not rely on slave labour (e.g. Canada, Scandinavian countries). Why is it then, that the Soviet rulers persist in using penal slavery when all other civilized societies abandoned this practice long ago?

The Organization of the Economy

As observed by Rusche and Kirchheimer, 'galley slavery, deportation and penal servitude at hard labour, which partially replaced capital and corporal punishment in the late sixteenth century' were not the result of humanitarian considerations, but of certain economic developments which revealed the potential value of a mass of human material completely at the disposal of the administration (Rusche and Kirchheimer, 1968: 24). Quite simply, it was at this time that Europe experienced an unprecedented increase in economic activities and opportunities, which was not matched by adequate numbers of available labourers. The large labour reserve typical of the preceding century suddenly disappeared. 'Capitalists of the mercantilist period could obtain labour on the open market only by paying high wages and granting favourable working conditions' (Rusche and Kirchheimer, 1968: 26). Forced labour, therefore, became one answer to the pressures of rapid economic development. Its usefulness was, however, greatly reduced and finally totally negated with the development of industrial capitalism when, on the one hand, machines replaced some of the human labour and, on the other, the high quality of merchandise in the competitive free market economy became vitally important. Penal labour was simply too wasteful and led to the production of inferior products. The employment of prison labour, therefore, was no longer considered economically profitable. As a result, modern prisons were introduced to isolate, punish and reform prisoners while simultaneously excluding them from the mainstream economy. Work, if present at all, was utilized as a form of punishment and not as a means of profit making.

In contradistinction to Western economies, the Soviet economic model has rejected the principle of the free market, introducing instead the regulatory measures of the centralized state. It is not private enterprise but the state which plays the dominant economic role and which controls all the processes of employment and production. Production is standardized and competition is precluded. While political indoctrination does not appear to provide sufficient motivation for high productivity and efficiency, economic incentives are nevertheless ideologically repudiated. In their absence, special coercive measures have to be employed by the state in order not only to assign people to specific jobs and localities but also to impose upon them the duty to work and to bind them to their workplaces (see Chapter 4).

Under such conditions, penal labour does not appear to be significantly less productive than free labour. Moreover, it has the advantage of being easily employable in order to ensure the fulfilment of those parts of the Central Plan, which, due to their exceptionally unhealthy or harsh nature, can be realized only under considerable coercive pressure. The competitiveness of the products and the value of the output are given less importance in the non-market economy. While the costs of transportation, accommodation, security and administration of labour colonies are considerable, the lack of any social control over the penal system permits the reduction of these costs to the lowest possible level. Permanent hunger, lack of medical care and primitive, overcrowded facilities are typical features of Soviet (and incidentally Polish) penal institutions. Moreover, prisoners receive only a small percentage of their nominal wages, the rest being paid towards the cost of their maintenance in prison. There can be no doubt that prison labour contributes considerably to the gross national product of both countries and that it plays an essential role in the fulfilment of the Central Plan. It is the state monopoly and the non-market nature of the centrally directed communist economy which make the utilization of slave labour compatible with the overall economic structure.

In addition, other factors which contributed to the disappearance of penal labour in Europe seem to be absent or relatively unimportant in the

Soviet Union (and other communist countries). One such a factor is the reaction of free labourers to the threat posed by the employment of prisoners especially at times of growing unemployment. Thus, the abolition of prison labour in France in 1848 was apparently prompted by a situation where 'instead of an upper class eager to obtain labour power from any source whatsoever . . . a working class mount[ed] the barricades to secure official acknowledgment of their right to work' (Rusche and Kirchheimer, 1968: 95). The issue of unemployment is somewhat different in nature within the Soviet Union. The centrally planned mechanisms of compulsory work assignments and the virtual elimination of choice in the selection of the workplace and the locality help to distribute the available manpower more evenly. As well, the preference for underemployment and meager wages over unemployment greatly reduces the visibility of the problem. Above all, however, the prohibition against both the organization of free trade unions and the engagement in labour negotiations deprive 'free' labourers in these countries of any control over their wages and working conditions in specific and the labour market in general.

The Political Organization of the State

The Soviet communist state, based on the totalitarian principle of one party rule, favours those forms of social organization which help to install total control over its citizens. The concentration of people in clearly delineated spaces greatly facilitates surveillance and the inculcation of desired forms of discipline (see e.g. Goffman, 1961; Foucault, 1977). It is not surprising, therefore, that the rates of imprisonization in communist countries (including hospitalization in mental hospitals) are so extremely high. The so-called total institutions (Goffman, 1961) are believed to be the best schools of mechanical obedience and passivity – the most sought after characteristics in these countries where initiative and creativity are systematically suppressed.

The imposition of hard labour from dawn till night has emerged as the most effective way of keeping people too busy and too tired even to think. Outside the prisons, in the society at large, the long working hours, the six day working week, the harsh conditions of everyday existence, the chronic shortages of food and other goods (i.e. long hours wasted in lines and in exhausting searches for necessities) and the overbureaucratization of all aspects of life, all seem to play a similar role. The preoccupation with the daily struggle to survive leaves little time for any nonconformistic thoughts or independent and creative activities. In comparison, prisons, forced labour, the duty to work and the general lack of choice within the vital areas of life, all seem to have the same function of limiting the avenues of human expression and diversity of behaviour. This reality is very distant indeed from Marx's idealistic visions of a society where 'labour which is determined by need and external purpose ceases' and is replaced by the 'development of human potentiality for its own sake, the true realm of freedom' (Marx, Das Kapital, 1867, reprinted in Bottomore and Rubel, 1963: 259–60).

Contrary to Marx's expectations, the division of labour has not been abolished under 'real-life' communism but has continued to play the essential role in maintaining industrial production and administration. While social mobility in Western capitalist countries is determined by birth, wealth and merit (with the latter having considerable weight), in communist countries this mobility is regulated by birth, wealth and political criteria, with the latter being of decisive importance. The absence of any separation between the state and the economy precludes any individualistic economic pursuits or initiatives and leads instead to alienation of second degree, whereby not only one's physical and mental energy is converted into an alien product, but one's spiritual and mental autonomy is violated by forced indoctrination and ideological conformization by the employer (the state). The seeds of this development can be found in Marx's vision of the communist society which foresaw the elimination of alienation through the total denial of individualistic values and interests:

> Human emancipation will only be complete when the real, individual man has absorbed in himself the abstract citizen, when as an individual man, in his everyday life, in his work, and in his relationships, he has become a *social being* and when he has recognized and organized his own powers as *social* powers, and consequently no longer separates this social power from himself as *political* power.
>
> (Marx, 'Zur Judenfrage', 1984, reprinted in Bottomore and Rubel (eds), 1963: 241)

This total fusion of social and individual perspectives may be initiated in various ways. The utopian Marxist proposal perceives it as a result of the genuine process of the abolition of class and power. Other, non-Marxist interpretations may identify such processes in any society with a high degree of consensus, even if they are, in fact, ruled by what Gramsci (1971) regarded as a perfect hegemony by the ruling class, that is, the skilful socialization of the citizenry in order to blind it from the exploitative conditions and conflicts of interests. Another possibility emerges when the hegemony fails, but nevertheless, no genuine social liberation takes place. In such circumstances an imposed 'liberation' may occur when faithful followers of the Marxist utopia do not hesitate to use coercion, suppression and penal slavery to root out the individualistic desires and pursuits seen as the legacy of the capitalist era. The mindless criminalization of various forms of behaviour in communist countries simply because they are perceived as 'capitalistic' or individualistic in nature, in conjunction with the persistent depiction of all crimes as remnants of the 'capitalistic mentality', attest to such a tendency.

As well, the lack of legitimacy among the power holders (in contrast to the legitimacy achieved in the West through the mechanisms of representative democracy) aggravates their insecurity and vulnerability. The continuity of their rule does not depend on the votes they are able to secure, but rather on their ability to stifle any opposition or other manifestation of social or political pluralism. The power-draining function of the prison (Mathiesen, 1974: 77) is, thus, much more obvious and vital to Soviet corrections than it is to the operation of the penal system in Western nations. The long list of political and economic offences punishable by penalties more severe than those meted out for ordinary crimes in addition to the actual imprisonment or psychiatric confinement of numerous individuals suspected of having unofficial political and economic influence, testifies to the dramatic importance of the penal system in purging the society of any signs of independent life.

Thus, the thesis that there exists a clear relationship between the penal system and the political and economic organization of the society is strongly supported by the example of their correlation in the Soviet Union. The similarities between the Soviet and Polish political, economic and penal organization which have already been examined make this thesis applicable to the Polish situation as well. Nevertheless, there does remain one characteristic of the Soviet penal system, namely the extensive use of psychiatric labels and institutions, which is not as visible within the Polish system. The question remains, then, why is there such an essential difference between the Soviet Union and Poland in the extent to which the blatant abuses of psychiatry are utilized in the efforts to achieve this total political submission and conformity? At first glance, professional tradition and the integrity of Polish psychiatrists may serve as a tentative and partial explanation. Yet, surely, some Polish psychiatrists could be forced to violate professional standards if the pressures applied were of a more malicious nature. It appears, therefore, that the Soviet state expects greater conformity and is, in general, more resolute than the Polish state in applying police methods of control. This reality appeared accurate, at least, until the violent suppression of the Solidarity movement in 1981 and the subsequent political developments.

In general, it seems that civil liberties and individualistic attitudes have traditionally been treasured by the Poles while given far lesser importance in Russia. Differences in the historical pasts, political heritages, religious traditions, civil fortitudes, and the endurance of cultural contact with the rest of Europe are among the factors which must be taken into consideration in any attempt to explain the divergent patterns of popular political culture within these two countries. The prominent place of national independence and individual rights among the values cherished by the Poles explains their involvement in repeated outbursts of protest and rebellion against communist authorities. Even when violently suppressed, these events are usually followed by some form of liberalization which, in turn, helps to provide channels for the release of the anger and bitterness whose accumulation proves to be so dangerous to the system's stability. It appears that, while political curbs applied to the Poles are very severe, the Polish authorities and their Soviet masters tend to rely more on the application of economic hardship as a form of punitive control over that society marked, as it is, by strong constitutionalist and democratic traditions. Many Poles, in fact, believe that they, as members of a 'civil society', do trade some economic advantages for their extremely limited individual freedoms, which, despite their restrictions, are still greater than those of many other communist countries. Hungary and East Germany are often quoted as examples of the opposite situation where populations submit to greater political controls in exchange for some economic gains.

The Soviet people, on the other hand, seem to be totally deprived of both freedom of expression and economic opportunities. In order to subjugate them in this way, a massive system of indoctrination, total isolation from the West and prohibition of information has been in operation for more than 65 years. The Stalinist years of dehumanization and savage terror left that society paralysed with fear and morally crippled. It was only the quiet suppression which followed that seemed to increase substantially the chances for individual survival and it is this survival which has been the main objective of many Soviet citizens since. It, in turn, involves many complicated everyday operations to secure material necessities, to make political connections, to bribe, to avoid trouble, in short, to continue living under the conditions of permanent shortages, economic disorganization, overbureaucratization and totalitarian political control.

Such are realities of life for the average citizen within Soviet society. One has to make many adjustments and compromises in order to survive. The only way to neutralize the feelings of disgust and humiliation which one feels is to convince oneself that no sane individual would do otherwise, that no one desires to bring upon him or herself inevitable destruction. Dissident, nonconformist, fervent religious believer – each one of these seem to be able to deny the validity of the assumption that 'everybody gives in because everybody wants to live'. The actual scepticism regarding their authenticity ('they are probably sent by the KGB to provoke us') and their sanity (there is probably, after all, some truth in the earlier quoted statement by an American psychiatrist) seem to be justified insofar as these individuals represent an assault on the self-respect of the average members of a society of survivors. They put in question each citizen's moral integrity and awaken his/her conscience. No individual likes to be reminded about the mediocrity and mendacity of his/her existence. To some extent at least, the Soviet people do want to believe that those who have the courage to protest are either crazy or self-destructive rather than morally superior. Without this justification, the example set by these dissidents would oblige others to participate and, consequently, to abandon their routine ways of survival.

While there may be some merit in the claim that average members of Soviet society question the motivation of those citizens who consciously appear to jeopardize their own survival, it is impossible to place any credibility in the motivation of Soviet psychiatrists in their assessment of these citizens. In short, it is difficult to accept that the top Soviet psychiatrists, highly educated and intelligent people who sell their services to the KGB, actually believe that their ingenious invention, the so-called sluggish schizophrenia, is anything else than a convenient tool of political repression.

Given this overall picture of the patterns of incarceration in the Soviet Union and Poland, it is very clear that the relationship between prisons, politics and the economy is not only very pronounced but also crucial for their political stability.

Part Two: The Withering Away of Crime?

6* Crimes of the Political Elite: 'Red-Collar Crime'[1]

Crime committed by the ruling party élite is not restricted to economic and political corruption. Indeed, the later chapter on economic crime will examine some of the other criminal ventures of this group. It is the corruption among the top officials, however, which constitutes a type of crime whose analysis may best enhance the understanding of the mechanisms of power prevalent in communist countries. It is often believed that corruption is a part of human nature and that it is omnipresent. For the purposes of this chapter, however, the focus will be, not on corruption in general, but rather on those specific forms of top level corruption which occur with high frequency under the concrete political and economic conditions of two selected communist countries: the Soviet Union and Poland. The latter will be given greater emphasis since the nature of corruption in Poland is rarely explored in other than brief journalistic accounts; easily accessible English language literature on Soviet corruption, on the other hand, is relatively abundant. Before discussing top level corruption in these countries, however, the key concept of 'nomenklatura' has first to be introduced.

NOMENKLATURA

Michael Voslensky (1980b) claims that 'nomenklatura' and 'gulag' constitute two key elements of the Soviet reality. Simply stated, nomenklatura is a secret list of these important positions at all levels of the economic and state administrations, and, indeed, all other areas of institutional life, which are formally reserved for loyal communist party members. While all appointments, and even those of a totally subordinate nature, have to be approved by the local party cells, the party has the exclusive right to nominate appointees for nomenklatura positions (see e.g. Voslensky, 1980a: 28). These positions include key posts in such areas as state administration, the state economy, the secret police, prison administration, the army, education, youth organizations,

*This chapter incorporates many ideas from Łoś, 1984.

science and the media. In other words, the holders of nomenklatura posts, together with the party apparatus itself, represent the ruling bureaucratic élite or, as some prefer to call it, the 'red aristocracy' or 'the new bourgeoisie' (for a more detailed discussion of the 'new class' thesis see Chapter 1; also Voslensky, 1980a: 33–41; Nove, 1975).

Yet, nomenklatura is much more than just a list or just an élite; it is a mechanism by which the ruling monopolistic party exercises its control over all areas of political, economic and socil life. It is the essence and main vehicle of the communist power as it provides the party with a network of trusted functionaries who occupy all the strategic administrative positions, which, in the USSR, includes both the all-union and union–republic levels. It should not be surprising, therefore, that, as noted in Chapter 2, no demand by the striking Gdańsk workers and later by the Solidarity Union was met by such a determined refusal even to negotiate the issue as was the workers' bid for the right to veto the nominations for the directors of their factories or to request the dismissals of the current directors. Clearly, if such a right was granted to the employees, few party protégés would retain their posts and the neat scheme which promotes the transmission of command from the top to the bottom of the loyal bureaucratic pyramid would collapse.

The function of nomenklatura as both a transmission belt and a unified, vertical system of control, therefore, is crucial to the continuity of the political and economic organization of these countries. Moreover, in the case of Poland, it also represents the only network accessible to direct Soviet supervision and intervention. Within the Soviet Union, it facilitates Russian domination over the non-Russian republics since the post of the second secretary of the Central Committee of the Communist Party in those republics is, as a rule, reserved for a Russian from Moscow. The same appointment qualification is applied for the posts of the chairman of the KGB and the police chief. While other important positions are given to both Russians and autochthons, the latter are often selected among functionaries who spent several years of their service in Moscow (Voslensky, 1980a: 405–6).

Membership within the system of nomenklatura is either inherited or achieved by cooptation on the basis of 'connections' and loyalty to the political subculture and lifestyle of the party élite. There is no equality within this élite. On the contrary, a strict hierarchy of positions exists and relations of command and subordination dominate its inner structure. These are modified however by personal relations of blood, friendship or hatred which, in turn, provide additional mechanisms of communication and decision making. The interests and aspirations of the members of the élite are usually quite particularistic, concentrating on the preservation of their places within nomenklatura and aspirations of upward mobility within the hierarchy. Yet, criteria for promotion and demotion seem to be rather whimsical, making the degree of insecurity and anxiety quite high within nomenklatura circles. It is the fear of the temporary nature of their good fortunes, whose duration depends entirely on some secret decisions made by key bodies of the Communist Party which may, in fact, be one of the crucial factors contributing to the greed and hasty pursuit of personal gains by these officials. This fear appears to coexist, however, with both their belief in their absolute superiority and importance and their tendency to enjoy power to the full, while it lasts.

This chapter focuses on corruption within the top level nomenklatura circles,[2] and thereby includes:

1. Individual corruption of high ranking officials who use public money, resources, means of production, manpower, etc. to satisfy their own needs (this may include spectacular but wasteful investment decisions which serve their short-term goals and ambitions, enhance their prestige, power, and so forth).
2. Mutual corruption within the network of ruling cliques (this is a process of reciprocal bribing among officials out of the public pocket in order to maximize individual profits, secure mutual support and keep each other in check).

The following discussion concentrates on the political and economic sources of top-level corruption as well as on their interrelations and transformations.

THE EXTENT OF THE PROBLEM AND SOURCES OF INFORMATION

During the period of the relatively free operation of the Solidarity movement in Poland, between August 1980 and December 1981, the censor's control over the Polish press was considerably relaxed. Many critical articles which appeared in the daily papers and weekly magazines dealt with matters which previously could not be publicly discussed. In those 16 hopeful months the Polish media experienced a similar wave of renewal as did most other institutions in that country. The material they presented has, therefore, an exceptional value for any study of social and economic problems of contemporary communist states.

In the present attempt to analyse the nature and sources of corruption in Poland, various publications which appeared in the Polish press in the period following the strikes of August 1980 have been utilized.[3] They paint a bleak, deeply disturbing picture of a country plagued by injustice, corruption and exploitation. Yet, given the censorship and other constraints of freedom of expression always present in a totalitarian country, it must be assumed that they present a rather cautious diagnosis, more likely understated than overstated.

The systematic scrutiny of these publications reveals, above all, those aspects of corruption during the period of Gierek's rule, which were perceived by journalists as most irritating and conspicuous; they never attempted any global analysis. In order to take advantage of this unique material, however, this chapter will extrapolate the main concerns of these reports and attempt to convey their style and tone through the use of numerous quotations and examples derived directly from them.

Since there has been no comparable period of relaxation of censorship in the Soviet Union, the value of articles published in the Soviet press seems to be much more limited. They do provide, however, many examples of the corrupt practices prevalent among Soviet officials and do give some indication of the type and extent of criminal prosecution of them. Additionally, the extensive literature published in the West on the nature of corruption in the USSR offers a wealth of information which will be also referred to in this chapter.

The extent of corruption among the top members of nomenklatura is difficult to estimate. Both recent press reports and popular opinion in Poland and the USSR suggest that it has been very widespread indeed, but naturally, no precise figures can be provided.

Recent, well-publicized cases of the indictment of high party officials in the Soviet Union[4] include: a case of high level corruption and malversations in the Azerbaidshan Republic which resulted in 5 executions and 59 prison sentences (Smith, 1980: 122); a case of the USSR Deputy Minister of the Fish Industry who was sentenced to death for extortion and bribery (Rekunkov, 1982: 3); a case of a Minister of Finance in the Georgian Republic and 2 other senior officials jailed for 13 years for corrupt dealings in diamonds and state-owned luxury cars ('Ex-Official . . .', 1982: 7); a case of a Chairman of a Borough Soviet Executive Committee in Tbilisi who was sentenced to death for heading a gang of influential bribe takers and speculators ('After the trial', 1980); a case of a public prosecutor in the central Asian republic of Kirgizia executed for corruption (Cullen, 1983: 23); and a case of two officials of the State Committee for Foreign Economic Relations executed for systematically taking bribes ('Two Soviets . . .', 1984: 14).

The convicted officials also include many directors of state enterprises and state farms who were charged with fraud, embezzlement, bribery, report padding and other economic offences. Many officially reported sentences for these kinds of offences range from 8 to 12 years of deprivation of freedom. It must be remembered, however, that such illicit economic and official activities are very widespread among the managers of the economy and prosecution is applied in a very selective way. Trials of economic managers, similar to trials of selected politicians, are designed to serve some symbolic, political functions as well as to facilitate the removal of inconvenient executives who are no longer useful to the party or to its influential local or central groups.

In Poland, before 1980, it was extremely rare that a relatively high official would actually be taken to court. The prosecution for economic crimes and corruption concentrated rather on low and middle level participants, leaving untouched those who knew about, profited from and often directed criminal rings, but who were protected by their respectable party positions. It was the Solidarity movement which broke the silence surrounding corruption and unrestrained criminality among high level officials. At numerous meetings, workers, and even rank and file party members, demanded that the full truth be revealed concerning the extent of abuses of office and of public property by the party bosses. Public opinion was consolidated behind those demands. A daily paper summarized workers' common sentiments in the following sentence: 'For taking just one plank one could be fired, while at the same time far greater abuses were never punished' (Guzowska, 1981: 3; this author's translation from Polish).

Numerous reports were submitted to prosecutor's offices by work crews, union commissions and individual citizens. Most frequent accusations covered the appropriation of social property, forgery, the extortion of valuable gifts, foreign currency, and other forms of bribes, illegal traffic in permits to purchase cars, report padding, speculation in scarce commodities and black market operations ('Komunikat Prokuratury . . .', 1981: 2).

The Superior Office of Control (NIK), which deals with the cases of violation of law by the state agencies and their representatives, received three times as many complaints in 1980 as in 1979, with the majority of the complaints lodged after August 1980 (the date of birth of the Solidarity Union). Of 19 237 cases, 40 per cent were related to corruption, nepotism, economic crimes and wasteful management of economic resources. More than half of the complaints were judged to be legitimate. By March 1981 the investigations of 4000 cases were completed and 324 cases (among them 215 complaints against the members of nomenklatura) were found sufficiently 'sensitive' to be transferred to the Party Control Commission ('Ludzie . . .', 18 March 1981). The Warsaw Party Control Commission received 1145 complaints between July 1980 and March 1981. By March 1981, it considered 686 cases and made 116 recommendations. Among them: 35 recommendations of expulsion from the party, 42 decisions to apply some disciplinary measures and twelve decisions to transfer cases to the Public Prosecutor's Office ('Dzialalność . . .', 31 March 1981).

The demands made by the Solidarity Union and the exceptional intensity of public indignation resulted in relatively vigorous action by the prosecutor's offices. According to the information issued by the General Prosecutor in June 1981, among the investigated cases were those of four ministers, seven deputy ministers, five first secretaries and two other secretaries of regional party committees (Ptaczek, 1981: 23). As of December 1981, criminal charges were brought against 263 prominent officials. Temporary detention was applied to 101 persons. The investigation was completed in 181 cases and indictments were submitted to the courts against 154 persons ('Investigation . . .', 1982: 11). Among the charged officials were one minister, one deputy minister, two heads of regions (*voievodships*), three deputy heads of regions, the chairman and deputy chairman of the Committee for Radio and Television (subsequently sentenced to eight years in prison), and several directors of both large industrial companies as well as ministerial cabinets. Among the officials under investigation were the former General Secretary of the Central Committee of the Communist Party (Edward Gierek) and two former Deputy-Premiers ('Komunikat . . .', 1981: 2). Moreover, an official press report on police activities revealed that the police had been gathering information about some of these people since 1971. It claimed that the police had long lists of:

> omnipotent people, that is, criminals who used methods of corruption, abused their official positions, and made illegal multimillion fortunes. As early as 1973, these lists already included more than 2,500 names.
>
> (Markiewicz, 1981: 4; this author's translation from Polish)

Two prominent Polish journalists, specializing in legal matters, demanded amnesty for all those who had been sentenced for years in overcrowded prisons for relatively petty offences against state property and called for appropriate punishment for those criminals guilty of economic crimes involving millions of zlotych. They criticized the widespread practice of similar treatment given all participants of criminal rings in a nationalized economy regardless of the role they played. As a result, 'criminal proletarians', who had to steal in order to survive, were sentenced to long years in prison for their marginal association with criminal schemes operated by a 'criminal élite' whose members stole in order to live in luxury without fear of apprehension (Podemski, 1981b: 3; Falkowska, 1981c: 13).

In Poland, as in the Soviet Union, any potential criminal charges against the members of nomenklatura are first considered by special party commissions and eventually brought to the attention of the prosecutor's offices in exceptional cases only. (This practice persisted during the Solidarity period despite the relaxation and even removal of many manifestly authoritarian practices.) Party commissions' sanctions are generally limited to a reprimand, a recommendation of transfer to another post or retirement, or, in extreme cases, expulsion from the party. Although it is not formally expressed in any legal regulation, the police and the prosecutor's offices are expected to apply to party committees for authorization if they wish to initiate an investigation against any party official. Functionaries of Polish legal agencies are reminded of the existence of such rules during employees' meetings and conferences (Holwiński, 1981: Spotowski, 1981; Czabański, 1981b). According to a former Soviet jurist, Shtromas, a special secret instruction exists in the Soviet Union which recommends that a party member cannot be convicted by a court before the fate of his party membership is decided by an appropriate party committee (Shtromas, 1977).

Within the Soviet Union, the importance and indispensability of party control over the legal system is constantly emphasized in political as well as legal documents. This is, in fact, the essence of the 'socialist legality' which has been the guiding principle within the Soviet law (see Sharlet, 1979, for a detailed analysis of the relations between the Communist Party and the administration of justice in the USSR). While, however, the principle of party control had been especially strongly stressed in Brezhnev's law and order campaigns, his successor, Yuri Andropov, tended to rely more on the supervision exercised by the KGB. In Poland, the official rhetoric emphasizes party guidelines rather than party control and supervision; yet, measures similar to those in the Soviet Union are actually implemented. In both countries nominations and appointments to all important positions within the administration of criminal justice as well as the appointments of judges and even lay assessors, have to be approved at the appropriate party levels. This process provides an extremely effective way of controlling the daily functioning of the legal apparatus by assuring that all its participants are fully aware that they 'cannot be reappointed, renominated, transferred, or even relieved of their office except again with the prior approval of the party organs' (Sharlet, 1979: 327).

In Poland, after the legalization of the Free Trade Union Solidarity, a number of press publications openly criticized the absence of legal guarantees of judicial independence and the common practice of political intervention and control over the courts of law. In one quoted case, six judges submitted a written statement to a Solidarity commission in which they complained that binding directives had been issued in individual cases, and especially in those involving workers who had participated in the 1976 strikes and in those of local officials or influential underworld figures (Falkowska, 1981a). Other articles criticized prevailing personnel and remuneration policies as well as the criteria of evaluation of judges which foster opportunism and servility among judges (Strzelecka, 1981a; Dankowski, 1981). Similar criteria also apply to Supreme Court justices whose term of office is limited to five years and may or may not be renewed, depending on the political evaluation and personal connections of the individual judge involved (Dankowski, 1981). Thus, in Poland, as in the Soviet Union:

> all those who investigate, prosecute, preside, defend, and even study the administration of justice . . . first must pass through a system of political filters before they can take office or assume their responsibilities. (Sharlet, 1979: 327)

As well, there exists a strong tendency to appoint as many party members as possible to all levels of the criminal justice system in order to ensure that the secret instructions of the party be carried out. A primary party organization exists in each court and in every other legal agency. Its main role is to guide, supervise and evaluate the judges' performance in accordance with the dominant criminal policy. It must be stressed, however, that the interests of a local party organisation are not always fully consistent with those of superior party bodies. As a result, their actual functions involve not only the main function of transmitting and implementing the centrally determined political line but also many private and local interest games and network influences. Incidents of corruption and, consequently, protection of illegal interests of the local élites or powerful criminal rings are not infrequent. To quote the USSR Prosecutor General R. Rudenko:

> In exercising supervision of legality, prosecutors encounter attempts by some local executives and officials or higher level administrative agencies to shelter lawbreakers from responsibility. ... Unfortunately, not all prosecutors display firmness in such situations. Some of them, yielding to persuasion from local executives, show themselves to be spineless. (Rudenko, 1980: 6–7)

POLITICAL DETERMINANTS OF TOP-LEVEL CORRUPTION

One obvious and frequently quoted cause of top level corruption is the political inertia and lack of accountability among the power élite, characteristics of any one-party system, which is based on political absolutism and on lack of legally guaranteed mechanisms of power change. This explanation applies equally to the Soviet Union and Poland.

The system of nomenklatura itself contributes considerably to the corruption of its members. According to numerous accounts, the desirability of nomenklatura positions makes their illegal sale in exchange for bribes a very profitable business for influential party officials. Price tags for some of those posts appear to achieve truely astronomical proportions (see e.g. Zemtsov, 1976, 1979).

A second often cited cause of corruption within top political levels stems from the official respect which those who occupy chief offices within the official hierarchy are given. They are presented as representatives and, indeed priests of the communist party. Thus, any criticism raised against them is viewed as equal to an attack on the party. In turn, any criticism of the party is synonymous with a critique of communism itself, an action which calls for the most severe of penalties. Above all, this reverence provides a convenient shelter to those in the position to monopolize power, and allows them to be totally exempt from public scrutiny. There is little doubt, therefore, that they may be tempted to indulge in some profitable but corrupt practices. The lack of any inhibitions on their part is clearly confirmed by many lower rank functionaries and managers of industry, interviewed in 1980–81 by Polish journalists. They stressed that they had to obey even the most extravagant requests of the party bosses out of fear of being accused of disrespect or disobedience to the party. Thus, the difference between communist and multi-party capitalist countries in this respect is quite clear. 'Under capitalism, a critique of the given ruling élite is not synonymous with an attack on the principles of the political system, and, normally is not treated as such by anyone', states one of the authors in an issue of the weekly *Literatura* published during the period of 'renewal' in Poland (Chlopecki, 1980: 4; this author's translation from Polish).

A third cause is often seen to be the amount of control practiced by the political élite over the legal agencies, control which is buttressed by the group's omnipotent status. As mentioned earlier, there exist a number of mechanisms which make criminal prosecution of party officials especially difficult. In Poland it has been openly admitted that the direct political control over the legal system makes it easy for those who occupy more influential positions to manipulate the law in order to obtain material gains and to secure their own impunity. Moreover, both in Poland and the USSR, these officials actually accept considerable bribes or regular pay-offs ('protection money') in return for assuring the impunity of those members of local cliques who are involved in criminal dealings but lack direct political influence (see e.g. Simis, 1979: 43–6; Staats, 1972: 44–5; Pomorski, 1983: 14). As well, local power élites tend to develop extensive links with the organized crime networks including both conventional criminal underground networks and organized perpetrators of economic crimes. Their profitable yet illegal operations allow these criminals to offer exorbitant bribes for the promise of protection and freedom from prosecution. As Simis points out, the bribes tend to be considerable

> [because] they are mainly given for freeing black marketeers who have large funds at their disposal and, because the bribe-takers are sufficiently highly placed in the party hierarchy for small-scale bribes to be of no interest at all to them. (Simis, 1979: 45)

While the probability of public disclosure of such cases is generally very low, in the period from mid-1960s to the late 1970s the corruption dealings and involvement with the underworld of the entire ruling élites of several Soviet republics were exposed by the KGB. They include the entire leadership in Kirghizia, which:

> had been in the pay of a highly ramified network of black marketeers and underworld racketeers for many years. It had been established that the latter had set up dozens of clandestine factories, collective

> farms and plantations of opium and cannabis, which were not officially registered, for which no state taxes were paid and the income from which was shared out between those engaged in these criminal operations and the rulers of Kirghizia. (Simis, 1979: 47)

Similar involvement by the entire power hierarchies in the Azerbaidzhan Republic as well as in Georgia, Armenia and Uzbekistan has also been revealed. Nevertheless, the penalties tended to be relatively mild and most high-ranking bribe-takers went unpunished. 'The people who ended up in dock were the bribe-givers, large-scale underworld racketeers and individuals who had been engaged in the purchase of office' (Simis, 1979: 48).

More recent reports published in the Soviet press regarding such activities in these republics indicate that the personnel changes and the imposition of some criminal sanctions have brought little change in the corrupt habits of their ruling cliques. While these press articles avoid any generalizations, it is clear that the various reported incidents of abuse of office are indicative of the prevalence of corruption in the highest circles of power in these republics. For example, in 1979, only several years after the thorough re-organization within the hierarchy of the Azerbaidzhan Republic, heads of three ministries were dismissed from their posts for, as *Pravda* reports, they had 'connived at bribery, defrauding the state and embezzlement' (Tairov, 1979: 2). One of the ministries concerned was that of Public Health where the Minister and several executives were found guilty of glaring violations, notably 'favoritism, nepotism and localism' as well as the toleration of 'embezzlement, bribery, extortion and use of official position for mercenary purposes' all of which were widespread in the medical establishments ('In the Azerbaidzhan . . .', 1979: 2).

As well, a large scale bribery scandal which involved many local functionaries was disclosed in 1982 in one district of Azerbaidzhan. In addition to the officials of the District Soviet Executive Committee and local managers 'several officials of the people's court and the district internal affairs department were guilty of flagrant violations and abuse of office' ('In the Azerbaidzhan . . .', 1982: 14). Although the report did not name any party officials, it did suggest the party's direct involvement and responsibility:

> [the] District Party Committee knew about all this, but it took no effective steps to stop the violations. . . . Because exacting party control and devotion to principle were lacking in the district, little was done to combat manifestations of a petit bourgeois, consumer

> psychology, private-ownership tendencies and other negative phenomena. ('In the Azerbaidzhan . . .', 1982: 14)

As in Azerbaidzhan and several other republics, the disclosure of a high level criminal ring in the Soviet Republic of Georgia in the early 1970s and the subsequent dismissals and trials have not had any visible deterrent effect. For example, in 1982, the finance minister and two other senior officials in Georgia were found guilty of corruption. It was very clear, however, that they were part of a large scale criminal network including many high-ranking officials who themselves managed to escape prosecution ('Ex-Official . . .', 1982: 7). It seems, therefore, that isolated cases of disclosure and punishment fail to weaken the general faith of the members of nomenklatura, in their impunity.

There are also many indicators that, among the members of Polish nomenklatura, such a belief in their superiority and impunity was well established before August 1980. In many officially published descriptions of corruption and blatant abuses of office by influential functionaries, there is striking evidence that these members frequently abstained from taking even elementary precautions against possible legal inquiries into their actions; they felt totally confident of the protection granted by their offices. For instance, several articles portray typical methods by which the influential party officials were able to secure luxurious villas in the most attractive regions of the country without ever having to pay for them with their own money. In one quoted case, for example:

> the house owners were expropriated on the basis of that law which allows for such a procedure when it is vital for the satisfaction of some public needs. Then, those houses were luxuriously equipped and sold to the deputy-head of the region and the regional police chief. . . . The National Treasury paid 4 million 475 thousand zlotych for these transactions. It was not uncommon that the occupants of a house, which has been singled out by someone influential, were evicted by the police. (Loch, 1981: 5; this author's translation from Polish)

In another case, a picturesque spot attracted the attention of the bosses of the gigantic Katowice Foundry and of the Ministry of Metallurgical Industry:

> Lands for them and their families were extorted from the peasants without the slightest effort to give any appearance of legality or decency. In exchange, these visitors offered to their hospitable host (the head of the town and region), his people, and his beautiful town

> cement, steel, special authorizations to purchase cars. . . . These kinds of reciprocal transactions constituted in the 1970s an absolutely normal and generally accepted style of work.
>
> (Wesolowska, 1981: 5, this author's translation from Polish)

According to the quoted report, this particular deal (which was one of many) also included the construction of a private highway, the introduction of electricity,[5] the landscaping of private parcels, and so forth. All of these projects were financed by public money apportioned by the head of the region and the local party secretary. Needless to add, all the gifts with which their hospitality was reciprocated, came from the public pocket as well.

In the same town, 2000 families (out of the population of 15 000) were practically homeless, living in deteriorated slums and other virtually uninhabitable dwellings (Wesolowska, 1981):

> The greed and the limitless desire to possess, the faith in the invulnerability of their position, in their power and their immunity, were responsible for the fact that all appearances were eventually forgone and they resorted to common robbery.
>
> (Biedzki, 1981; this author's translation from Polish)

> The brutality of this acquisitiveness was caused by the dominant system of relationships. For this reason, not only the individuals but also the system should be judged.
>
> (Wesolowska, 1981: 5; this author's translation from Polish)

The Soviet press reports many similar situations. For instance, an article in *Pravda* describes a case where:

> the head of a department of the USSR State Construction Committee's Chief Administration . . . diverted scarce state-owned building materials for the construction of his dacha. . . . A brigade of workmen had been brought in from hundreds of kilometers away to do the job – at the expense of the Beryozovka Mine. Scarce building materials had been brought in from 300 km away.
>
> (Astafyev, 1983: 22)

And again in another Polish article, the author explains how luxurious villas and mansions[6] for the powerful were routinely erected and lavishly furnished by the state enterprises. They were nicknamed 'constructions S' (special constructions) and were normally initiated by a telephone call from a high-ranking individual. In most cases, they were built in place of another project which was originally included in the official plan. In some cases, the best construction materials allotted to the enterprise were invoiced as deteriorated and unusable, when, in fact, they had been assigned to a 'construction S'. The engineers and construction workers involved in these constructions expressed strong sentiments towards these projects:

> [they] spoke about them with a real hatred, with a hatred of the very idea. They could not comprehend how it was possible to force state enterprises, which did not have sufficient materials, equipment and people necessary to fulfill their planned tasks, . . . to build luxurious villas and cottages, and to do it in an atmosphere of constant threats, disdain and insolence.
>
> (Moszyński, 1980: 5; this author's translation from Polish)

In most of the cases, the self-confident officials neither attempted to cover up the illegality of the transactions nor pretended that they were paying their bills. They treated these projects as a tribute, due to them in virtue of their office. Only when the newly created Solidarity Union initiated vigorous investigations into the extent of corruption in Poland, did they realize that they might not be above the law:

> Receipts have now become a dream of many. The 'Clients S' have launched a Receipt Campaign. 'Can you imagine, one of the clients who had never honoured us with a visit, who had summoned the directors whenever anything was wrong with his construction, this week visited us twice. He tried to fix some receipts.' . . . He also tried to obtain written statements from the people who worked for him claiming that they had received separate payments from him and that they had worked after their normal working hours.
>
> (Moszyński, 1980: 5; this author's translation from Polish)

In sum, this closed network of cliques[7], totally alienated from the rest of society, has acquired a feudal mentality, whereas they treat the country as their own property and the citizens as their serfs. The three aspects of the political organization of communist societies noted in the preceding pages clearly enhance such attitudes. Moreover, they serve to preclude any effective controls over those called by the party to assume offices of key importance in the party itself, in the state administration, in the police force, and in the economy. The pattern of corruption subsists mainly through the totally unhampered use of public resources. These top officials aim at organizing their mutual relationships in such a way that every member of the clique has an opportunity to take advantage of the resources controlled by other members. The shares of various participants may differ according to their position within the hierarchy, but the pattern remains the same in most cases. A Polish journalist's words sum it up well: 'No one in our story will act alone, everyone will be linked with others and dependent on them' (Wesolowska, 1981: 5). Another reporter adds: 'It did not stop at the individuals. Among those who participated were various units of the state economy, ministries, cities, and regions. Scrambling for resources and opportunities, snatching them from each other, bribing to obtain planned deliveries, constructing luxurious facilities under the pretense of social programs . . . falsifying statistics to profit individuals and organizations. . . . The boundaries between social and private have been blurred' (Skalski, 1980: 7; this author's translation from Polish).

In short, the lawlessness of the priviledged has been exalted and protected by them and their new ideology; their management of the country has become synonymous with their ownership of it, that is, with their unfettered access to it. When such a vast pool of resources falls into the hands of one small group, there is no concern for the economy and its rational expansion. The shares are so immense that the rulers, who at the earlier stages of the development of the communist system in these countries were drunk with power, are now additionally satiated with opulence.

As one of the journalists of a local weekly from Lódź puts it: 'Unfortunately, we had too many private owners of the region who were building here, for themselves and for their colleagues from the region and from outside, a private 'second Poland' (Indelak, 1981).

ECONOMIC ROOTS OF TOP LEVEL CORRUPTION

Clearly, the economic determinants of corruption among the top officials are closely related to the political ones. One of the most obvious explanations stems from the economic organization itself. In a system where the economy is nationalized and totally subordinate to political management, it becomes an area of contest between various political figures. It adds a real, material dimension to their political games and ambitions. Influential officials have the power to both shape economic policies and dictate concrete economic decisions. This, in turn, gives them direct access to material resources, which serves to enhance their prestige and dictatorial powers.

The lower level economic managers are reduced to the role of 'a vassal who squeezes out from his estate a sizeable fief for his master' (Indelak,

1981). The economic advisors and experts are simply pawns who must invent economic rationalizations for the whims and dreams of their superiors or be accused of a heresy and disloyalty. No economic laws are respected; the party élite feels not only above the law, but also above economic logic. Their feeling of omnipotence, derived from their absolute political power, leads party officials to believe that the economy will always obediently respond to their wishes and expectations, since all individuals at all levels of the economic hierarchy must comply with their orders.

The construction of the Katowice Foundry in Poland in the 1970s provides an excellent, though tragic, example of this pernicious nonchalance of the political leaders. *Zycie Warszawy*, the most popular daily paper in Warsaw, called it 'the biggest fraud in the whole world' (Zycie i Nowoczesność, 1981). The initial idea was quite noble: to build a gigantic, modern foundry in order to eliminate several older ones, which were unhealthy for the workers, polluted the environment, etc. Yet, it also provided a great opportunity for top politicians to enhance their images and their political interests. The General Secretary of the party, Edward Gierek, and his close collaborators wanted the foundry built in Slask's region (Silesia), where they were from and where they had ruled before Mr Gierek's promotion. Several experts argued that it would be impossible to organize the efficient transportation of Soviet or western ore to Slask, because of the already constant transportation of coal and the resultant general congestion of the highly urbanized area, as well as the considerable distance from both the Soviet border and the sea. They were quickly silenced, however. The specific location was determined irrespective of any rational advice. The Deputy Minister of the Metallurgical Industry wanted to leave a lasting monument to commemorate his triumphant career, and he therefore chose his place of birth as the site for the gigantic construction. It was an absurd decision, which has had disastrous consequences for the whole region. For example, it has deprived the neighbouring, highly populated area of drinking water, it has devastated the green belt created purposefully to improve air in the mining district, it produces dangerous dust whose effects are felt in neighbouring Cracow, the old capital of Poland and a beautiful, historic city. All other decisions concerning construction, technology, costs, investments, imports and so forth were made in a similar fashion. Only those experts who were prepared to lie were accepted to the project:

> They knew what it would lead to, but for their silence they were rewarded and praised. They were called 'our men'. . . . Total

> conformity. Each of them knew what he was doing. . . . It was such a time that it was enough to blink to be dismissed . . . it was enough to show some doubts . . . (Zycie i Nowoczesność, 1981; this author's translation from Polish)

Katowice Foundry will always result in enormous losses to the country. It is too complex to be dismantled and thus it will remain as an ominous monument to the principle of the political management of the communist economy.

Another economic determinant of top level corruption is the peculiar nature of the central plan, which must be strictly obeyed by the producers, but can be quite arbitrarily altered and manipulated by those in the positions of power. (For example, Katowice Foundry, which cost approximately 500 billion zlotych,[8] was never included in the State Plan.) This opens to the privileged few an unlimited opportunity to re-direct funds from some projects to others, including their own private enterprises. As well, it has a demoralizing effect upon the middle level managers of production, who feel disoriented and incapacitated. Such a system, in turn, breeds passivity, detachment from the real economic goals, concentration on self-interest and a readiness to fulfil any wishes of the higher party officials. Without a doubt, it also creates a tendency on the part of the middle level functionaries to take advantage of the chaos and waste brought about by the arbitrary changes and to secure extra profits for themselves. Indeed, the middle level functionaries are expected to promote the appearance of chaos and confusion in order to divert attention from the real causes of the economic losses. They are also encouraged to falsify their production reports and statistics to cover up for any abuses caused by private greed, incompetent decisions, political interference, and all the other routinely occurring factors.

A third cause of top-level corruption to be noted here is related to the strictly vertical structure of the economy which is a result of the basic principle of the central plan. Only a vertical or hierarchical structure, suited for the transmission of commands, is politically significant and, therefore, fully legitimized. The lack of a horizontal economic structure, which would allow the development of both cooperation and competition among the producing units, creates room for illegal bargaining, speculation, and corruption. It also facilitates the exploitation and manipulation of the lower units by superiors. Clearly then, an economy which is based on the principle of obedience and subordination and on the artificial isolation of functionally related units serves to facilitate the abuse of power and the transmission of some private demands from the top to the bottom of the hierarchy. In addition, it breeds the attitudes of servility expressed in the willingness of the lower levels to satisfy their superiors' personal desires in order to gain some freedom of movement.

The fourth and final cause can be found in the progressing monopolization of the economy. It is expressed in the forced mergers of smaller enterprises, the growing number of gigantic combines, and the overwhelming tendency to attribute to the highest levels of administration a total monopoly over all economic decisions. This super-monopolization (or progressive concentration within the already monopolized economy) causes a further decrease in the autonomy of the directors of individual enterprises; they become puppet-figures obliged to serve the political administrators and constantly threatened by them. The ever growing concentration of management has reversed the promised direction of development from the nationalization to the socialization of the means of production. Under such conditions, the gap between the decision-makers and the shop-floor workers becomes too vast to be bridged. No grass-root criticism or blame reaches the upper echelons. The workers cease to exist as acknowledged participants of the economic process and simply become a part of the vast resources at the disposal of the top administrators and party officials; they are not perceived as a part of the economic structure by the totally alienated, self-perpetuating and self-corrupting powerful cliques.

DISCUSSION

Top level corruption is very widespread and seems to have common causes in both studied countries although its specific forms may differ slightly. The prevalent pattern of corruption in Poland in the 1970s was connected with the existence of closely knit networks of cliques formed by those people who occupied key positions in the party, state administration, police and economy. They needed each other in order both to acquire direct personal access to various state-controlled resources and to secure impunity and political credibility. They never paid for favours out of their own pockets. The bribes they offered to each other included public money, property, free labour, the services of the employees of state enterprises, political privileges and legal protection. The process of the ever growing concentration of the economy was paralleled by a process which may be likened to its gradual secret reprivatization.

Various studies of corruption in the Soviet Union (e.g. Staats, 1972; Kramer, 1977; Schwartz, 1979; Simis, 1979, 1982; Jowitt, 1983) present a very similar picture. '*Krugovaia poruka*' or mutual guarantee seems to be a common feature of corrupt cliques (see e.g. Staats, 1972: 44–5; Kramer, 1977: 223). It ties participants together through the need for mutual assistance as well as the availability of mutual blackmail. This 'krugovaia poruka' inevitably includes those individuals who are charged with the duty of preventing and exposing corruption. This reality serves to consolidate further the illegal alliances among representatives of various sectors of public life and provides them with feeling of absolute freedom. This solidarity among the powerful is, however, precarious as they are involved in never ending political competition and power struggles. The criminal justice system is occasionally used as a weapon in these games. Those officials who become its targets are usually selected by their more powerful and equally corrupt associates and superiors. The final choice of scapegoats is essentially a political decision.

Recurring anti-crime campaigns (which include the energetic campaign launched by Andropov in the early 1980s) do not seem to touch the core of the problem and, in fact, do not even attempt to do so. Their main function is symbolic; moral campaigns are cheaper and ideologically much more acceptable than economic and political reforms. They are designed to convey to the population the impression that some prevalent sources of evil are being dealt with. Despite their symbolic function, however, these campaigns do fulfil, to some extent, their ostensible purpose of confronting the problem of corruption. They serve to prevent it from becoming so overt and ostentatious as to be not only embarrassing to the ruling élite, but also clearly against its long-term interests. The ruling group is forced, therefore, to possess and sometimes implement some means of neutralizing (rather than eliminating) the most conspicuous symptoms of its decadence.

To understand fully the sources and specific features of the all-prevading corruption which characterizes the Soviet-style élite, it is necessary to recognize its historical roots. The communist élite was conceived by Lenin as a revolutionary stratum, a vanguard trusted with a clear, dynamic mission and blessed with charisma. As noted by Jowitt (1983), the time of stabilization and the transformation of 'combat' tasks into 'maintenance' tasks has removed this group's charisma and left it with no clear political identity, thereby producing an overwhelming need for the routinization and maximization of its security. As a result, the communist élite has become totally inward-looking, preoccupied with its own mission of comfortable survival under conditions which lack the democratic mechanisms and traditions of openness or inter-class communication. In fact, it may be claimed that:

> the Soviet élite cadre has succeeded where the Soviet working class has failed; it has become a group 'in itself and for itself'. It has successfully identified, or better confused, the party's general interest with its particular status interests of career and personal security, privileged material, and superior political position. In doing so it obstructs the emergence, inside as well as outside the party, of any political force able to demonstrate the relativity of cadre interests.
> (Jowitt, 1983: 286)

Indeed, the only missions which seem to revitalize the revolutionary spirit of this post-revolutionary élite are the external combat tasks (Jowitt, 1983) expressed through imperialistic ventures in various parts of the world and the obsessive preoccupation with augmenting the Soviet military might.

In sum, the combination of a non-democratic political system with a nationalized economy inevitably seems to produce an environment where opportunities for corruption are practically unlimited. The total monopolization of both the power and economic resources in the hands of the dominant political élite, which, in turn, is neither controlled nor influenced by any other social group or organization within society, makes any piecemeal programmes of corruption and crime prevention a futile exercise. Even if some members of the élite are singled out from time to time as scapegoats responsible for the evident economic and political failure of communism, this is a purely symbolic manoeuvre by an élite which wants to assure its own continuation and unlimited power.

7 Crimes of the Functionaries: Bribery, Extortion and Favouritism

CORRUPTION WITHIN THE STATE BUREAUCRACY, SERVICES AND TRADE

Top-level corruption does not exhaust the totality of corrupt practices in communist countries. Lower-level corruption, which occurs in the daily encounters between lower-rank functionaries and the rest of society is not only extremely wide-spread, but appears to be inevitable under the political and economic conditions prevailing in these countries. Indeed, it results from the inefficiency of the centralized, politically managed economy, and chronic shortages of goods as well as from the tendency of communist states to control every aspect of citizens' lives. The rigid and politically controlled distribution of various goods, services and opportunities invites corruption and manipulation by giving almost uncontrollable power over those commodities to the functionaries of the state administration and the state trade.

Intrinsic shortcomings of the centralized state economy and administration lead to the development of a variety of black markets and to a peculiar economic underworld. They also lead to the thorough corruption of the bureaucracy at all levels (see, for example, Staats, 1972; Simis, 1979, 1982; Smith, 1976). These developments are complicated even more by the preponderance of political criteria in the system of promotions and privileges, as well as in the distribution of some restricted goods (for example, apartments, telephones, and fur caps), social services (child care, reduced price holidays, hospital admissions, and the like), or other opportunities (entrance to university, passports to travel abroad, and so on). Therefore, '[w]hat the élite get legally through their special stores and system of privileges, ordinary people are forced to seek illegally in the country's countereconomy' (Jacoby *et al.*, 1977: 39).

Ways around these political and bureaucratic barriers may be opened if one is able to find either suitable 'connections' to reach informally the responsible clerk or official or the appropriate way to hand him a bribe or arrange a mutually acceptable exchange of services (favours). Very often a 'go-between' is used who can discuss more freely with both parties the conditions set by each; the chain is broadened and often turns into a long network of mutual favours. If, for instance, a telephone official insists on having an imported coffee set, the telephone applicant tries to find someone with a 'contact' in the shop which might have received imported china. A workmate may promise help because his girlfriend knows a sales clerk in such a shop. Therefore a small gift for the kind colleague and flowers for the girlfriend are in order. The sales clerk may in fact be able to 'put aside' one of the sets which reach the shelves of the store, but she would expect a place in the nursery for her child in return. The search for an appropriate person continues. In the end, all claims are miraculously satisfied, and the telephone clerk receives an attractive coffee set which he could not buy directly from the shop. Instead of an impersonal and prosaic transaction in a state store, a whole new network has developed and a number of people have managed to satisfy their particular needs. It does not follow, however, that these arrangements have made those people more satisfied than they would be otherwise. The overall social costs of 'mutual-favour-networks' are enormous: witness the loss of time, the humiliation of the experiences, the inevitability of using one's own friends as middlemen in dubious transactions and negotiations, and the demoralization of employees who constantly abuse their offices to respond to the pressures and to settle their own problems. In addition, the network mechanisms work to the advantage of those better off and well connected who have stronger bargaining power, as well as of those who have fewer moral scruples.

It is interesting, however, that such complex networks of corruption serve clearly as a stabilizing factor; any change would disturb dangerously the existing, tested, and familiar arrangements and could bring to light common involvement in law violations. It can be maintained that, in fact, it gives to the system some sort of peculiar legitimacy, as Podgórecki argues in his analysis of 'tertiary social control':

> If behind the legal system (which is rejected by the population at large as unjust, undemocratic, etc.) there operates a complicated infrastructure of mutually interdependent interests then this legal

> system may become accepted, not on the basis of its own merits, but because it creates a convenient cover-system for the flourishing phenomenon of 'dirty togetherness'. Then each institution, factory and organization serves . . . as a formal network which gives a stable frame of reference for an enormous amount of mutual semi-private services, reciprocal arrangements. (Podgórecki, 1979: 203)

The occurrence of such arrangements may not always be triggered by a spontaneous and grass-roots self-defence of the people who want to survive. Some of their forms may be manipulated and stimulated by the official power centers to counterbalance 'private' cliques and to control profits flowing from corruption and fiddling:

> The bureaucratized administrative apparatus especially in the case of state-owned economy becomes so routinized, inelastic, decentralized, and powerless that the central organs may see no other way to keep this apparatus functioning than by saturating it with their own ramified 'mafia'. (Podgórecki, 1979: 200)

Hedrick Smith makes a similar observation in his one-time bestseller, *The Russians*:

> Strangely, for all its protestation about corruption, the regime seems to have ambivalent feelings toward the counter-economy. . . . In a way, one economist suggested, the authorities reluctantly tolerate the personal commerce of 'the little people' as a necessary outlet for their consumer frustrations and a diversion from any more serious challenge to the system. The party knows, he reasoned, that people who are chasing after illegal goods in the counter-economy are not worried about reforms. (Smith, 1976: 133)

Moreover, as a Polish report by an independent discussion group 'Experience and the Future' suggests, 'the more inefficient the national economy, the more trumps the authorities hold to gain supporters by handing out privileges' (*Poland Today*, 1981: 68).

Many press reports, both published in Poland during the 'renewal' of 1980–81 and in the Soviet Union during the periodical anti-corruption campaigns, provide numerous examples of the extensive use of such means as monetary bribes, payments in kind, political influence or exchange of favours, to secure privileged treatment in such areas as the allocation of apartments, entrance into university, health-care, child-care and the acquisition of various goods in short supply. As well, many reports describe corrupt relationships between employees and managers, managers and inspectors or auditors, citizens and law enforcement agents and so forth.

For instance, the Soviet paper *Zarya Vostoka* cites the case of a woman sentenced to 10-years' deprivation of liberty with confiscation of property for the acceptance of bribes for services she could not actually deliver. She simply 'passed herself off as a lecturer at Tbilisi University and led her 'clients' to believe that she could arrange for the admission of their offsprings not only to the university, but to any other higher school' (Inoveli, 1983: 4). Her trial established that she succeeded in defrauding 23 people, who assumed that such payment would be an effective way to secure the desired admissions. *Izvestia* reports another case in which the head of a Housing Management Office in Kharkov, a lawyer by training, was sentenced to nine year's deprivation of freedom with confiscation of property for collecting substantial bribes over a period of three years for the allocation of service apartments to new employees of the office (Ryashchenko, 1980: 6). In another case, 36 bribe-takers were sentenced to lengthy terms of incarceration with confiscation of property and prohibition from holding positions of financial responsibility. They were involved in the extortion of bribes from the employees of and the job applicants to a garage of the Baku Motor Transport Association. The bribes were received in exchange for the right to obtain spare parts or gasoline, to take official business trips, or make illegal use of the garage's vehicles. The largest bribes were offered for the permits of purchase for new cars and for the opportunity to be hired at the garage ('From the Courtroom . . .', 1981: 4). Yet another report explains how inspectors of a district consumers' cooperative collected bribes from the managers of the district's stores and bars in return for a promise to destroy documents disclosing shortcomings in the observance of trade regulations. The extortionists kept detailed records of such payments made on a regular basis by the managers, who, in turn, usually tried 'to pass on the cost to the consumer, who ultimately [paid] for the losses caused by the swindlers and blackmailers' ('From the Courtroom . . .', 1975: 4).

While the above examples have been chosen from among many reports published in the official press, there are countless instances of bribery and extortion which are never disclosed and registered. They range from the most mundane efforts by the bribe-givers to secure necessities for their families to the most spectacular cases of large scale corruption in the economy, public administration and the criminal justice system. Their forms are almost identical in the Soviet Union and Poland. Indeed, it seems that corruption has become a part of the natural social landscape of these countries:

> The atmosphere of corruption has bred the conviction in the minds of the people that everything can be attained by bribery: a good job, a university diploma, or an undeserved judicial verdict. And although that conviction is far from justified in all cases, it has led to the climate of tolerance toward corruption that holds sway in Soviet society.
> (Simis, 1982: 248–9)

This observation applies equally to Poland. A rare survey of public opinion on bribery was conducted in 1976 by two Polish researchers, A. Rzepliński and A. Kutylowski (1981), based on a random representative sample of the adult population of Poland. Asked about the major causes of corruption, 63.5 per cent of 909 interviewees replied that it was caused by 'people's desire to obtain something that should be available, but was not'. As well, many respondents thought that 'people did not believe that it [was] possible to obtain positive treatment in a normal way', or that 'people did not know how to exercise their rights'. In response to the question concerning the intensity of the moral condemnation of bribery, 47.1 per cent of the sample indicated that it should be always condemned; 24.3 per cent stated that it should be often condemned, 21 per cent maintained that it rarely deserved condemnation and 4.4 per cent did not see any reason for condemnation at all. As well, the majority of the respondents were of the opinion that a reprimand and dismissal from work were sufficient penalties for bribery with the only exception being corrupt penal judges who, according to many interviewees, should be given prison sentences. Moreover in a survey of a representative sample of adult Warsaw inhabitants, 27 per cent indicated their total indifference and only 40 per cent expressed strong disapproval of bribery (Kwaśniewski and Kojder, 1979; Kojder and Kawśniewski, 1981: 94).

In a discussion of these findings organized by the Polish Sociological Association, the participants shared the view that corruption reached such proportions that it was no longer perceived by people as a deviant or unusual phenomenon. Indeed, it was stressed that bribery and other forms of corruption often constituted a necessary condition of 'efficient' economic action and/or the effective settlement of citizens' affairs. Many participants of the meeting were of the opinion that the roots of corruption were not moral but socio-political (for details see Kawśniewski, 1981: 111–15).

While the most evident and best documented corruption is that which occurs in the relations between the functionaries of the state trade and bureaucracy and their clients, other areas of social corruption should not be overlooked. For example, state-run health care is notorious for its susceptibility to wide-spread corrupt practices. In theory, medical services should be delivered free of charge to most employed citizens and their families. There are, however, hidden fees charged for many services delivered by doctors and nurses. A typical example is provided in a report in *Izvestia*, which describes the case of a Soviet doctor who 'charged a set "tax" on every kind of medical service, including his hypnosis treatments'. As well, he often charged patients for their medication far above the official price, claiming that the medication was in short supply or unavailable (Troyan, 1983a: 6). The notoriety of corruption in the Polish health care system is well portrayed in a press article in the weekly magazine *Polityka*. The author's description of the situation in Polish hospitals is clearly alarming:

> Dirt, worms, the rudeness of the orderlies, the impertinence of the doctors, bribery, the extortion of payments for bringing a bed-pan, for giving oxygen(!), for a nurse's presence during birth-giving, for surgery performed by a chosen doctor, for the right to humane treatment.
>
> (Mozolowski, 1983: 7; this author's translation from Polish)

Yet, admissions to these unpleasant institutions are considered a privilege and, both in Poland and in the USSR, doctors often charge special fees for hospital admissions, or at least expect expensive gifts from their patients. As Simis comments:

> [the] number of hospitals in the Soviet Union is obviously insufficient to cover the needs of the population. No amount of bribery can increase the number of hospital beds, but people willing to pay can have those beds redistributed in their favour. (Simis, 1982: 225)

As well, in order to avoid harsh treatment in the state hospitals, admission as a private patient, while expensive, is nevertheless often a vital and, by all accounts, common arrangement:

> The only way, then, to avoid free medical care is to go to the same free, state-run institutions, not, however, as a normal nonpaying patient but, rather, privately, by visiting a specific doctor by prior agreement and for a fee. (Simis, 1982: 225)

A Polish report by the group 'Experience and the Future' confirms this picture:

> Free health care for the vast majority of the population was once considered an achievement of People's Poland. But unfortunately,

today the situation is completely different. Irregularities and deficiencies in health care have meant that medical treatment now requires money, quite a bit of money, as well as connections and pull. They have led to a distressing situation; if one does not bribe the nursing staff, one does not get decent attention, and if one does not bribe the doctor, his care will be marginal. One now pays to get a bed in a hospital or an operation, to say nothing of medicine. Gradually the public is divided into two categories: those who can afford proper medical care and those who cannot. (*Poland Today*, 1981: 87)

The health care system, not unlike all other state services and provisions, suffers from overcentralization and 'overplanification', which paralyze its development and greatly limit its social utility. Difficult access to these services and their poor organization, combined with low wages and the lack of viable incentives for the staff, have resulted in unchecked corruption. It is not surprising, therefore, that citizens have lost their faith in the free delivery of any services by the state and have acquired the habit of paying for all such provisions twice: through direct or indirect deductions from their wages and through private fees, bribes, gifts and tips.

CORRUPTION WITHIN THE CRIMINAL JUSTICE SYSTEM

Another public sector worthy of note for its rampant corruption is that of law enforcement. Until recently, the authorities in both studied countries vigorously denied the existence of this problem. Yet, the anti-corruption campaign initiated by Andropov in the early 1980s chose the police as one of its primary targets. Suddenly, the silence was broken; many stories of police corruption appeared in the newspapers and charges of abuse of office were laid against numerous police officers. These developments took place almost simultaneously in the USSR and Poland.

Soon after his nomination as the General Secretary of the Communist Party, Yuri Andropov appointed as head of the Ministry of the Interior a career KGB officer, General Vitaly Fedorchuk, who had served for seven months as the chairman of the KGB. The Ministry was believed not only to be riddled with corruption, but also actively blocking KGB efforts to stamp out economic crime and corruption within the Soviet society. Since the Ministry is responsible for the uniformed police (known as 'militia'), the move was interpreted as an attempt to both quell police corruption and bring the two branches of the security organs closer together[1] ('Changes in security . . .', 1982). Numerous policemen were reprimanded, demoted or dismissed while many others, and particularly those caught taking bribes in the élite Administration for Combating Embezzlement of Socialist Property and Speculation, were sentenced to long terms in some of the harshest Siberian labour camps (Burns, 1983b). Soviet newspapers were full of praises for the work done by the KGB, the agency which has rarely been mentioned publicly since the times of Josef Stalin when this secret police organization acquired its notorious reputation. In his speech during the meeting of the Presidium of the USSR Supreme Soviet in January 1983, General Fedorchuk stressed the need for improvements in the work of the police and better coordination of the activities of all law enforcement agencies ('Meetings . . .', 1983: 1–2).

Among many examples of police corruption related in the Soviet press is the case of a corrupt inspector of the Krasnodar Department of Combating the Embezzlement of Socialist Property and Speculation, who was sentenced to twelve years in an intensive-regime labour colony; the case of a police captain who headed a criminal gang engaged in the theft of agricultural products from a collective farm; the case of an investigator in a Borough Internal Affairs Department who was convicted of repeatedly accepting bribes in exchange for releasing suspects from criminal liability; a senior inspector of a District Division for Combating the Embezzlement of Socialist Property and Speculation who was sentenced to 12 years' deprivation of freedom for bribery (Udachin, 1983a: 2), and finally the cases involving the head of a similar department at the city level sentenced to 11 years' confinement in an intensive-regime labour colony and a senior inspector of the same department sentenced to 8 years in an ordinary-regime colony for repeatedly accepting bribes from employees of the City Restaurant and Cafeteria Trust and for refraining from taking actions against them (Udachin, 1982a: 2; 1983b: 2).

A correspondent of *Sovetskaya Rossia* poses this question regarding the corruption within the police force:

> What made possible the appearance of criminals in the ranks of the police? There is one answer: an atmosphere of tolerance and low standards that has come about in the territory internal affairs administration and in many city and borough internal affairs departments. . . . Moreover, illegal actions are not always given a proper assessment by the top officials and political workers of

> internal affairs agencies. In a number of instances they have tried to excuse the lawbreakers' actions and to protect the offenders.
>
> (Udachin, 1983a: 2)

By all accounts, these practices are extremely prevalent and it appears that no narrowly focused anti-corruption campaign can root them out; they are part of a complex web of corrupt and illegal links which tie together people from different walks of life and different sectors in the power structure. This informal structure has achieved such a degree of stability that no measures short of radical political reforms could alter their perennial nature.

While the pattern which emerges from a number of press publications from Poland does not differ significantly, most of the press reports focus on the corrupt practices of policemen involved in street patrol work rather than on those of more senior police functionaries (see, for example, 'Ukaranie . . .', 1983: 4; 'Aresztowanie . . .', 1983: 6; 'Wydalenie . . .' 1983: 2). During the Solidarity period, a number of publications discussed the low moral standards within the police forces, however, the main preoccupation was with the issue of police brutality. These critiques increased public concern and triggered some official efforts to 'clean up' the police force.

According to the police statistics, 706 policemen were expelled in 1980 from the force. Among them, 264 were accused of causing accidents, 76 of physically abusing citizens, and 71 of offences committed for economic gain. As well, 6000 members of ORMO (the voluntary police force) were expelled for various, often serious, offences. Moreover, 400 preparatory criminal investigations were initiated against policemen and by August 1981, 117 policemen were charged. In 72 cases, investigations were conditionally closed and in 54, charges were dropped because of the lack of evidence. Another 26 cases were transferred to proceedings under private accusation and 131 cases were still under investigation. While most of the criminal investigations undertaken in 1980 were concerned with crimes against life and health, 101 cases involved the unjustified use of force during police intervention and 41 cases were related to illegitimate methods used during cross-examination. Other crimes included rape or attempted rape (six cases), family violence (five cases), fraud, false testimony and the purchase of stolen goods (Olszewska, 1981: 8–9). It is interesting to note that, at the time of the publication of these cases, corruption was not even mentioned. Nonetheless, it was a well-known fact that, for example highway police had a fixed 'tariff' for various traffic offences and drivers always tried to have enough cash with them to avoid prosecution for any violation they might be accused of. Equally well known was the fact that the extensive black market, as well as numerous legal and illegal private businesses, could function smoothly only if they made regular payments to the guardians of law and order. Yet, despite these incidents of corruption, it was the brutality of the police which seemed to be an issue of special gravity for the newly constituted Solidarity movement and the members of the opposition, many of whom had personally experienced police violence.

The press reports of that period expose the low moral standards prevalent among the police and fostered by the mendacity and hypocrisy permeating the police work such that different criteria are applied to the powerful law-breakers and to the ordinary offenders, and the law is flexibly interpreted and applied according to political pressures. As well, several publications point to the demoralizing impact of continuous expectations to doctor arrest statistics according to the political needs of the moment (Mikusiński, 1981: 10; Olszewska, 1981: 8–9). Most importantly, however, they criticize the constant interference of the party into police work and the very situation where the police are *de facto* subordinated at all levels to the parallel party organizations. A report by the group 'Experience and the Future', which included many party members and well-established academics, also stressed the negative consequences of the lack of any social control over the police force and the ever-increasing extent of the policing of the economy:

> The range of activities that the law enforcement apparatus is forced to carry out in the economic domain has been enlarged beyond measure by the legal muddle, and as a result, the size of the police apparatus has been increased to proportions more in keeping with a police state. . . . Thanks to the lack of control over the police apparatus there has been a growth of criminality within that apparatus itself, ranging from the extraction of material advantages from the exercise of power, . . . to the ever more frequent cases of robbery and beating committed by members of the police.
>
> (*Poland Today*, 1981: 40)

Information on the corruption within the courtrooms and prosecutors' offices is rather limited. The same Polish report presents the judiciary as very poorly paid, consisting of political appointees and subject to political directives and manipulation. It indicates that 'the period of repression following the events of June 1976 [and now the period following December 1981 may be added] showed how easy it is in

Poland to return to the old system of show-trials . . . by exerting the requisite pressure on the courts' (*Poland Today*, 1981: 40). The report adds that such political manipulation has become, for both the judges and the party, 'such an ordinary, everyday practice that it no longer shocks anyone' (*Poland Today*, 1981: 41). As well:

> [the] press does not even bother to conceal the fact that judges confer about implementing the recommendations of the latest party central Committee Plenums, which leads public opinion to doubt that any regard at all is paid to the principle of the independence of the courts. (*Poland Today*, 1981: 41–2)

Political corruption is thus perceived by the Polish critics of the judiciary as much more noteworthy than petty bribery, although this does exist as well. Interesting material concerning the extent of corruption within the justice system in the Soviet Union is provided by Konstantin Simis, a Soviet lawyer who emigrated from the USSR in 1977. He describes the 1940s and 1950s as the years of the most rampant corruption in the courts and public prosecutors' offices. According to his account, the scale and pervasiveness of corruption was the same in big cities and in more remote areas, but the forms of the prevailing corrupt practices differed greatly. Simis recalls visiting some of those isolated towns and regions where corruption was practiced in ways which appeared to him 'patriarchal and drably provincial' (Simis, 1982: 109):

> I was able to observe the local judge receiving callers. . . . The petitioners went in one by one. Almost everyone who entered the room carried either a package wrapped in a white scarf or a clay jug or a pot. They all left the room empty handed. . . . The concept of a bribe being a criminal act is lost even to the participants. The lawyer simply has a preliminary conference with the investigator or judge about the prospects of the case, the amount of money that the lawyer will receive from his client if the outcome is successful and how that money is to be divided. (Simis, 1982: 109–10)

The poorly paid positions of people's judges became very desirable as a result of the additional income derived from bribes and gifts. In fact, the prices required to be 'elected' as a judge, district prosecutor or investigator were, according to Simis, approximately twenty times higher than the annual wages paid to the holders of such posts (Simis, 1982: 112). At the beginning of the 1960s, however, a series of corruption trials were held in which more than 200 individuals involved in the dispensation of justice were convicted (Simis, 1982: 107). Moreover, special attention was paid to Moscow, where:

> in the space of one and a half to two years roughly twenty trials were held in which about three hundred investigators, prosecutors, and judges were convicted of taking bribes. There was not a single public prosecutor's office or court in Moscow (apart from the Supreme Court of the USSR) that did not see some of its staff on trial. A whole new staff had to be recruited in some of Moscow's districts, for in those places not a single people's judge, investigator, or public prosecutor remained. (Simis, 1982: 121)

Yet, this well-coordinated action did not erase corruption from within the Soviet justice system. The testimonies of numerous emigrants, as well as the Soviet press enunciations continue to bring stories about corrupt practices within the Soviet judiciary and 'procuratura'. Among the cases reported in the early 1980s is that of several officials of the people's court and the district internal affairs department who were found guilty of 'flagrant violations and abuse of office ('In the Azerbaidzhan . . .' 1982: 3) and the case of a public prosecutor in the central Asian republic of Kirgizia sentenced to death for soliciting Bribes (Cullen, 1983: 23). Some other cases, noted by Simis, involved judges of two districts of Moscow convicted of bribe taking along with several district investigators (Simis, 1982: 125).

While the period of 'blatant' corruption within the justice system has ended, the corruption itself has not disappeared; it has merely been curtailed and has become more discreet. 'Bribes are still given and taken, but now the dealings are surrounded by a cautious atmosphere of conspiracy' (Simis, 1982: 125). It seems almost inevitable that in the political context so conducive to corruption, where all other areas of institutional life are riddled by it, moral restraints would not be sufficiently strong to keep this vice away from the courts of justice.

THE CRIME OF BRIBERY: LEGAL ASPECTS

Both offering and receiving bribes constitute crimes according to the penal codes of the USSR and Poland. As well, instigating or aiding an offence of this type is considered a criminal offence. The penalties are strict, especially for the bribe takers. This offence may be committed only by 'officials', that is, individuals who represent authority or fulfil executive functions. The Soviet law predicts several types of 'the taking of a bribe'. In its non-aggravated version, this offence calls for imprisonment for three to ten years with confiscation of property. In special cases, when the bribe was extorted or when the official occupies a 'position of responsibility' or has been previously convicted of corruption or has accepted bribes on more than one occasion, the punishment is increased to imprisonment for 8 to 15 years with confiscation of property (and with exile for 2 to 5 years if the judge so recommends). If there exist 'especially aggravating circumstances', bribe taking may be punished by death and the confiscation of property.

The Polish Penal Code calls for penalties ranging from 6 months to 10 years for different forms of 'bribe taking'. If, however, the offender performs a function of special responsibility or has accepted a material benefit of great value or a promise thereof, he is subject to the penalty of deprivation of liberty for a term of not less than 3 years (the upper limit is left undefined).

Giving a bribe, in its simplest form, is punishable in the Soviet Union by 3 to 8 years' imprisonment. In its aggravated form, however, it is punishable by a prison term of 7 to 15 years, confiscation of property and exile (at the discretion of the court). The penalties for this offence in Poland range from a fine to the deprivation of liberty for up to 10 years. Instigators or intermediaries are liable to penalties similar to those for offenders who give or promise bribes. Both in the USSR and Poland, however, a bribe giver, an instigator or an intermediary who spontaneously reports the incident before the law enforcement authorities discover it is released from the responsibility.[2] This provision has been vigorously criticized by many Polish lawyers and intellectuals as being immoral and contrary to the longstanding legal tradition in Poland.

Important changes were introduced in September 1981 into the Russian Republic Criminal Code, which serves as a model for all other union republics. The amendments aimed at the more explicit criminalization of bribery in the areas of provision of services to the public (e.g. in stores, catering services, ticket offices, hotels and medical establishments). The essence of these amendments is such that they establish liability for rank-and-file employees of services and not just for 'officials' whose legal definition was never quite clear. A new section has been added which deals with the receipt of illegal compensation from citizens for the performance of work connected with the provision of services to the public. This offence is punishable by corrective labour for a term of up to 1 year or by a fine. When it is committed repeatedly or involves large sums of money it may be punished by the deprivation of freedom for a period of up to 3 years or by a fine. Similar penalties are listed in another new section which deals with the sale of goods from warehouses, depots and public-catering organizations and with the concealment of goods from consumers when such concealment is committed for material gain or out of other personal interests. The newly legislated amendments give 'extortion' a broad interpretation so that it is no longer limited to a direct demand for payment. According to this revised definition, extortion includes 'the deliberate creation of conditions in which a citizen is compelled to pay compensation in order to prevent consequences harmful to his legitimate interests' ('Blocking . . .', 1981: 3).

It is clear, therefore, that the law-makers are fully aware of the complete permeation of the economic and public life by private interests and private deals which govern the actual circulation of goods and the exchange of services. The 1981 legal amendments prove once more that symbolic and punitive measures continue to be preferable to real reforms and that the criminal law and not communist ideology or morality serves as the major official source of the regulation of the behaviour of individuals. These observations will be further elaborated upon in the following chapter on economic crimes whose common presence in communist countries is facilitated by the ubiquity of corrupt bonds and transactions within the state economy and administration.

8 Crimes of Managers and Entrepreneurs: Economic Crimes*

THE ECONOMY AND CRIME

Crimes against the communist economic order and economic relations are among the most publicized, widespread and persistent crimes in all communist countries. Since their commission normally involves at least some measure of corruption, it is practically impossible to clearly separate these two types of criminal activity in any systematic analysis of their nature and their control. This chapter will concentrate, therefore, on selected forms of economic crimes as well as on those types of corruption which are closely associated with and, often, necessitated by them.

It must be noted that most of the economic crimes in communist countries do not have exact counterparts in capitalist countries due to critical differences in the organization of their economies as well as in the nature and scope of their criminal laws. Types of economic crimes which are included in the criminal codes of all Soviet Republics involve: engaging in forbidden trades, falsifying figures or otherwise distorting reports on plan fulfilment, private entrepreneurial activity, intermediary commercial operations, issuance of poor-quality, non-standard or incomplete products, and illegal manufacture, sale and storage of alcoholic beverages (see *Great Soviet Encyclopedia*, 1973, vol. 2: 66; the Criminal Code of the RSRSR, Chapter 6, reprinted in Luryi, 1978: 171–5, or *Encyclopedia of Soviet Law*, 1973, vol. 2: 238–9). Thus, economic activities criminalized in the Soviet Union are, with the exception of moonshining, either legal or simply non-existent in capitalist countries. Since the Central Plan, according to which the communist economy is regulated, has the status of law, all economic deviations from the plan are criminalized. This implies massive legal intervention in the economy as well as a reliance on the criminal law as one of the fundamental means of stimulating efficiency and excellence of

*This chapter incorporates excerpts from M. Łoś, (1982a) and M. Łoś, (1983a).

economic production. Indeed, the penal law appears to play the role of a major regulator of the economy. For, while traditional, capitalist regulators, such as profit orientation, market laws and labour negotiations are void of any meaning under communism, no new dependable regulating mechanisms have been developed.

It would be misleading to examine the issue of economic crimes without commenting upon the contradictions, deviations and criminogenic nature of the economy itself. The main problem with the communist economy is that, contrary to the main assumption of Marxist theory, it is completely subordinated to an abstract political doctrine, not generated by but in fact completely divorced from the material base. As a result, the communist economy can make sense only on paper, and it is not surprising that the constantly emphasized economic success is supported by 'paper' evidence and ideological slogans which are in clear contradiction to the unsound and disorganized reality.

The one-party state monopoly over both the means of production, and the totality of the political and social processes, implies the full ideological unity of the official political and economic interests, and, therefore, the sheer impossibility of any legislation interfering with or curbing the centralized, plan-oriented organization of the industry. Even more significant is the fact that it excludes the existence of any trade unions representing the interests of the employees rather than employers (i.e. the state). Furthermore, the monopoly of the one-party state over the mass-media negates the possibilty of any counter-control or pressure by a non-party majority.

The state's economic monopoly and its power to fix prices paralyzes the mechanisms of self-regulation in the communist nationalized economy. The exclusion of competition, a practice which is usually seen as criminal in the western countries, becomes the guiding principle under communism. The economy is geared towards the fulfilment of the Central Plan and disregards the pressure of demand and unsatisfied social needs. The macro-economic decisions, especially the plan, cannot be criticized or adapted to the changing needs of society; their premises are secret, their directives legally binding.

Whatever is produced in agreement with the plan is considered automatically as adequate and socially useful, because the plan cannot be wrong. And, in fact, everything that is produced officially contributes towards the fulfilment of the plan since all the reports are prepared with the obligatory nature of the plan in mind. Any evaluation of the plan and all future planning, therefore, is based on distorted information contained in reports modelled upon legal expectations rather than real production. The plan is, thus, fully arbitrary, and its economic soundness can never be submitted to a systematic, practical test or any form of social control.

Another factor limiting the effectiveness of production in the communist countries is state ownership of the means of production. Not only workers are denied any share or say under this form of ownership, but even the enterprise directors, responsible for production, are totally subordinated to state command.

In his paper presented during a conference in Warsaw and later published outside the orbit of communist censorship, Stefan Kurowski, a Polish economist, clearly explains the important aspects of the economic failure of communism:

> In the area of ownership, the enterprise stage has been skipped, and, almost the highest level, that of state ownership, has been established. Thus, a new disproportion has emerged: state ownership of the means of production is not in harmony with the enterprise level of the production process, and this yields a new contradiction.
>
> (Kurowski, 1980: 18; this author's translation from Polish)

According to Kurowski, this contradiction emerges from the simultaneous existence of both the Central Plan, which embodies the principle of state ownership of the means of production, and the enterprises, which organize the process of production in reality. The conflict between the producing units and the planners has been emphasized by other authors as well. For example, Katsenelinboigen observes that:

> The system of planning in the USSR is, to a large degree, constructed on the principle of 'power play'. Throughout the entire vertical line, beginning at Gosplan and ending with the workplace, there is a struggle between the administrators and the persons administered in the assignment of a plan. As is well known, the persons administered attempt to receive the smallest possible plan for output and to include as many inputs as possible in this plan.
>
> (Katsenelinboigen, 1977: 72–3; see also Katsenelinboigen, 1978a, b)

Kurowski further argues that:

> The Central Plan focuses the main part of its efforts on the fight against the enterprises, in an attempt to subject them to its command, to limit their independence, to break the barriers which protect their

> separate existence, to weaken their mutual dependence . . . to acquire their information about the production process. . . . The enterprises, in turn, fight against the Central Plan, by circumventing its orders and prohibitions, concealing so-called reserves, building up unofficial networks in the form of a whole economic underworld ruled by its own criteria and economic motives contradictory to the Central Plan. . . . Ever greater enterprises are created, smaller plants are merged, ever more decisions are reserved for ever higher levels of administration and corporations, in order to facilitate the management from the pedestal of the Central Plan, in other words, to conform with the execution of state ownership.
>
> (Kurowski 1980: 18–19; this author's translation from Polish)

Clearly, this strategy implies an ideological somersault since it assumes that the introduction by force of 'more progressive' forms of production relationships will provoke appropriate changes in the sphere of the means of production. This is a typical case of 'putting the cart before the horse' when the only result can be that:

> the horse will fall down and the cart will fall apart. In the meantime, however, the central planner carries on this combat on two fronts: against the population, which acts as consumer, and against the enterprises. He is eager to ensure, therefore, that his two enemies do not join forces to act in their common interest, which could be realized in the market.
>
> (Kurowski, 1980: 20; this author's translation from Polish)

Such a union, although officially prohibited, emerges in the form of a black market, a second economy, and many other illegal, semi-legal or merely informal arrangements, all of them vital to the survival of both the economy and the individual members of the society.

CRIMES AGAINST THE CENTRAL PLAN

The aspirations of early communists to nurture a new kind of morality and a genuine commitment to the nationalized economy faded long ago through confrontation with popular dissatisfaction and workers' estrangement from the communist economic order. Not surprisingly, the coercive nature of the over-centralized and overplanned economy, based on the totalitarian principles of complete subordination of individual activity to an all-embracing programme, has not promoted sentiments of co-responsibility and cooperation. The sense and purpose of any economic activity must be lost when its importance is reduced to the dry figures and indicators of the omnipotent plan which, in turn, do not correspond with the real production processes and real social needs. All that is required is a symmetry between the officially expected figures and the officially reported ones. Thus, a new form of alienation has been created: the alienation of the workers whose labour and productive effort is 'paperized' or converted into an official reality of the fulfilled (or unfulfilled) plan independent of the real material outcome and the conditions under which it was achieved. Since each level of the economic administration is interested primarily in transmitting positive messages about satisfactory production results to the higher levels, the bureaucratic circulation of paper effectively replaces the circulation of real products. Human labour does not result in commodities which are subordinated to the capitalist market laws. Rather, it is turned into abstract figures, seductive playthings used by the rulers to support their ideological claims and political careers while further oppressing workers and repressing their desire for authentic production. The Central Plan, essentially a political tool of the exercise of power over the working people, not only helps to control but also to impoverish them. It facilitates a purely political management of the economy by the Communist Party élite which is afraid to face the complex economic reality. It desperately clings to the ideologically manufactured, fictitious images of a machine-like society, a society which follows precisely and eagerly all formal instructions and demands.

Participants of the production process live in constant fear that the discrepancy between the imagined and the real will be uncovered and that they will be held responsible for producing this false reality. The irony is that, faced with no other option and under the threat of criminal and political sanctions regardless of culpability, they do in fact contribute to its creation, constantly turning real life outcomes into well rounded figures. In this well planned system, both the failure to fulfil the plan as well as the provision of false information about its fulfilment, are treated as criminal offences, anti-state activities and signs of disloyalty to the party. It is only the preparation of an unrealistic plan which is incompatible with reality that is not subject to any legal sanctions and is exempt from scrutiny and criticism, sanctified by its party origin and ideological validity.

Under Soviet criminal law, a deliberate distortion by an official of accounting data concerning the fulfilment of plans is treated as a crime.

Liability for additions was set by a decree of the Presidium of the Supreme Soviet of the USSR dated 24 May 1961, which emphasized the nature of such offences as anti-state acts harmful to the national economy. According to article 152(1) of the Criminal Code of the RSFSR, false reporting is punishable by deprivation of freedom up to 3 years (see *Great Soviet Encyclopedia*, 1973, vol. 20 or Luryi, 1978: 1066). While there are no special provisions in the Polish Penal Code dealing directly with false reporting, the Code does contain some more general categories of crime which can be applied to these cases.[1]

Report padding is a very common activity in all Soviet-style economies. It involves misrepresentations of the quantity, quality or the very nature of economic output. Such operations often generate substantial profits for the management (and occasionally for the workers as well), by making them eligible for special financial bonuses resulting from the fulfilment or overfulfilment of the plan. While it usually involves reporting of fictitious achievements, in some cases, false reporting may also aim at concealing an excess portion of actual production. In such cases, this fabrication is done in order to avoid increases in the following year's plan or to build up reserves of materials or end-products to be used in cases of any future difficulties in achieving the planned quota. Naturally, report padding is frequently committed to cover up or to facilitate large scale theft of state property or illegal production and/or illegal sales of produced goods. While these falsifications are normally committed by managers, others do profit from them as well. As stated by Pomorski:

> The group of beneficiaries includes some of their subordinates whose professional careers and earnings also directly depend on plan fulfilment. . . . Then come formal and not so formal superiors. . . . There is a definite community of interests and goals among all these people, interests and goals which often do not coincide with those of . . . the central planners. (Pomorski, 1978: 303)

In Poland, the habit of report padding is as widespread as in the Soviet Union. Numerous controls initiated by the Free Union Solidarity during its short legal existence confirmed that practically all the economic reports were false (see for example Mońko, 1981, an article published in Poland in a censored weekly magazine). Various other inquiries undertaken by Polish journalists during the same period led to similar conclusions:

> Many bosses falsified statistics on their production and costs. Many

went even further, selling goods which were not yet produced and accounting for them in the reports on the fulfilment of the plan . . .
(Oseka, 1981; this author's translation from Polish)

In 1980, an official from the Supreme Chamber of Control revealed during a session of the Polish Diet that:

> For years, the Supreme Chamber of Control was informing the leaders of the state and the party of the dangerous phenomenon of fabricating statistics in order to show economic results better than the actual ones.
> ('Posiedzenie . . .', 1980; this author's translation from Polish)

Yet, given these occurrences, law enforcement and other agencies of control are remarkably passive and reluctant to intervene. Even in the Soviet Union, despite strict legal provisions and special guidelines issued by the party and central legal agencies, law enforcers are rather cautious towards this type of crime. Very few cases are investigated and prosecuted. Sanctions rarely involve the deprivation of freedom, which is the statutory penalty, and offenders are often allowed to continue in their managerial jobs or move to other posts similar in nature. Only minor cases are prosecuted and even then:

> typically, only secondary figures [are] brought to responsibility, whereas the real architects of the criminal schemes [are] left immune. The mood of permissiveness and compassion also [prevailes] in the courtrooms. . . . With respect to many architects and organizers of eyewash – notably local state and party dignitaries, leaders of provincial élite groups – local procurators are utterly powerless. *It may hardly be expected from the Soviet judge that he would eagerly send to a labour colony a respected comrade who engaged in what comrades in his position are routinely engaging in every day.*
> (Pomorski, 1978: 305; italics added)

Practically all important local officials have an interest in the plan-related 'eyewash'. They all have some official responsibility for overseeing that the plans for a given region are fulfilled. They all want to be left alone by the superior levels of command in order to continue with whatever illegal or semi-legal schemes they are involved in. Any reporting of unsatisfactory results threatens to bring outside controllers or investigators into their community. The existence of a tight network of mutual favours, corruption and exploitation of state resources depends on a prudent and stable social environment. Such networks perpetuate themselves through relationships of interdependence and support as well as a collective eagerness to participate in covering up all improper operations. Moreover, their impunity is greatly enhanced by the fact that they usually include most prominent local representatives of the police, the judiciary and other legal agencies. Any real attempts at more vigorous law enforcement and effective prevention of criminal report padding would have multiple negative effects for the central authorities as well. First of all, it is a crime committed almost exclusively by people in positions of relative power (which are held normally by party members) or at least with their direct knowledge and endorsement. Moreover, it is a crime which they practically cannot avoid. A truely comprehensive law enforcement would mean the actual criminalization of this very large group of people on whom the party has to rely for its everyday exercise of power. This, in turn, would have at least two politically undesirable consequences. First, it would officially label this key group as unworthy, and, second, it could provoke a hostile reaction and a further deterioration of relations between the central planners and the lower level managers. The party leaders could hardly afford such a move. Besides, they seem reluctant to obtain true production figures since this would force them to make an embarrassing choice between, on the one hand, disclosing the truth about the dismal state of the economy to the national and international public, and, on the other, instructing the central statistics offices to disregard completely all reports received and to prepare instead their global statistics purely on the basis of detailed political directives. This is not to suggest that, at present, statistics are not 'doctored' at the central level, but it seems that at least some effort is made to go through the bureaucratic motions of summing up all the partial reports. If the productive units suddenly started to provide accurate figures, this exercise would be even more spurious and redundant.

In addition to the mainly political reasons for the non-enforcement of the laws against report padding, there exist purely technical difficulties in the investigation and prosecution of such offences. One of the most obvious obstacles is the 'information flood' which is so characteristic of the communist economy. The requirement of constant reporting to the superior bodies leads to such overlapping of statistical information that any systematic verification becomes practically impossible (see Shenfield, 1982).

Whatever the reasons for the non-enforcement, it must be realized that the crime of falsification of economic information is a crime of the local establishment aimed at the central planners (see Pomorski, 1978).

It is, thus, an expression of objective conflicts of interests within the dominant communist group. As such, it does not have a counterpart in capitalist countries. Its general acceptance and political usefulness do not alter the fact that it has a profound negative impact on the functioning of the communist economy. It prevents any realistic planning and leads to an escalation of dangerous fiction which, in turn, becomes an organizing principle of the whole economy. An article in a Polish magazine published in 1981 talks openly about a 'suffocation of reality by the paper fiction'. The author observes that:

> A false report becomes a starting point for erroneous planning, forecasting and style of management. False planning and false information about the plans and about the reality make it impossible to manage the economy.
>
> (Mońko, 1981; this author's translation from Polish)

As a rule, therefore, central planning gradually leaves 'the terrain of reality and creates a fictitious reality which becomes autonomous from the real production' (Besançon, 1981: 43; this author's translation from French). The planning of production consists essentially of the planning of future statistics and not of future outputs.

It would be false, however, to claim that the fictitious functioning of the economy is caused by the prevalence of report padding on the local level. Such crimes against the Central Plan may contribute to the perpetuation and escalation of falsehood, but they themselves are necessitated by the very organization of the centrally planned economy. Any genuine critique of these processes, therefore, has to start with an analysis of the consequences which result from the principle of central control of the economy by a monopolistic political party, and not with its criminal abuses. Moreover, it must be noted that, even if this principle has been proven economically unviable, it cannot be abandoned. An abolition of the central planning of the economy would precariously weaken the party's central control over the society. Economic and political control mechanisms simply constitute two sides of the same process and are based on the same set of structural principles.

CRIMES AGAINST COMMUNIST PRODUCTION

The common characteristics of communist production – which include the lack of incentives and the waste and ineffectiveness of the organization of production – open opportunities for the introduction of illlegal incentives and increased productivity, the fruits of which are illegally appropriated. For example, Majchrzak (1965) describes in detail the activities of criminal groups in the leather tanning industry in Poland. One of the typical patterns consists of the introduction to a tannery of large amounts of illegally bought raw skins together with the legal ones and, at the end of the processing procedure, their withdrawal for black market sale. The participants of the 'gang' are selected according to their positions in the factory; all they are required to do is avoid mixing up the two lots of skins and some double recording.

The cooperation of selected truck drivers, convoyers, guards, and so forth is also crucial for the completion of these tasks. If the goods are to be distributed through state stores (instead of the black market), some of these store employees have also to be included in the scheme. To achieve a satisfactory level of protection and security, it is usually necessary to buy the collaboration of internal and external auditors and inspectors, as well as that of the director of the enterprise. While workers labour harder, often with no extra pay, they may get some satisfaction from working in an unusually well organized enterprise, with staff who care about the results and do everything to facilitate production processes, to avoid any unnecessary stoppages and to achieve high standard products. This technique for the creation of a parallel illegal enterprise within a legal one has been utilized in many other branches of production, including, for example, the meat and food processing industry. Indeed, modified versions of such a procedure can be introduced successfully into most state enterprises and various sources indicate that it appears to be very wide-spread in both Poland and the Soviet Union. For example, Chalidze maintains that 'unregistered production within a state enterprise' is very common in the Soviet Union, and 'those who are brought to book for such activities are generally also charged with stealing socialist property and abusing their official position' (Chalidze, 1977: 169–70; see also Grossman, 1977: 31).

It has been widely documented that securing the cooperation of the people who occupy strategic positions is, as a rule, very easy, whether through the use of bribes (as in the case of controllers, etc.), special payments for extra jobs (e.g. drivers), or shares in the profits (directors, bookkeepers, foremen, etc.). Of course, in the event of trouble, various forms of blackmail or even physical terror may be employed. Moreover, the operators of such criminal cliques usually have splendid political reputations, skilfully use current ideological slogans and have convenient connections with influential people. They easily deal with critics, either on political grounds or by charging them with defamation (Majchrzak, 1965; Daszkiewicz, 1971).

It is worth emphasizing that the existence of a double structure and the double recording of the ongoing productive processes is possible only because of the typical occurrence in communist enterprises of complicated patterns of spurious activities which easily accommodate further expansion of fiction. Within the communist economy where the only officially relevant and clearly formalized dimension of management is an hierarchical one and the only relevant types of activities are planning and reporting back on the fulfilment of the plan, there is much room for illegal economic production.

Besides the illegal production which is fully simultaneous with the legal one, there exist many forms of private subsidiary shops in the factories, collective farms, service enterprises, and so on (see, for example, Grossman, 1979). Their organizers share the profits with the 'parent' enterprises in exchange for formal cover and protection. They often use stolen materials and as a rule 'borrow' machines and other equipment from their legal hosts.

Rather large illegal gains are also obtained due to the often too tolerant estimates of both materials and labour needed for the planned production and the size of the inevitable losses and waste. There are many ways in which such favourable norms can be secured including bribes, false reports about past performance, etc. The surplus can easily be sold on the black market or utilized for private production. Organized crime flourishes within state trade and services (e.g. home repairs, appliance repairs, catering, etc.) to the same degree as within industry; in this situation, however, private consumers are often the immediate victims.

Although cases of very harsh penalties for the participants in organized gangs are known to have been meted out, communist law enforcement is usually rather lenient towards them. Moreover, there are many instances where people with previous convictions for economic crimes nevertheless hold responsible positions within the state economy. For example, in a survey of 150 persons convicted for organized crime in light industry in the years 1959–64 in Poland, it was found that in 1968, 57 of them were holding executive positions or posts connected with considerable responsibility for state property (Pawelko, 1971: 182).

Frequent campaigns against economic crime are designed to play a mainly ritualistic function aimed at mobilizing official agencies and public opinion in support of general goals fixed by the party and the central planning agencies (see Smith, 1979 for a discussion of anti-crime campaigns in the Soviet Union). They also hope to divert attention from the economic hardships experienced by people and from those officials directly responsible for the mismanagement of the economy. Campaigns against economic offenders in the Soviet Union have shown a recurring pattern and their frequency has increased in recent years to keep pace with the clearly accelerated succession of economic crises. They are also coordinated with political pressures created by the five-year planning cycle, a fact which has been well-documented in Smith's study of procuratorial anti-crime campaigns:

> The overall trend of procuratorial supervision since 1968 has been associated clearly with the planning period. In the first two years of the plan, procurators supervise a wide array of violations. . . . But as the pressures to fulfill production quotas rise in the fourth year, procurators institute campaigns against theft and other economic violations which might threaten production. During the final year of the plan, particular attention is given to padding and falsification of reporting records. (Smith, 1979: 153)

During these waves of mobilization of anti-crime efforts and sentiments, there are always some people selected and sacrificed to fuel the campaign, to promote an image of the effectiveness and diligence of the criminal justice system and to demonstrate that the threat coming from those selfish individuals is very real and accounts for current malaises of the economy. Nothing can better serve those ends as well-publicized trials resulting in one or more executions. By including some relatively high officials among the sentences it is hoped that the publicity will build up public trust in the impartiality of the legal system as well as provide further support for the claim that economic difficulties can be tackled by a diligent application of the criminal law.

In addition to the illegal production, both the wasteful or improper use of economic resources and the issuance of poor quality or incomplete products are criminal acts in the studied countries. While, however, the wasteful organization of the economy inevitably causes great losses, its underlying principles cannot be criminalized by the state. Only concrete cases of waste, usually on the level of individual enterprise, can be penalized in the light of existing law, although this rarely occurs. It is often difficult to separate wilful waste or negligence on the part of the individual employees from that caused by unrealistic, contradictory, or outdated plans. There are countless ways of wasting material resources and human labour. For example, the lack of any insight into consumer demand, and the low quality of many consumer goods lead to growing stocks of unsaleable products. Lack of coordination between the production of parts and the planned amount of the final product causes enormous losses in scrapped parts and half-completed products. Great losses are also brought about by delays in the delivery of necessary materials and parts, which cause frequent stoppages in the production processes. The conventional penalties do not have any deterrent effect since the fines paid by the unrealiable supplier to the receiving enterprise are usually compensated by the penalties paid to this supplier by his other cooperators who, in turn, have been unable to meet their schedules (see Pawelko, 1971: 202). In any case, the fines, as observed by a *Pravda* commentator, 'come out of the state's pocket, [and] the plants don't feel them any more than they would a mosquito bite' (Timofeyeva, 1983: 3). Moreover, enterprises have a tendency to order more materials than they actually need because they know that their orders are often reduced. Additionally, they need some reserves to avoid at least some of the stoppages caused by the cancelled, delayed or thoroughly unusable deliveries. In some cases, this will mean simply depleting accumulated stock to continue production while in other cases, the given enterprise will trade some of its less attainable articles for the urgently needed materials or parts which are not kept in stock. Both the lack of reserves and the exaggerated stock-piling may create great losses, yet both these practices are very common in the communist, planned economy.

The examples of wasteful investment decisions are also numerous. Industrial plants, half-built and abandoned because of one individual's change of plans; new, costly factories or machines, immobilized by the prohibiting costs of either the transportation of raw materials from distant parts of the country, or of the importation of necessary elements from abroad, or of the training of workers to use and service the modern equipment not yet synchronized with the prevailing traditional nature of production. Since the economy depends fully on political decisions made by party officials who are experts in ideology rather than economics, the tremendous scale of waste and carelessness can be logically anticipated. This waste, fostered by political decisions, is not penalized, however, and any penalties are reserved for individual plants or economic units. These sanctions, in turn, are largely symbolic, and the cooperators or the trade organizations prefer not to press charges or demand fines in an effort to preserve good mutual relationships (Sadikov, 1983: 3). In any case, 'the volume of production at large and even medium-sized enterprises is so great that economic sanctions against them for shoddy output have little effect' (Sadikov, 1983: 3).

Sanctions are also sometimes applied to individuals, but, according to *Pravda*:

> this happens very rarely. Suffice it to say that in the past three years, agencies of the Russian Republic Chief Administration of State Quality Inspection of Goods and State Trade Inspection have turned over approximately 1,200 such cases to investigative agencies, but few offenders have been brought to trial'. (Sadikov, 1983: 3)

Immense losses are also caused by incompetent or dishonest export agents (Naumowicz, 1970: 9). Jobs in foreign trade often tend to be distributed according to political rather than rational, professional criteria. They are considered to be not only politically sensitive, but also very attractive and, as such, are often given to incompetent, but politically worthy people, either in reward for their merits or as consolation for their deprivation of other, more desirable offices. Several cases of gigantic criminal schemes by foreign trade agents were uncovered and prosecuted during the early 1980s in both the USSR and Poland (see, for example, 'Handel i Etyka', 1980: 17–18; 'Przyjmowali . . .', 1983: 6; 'Two Soviets . . .', 1984: 14; 'Kary śmierci . . .', 1984: 4). Information about this kind of economic wastefulness is usually fully suppressed, however, and is disseminated largely through informal channels. This tendency to conceal the real facts is even more pronounced in cases of waste of both resources and human potential caused by the ideological mismanagement of the economy which is founded on fictitious premises and ruled by secret decisions and policies.

CRIMES AGAINST THE COMMUNIST DISTRIBUTION OF GOODS

As is generally known, the centrally planned distribution of goods in communist countries is not very effective. And, since the supply of goods is almost always insufficient and of poor quality, informal access to the legal as well as illegal system of distribution becomes one of crucial importance. Private middlemen and speculators play an extremely important role in an elaborate world of illegal or semi-legal redistribution of foodstuffs, consumer goods, building materials, and other scarce commodities (see Simes, 1975; Grossman, 1977; Katsenelinboigen, 1977 and 1978b; O'Hearn, 1980, for a more detailed analysis of Soviet illegal markets). It can be argued that such enterprising individuals or organized gangs introduce to the communist economy the capitalist market laws of supply and demand. Yet, in countries where all economic activity is supposed to be under the control of the government:

> [t]he type of individual initiative which is widely considered praiseworthy in a country such as the United States, can be criminal. In fact, increasing success in individual economic endeavors tends to bring increasingly severe penalties, culminating in the death penalty for persons who are exceptionally successful.
>
> (Barry and Barner-Barry, 1982: 305)

The problem is, however, that citizens of these communist countries seem to understand better the logic of the capitalist economy with its rivalry, injustice and pursuit of profits, than the communist logic of repression and strangulation of private initiative through the strict controls of the central command. Their economic instincts urge them to search tirelessly for ways to redistribute scarce resources in order to satisfy most adequately the existing demand and ensure their own personal profit.

The Criminal Code of the RSFSR includes several crimes of this type:

> S. 153. Activity as a commercial middleman carried on by private persons as a form of business for the purpose of enrichment shall be punished by deprivation of freedom for a term not exceeding three years with confiscation of property.
>
> S. 154. Speculation, that is, the buying up and reselling of goods or any other articles for the purpose of making a profit, shall be punished by deprivation of freedom for a term not exceeding two years with or without confiscation of property, or by correctional tasks for a term not exceeding one year, or by a fine not exceeding 300 rubles. Speculation as a form of business or on a large scale shall be punished by deprivation of freedom for a term of two to seven years with confiscation of property.
>
> (The Criminal Code of the RSFSR reprinted in Luryi, 1978: 173–4)

In addition, speculation in currency or securities on a large scale is punishable by deprivation of freedom for 5 to 15 years with confiscation of property, with or without additional exile for a term of two to five years, or by death with confiscation of property. According to the Polish Penal Code, anyone without a commercial licence who accumulates goods for the purpose of reselling them at a profit (s. 222), or anyone employed in a unit of the socialized economy who sells his own or another person's goods without authorization to do so (s. 223(1)), is subject to the penaly of deprivation of liberty for up to three years. But, if in the commission of the latter type of crime, the perpetrator is gleaning a regular source of income, the penalty is increased to a term of 6 months to 8 years (s. 223(3)). Moreover, anyone employed in a unit of the socialized economy who disposes of goods with the purpose of reselling them at a profit is subject to the penalty of deprivation of liberty for from 6 months to 5 years. But if the perpetrator made the commission of such offences a regular source of income or if he has committed the offence in relation to property of considerable value, the penalty is increased to up to 10 years (*The Penal* . . . , 1973: 95–6, s. 221). Additionally, two temporary laws on combating speculation, passed in 1981 and 1982, went far beyond the existing criminal code provisions.

Despite their harshness, these laws do not seem to have a strong deterrent effect on potential perpetrators. Speculation is present everywhere, from agriculture to medicine. A typical example of the illicit redistribution of medical materials, which is not well publicized in the western literature but is nevertheless very common in communist countries, is quoted in one of the issues of *Pravda*:

> In a number of medical institutions, cases have come to light of the hoarding of medicines and their resale at high prices and the misappropriation of food intended for persons undergoing inpatient treatment (Tairov, 1979: 10)

Much better known in the West are numerous examples of speculation in meat, a commodity very highly valued but always in short supply in both the Soviet Union and Poland. A recent report in *Pravda* indicates that, in 1981, several hundred meat pilferers were detained in the southern Ukraine alone. Their method of operation is as has been described thus:

> The 'miracle' begins when the carcass is placed on the slaughter shop conveyor for cutting. In places where a soiled or ragged spot should be gently excised, the butchers cut off a kilogram or two of good meat. Brisket, tenderloin and other parts of the carcass often wind up as trimmings. As carcasses are being processed, unauthorized personnel slip into the shop under various pretexts. Few leave without trophies. The directors of many farms . . . have complained about how their livestock 'lost weight' at receiving centers and slaughterhouses.
> (Kucherenko, 1982: 21)

It is not only the methods of committing crime which are typical in the described cases. The recommendations for reform often resemble the one proposed by a *Pravda* journalist:

> The selection and placement of personnel must be improved, as must upbringing work. Can one possibly consider normal the situation at the Odessa Meat-Industry Production Association, where communists account for only 1 percent of the 800 employees who handle valuable goods or money? (Kucherenko, 1982: 21)

Since almost all goods are scarce in the Soviet Union and Poland, practically every factory has its own long record of pilfering, dealing and reselling. The Soviet press is full of examples:

> The fence around the Dyatkovo Crystal Factory is full of holes, some big enough for a man to walk through, and a well-trodden path lies at the bottom of a ditch running under the fence . . . Dyatkovo's market presents a depressing sight. Individuals carrying baskets and bags fearlessly offer a wide assortment of crystal at reasonable prices. 'Peddlers' stroll through apartment houses and office buildings hawking items at the wholesale prices. The hotel is always full of characters who are 'making contacts'. (Pyrkh, 1982: 16)

The recommendations for improvements are again typical: improved control, better checks at the factory gate, stricter methods of record-keeping, and so forth. In yet another case, reported in *Izvestia,* a group of enterprising individuals sold tens of thousands of flowers in the market-places of large cities. This time, however, the product came from their own, legitimately owned plots:

> A person can grow anything he likes on his private plot, of course. But some speculators go so far as to build their own greenhouses for commercial purposes. (Bablumyan, 1982: 19)

Thus, the very idea of producing something for profit is in itself criminal. As well, it engenders further crimes since, in the case of the flower sellers, a private individual is not legally allowed to buy the necessary tools and materials to build a greenhouse and must therefore steal them from the nationalized economy or obtain them through the black market. Some recommendations concerned with the prevention of this type of crime are a bit more perceptive than those in the previously quoted cases. For example:

> . . . the speculation in flowers would not have such deep roots if the organization whose job it is to supply the public with flowers provided

> any serious competition for the private entrepreneurs. I have in mind the republic Ministry of Agriculture's Flora Association which fails to meet its flower-growing plans from one year to the next and whose products are far inferior in quality to those found in the marketplace. (Bablumyan, 1982: 19)

Western commentators as well as 'samizdat' authors in communist countries naturally go further in their interpretations of the role of black markets in a Soviet style economy. For example, in an article circulated originally as a samizdat publication in Moscow, its author claims that:

> The black market is the very basis of the Soviet economy, the foundation on which the planned economy structure rests. The black market is the socialist mechanism of power and exploitation, the very essence of our socio-economic system. . . . The commodities which circulate in it support the existing political and social order. (Timofeev, 1982: 5)

In Poland, speculation is as prevalent as in the Soviet Union. At the beginning of the 1980s, it became the target for a new anti-crime crusade initiated by the government, desperate in the face of the growing Solidarity movement. The media were full of descriptions and condemnations of rampant speculation and the growth of illegal markets. Special anti-speculation squads were created and manned by policemen, soldiers and volunteers. They concentrated mainly on the most visible, but relatively small-scale operators, while the activities of more serious, wholesale dealers continued unhampered. The squads regularly raided flea markets and other places where private vendors were likely to be found. Newspapers reported daily on their successful operations as well as difficulties they had to face. The following citation illustrates well this carefully balanced political mixture of optimism and pessimism:

> It is true that after just two weeks of the intensified anti-speculation campaign, the black market is now on the defensive. . . . Yet, we are still a long way from the total elimination of this unacceptable social phenomenon. (Olszewski, 1981; this author's translation from Polish)

In the first 7 months alone of 1981, these anti-speculation raids on Warsaw private markets resulted in 212 cases being prosecuted by petty offence penal boards and 98 referred to criminal courts. In addition, 233 speculators were fined immediately ('Kontrola rynku', 1981: 8). This well-publicized war on speculation was expected to convince the public that an economic recovery of the country tormented by food shortages and general economic collapse depended mainly on the successful suppression of speculation and the operation of black markets. Such a task, it was implied, could not be accomplished by a free union movement, but rather, only by a full mobilization of the repressive forces in the society. A new bill on the 'struggle against speculation' was hastily prepared which proposed that an almost unlimited power be granted to the police and special penal boards whose decisions, in turn, could not be appealed to the courts or to the prosecutor's offices. As well, the proposed penalties were to be significantly more severe than the existing ones. Many lawyers and other social groups protested against the harshness and lawlessness of the proposed measures. A resolution of the Association of Defence Lawyers sharply criticized the draft, concluding that:

> [o]nly a socio-economic reform which would respect market laws, genuine workers self-governments and trade unions, and would secure appropriate prices and agricultural policy, could eliminate speculation or at least push it away from the mainstream of social life.
>
> (Górski, 1981: 2; this author's translation from Polish)

A slightly modified Bill was passed in October 1981 as a temporary law. Its scope was farther extended in October 1982, thus suggesting that the law was more than just a temporary measure. Despite great political changes, speculation has continued to be portrayed as one of the major aspects of the Polish economic crisis of the 1980s. And the voices demanding radical socio-economic reform in lieu of individualized criminal repression have once more been suppressed.

In the following years, the anti-speculation campaign has continued to be vigorously promoted by the Polish authorities, and the daily press has remained preoccupied with the issue. In 1983, 8105 persons were charged and 6712 were convicted on charges of speculation. The latter figure represented a decrease in convictions in comparison to 1982 when several thousand more speculators were convicted by the courts ('Spekulacja . . .', 1984: 6). The press reports stressed, however, that cases prosecuted in 1983 involved more highly organized criminal rings than in previous years. Such groups intercept large quantities of goods before they reach state stores. They normally act in collusion with the managers of state enterprises who even go so far as to adjust their production to the needs and preferences of the speculators ('Spekulacja . . .', 1984: 6; 'Narada . . .', 1984: 2; 'Nowe . . .', 1982: 2). In one quoted case, for example, the production process was altered when a gang of speculators requested large quantities of fabric meant to imitate imported ones ('Narada . . .', 1984: 2).

Another criminal ring was involved in a highly organized scheme, whereby the newly produced expensive consumer goods (such as furs, furniture, electronic equipment, electric household appliances, etc.) were received at the factory gates and sold on the black market while the stores for which the goods were intended were offered cash equivalents calculated according to the official prices and augmented by handsome bribes. In connection with this criminal scheme alone, 74 persons were charged, among whom were 6 presidents of various organizations, 28 state store directors and 9 drivers and convoyers ('Siedemdziesiat cztery . . .', 1984: 6). In another case, a well-organized gang speculated in food rationing cards which were introduced in Poland in the early 1980s as a result of acute food shortages ('Spekulacja . . .', 1984: 6). As well, speculation in books which are printed in very inadequate quantities appears to be very common. Textbooks, novels and instruction manuals seem to be in great demand which cannot be satisfied by the limited supply. The situation is additionally worsened by the recent closure of more than 15 000 libraries across Poland, apparently for economic reasons. While traditionally, the stocks in state bookstores were depleted by speculators, recently more efficient methods have been developed whereby large quantities of books are 'allotted' to the speculators directly from the printers or during transport ('Jak ukrócić . . .', 1983: 2; for a Soviet example see Bablumyan, 1983: 6).

Finally, various Polish press publications analyze a more general phenomenon which consists of the total subordination of the market to the producers. In the situation of the chronic scarcity of goods, producers are able to terrorize the state trade to the point that the stores are forced to accept with gratitude substandard or dated articles while large quantities of state produced goods are diverted from the state market altogether. Goods are often exchanged among producers without the use of stores; as well, newly produced articles frequently are sold immediately to employees in quantities which suggest that speculation may be involved ('Nowe . . .', 1982: 2). Unlike western countries where the supply of goods is usually greater than demand and producers have to fight to secure markets for their products, within Poland and the Soviet Union, the 'producers' market' coupled with the rigid state trade structure leads to the creation of huge black markets which gradually replace the legal ones.

CRIMES RELATED TO THE 'PRIVATE SECTOR' OF THE ECONOMY

The communist economy, based on the principle of state ownership of the means of production, has been gradually forced to accommodate some margin of private economic enterprise. It has become apparent that the rigid system of long-term planning and hierarchically centralized management is not able to respond to the changing demand in the consumer market and to the individualized expectations in the area of some personalized services. After 1956, both the Soviet Union and Poland partially relaxed their ban on private craft and small enterprise. Nevertheless, involvement in prohibited types of trade or industry persists as a crime. Naturally, the extent to which private initiative has been actually legalized varies from one 'ideological wave' to another.

While the dependence of the illegal producers on the black market for the supply of tools and raw materials as well as for the sales of their products is quite understandable, more striking is the fact that the legally established private enterprises have to rely on them as well. The ideologically determined regulations of the market make it practically impossible for a private person to buy machines, materials or other items necessary for carrying on production:

> Most people would doubtless prefer to buy their necessary supplies honestly, but the state makes this impossible. For instance, one cannot buy leather to make shoes, upholster chairs, or bind books. So when a man is charged with making shoes illegally, he is usually also charged with stealing leather from the state – an excellent example of how, by prohibiting a harmless activity, the state incites people to commit more serious offences. (Chalidze, 1977: 166)

A private producer may obtain authorization to purchase limited amounts of required articles, but if he wants to make a profit and be also able to pay taxes, he has to produce and sell more than he is permitted, and, more than he is prepared to reveal to the revenue officer. He is forced to pay black market prices (or bribes), therefore, for the materials essential to his production if his business is to succeed economically. Moreover, the officially allotted supplies may be of such low quality that the profit-oriented producer may be better off paying black market prices for more suitable materials.

In some cases, tools, raw materials, construction materials or chemical substances (for example, fertilizers) can be purchased legally only in the 'hard currency' stores. In these cases, however, the producer has to buy hard currency from the black market dealers (there is no legal exchange), or engage in even more risky criminal operations which involve smuggling and contraband. There is no way by which legitimate private business in communist countries can be free of either the criminal stigma or the necessity to cooperate with the criminal underworld unless the basic principles of economic organization are rethought.

In his book on the prevention of economic crimes published in Poland, Witold Pawelko emphasizes the high concentration of criminal activities in areas where the state and private sectors interact. Utilizing the official data of the state agencies of control, he concludes that especially frequent are:

> abuses connected with the purchase of materials by state enterprises, institutions, and offices from the private sector. The second opportunity for abuses exists in cases where private industry and trade provide supplies for the state market. The underdevelopment of the production of some groups of consumer goods and services in the nationalized economy provides the premise of both types of crime. . . . The third area where the two economies meet . . . is the purchase of raw and other materials by private enterprises from nationalized sources. Delimited allotments from these sources do not allow the producers to broaden their activity beyond the global value of return set for them. . . . Hence, attempts to bribe employees of supplying agencies who determine the amount of the allotted material occur.
>
> (Pawelko, 1971: 74; this author's translation from Polish)

Even such plain recognition of the failure of the state economy and disclosure of the mechanisms of the inevitable criminalization of the private sector, however, cannot trigger any effective corrections of the status quo, since the required changes would violate the principles of the binding doctrine.

CONCLUSIONS

Economic crimes are defined in communist countries as:

> socially dangerous activities, which infringe directly on socialist property relations, rules of production, trade and distribution of material goods, and which are contrary to general societal economic interests.
>
> (Pawelko, 1971: 16; this author's translation from Polish)

This definition is based on an obvious mystification. It assumes that there exists an actual coincidence between general societal interests and the interests of the communist rulers who derive political power from economic relationships based on centralized ownership. The extraordinary protection which the criminal law lends to these relationships represents the real nature of the power structure of communist societies.

The definitions of economic crimes focus on the activities of individuals and on their private gain. They do not seem to include the crimes against people which are committed daily on an enormous scale by communist industries, for example, and which involve both disastrous levels of poisonous pollution (Topiński, 1981: 11; 'Pollution . . .', 1982; Komarov, 1980, 1981; Poprzeczko, 1984: 8; Jacyna, 1984: 12–17; Ogórek, 1982: 5; Walczak, 1984: 6; Loch, 1980: 3) as well as a drastic lack of consideration for safety standards (see, for example, Weschler, 1982: 167 and 1983: 112)[2] and the needs of workers and consumers. Information about such crimes is normally suppressed.[3] It is only the crimes directed against some ideological, economic principles which are given official publicity, attention and political visibility. It is evident that their well-publicized prosecution is expected to reinforce the binding force of these fundamental, ideological principles and not to improve the lives of the citizens of communist countries.

The nature and extent of economic crimes in any country cannot be explained without references to the specific features of its economic organization. It may be argued that the enormity of economic tasks entrusted to the communist state must lead to the constant growth of state power and bureaucracy. Such a tendency is obviously contrary to the Marxist thesis regarding the inevitable progress towards the withering away of the state. Within democratic capitalist countries, the relative independence of the dominant economic interests from the political ones, keeps in check the totalitarian tendencies of the state. Such tendencies remain unrestrained when the economic interests are unified with political ones and subordinated to a single dominant ideology.

The only solution to the profit seeking habits of many executives in communist countries is the creation of parallel production which is profitable, and which is not controlled by the state. Such private initiative counters and discredits the ideologically based state economy, because of its effectiveness elasticity and genuine human involvement, the features notably absent in the state enterprise. Being illegal, the private counter-economy certainly results in significant financial losses to the state. On the other hand, however, the state's tacit acceptance of its existence testifies to this countereconomy's vital functions as both the substitute and a cover up for the grossly inefficient official economic organization.

The dominant economic organization, with characteristic hierarchical relationships designed to transmit economic command, does not provide a sufficient base for carrying out production. The hierarchical relationships secure the routinized circulation of fictitious information (plans, reports) which inevitably loses touch with real production. Production related relationships, exchanges and cooperation are not incorporated into the ideological structure of the economy and, therefore, have to develop spontaneously, in an unplanned, and hence banned, manner. Indeed, they must be outlawed since they evade the Central Plan, that fundamental legal document according to which economic processes are to be organized. Yet, without these intricate illegal production relationships, the economy would exist only on paper. The inevitability of the development of an underworld economic markets is furthermore strengthened by the contradiction between the social and economic necessity of the existence of a private economic sector and the ideological unfeasibility of providing a legal and economic base for its functioning.

Economic crimes within communist and capitalist countries have some features in common, but they also differ significantly. These differences are a result of the contrasting ideologies and economic realities of these countries. Capitalist ideology is discreet and hidden, it has acquired a high degree of consistency with the economic reality, which it has been able to mould effectively. Moreover, it has become more or less absorbed and legitimized by the beliefs and life styles of the people. Economic crimes are shaped by the dominant values and are conditioned by market forces and economic cycles. Communist ideology, on the other hand, is coercive and doctrinaire, it has influenced the formal structure of the economy, but has never been embodied in real economic practice. Moreover, it has not been accepted, or even absorbed by the social consciousness. Economic crimes are motivated, to a large extent, by a counter ideology (a capitalist one?) which cannot be accommodated within the rigid structure of the communist economy. Both economic crimes and the country's economic development depend to a large extent on the existence of black markets and social corruption which are generated by the official economic structure.

9 Crimes of Workers and Peasants: Pilfering, Stealing and Dealing and 'Free-Unionizing'

WORKERS' CRIMES AGAINST STATE PROPERTY

A problem which greatly concerns the authorities in communist countries is the common lack of respect for nationalized property. It manifests itself above all at the work places where theft is not only widespread, but is seen as justified under circumstances which are often perceived as unfair and despotic. Chalidze describes bitterly the early origins of this attitude:

> To obtain funds, both the Social Revolutionaries and the Bolsheviks were active in organizing armed robberies, which were euphemistically known as 'expropriations.' . . . [During the Revolution, the Bolsheviks] declared that in the future all property of any magnitude would be held in common, and they incited the proletariat to pillage. In the name of the State they plundered the churches and took over the private possessions. In the course of time the proletariat came to realize that communal ownership meant simply that property, instead of belonging to an individual, now belonged to a superproprietor, the State; but initially they believed that they were seizing property in order to make it their own, although it was to be held in common and not individually. . . . With all its propaganda, the new regime did not succeed in persuading people to protect state property as their own; they continued to regard it as someone else's and treated it accordingly. This seems to be true today of the entire population; everyone steals a bit here and there. (Chalidze, 1977: 21–2, 28)

In addition to the common feelings of hostility against 'them' (those for whom one works), there are also other factors at work. The wasteful organization of work and the mindless subordination to the Central Plan discourages genuine involvement in the productive tasks and stimulates individualistic orientation which facilitates pilferage and cheating of the employer. While inadequate wages made moonlighting a necessity, there are no legal ways to acquire the parts, materials, or tools necessary to carry out this work (as the 'means of production', they cannot be owned or purchased privately). Thus, 'a typical feature of Soviet life is that people often steal socialist property not for personal use but as a means of carrying on their lawful occupations' (Chalidze, 1977: 195).

The state ownership of the means of production constitutes one of the crucial aspects of the economic organization of communist societies. Due to the ideological assumption that under communism there can be no conflict between the state and the people, state ownership is officially described as 'social', 'public' or 'socialist' ownership which falsely suggests a popular participation in the management of the economy. This is another fiction which is used as an excuse in the ruthless pursuit of the political exploitation of workers. Since there can be no conflict between employees and employers where employees are portrayed as owners and co-managers of their enterprises, workers are forbidden to organize, unionize, or voice their dissatisfaction with working conditions.

Thus, it should come as no surprise that workers, who see very clearly how ideological dogmas are used against them, not only perceive them as dangerous political tactics, but also try, in their own ways, to neutralize their oppressive nature. One of the most conspicuous consequences is a widespread lack of respect for both state property as well as other aspects of the dominant politico-economic relations. As a result, economic offences committed by workers, mainly in the form of theft, destruction or re-sale of state property, are not always seen by them as immoral and are generally treated with tolerance by their peers, their families and, often, their immediate superiors. The perpetrators of these offences, usually have great respect for private property and would never steal or willingly damage another's personal property. As Pomorski argues in his well-researched article, in the USSR, 'stealing socialist property has become very much a part of everyday routine, a fairly common way of livelihood, which is no longer perceived by many as deviant behaviour' (Pomorski, 1977: 240).[1] The reality of high involvement in petty stealing and dealing does not, automatically mean, however, that these offences are morally condoned. Rather, they are perceived as a regrettable yet almost inevitable outcome of the poorly organized, unfair economy. The wide spread occurrence of this type of legal violation seems to coexist with anxiety about the deplorable deterioration of moral standards.

According to available data, crimes against 'socialist' ownership, committed by both workers and managers, constitute the second largest group of officially processed crimes in the Soviet Union after hooliganism and represent up to 25 per cent of all prosecuted offences' (Pomorski, 1977: 239). An even higher proportion of crimes against 'socialist' property and other economic crimes can be found in Poland, where they represent 30 per cent of all prosecuted offences and are second only to crimes against private property, which amount to 37 per cent (see official statistics for 1979 in *Rocznik* . . ., 1980: 479). Nevertheless, economic crimes are among the most underreported types of crime, and, therefore, the actual rates must be many times greater than those indicated by the official statistics. The prevalence of such offences committed against nationalized property can only be interpreted as resulting from a failure of the communist ideology to have any real impact on the values and moral judgements of the citizens of these countries and indicates problems with legitimacy of the dominant property relations under communism.

Causes for the common disdain for the state property cannot be understood, therefore, in purely economic terms. While state property is certainly not seen by the people as their 'common' property as it is defined in the Soviet Constitution,[2] it is not always perceived as belonging to no one, as many commentators tend to see it. It is rather intuitively understood as one of the pillars of the monopoly of power by the party élite over the whole nation.

Constitutions, criminal codes and criminal policies of communist countries indicate clearly how important this kind of property is to the ruling élite. They actively confirm and reinforce the ideological dogma that the individual, as well as his personal property, has to be sacrificed in the process of building the new society, and that the sacred value of state property has to be preserved above all. The extraordinary severity of sanctions for violations against it, is the best indicator of its ideological importance. As Tony Cliff comments:

> It is odd that although the people thus, through the state, own the country's wealth, the Russian state should go to such extraordinary lengths to defend this wealth from them! That the severity of this branch of Soviet law is in marked contrast to the relative leniency with which murder, kidnapping, and other violent forms of crime, are dealt with, is highly significant. It becomes clear that in Stalinist Russia, the individual is rated much lower than property.
>
> (Cliff, 1974: 59–60, 62)

A law 'On the Protection of the Property of State Enterprises,

Collective Farms and Cooperatives and Institutions of Socialist Property' passed under Stalin in 1932, and described by him as the corner-stone of revolutionary legality, is the best example of this tendency. It declared that 'social ownership' (state, kolkhoz, co-operative) constituted the very foundations of the Soviet system, it was sacred and inviolable, and, therefore, persons who infringed upon it were deemed 'enemies of the people'. Under this law, any theft of the state or collective property became punishable by death by shooting, accompanied by the confiscation of all property. In cases where mitigating circumstances existed, the death penalty could be replaced by imprisonment for no less than ten years and confiscation of property (for more details see Pomorski, 1977 and Cliff, 1974). The scope of this law was soon broadened to include such offences as intentional slaughter of livestock and secret grinding of grain. This law was repealed by an edict on 4 June 1947 which distinguished between stealing state property (7 to 10 years in a correctional labour camp) and social property (5 to 8 years). As well, it introduced a new offence of aggravated stealing of state and social property (10–25 years and 8–20 years, respectively, with mandatory confiscation of property). Petty theft by first offenders, previously punished by a mandatory 1 year imprisonment term, was now included in the first category of theft with a required minimum sentence between 5 and 7 years in one of the concentration camps of the 'Gulag Archipelago'.

As Alexander Solzhenitsyn reports in his monumental work on the giant 'correctional' network in the Soviet Union:

> In the years immediately following the decree whole 'divisions' from the countryside and the cities were sent off to cultivate the islands of Gulag in place of the natives who had died off there. If a young girl sent into the field to get a few ears of grain took along two friends for company ('an organized gang') or some twelve-year old youngsters went after cucumbers or apples, they were liable to get twenty years in camp. (Solzhenitsyn, 1974, Vol. I: 89)

Such were the educational tools used by the Stalinist regime to inculcate people with the proper respect for the new type of property relations. Needless to add, they were based on a very mistaken concept of human nature and only provoked the escalation of hatred towards and social rejection of the repressive regime.

The current Soviet codes preserve the superiority of socialist property over private property both through their penalty structure and their legal definitions of crimes involving state and private property. The distinctions between social and state ownership has been abolished and replaced by the global concept of crimes against socialist property. The maximum penalties for such crimes are about 30 per cent higher than those for theft of personal property and there are several aggravated forms of these offences which carry heavier penalties (*Encyclopedia of Soviet Law*, vol. II, 1973: 676). Most significantly, capital punishment was introduced in the early 1960s as a penal sanction for large scale appropriations of state property. This clearly indicates that crimes against 'socialist' property relations continue to be considered more serious than crimes against life, health, and the liberty of individuals.

In Poland, two decrees of 1953 and two special legislations of 1958 and 1959 introduced extraordinary penalties for crimes against state property. In the present Penal Code, however, the differences in the penalties for theft of private property and state property are not as evident. The main differentiation consists in the fact that, while in cases of offence against private property the death penalty may be applied only when the use of a firearm was involved, the perpetrators of non-violent but especially serious crimes against state property are liable to capital punishment. The penalties for simple theft, however, are the same for both types of property and involve up to 5 years of deprivation of liberty (*The Penal Code . . .*, 1973: s. 199 and s. 203). Nevertheless, the judicial practice seems to continue to treat theft of state property as a more serious offence. Indeed, citizens seem to be convinced that there exists a clear difference in the degree of legal protection extended to state property and to personal property. A survey of a representative sample of the Polish population conducted in 1975, found that 52.2 per cent of the respondents believed that courts punished perpetrators of offences against 'social' property more severely, while only 2.7 per cent thought that they treated offenders against private property more harshly (35.5 per cent assumed that the courts do not differenciate between these two types of offenders) (Gaberle, 1978: 154).

Despite these findings, however, there are many indications that private property is granted much more moral respectability and legitimacy than 'socialist' property. Interviews with a representative sample of the adult population of Warsaw (487 interviews) conducted in 1976 clearly confirm this thesis. The authors, J. Kwaśniewski and A. Kojder, found that, while 91.6 per cent of the respondents strongly condemned theft of personal property (specifically, theft of a wallet), only 60.6 per cent expressed the same attitude towards theft of 'social' property (the theft of expensive tools from the factory). Moreover, the majority of interviewees recommended deprivation of liberty (52.6 per cent) or a fine (17.9 per cent) as an appropriate punishment for the theft of a wallet, while admonition (30.8 per cent), a fine (20.3 per cent) or dismissal from work (18.3 per cent) were among the most frequently suggested responses for the theft of factory tools (Kwaśniewski and Kojder, 1979: 162–5; see also Kwaśniewski, 1984: 45–7).

It is worthy of note that, while employee offences constitute a very high proportion of the cases handled by the ordinary courts, law enforcement in the area of petty employee theft does not appear to be particularly vigorous. In both Poland and the USSR, workers' courts (or comrades' courts) are entrusted with these types of cases, but they do not seem to be very active and their prestige is extremely low (see Chapter 3). And, thus, two prominent Soviet law enforcement officials expressed serious doubts about the usefulness of the comrades' courts in the fight against theft by workers:

> the comrades' courts do not everywhere and always have the desired effect on lawbreakers. The opinion of the citizens, most of whom favor the strictest punishment of lawbreakers, frequently changes by the time a case goes to trial in a comrades' court or gets discussed at a meeting, with the result that while everyone is against thieves and hooligans in general, they come to feel that 'their own' lawbreaker is not really all that dangerous and that allowances should be made.
> (Sharakhin and Ivanov, 1975: 5)

In some, even very petty cases, however, criminal proceedings are instituted and strict sentences meted out by the ordinary courts. While, overall, law enforcement appears to be very erratic, unfair and ineffective, it is important to note, that some forms of theft of state property by workers are rather serious and involve organized groups acting in conspiracy. Frequently, this type of crime is committed in collusion with truck drivers whereby the members of the group divert loaded trucks from their official destinations and sell the goods to private entrepreneurs or individual clients. In such cases, sentences tend to be much harsher, as illustrated by the fate of a three-person gang caught in one of the Soviet republics with a truck loaded with bricks who were sentenced to penalties ranging from 3 years of mandatory work to 3 years' deprivation of freedom (Bragin, 1982: 5), or, by the case of several interconnected groups of workers who repeatedly drove trucks full of galvanized steel from plants' warehouses and who were sentenced to different terms of deprivation of liberty (with 6 sentences in the range of 7 to 13 years' imprisonment and a number of sentences involving shorter terms; see Smirnov, 1982:6).

To recapitulate, petty theft and fiddling in the state economy is at least to some extent, caused by the workers' realization that what is not stolen is going to be wasted anyway. As well, the chronic shortages of goods in state stores contribute to the acceptance of theft as a viable way of acquiring articles in short supply, both for personal use and to barter for other commodities. Compounding the issue is the hypocrisy of the political and economic system and its laws, such that ideological slogans about the workers' ownership of the means of production, entirely contradicted by the reality, provoke feelings of bitterness, cynicism, and disrespect for the state property.

Stewart Steven, in his book *The Poles*, cites a very telling comment made by one of his Polish friends:

> There is much talk here about the so-called dignity of labour, without anyone's giving too much thought to what the expression actually means. The act of laboring is not in itself dignified, otherwise it could be held that slaves have dignity, which clearly they do not. Labor confers dignity on a man only if, through it, he is able to purchase independence by providing for his family needs and comforts, by alleviating his poverty through his own efforts. . . . All the Polish economy has been able to provide is the bare minimum for most of its people most of the time. No wonder then, that the work ethic has all but disappeared. (Steven, 1982:378–9)

When the work does not fulfil, even in a very minimal degree, these human needs for dignity and existential independence moral norms cease to be perceived as binding in the workplace. As a Polish sociologist observes, in post-war Poland morality has been reduced to 'the sphere of personal ties and relationships. Morality has ceased to play a role as an effective regulator in the area of the most important social roles, notably those related to work' (Kiciński, 1982: 11, this author's translation from Polish).

CRIMES OF PEASANTS

There is a great difference in the organization of agriculture in Poland and the Soviet Union. Polish agriculture is based on the principle of private ownership of farms and at least 70 per cent of the tilled land belongs to individual farmers. In the Soviet Union, on the other hand, all peasants are expected to work for state farms and are only allowed to own very small allotments which do not represent more than 2.5 per cent of the cultivated land. Nevertheless, peasants in both countries experience many similar pressures, fears and frustrations.

Polish peasants remember well the dark Stalinist era, when a massive attempt at forced collectivization of agriculture was made. The haunting memories of violence, mass arrests, and general terror of the collectivization campaign are still alive in the Polish countryside. These memories, coupled with continuous attempts by the authorities to expand state farms and to restrict private ownership, create a general feeling of insecurity and mistrust among farmers. Moreover, while peasants are allowed to own their farms, the individual purchase of machinery is made difficult for ideological reasons.[3] Private marketing of farm products is also very severely restricted. Polish peasants are caught, therefore, between the ethos of decentralized private farming and the reality of the rigidly centralized system of distribution and the collective ownership of the tools of production. This situation involves a clear contradiction between the farmers' desire for autonomy and profits and their subordination to the dictates of the bureaucratic machinery of the state market and the Central Plan.

In their attempts to achieve their goals, farmers use illegal means to purchase adequate quantities of fertilizers and pesticides, to construct necessary buildings and to secure needed tools and machines. As well, they must resort to illegal markets to sell their surplus produce in order to obtain funds to finance these investments. They perceive the state trade channels as uneconomical, not simply because of the low wholesale prices paid to farmers, but also because of the poor organization of transport and of state purchasing centres which mean that farmers must wait in endless lines while their products often deteriorate and thereby depreciate.

Various legal enactments are constantly introduced to help stamp out illegal markets and the door-to-door and 'street corner' sales of meat, eggs, fruit, vegetable and flowers by vendors. Recently, a special law was passed which forbade the transportation of meat in any quantities larger than these designated by the system of food rationing ('O przewozie . . .', 1983:8). This enactment must have rekindled within the Polish countryside the hateful memories of the German occupation when a similar law was imposed on the Polish population. Yet, both then as now, many people and especially peasant women, are prepared to take the risks involved in perpetuating this private 'food line' from the countryside to the cities. The scale of unmet demand is certainly extensive enough to provide the perpetrators of these types of offences extremely powerful economic incentives.

In the Soviet Union, the extent of misery and deprivation in the rural areas is much greater than in Poland. The collectivized farming results in enormous losses and breeds unchecked corruption and economic crime by farm managers and their associates. Small rural plots, on the other hand, which are officially intended to provide food for kolkhozniks' families, develop into highly productive private enterprises whose production is destined in part for illegal and semi-legal sales. Indeed, they seem so vital to the economy that, as Timofeev demonstrates in an interesting article, without these small peasant plots 'the socialist economy would not survive a day' (Timofeev, 1982:8). Due to a total failure of the communist, collectivized agricultural scheme, these small allotments, based on private initiative and the peasant family's desire to survive, have been forced to adopt very serious economic tasks. Indeed, 'the share of the peasants private parcels, with their 2.5 per cent of tilled land, is much more than half' of total agricultural production (Timofeev, 1982:7). Not only does it feed all rural inhabitants (40 per cent of the total population of the Soviet Union), but a significant portion is distributed in towns and cities through a network of illegal and semi-legal markets. While many Western observers praise the efficiency of these private allotments, they rarely realize the human cost at which these results are obtained. They rarely appreciate the extent of Soviet rural exploitation where all able-bodied male inhabitants are forced to work all day for totally unprofitable collective farms virtually without payment. Consequently, three quarters of the work done on the private parcels is done by women, and much of the remaining work is performed by children and the disabled (Timofeev, 1982:12). In Timofeev's words:

> A peasant family is a microcapitalist enterprise where the head of the family is required to exploit the labor of his dependants, to obtain from the personal farm the maximum surplus value and so make up for the necessary product not received by them on the collective and state farms. This exploitation is carried on, as a rule, by completely barbaric methods, without any modern agricultural methods, without machines, without the application of modern achievements. . . . Spade, wheelbarrow, sack, basket – these are almost the only tools. (Timofeev, 1982: 13)

Naturally, all obvious ways of increasing the rationality of effort on these allotments, such as the unification of several plots or the purchase of more advanced tools and fertilizers, are strictly prohibited. By allowing them, the productive superiority of this private agriculture would become too obvious and the visibility of its success too embarrassing.

As a result, the productivity of these family allotments is kept within accepted limits and the distribution of their products is strictly controlled by the anti-speculation laws and other regulations. This capitalist form of economy and distribution is allowed to exist in order to save the population from starvation, but it is publicly denied any legitimacy. Rather, it is submitted to numerous prohibitions and regulations in order to fix its productivity at an ideologically acceptable level, thereby preventing peasants from becoming economically independent agents:

> This thick web of prohibitions prevents the market from developing to full strength, prevents production from becoming directly connected with consumer demand. The black market remains under the control of the administrative authority, which dictates harsh conditions of constant exploitation of the peasant on the collective farm, the state farm and private parcel. (Timofeev, 1982: 10)

These mechanisms are very well analysed in Besançon's 'anatomy' of communism. He discusses the ambivalent attitude of the Soviet authorities towards those ever-present forms of capitalist production and distribution coexisting with the planned communist economy. The essence of his 'realism principle' is well summarized in the following excerpts:

> the economy remains socialist . . . when the decision to make a compromise and to introduce some principles contradictory to the spirit of socialism constitutes a necessary price for maintaining power and, consequently, for the possibility of promoting socialism in the future, when the opportunity arises.
>
> The principle that capitalism should be destroyed . . . is, thus, paralleled by another principle which says that enough capitalism should be preserved so the [communist] power will not be threatened by its own material and political base.
>
> (Besançon, 1981: 52, 49; this author's translation from French)

Periodical anti-speculation campaigns are supposed to achieve the same goals as other anti-crime campaigns in communist countries, namely to blame the 'persistent remnants of capitalism' for the failures of communist economic and social policies. Thus, the very devices which are secretly designed to keep this economy going can be publicly held responsible for its unsatisfactory performance. As a result, kolkhozniks are trapped in a situation where they must violate the law if they want to survive and where, in turn, their crimes are vital to the survival of the Soviet economy.

CRIMINAL DREAMS ABOUT TRADE-UNIONS

> Fifty workers have been given prison sentences of up to 30 years and five of them were given death sentences for having tried to organize free trade union in Cuba. Although the death sentences have been commuted to 20 years' hard labour, the possibility of the executions being carried out is not totally excluded. . . . The ICFTU [International Confederation of Free Trade Unions] has since learned that the lawyers who defended the five workers in question have in turn also been arrested, as well as a judge who protested against the sentences. ('Cuba . . .', 1984: 9)

This incident could have happened in any other communist country and, certainly extremely harsh sentences have been repeatedly meted out to organizers of free trade unions in both the Soviet Union and Poland. A challenge to the monopoly of the state trade unions is deemed to be one of the most serious offences, and consequently, anyone, even a lawyer, who attempts to defend such offenders, is considered an enemy of the party (as in the case of a Polish attorney, Mr Sila-Nowicki, for example, who was charged in 1984 with degrading the Polish nation, Poland, and/or its system, an offence which involves a maximum penalty of up to five years' deprivation of liberty; see 'Zarzuty . . .', 1984: 6).

While the Polish Constitution guarantees the right to form associations under section 84(1), the type of association is restricted. Only those associations which do not collide with the socio-political system and/or the legal system of Poland are permitted as stated in section 84(3). Such a condition gives the Polish authorities a very broad margin of discretion and, in practice, legalizes state repression of any activities or organizations which may weaken the monopolistic position of the party. Likewise, the Soviet Constitution states that:

> [i]n accordance with the aims of building communism, citizens of the USSR have the right to associate in public organizations that promote their political activity and initiative and satisfaction of their various interests. ('Constitution . . .', 1977:s.51)

Such a formulation of the right to associate is based on the party's definition of which organizations are 'objectively' in the interest of citizens and which are not.

Both Constitutions also list such rights as freedom of speech, of the press, and of assembly, meetings, street processions and demonstrations. The Soviet Constitution includes additionally a section which explains, that the

> [e]xercise of these political freedoms is ensured by putting public buildings, streets, and squares at the disposal of the working people and their organizations, broad dissemination of information; and by the opportunity to use the press, television, and radio.
>
> ('Constitution . . .', 1977:s.50)

All the existing evidence suggests, however, that any attempt to interpret these rights as universal, granted to all individuals and groups which want to express their views in peaceful ways, is bound to be suppressed and punished. 'Public buildings, streets and the media' are clearly put at the disposal of the supporters of only one party and one ideology. Thus, the numerous causes of discontent among workers are aggreviated by the total absence of channels to express their claims, grievances and challenges to the prevailing solutions. A Polish sociologist, Jacek Kurczewski, commented on this political defficiency in a publication inspired by the rise of Solidarity in 1980:

> In what is called real socialism there are very few ways of manifesting a conflict, and even those which remain become blocked because conflicts are excluded on doctrinal basis. . . . Western democracies have at their disposal a wealth of the various conflict managing institutions, and adoption of that wealth of forms in Polish public life is clearly the need of the moment. . . . At present, the Church laudably undertakes that role. In the future it would be much better, if, regardless of such or other *ad hoc* mediations, that role were played by impersonal law and independent courts. (Kurczewski, 1982:31)

Solidarity constituted such an attempt to create avenues for working people to articulate and defend their interests, preferences and grievances. The analysis presented in Chapter 2 as well as numerous collections of materials, books and monographs published recently by many groups and individuals, provide good insight into the process of the strangulation of this movement (e.g. *La Repression* . . ., 1982; Ruane, 1982; *Survey*, 1982; *Les Droits* . . ., 1983; Jain, 1983; *Committee in Support of Solidarity Reports* (a periodical publication); *Kontakt* (a monthly magazine published in Polish); also many articles in *L'Alternative*).

This process of suppression has involved arrests, interments, trials, long sentences, the use of armoured vehicles and firearms by the police to break strikes and peaceful demonstrations, police brutality, secret killings, torture and blackmail. Less violent methods of terror and harassment of working people associated with Solidarity have involved dismissals (see *Les Droits* . . ., 1983:238–45, 249–56), demotions, transfers to especially unpleasant tasks or distant localities (*Les Droits* . . ., 1983:262–4), evictions from apartments, threats, intimidation, pressure to sign loyalty oaths, restrictions of freedom of movement and communication and compulsory draft to the army. The employment of these measures has been facilitated by the introduction of political commissars and secret agents into the workplace, the militarization of all major industries which has rendered invalid the Polish labour law and has turned employees virtually into slaves deprived of any rights at all, and the imposition of new obligations upon management facilitating their more penetrating and relentless political control of employees.

Yet, the activization of this massive system of repression and terror has not been achieved easily. With the exception of the security forces and some groups within the party and army apparatus, those charged with the enforcement of the military rule seem to lack enthusiasm for the roles with which they have been entrusted. Not only many managers and administrators, but also numerous functionaries of the criminal justice system have attempted to resist the pressures and sabotage the orders to prosecute workers. Soon after the imposition of the state of war, for example, 40 judges were dismissed by the State Council as 'unreliable'. Many others were harassed and subjected to disciplinary penalties for their decisions to acquit Solidarity activists or apply punishments considered to be 'too lenient'. In fact, in many cases these 'lenient' sentences have been adjusted subsequently by the superior courts and those judges displaying such 'dangerous' tendencies have been gradually excluded from political cases ('Oddajmy . . .', 1983:12–13). The exodus of judges from the profession has become so alarming that the authorities have been forced to offer an explanation. Such an explanation was given by the then Minister of Justice, Lech Domeracki, who chose to blame low wages as the sole reason for the judges' decisions to leave. He estimated that approximately three times as many judges left their posts in 1983 than in previous years (Kucharski, 1983:1; 'Sedziowie odchodza . . .', 1983:5). This is not, however, a fully convincing explanation since judges' salaries have been inadequate for years and yet, in the past, considerably fewer judges changed their professional status.

According to labour law, workers who are dismissed from work may lodge appeals to special labour commissions of appeal whose bench consists of one professional judge and two lay members (for more details see Łoś, 1978:801–11), and from 1982–83, these commissions became known for their tendency to reverse decisions concerning political dismissals ('Oddajmy . . .', 1983:13). Yet an enactment by the Supreme Court on 27 February 1982 has limited considerably their role by effectively barring appeals of decisions made by directors of militarized companies (*Les droits* . . ., 1983:239). Furthermore, on 18 May 1982, a special conference was held during which two colonels representing the Ministry of Justice instructed judges involved in labour commissions of appeal to follow political guidelines and threatened them with disciplinary sanctions for any signs of support for workers (*Les Droits* . . ., 1983:243).

The free trade union movement in the Soviet Union became noticeable in the late 1970s, when the Free Trade Union Association was established in January 1978 by a group of unemployed workers (see Chapter 4). Most of the members of the Association were soon imprisoned or committed to psychiatric institutions (Haynes and Semyonova, 1979). The formation of the Association was preceded by the circulation of three 'open letters' on Soviet working conditions and neglect of workers' complaints. The main concern of this group of involved activists focused on dangerous working conditions, embezzlement and corruption, and serious worker–management conflict (Gidwitz, 1982:35–6).

In April 1978, another group announced the formation of the Independent Trade Union of Workers of the USSR. A third attempt was made in October 1978 when the Free Interprofessional Association of Workers was formed. Its leader, Mark Morozov, declared that the group had no political intentions, but aimed at providing legal, moral and material assistance to its members and at establishing a variety of voluntary cooperative associations including a credit union, health care programmes, vacation homes and child centres. It also intended to form a number of 'working groups' to investigate human rights abuses of its members and to publish regular reports. By mid-1979, 4 out of the original 8 members of the Council of Representatives of the Association had been arrested and two other members forced to emigrate. Despite constant harassment, which has made the work of the Association extremely difficult, it has continued to exist and in 1982 counted approximately 300 members in various republics (Gidwitz, 1982:36–7).

Needless to add, the official trade unions do not fulfil any of the functions requested by the workers. As Gidwitz put it:

> [t]he notion of trade unions as 'transmission belts' from the party to the masses dates from Lenin's time. Today trade unions have been turned into a means for the direct subordination of working population. In the USSR, trade unions deal with problems of production, plan fulfillment, labour discipline, and indoctrination. . . . Their defence of workers' interests is marginal at best.
>
> (Gidwitz, 1982:29)

Worker unrest has a long history in the Soviet Union. In a recent review Gidwitz indicates that there has been some shift in the reaction by Soviet authorities to strikes and workers' protests. While in the 1950s and 1960s army troops were normally used to 'restore order' and heavy casualities were practically unavoidable, the 1970s witnessed an increased willingness to listen to workers' grievances and to satisfy, to some extent, their immediate demands. Only afterwards, when the crisis situation is diffused, may some people be quietly arrested or dismissed from work. The most frequent complaints focus on food shortages, unsafe and generally inadequate working conditions, increases in production norms and low wages. In some republics, labour unrest has been accompanied by anti-Russian and anti-Soviet ethnic movements (Gidwitz, 1982:32–5).

One of the most alarming features of the working conditions in the USSR and Poland is the high accident rate which results from poor safety standards and the unreasonable pressure on workers during the end-of-month or end-of-plan 'storming' periods. In his analysis of the situation in the Soviet Union, Eberstadt referred to 'carnage in the factories' and identified accidents as a principal cause of declining life expectancy (Eberstadt, 1981:24). Unfortunately no relevant statistics are ever published. In Poland, on the other hand, while such work accident statistics are published, their reliability is generally questioned. According to the official data, in 1981 there were 200 399 such accidents in the nationalized economy. This figure represented approximately 1.5 per cent of the total number of 13 million employees in the state economy in that year. The number of accidents includes 1203 cases of fatal injuries (*Maly Rocznik* . . ., 1983:53). It is important to note, however, that according to some Polish experts, about 20 to 50 per cent of work-related accidents are normally registered as not connected with work (Sokolowska, 1982:96).

Especially tragic appear to be conditions of work in the Polish coal mines. The imposition of the state of war was accompanied by the increased norms of production, forced overtime work, duty to work on Saturdays and Sundays, total disregard for safety precautions and technological requirements, which have led to a dramatic increase in serious accidents. Thus, according to a report in a miners' paper published clandestinely:

> Between 1 January and 12 December 1981 [Solidarity period] no single miner was killed in the mines. On 13 December the mines were militarized, quitting one's job became punishable by three years'

> imprisonment; such action might also, however, be treated as desertion, punishable by death. . . . Between January and September 1982, in the first nine months of the state of war, 161 miners and members of rescuing teams were killed in the Polish mines.
>
> ('Wegiel . . .', 1983:6–7; this author's translation from Polish)

In the 1980s, some official publications have broken finally the silence concerning the long-hidden issue of health hazards caused by industry. An article in a Warsaw daily, for example, quoted the figure of 1.5 million workers (including 260 000 women) as being exposed to highly dangerous working environments ('Zagrożenie . . .', 1984:2). In addition, there are those who do not work in these plants, but who suffer health damage as a result of the pollution of air, water and soil caused by these industries. In 1980, Polish experts located 27 regions in which the population was exposed to extremely high levels of at least 2 types of toxic agents (Jacyna, 1984:15). Millions of people live, work and are born in these areas. The rates of chronic diseases, birth defects and infant mortality which are generally very high in Poland, are extremely elevated in these dangerous districts.

Thus, any analysis of crimes committed by workers has to include also the degree of their victimization by the crimes of others. It is true that workers steal, pilfer and sabotage the state economy, but it is the nature of the economy, and above all the nature of the economic and political subordination and enslavement that alienate them and motivate their petty acts of greed and vengeance, on the one hand, and most dignified manifestations of solidarity and organized resistance, on the other.

10 Crimes of Women: Offences Against the New Ethics*

THE TRADITIONAL IMAGE OF THE FEMALE OFFENDER

In Poland and the USSR, just as in other countries, men seem to be more involved in crime than women or, at least, they manage to be officially recorded with far greater frequency. While, however, there exists in the West a growing body of criminological literature which explores the significance of gender in crime and the criminal justice system, Soviet and Polish literature offers very limited insight into this phenomenon. Numerous recent western publications present an analysis of cultural and structural differences in gender roles as well as biased practices of male-dominated agencies of criminal justice operating in the social world structured according to male interests (see, for example, Smart, 1977a, b; Hagan *et al.*, 1979; Bertrand, 1979). While this type of approach is virtually absent in the studied countries, these nations do offer an interesting case for students of female criminality especially since women and men in both of them have very similar levels of both education and involvement outside the home. In addition, the criminal justice systems of these countries employ very high numbers of women.

Despite this apparent equalization of male and female status, little is known and published about crimes committed by women and the punishments meted out to them. Similarly, a serious analysis of various aspects of the unique status of this gender group in the social structure is practically absent. Superficial political declarations about full equality and emancipation of women are often substituted for more reliable and realistic research and analysis.

While frequent press reports on individual cases of female involvement in bribery, speculation and theft of public property suggest that women are active in these areas of nonconventional crime, most of the analysis offered by academics focuses on those traditionally female forms of deviancy, such as prostitution, immorality, infanticide and vagrancy. Among the Soviet authors, M. N. Golodniuk displays the most consistent interest in the female offender. One of the studies,

*This chapter incorporates excerpts from Łoś, 1983b.

conducted by Golodniuk in the 1970s, looked at female recidivists serving time in a Soviet labour colony of ordinary regimen. A variety of methods of study were used including surveys, individual interviews with the inmates, studies of case files, interviews with guards and observation of inmates; all of them were employed in the search for the unique criminal personality of female recidivists. The author concluded that female criminality is not determined by biological factors, but rather by 'moral personality', social roles, as well as psychophysiological characteristics including liability of nervous systems, heightened emotionalism, impressionability, and so forth. According to this study, it is the difference in male and female personalities which can explain the differences in rates of criminality between the sexes (Golodniuk, 1975).

The most prevalent crimes for which female recidivists investigated by Golodniuk were convicted included: theft of personal property, hooliganism, theft of socialist property, thefts in connection with vagrancy, refusal to take jobs (parasitism), violations of internal passport regulations and illegal abortions. The participation of women in both crimes against persons and crimes with violence was very low. When committed, such crimes were, as a rule, triggered by difficult personal relationships with victims, who were usually relatives or acquaintances. Approximately half of the total number of women studied were intoxicated at the time of their most recent crimes. In turn, many of the women who drank to excess began drinking as a result of psychological trauma, deaths of loved ones, family troubles, etc. The process of their alcoholic degradation was very fast. In the interviews conducted with the female recidivists, one-third of them cited material hardship as the motive for their mercenary offences.

Overall, the data showed that difficult personal relationships and family disorganization, economic hardship and alcoholism had considerable influence on the criminal involvement of these women. Moreover, it was found that many of them had no faith in themselves and nurtured dreams of finding a strong man who would provide leadership and protection.

The family status of the studied recidivist women was not typical of the general female population, nor that of the first offender population. Instead, they were mature women between 30 and 50 years of age, of which only 23.2 per cent had families (as compared to 55 per cent among first offenders). Moreover, 36.8 per cent of the recidivists, compared to 11.3 per cent of the first offenders, were divorced. Family stability was greatest among those female recidivists who were convicted of stealing state property. Among women convicted for other crimes, the author found much instability, frequent drunken brawls with spouses or live-in companions and repeated incarcerations of their husbands. Half of the women studied by Golodniuk had been working before their arrest, many at unskilled, heavy labour.

The author suggests that to rehabilitate these women it is necessary to provide them with lighter, meaningful jobs, with housing and with moral support. In light of the obtained data, they appear to be destitute women, degraded and stripped of hope by the alcohol and unbearable hardships of life. Women who were, on the one hand, exposed to unusual pressures and pitfalls and, on the other, were somewhat inferior in their abilities to cope and to endure against the odds.

Similar conclusions are drawn in a more recent publication by the same author (Golodniuk, 1980), but far less attention is paid to the alleged criminal personality of female offenders and much more to social and economic conditions. As well, the analysis is more directly focused on offences committed by working women against state property. The author claims that a considerable proportion of women convicted of crimes for gain related to their jobs were engaged in physically heavy, unskilled labour (in industry, warehouses, etc.). Such crimes are also frequently committed by women working in food stores where they have many opportunities to deceive customers. These types of work produce fatigue, irritability and disillusionment with respect to the occupation. While they are physically demanding and involve financial responsibility, they are very low-paid. Golodniuk stresses that the use of equal standards for men and women at jobs requiring considerable physical effort places women in disadvantageous conditions. As well, female responsibility for home-making and child-rearing inhibits their professional careers, excludes them from any forms of skills-upgrading and causes excessive physical and nervous stress, all of which contribute to both work-related and domestic crimes.

This 'double burden' of work and home responsibilities, the official indifference to the needs of working women, the increasing rate of family breakdown, the unworthy behaviour of husbands, the psychological trauma of divorce and the financial difficulties of divorced women left with children, are all factors presented by Golodniuk as being crucial to the incidences of female crime. Given these identified causes of criminality among Soviet women, the main message of this more recent publication with respect to the prevention of such crime emphasises the implementation of a set of measures, socio-economic, political and ideological in nature, aimed at improving the social position of women (Golodniuk, 1980: 41).

A number of studies in Poland (most of them conducted by M. Jasińska; see 1967, 1976 and 1982) inquired into the plight of women involved in prostitution. Despite the non-criminal status of prostitution in Poland, it is by no means a trade free of stigma and criminal status. There exist special morality squads whose main task consists of controlling prostitutes and their criminal connections. In effect, prostitutes are very often arrested on charges of disturbing order and stealing personal property from drunken clients. In recent years, they have also been frequently arrested and convicted by the petty offence boards for failing to have a valid medical certificate. In comparison to the earlier period, however, the actual criminal involvement of contemporary prostitutes appears to be far less serious and widespread.

Two large-scale studies, which involved interviews with prostitutes, their families, policemen, doctors and restaurant and hotel staff, were conducted by Jasińska at the end of the 1950s and at the end of the 1970s. Both provide interesting insights into the changes of the size, structure and demographic composition of the population of young prostitutes. First of all, the author found that the number of women under 25 years of age involved in prostitution has increased considerably during the 20 years between the 2 studies. While, however, street prostitution was more prevalent in the earlier period, the more recent research shows an overwhelming preference for more discreet forms of solicitation in such establishments as restaurants and hotels, where the staff act willingly as intermediaries between the prostitutes and potential clients. Taxi drivers constitute another group heavily involved in such procuring, an offence punishable by up to 10 years' imprisonment. In fact, only about 20 per cent of the interviewed women appeared to be working for pimps. Moreover, in the late 1970s, the proportion of foreigners among patrons of female prostitutes was much higher than in the 1950s, a fact which had clearly beneficial consequences for the incomes of the women in this profession.

Over 60 per cent of the young prostitutes interviewed at the end of the 1970s and at the beginning of the next decade came from 'blue collar' backgrounds. The earlier research, on the other hand, showed a higher percentage of 'underclass' prostitutes and found that 72 per cent of their parents had never completed elementary education. Similar to the earlier study, however, the recent data indicate that the family background of young women involved in prostitution is extremely unstable and inadequate. Over 50 per cent were not raised in a two-parent family as a result of one parent's death, parental divorce or an unknown father. Forty-five per cent were brought up at least partially during their childhood by people other than natural parents. Over 50 per cent lived for some time under the same roof with an alcoholic. In 30 per cent of the cases, mothers or fathers of the prostitutes changed partners very frequently and several fathers or stepfathers maintained sexual relationships with their daughters.

Approximately half of the interviewed women ran away from home during their childhood or adolescent years. Most of them dropped out of school quite early. Approximately 25 per cent of the interviewed women began working as prostitutes between the ages of 16–17, about 40 per cent between 18–19, while the remaining 35 per cent became involved in prostitution when they were at least 20 years old. Practically one-third of the interviewed prostitutes drank heavily, most had long histories of venereal diseases and gynaecological problems. Thirty per cent had children residing with relatives or in orphanages (Jasińska, 1982: 85–8).

In sum, it appears that, just as in other countries, prostitution becomes a viable choice for women coming from problem families, who leave home early to escape abuse or hardship and who do not have any competing professional options due to the lack of qualifications and generally lower legitimate financial opportunities for women. It is, however, striking that no effort is made to open some other avenues for these women, and the only services extended to them are compulsory venereal disease tests and 'rehabilitation' efforts by the police.

Contrary to the claims of the Soviet authorities as well as some western experts (e.g. Mandel, 1975), prostitution is quite common in the USSR as well. There again, economic aspects play an important role:

> What are the real reasons that women become prostitutes in the Soviet Union? Apart from the boredom of daily existence, which is particularly acute in the USSR, it is mostly a question of material incentives, even though Soviet propaganda still asserts that the material conditions that contribute to prostitution have long since disappeared. The government maintains that a subsistence level income is ninety-two rubles, fifty kopecks a month; the average per capita income is about sixty-five rubles a month. Thus a prostitute can take on only a handful of customers a month and still get by.
>
> (Stern, 1980: 195)

As in Poland, prostitution is not a crime in the Soviet Union. Nevertheless, Soviet prostitutes are subject to anti-parasite laws which lead to their frequent arrests and exiles from large cities. For this reason, many of them secure some type of employment for the sake of appearance. (The same situation exists in Hungary, see Volgyes and

Peters, 1978: 38, but not in Poland where parasitism is an offence only when committed by men.) As in Poland overt soliciting is not prevalent in the USSR. While it does exist, especially at railroad or subway stations, it has been largely replaced by the active involvement in procuring by employees of restaurants and hotels, shoeshine boys and, above all, taxi drivers. (Procuring is punishable by five years of hard labour followed by internal exile.) The level of education of Soviet prostitutes is very low, alcoholism rampant and health problems numerous. In the absence of adequate health care services and modern contraceptives, Soviet prostitutes 'often contract and transmit venereal disease, and illegal abortion is the standard method of contraception – either performed by helpful friends or self-administered' (Stern, 1980: 195).

It appears, therefore, that neither Polish nor Soviet authorities have succeeded in their efforts to eradicate prostitution, which they have declared to be just another relic of the capitalist past. The hope that the new conditions as well as the severe penalties for those who exploit prostitutes will liberate women and remove any need on their part to engage in this old trade has clearly not been fulfilled.

THE EMANCIPATION OF WOMEN

The question may be asked whether the Polish and Soviet situations confirm or disprove those theories which predict significant increases of female criminality with the process of 'liberation' of women and their incorporation into the official, organized structure of society. While superficial theories can be easily proved or disproved by superficial generalizations about the facts, such exercises do not contribute much to the understanding of the complexity of social reality. Two articles (Adler, 1977 and Pleńska, 1980) which attempt to answer the question of why the emancipation of women in Poland has not produced significant increases in crime, touch upon some of the important aspects and factors involved, but overlook others. This chapter is another contribution to the discussion started by these authors. It attempts to deal with the problem in question in a phenomenological fashion, by reconstructing some key subjective aspects of objective changes in the societal organization. It does not offer a rigorous empirical analysis, nor does it present a synthesis of criminological studies in this area since none have ever been undertaken.[1] Rather, references to official statistics are provided only as a necessary starting point for the discussion of changes in the extent and structure of female convictions.

There are so many possible interpretations of emancipation that there can be no one clear answer to the question of whether or not Polish and Soviet women are emancipated. The following discussion will focus on the Polish situation, but similarities between Poland and the USSR in this respect are evident. The developments in both countries prove that the emancipation of women communist style is not a smooth and unequivocally beneficial process. A female journalist recently made the following observation in a Polish weekly:

> It is truly sad to look at them in the streets: gray and tired, burdened with bags, not a trace of glamour and coquetry. Some move slowly, apathetically, others run breathless, always afraid to be late. . . . Those elegant have disappeared, and remained those gray, standing for ever in lines, disappointed, resigned, disillusioned, fully aware that they have lost their race for modernity. Today they do not even understand any more why their predecessors so badly wanted to be equal to men.
> (Starczak-Kozlowska, 1982: 4; this author's translation from Polish)

This journalist is skeptical about the gains Polish women derive from their glorified emancipation:

> Once upon a time, spouses' functions were clearly defined, reinforced by tradition: man was the provider, she occupied herself with homemaking. Now she earns money side by side with him and continues to take care of the home as an unpaid housekeeper. Representative surveys of the Polish population show that in 83 percent of married couples, women do the shopping and cook dinners . . . in 78 percent women wash the dishes and in 71 percent they wax the floor.
> (Starczak-Kozlowska, 1982: 4; this author's translation from Polish)

And yet, outside the home, women's involvement in work is not much less than that of the men and they account for 46 per cent of the workforce; 75–80 per cent of women between 25 and 40 years of age who have one child hold regular jobs outside the home as do 58 per cent of those with four children (Pleńska, 1980: 465). In the Soviet Union, the proportion of women in the total labour force equalled 51 per cent in 1978 (Barry and Barner-Barry, 1982: 199). It should be noted, however, that this equalization in the level of employment has not been achieved by way of a genuine change in the societal gender structure. Rather, the needs of the Stalinist-style industrialization called for the full mobilization of all able-bodied members of the society, independent of their wishes and aspirations.

There can be no doubt that life is extremely difficult for working mothers in these countries. They work till the last days of pregnancy. In their rented rooms, tiny apartments or crowded accommodations shared with their relatives, young parents do not have the benefit of disposable diapers, instant baby formulas and convenient baby clothes, utensils, and appliances, which make western mothers' lives so much easier. They might purchase some of these articles in hard currency stores, provided they have the currency, or on the black market if they are wealthy enough. After spending their paid maternity leave at home, mothers face the choice of going back to work or staying at home to look after their children. Since, however, their husbands' salaries will not be enough to support three people, the choice quickly becomes the agonizing question of what to do with the baby while they return to work. They may consider a state nursery, but this option is considered by medical experts, psychologists and mothers themselves to be the cruellest of choices. Nursery children are constantly sick and their development is significantly retarded because of physical infections and a lack of human interaction (nurseries are literally baby storages, with one nurse caring for 15 to 25 children). In 1980, only 8.5 per cent of all Polish children under three years of age were placed in nurseries, a figure which reflects the poor quality of a very limited number of services (Mankiewicz, 1981b: 4–5).

Desperate mothers can try to force their parents, grandparents or any other retired relatives to care for their babies and this is, in fact, the most frequent solution. If they have relatively well paid jobs, they may try instead to hire a 'woman'. The costs often outweigh their worth, however; they are often unreliable and tend to disappear after a few days, weeks or months taking with them whatever valuable objects they can steal. In essence, since 'servants' are considered a capitalistic luxury, domestic and baby-sitting services are neither organized nor subject to any controls.

Working mothers, who somehow manage to solve the problem of baby-care during their working hours still have to stand in lines every day in order to buy family groceries after work (the lack of a car, freezer or large refrigerator, necessitates this daily shopping). They then have to cook, clean, wash (automatic washers are rare, drying machines are practically non-existent, and laundrettes unknown), and mend socks, stockings and baby clothes (items very rarely available in stores). These are but a few activities typically performed by women, and research shows that Polish mothers of two spend seven hours every day working at home in addition to the eight hours spent at work. This estimate, it must be noted, does not include time spent shopping (Starczak-Kozlowska, 1982: 4).

The situation among Soviet women is not different. A Soviet expert determined that a husband's work week (including housework) is about 50 hours, while that of the working wife is 80 hours (see Barry and Barner-Barry, 1982: 199). Lining up for food and other necessities is equally or even more prevalent in the Soviet Union. A recent article in the weekly *Nedelya* stated that women spent on average 5.8 hours a week in lines and only 4.5 hours with their children. Moreover, the goods they buy after having waited so long are often spoiled or faulty ('Soviet Women . . .', 1983).

After the child's third birthday, he or she theoretically becomes eligible for placement in a child centre. According to an article in a Polish women's magazine, however, many such applications are not even considered in many centres due to chronic overcrowding and the inadequate number of facilities[2] (Mankiewicz, 1981a: 3). The chances for older children are not much better. Only six-year olds have a more or less assured place in child centres in order to prepare them for school. According to the official statistics, the total number of three-to six-year-old children attending child centres in 1979 amounted to approximately 34 per cent of all children in this age group (*Rocznik* . . ., 1980: 415). This suggests, in turn, that the percentage of those children five-years-old and younger, whose parents are lucky enough to secure a place in a child centre, must be very low (see Sidorczuk, 1981: 3). While the fees for these facilities depend upon the family's economic situation, they do constitute a very significant burden on the budgets of young families. In addition to the regular fees, families often have to pay handsome bribes in order to secure admission for their children while remembering gifts for teachers' birthdays and other occasions. Those parents whose applications are rejected by the state institutions often turn to privately run child centre's where they must be prepared to pay one parent's full salary for their child's pre-school education. Despite the cost, there are advantages to privately run child centres among which is the relatively small size of the group under the care of one teacher which is significantly lower than the usual 35 or more in the state centres.

These few examples of the problems which the majority of women experience daily are cited in order to expose this side of women's life which appears to be largely unaffected, or rather negatively affected, by their social emancipation which is partial and one-sided. Due to the needs of the rapidly expanding economy in the post-war period, Polish women have been effectively forced to handle two full-time jobs in place of the one which they traditionally held. Their inclusion into the workforce was also dictated by the desire of the new communist authorities to subject them, as society's major socialization agents, to comprehensive ideological indoctrination which, in turn, can be more easily conducted at the workplaces than in the isolated world of their private homes.

There does exist, however, another side to the social liberation of women which cannot be portrayed in such clear-cut terms. For example, many women do enjoy their jobs and take full advantage of the occupational opportunities open to them. Moreover, Polish women are equally or even better educated than men, which shows how far the society has accepted the idea of equal educational opportunities for both sexes. However, there remains a relatively strong division between male and female occupations. Not many boys are found in vocational schools for hairdressers, salesclerks, secretaries, nurses, and so forth. Similarly, very few girls attend schools for mechanics and technicians. At the university level, languages, pedagogical and librarian as well as medical studies (the latter of which lasts many years and leads to relatively low paying jobs) are totally dominated by women. Men continue to be preponderant in studies such as engineering which lead to the best paid jobs. Women tend to be employed in education (they constituted 76 per cent of those employed in this field in 1981), in health care and social services (81 per cent of all employees and 59 per cent of all medical doctors and dentists), administration and the criminal justice system (61 per cent), and in retail trade (70 per cent). They are, on the other hand, underrepresented in industry (37 per cent), constructions (19 per cent), agriculture (27 per cent), and transport (26 per cent) (*Maly Rocznik* . . ., 1983: 45). Similarly, a small proportion of Soviet women 'work in construction and transportation, whereas retail trade, banking and insurance, and the health professions are overwhelmingly populated by women' (Barry and Barner-Barry, 1982: 199).

Despite their higher levels of education, the official 1984 data indicate that Polish women earn about 73 per cent of the salaries earned by men (Leśnicka, 1984: 3; see also Coser, 1980). They also tend to occupy rank and file, dead-end positions, and are very rarely promoted to any managerial posts. Moreover, they are virtually absent from the executive bodies of the Communist Party and in the government and are grossly underrepresented in the Diet, where they constitute 23 per cent of all deputies. (The proportion of women among deputies has ranged from between 4 per cent to 23 per cent between 1952 and the early 1980s; *Maly Rocznik* . . ., 1983: 16).

An article published in a national daily newspaper during the relatively liberal period of relaxed censorship in 1981, summarizes bitterly the range of advantages brought to women by their occupational 'liberation':

> The only right which women have won during the long years of struggle for liberation is the right to work hard. When the country needed to mobilize the labour force, they urged women to raise their qualifications, they excited their aspirations, they tempted women with the vision of promotion from a worker to director. Now, when they think about drastic employment reductions, especially in administration. . . . they persuade women that their real calling is rearing children, creating a cosy home environment for men. . . . There are no women in the government, in the party apparatus, in the teams of experts, at the negotiation tables, even where decisions are made about meat rationing or concering the definition of the social subsistence level.
>
> (Jakubowska, 1981: 8; this author's translation from Polish)

These sentiments are echoed on many pages[3] of the Polish women's magazine, *Kobieta i Zycie* (Woman and Life). For example, one journalist who strongly stresses her party affiliation, claims that:

> . . . while giving women education and encouraging them to engage in ambitious, creative work, we have bashfully concealed the fact that these expectations are not accompanied by conditions which would allow them to realize those aspirations. . . . Periods of development meant that women were encouraged to get involved in professional and public life. Economic stagnation means that women are praised as priestesses of the family nest.
>
> (Sidorczuk, 1981: 15; this author's translation from Polish)

Although professionally 'liberated', Soviet women are also greatly underrepresented in management and supervisory positions. As well, their participation in the government and the party is minimal. While, in recent years, they have made up approximately 30 per cent of all deputies to the Supreme Soviet (a 'rubber stamp' body without real power), their participation in other political bodies has been much less pronounced. For example, in 1981, there were 17 female members (or 3.6 per cent) among 470 members of the Central Committee of the Communist Party, and nine of them were only candidate members (Barry and Barner-Barry, 1982: 136). There are currently no women in the Politburo, the body in which the real power is concentrated. Indeed, in all Soviet history, there has been only one female member in the Politburo. (In Poland, the first woman was introduced to the Politburo in 1981.) There are no women in the 109-member USSR Council of Ministers (Barry and Barner-Barry, 1982: 90).

While women have accepted the importance of their work as an indicator of their status, they are fully aware that they are simultaneously evaluated in terms of the quality of their performance as mothers and home-makers. This, of course, means that they are constantly subjected to the stressful consequences of this acute role conflict, split identity and troubled conscience, regardless of their individual style of adaptation to these opposing pressures. This also means that they are still under the influence of traditional cultural patterns of expectations and gender norms, which promote different moral standards and virtues for men and women. In essence, their paramount responsibility for the upbringing and moral education of their children strengthens their ties with the Church and traditional community values which are generally perceived as being threatened by the opportunistic and hypocritical political culture imposed on children through the schools and the mass media.

By introducing their children to the national cultural tradition, women hope to strengthen their integrity and moral convictions in the current world of new alien values and massive attempts to construct a 'new socialist man'. Historically, in Poland, this tradition has included a model of the Polish Mother who sacrifies herself to the family, who cares for children, educates them in patriotic values, and remains faithful to her husband when he goes to endless wars to defend the homeland against its enemies. She is infinitely brave, patient, dutiful and virtuous, a person in her own right, but choosing inevitably to live for others. A delicate creature, she can, however, be both a tender mother and a resourceful provider for her children bereaved by their hero father fallen on the battlefield. The combination of these two roles and the attempt to perfect their performance in both is not new for Polish women for history has forced them again and again to fill the places left empty by their men called through their patriotic duty into the services of the fatherland.

The same is true for Soviet women, as they too, during many wars and recently during the years of communist economic mobilization, have been forced to carry the double burden of these two demanding and often conflicting tasks, the burden of a 'double working day' as they often call it. It must be noted, however, that any spontaneous feminist organizations or attempts to create a women's liberation movement are of course banned, just as are any other types of grass-roots organizations. A women's group, organized in the Soviet Union in the late 1970s, which even began publishing a *samizdat* feminist journal entitled *Women in the USSR*, was soon brutally suppressed and most of its leaders forced into exile abroad.

THE EMANCIPATION OF WOMEN AND CRIME

It has been noted by Adler (1977) and Pleńska (1980) that the ratio of female to male crime rates increased somewhat in the post-World War II period in Poland, when women were integrated en masse into the socio-economic mainstream, but decreased after approximately one decade. Alder believes that normative controls over women, exercised by the Church and state, have continued to operate and that the emancipation of women transcended them only temporarily. In other words, a vocational upgrading has not, in fact been followed by a psychological and moral liberation of women.

Pleńska seems to share these views. She goes beyond them to claim that the upswing in the number of convictions of women in the period of intensive industrialization after World War II was due to the increase in opportunities to commit crimes against state property. According to the statistics, economic offences did indeed account, to a great extent, for the increase in female criminality in Poland. Pleńska attributes the subsequent diminution in female conviction rates in part to the legislative changes of 1953, which decriminalized minor crimes against state property. She also notes that, while the penal law in Poland has been traditionally oriented towards controlling male deviance, prostitution and other 'moral delinquences' have not been criminalized, and thus increases in these types of deviance may go unnoticed.

In the 1940s and the 1950s, the increase in recorded female criminality relative to that of males cannot be explained simply in terms of female emancipation. Literally, emancipation implies a process in itself, a struggle for fuller participation and liberation. The rapid increase of women's employment and involvement in traditionally male roles in Poland, however, was necessitated by various external, objective factors. Among the circumstances which are often overlooked is the much higher proportion of men relative to women among the 6 million Poles killed during the war. As well, greater numbers of men than women were out of the country at the end of the war and the subsequent communist takeover in Poland, because of their involvement with the

Polish armed forces in the struggle against the German army in other parts of Europe. While large numbers of these war veterans settled in the West, thousands of those who returned or who were members of the Polish Home Army were subjected to vigorous persecution and often long years of imprisonment.

The magnitude of male casualities of the war and post-war periods explains, to some extent, the necessity for the maximum involvement of women in the reordering of the country and its economy. As well, it highlights the purely demographic aspects of the higher proportion of women found in official crime statistics. Indeed, it may well be, that if the numerical changes in the proportions of both sexes in the total population were properly accounted for, the significance of the shift in the conviction ratio would actually disappear. Similarly, the unusually high ratio of female to male convictions (2:1) in 1946 in the Soviet Union could be explained by the vast reduction in the male population (Zeldes, 1981: 77).

In any event, it must be noted that increased occupational activisation of women was but one process among many interrelated, traumatic social and economic transformations experienced by Poland after World War II. Intensive industrialization and collectivization of agriculture patterned on the Stalinist model, meant a total subordination of individual needs and values to the requirements of the economy and ideology.

The massive population exodus out of the countryside and into the cities and new industrial centres led to the destruction of community ties and traditional controls. Millions of young men and women left their villages to look for better lives and new economic opportunities.[4] While most of the unskilled male immigrants were finding work in the construction of new industrial plants, many women, unable to find jobs within the underdeveloped services and unwilling to perform heavy construction tasks, eventually turned to prostitution. In this way, they served the needs of large communities of men isolated both from their rural families and mores and from the urban culture and opportunities.

The post-war change of the Polish borders necessitated yet another significant shift of large numbers of the population, mainly from the eastern parts of Poland, taken over by the Soviet Union, to the newly recovered western territories. These new settlers, completely uprooted and culturally alienated, were faced with the harsh realities of a land devastated by the withdrawing German army, void of any social infrastructure and torn apart by hostilities between various ethnic and cultural groups dumped together by the cruel forces of history.[5] For many, the turmoil of their forced exodus was too stressful and they became typical displaced, transient people, never able to settle and develop roots in the new land. As the Polish literature on the subject well documents, all indicators of social disorganization, such as alcoholism, psychiatric hospitalizations, crime, juvenile delinquency and family breakdowns, reached record proportions in these regions (see, e.g. Maroszek, 1963, 1975; Kobus, 1975 and Kryczka, 1978). Statistically speaking, the drastic increase in crime in this part of Poland had a significant impact on the national crime rates and delinquency during that period. It probably also affected considerably the general picture of female delinquency especially as usual controls and traditional values lost importance under the conditions of cultural conflict and anomie.

In sum, it would seem rather inappropriate to link any of the temporary post-war increases in the proportions of female criminality, be they real or spurious, to the women's social emancipation without considering the very complex circumstances and social transformations of that tumultuous period of Polish history. A similar conclusion applies to the post-revolutionary and post Second World War periods in the Soviet Union.

STATISTICAL DATA ON FEMALE CONVICTIONS

While some general statistical information on convictions of women in Poland is periodically published, this is not the case in the Soviet Union. What follows is a detailed analysis of the nature and dynamics of female convictions in Poland, supplemented whenever possible by Soviet data.

According to the official Polish statistics, in 1981 there were 13 000 adult female convictions compared to 116 000 male convictions, a ratio of 1:9. This ratio did not vary significantly during the last decade, and was approximately 1:8 in 1980. It was, however, relatively higher in the 1960s when it ranged from 1:5 to 1:8, and it exhibited its highest level in the 1950s when it ranged from 1:3 to 1:4 (*Maly Rocznik* . . ., 1983: 288 and Łoś, 1983b: 49). Soviet data for the 1960s indicate that the ratio of male to female convictions fluctuated between 1:4.5 to 1:7, and was not much different in the 1920s when it ranged from 1:6 to 1:7 (Zeldes, 1981: 77–78).

In 1979, 11.2 per cent (17 406 cases) of all adult convictions in Poland involved women. The types of offences common among men and women were quite different as illustrated in Table 10.1 (A and B). While female

Table 10.1(A) Valid convictions by the courts in 1979 in Poland (men and women)

Type of offence	*Total*		*Men*		*Women*		*Ratio men to women*
	no.	*%*	*no.*	*%*	*no.*	*%*	
Against state property	43 270	27.8	38 688	27.9	4 582	26.3	8.4:1
Economic offences	5 811	3.7	2 245	1.6	3 566	20.5	1:1.6
Fiscal offences	3 144	2.0	2 238	1.6	906	5.2	2.5:1
(Against state property, economic and fiscal offences together)	(52 225)	(33.5)	(43 171)	(31.2)	(9 054)	(52.0)	(4.8:1)
Against private property	39 231	25.2	35 690	25.8	3 541	20.3	10:1
Against life and health (including rape)	15 426	9.9	14 418	10.4	1 008	5.8	14.3:1
Against family and guardianship (non-payment of alimonies, bigamy, child abduction and abuse, etc.)	20 641	13.2	20 065	14.5	576	3.3	34.8:1
Against public safety and the safety of land, water and air traffic	9 046	5.8	8 780	6.3	266	1.6	33:1
Against state institutions and functionaries (including the police)	6 025	3.9	5 325	3.8	700	4.0	7.6:1
Against honour and personal inviolability (false allegations, insults, etc.)	3 701	2.4	2 899	2.1	802	4.6	3.6:1
Against criminal justice system and against documents	5 111	3.3	4 383	3.2	728	4.2	6:1
Against public order	1 161	0.7	919	0.7	242	1.4	3.8:1
Other	3 309	2.1	2 820	2.1	489	2.8	5.8:1
TOTAL	155 876	100.0	138 470	100.0	17 406	100.1	8:1

Source: This table has been constructed on the basis of tables 16(772) and 19(776) in *Rocznik* [illegible] 1980: 483 and 484

Table 10.1(B) Valid convictions by the courts in 1979 in Poland (men and women)

Type of offence	*Men* no.	*Men* %	*Women* no.	*Women* %	*Total* no.	*Total* %
Against state property	38 688	89.4	4 582	10.6	43 270	100.0
Economic offences	2 245	38.6	3 566	61.4	5 811	100.0
Fiscal offences	2 238	71.2	906	28.8	3 144	100.0
(Against state property, economic and fiscal offences together)	(43 171)	(82.7)	(9 054)	(17.7)	(52 225)	(100.0)
Against private property	35 690	91.0	3 541	9.0	39 231	100.0
Against life and health (including rape)	14 418	93.5	1 008	6.5	15 426	100.0
(Homicide)	(273)	(86.7)	(42)	(13.3)	(315)	(100.0)
Against family and guardianship (non-payment of alimonies, bigamy, child abduction and abuse, etc.)	20 065	97.2	576	2.8	20 641	100.0
Against public safety and the safety of land, water and air traffic	8 780	97.1	266	2.9	9 046	100.0
Against state institutions and functionaries (including the police)	5 325	88.4	700	11.6	6 025	100.0
Against honour and personal inviolability (false allegations, insults, etc.)	2 899	78.3	802	21.7	3 701	100.0
Against criminal justice system and against documents	4 383	85.2	728	14.2	5 111	100.0
Against public order	919	79.2	242	20.8	1 161	100.0
Other	2 820	85.2	489	14.8	3 309	100.0
TOTAL	138 470	88.2	17 406	11.2	155 876	100.0

Source: This table has been constructed on the basis of tables 16 (773) and 19 (776) in *Roczhik* . . . , 1980: 483–4.

convictions accounted for 6.5 per cent of all convictions for crimes against life and health (13.3 per cent of convictions for homicide), 2.9 per cent of all convictions for crimes against public safety and the safety of land, water and air traffic and 2.8 per cent of convictions for offences against family and guardianship, the female share of convictions for economic crimes was a staggering 61.4 per cent, for fiscal offences 28.8 per cent and for offences against public order 20.8 per cent.

In order to understand the legal and social meanings of these data, the specific types of offences in which women seem to be relatively over-represented must be examined. For example, despite the rather low overall representation of women in convictions for crimes against public property (10.6 per cent), their share in crimes involving simple usurpation of state property, usurpation of property of great value and property for which one is responsible, as well as usurpation of property in collaboration with other persons, is relatively higher (13.4 per cent). It appears that it is crimes against state property which involve the use of force or violence for which women are particularly rarely convicted; they represent only 2 per cent of all convictions of this type.[6]

As indicated earlier, women accounted for 61.4 per cent of convictions for economic crimes. Convictions for these crimes constituted 20.5 per cent of all female convictions, but only 1.6 per cent of male convictions. Moreover, the share of economic crimes, fiscal offences and crimes against state property was a full 52 per cent of all female convictions as compared to 31.2 per cent of all male convictions. These data indicate clearly that convicted women are much more likely than men to be sentenced for offences related to the communist economic order, while men tend to be more frequently convicted for more traditional crimes involving violence, neglect of family and guardianship responsibilities and violation of private property. This tendency seems to be consistent with Soviet data. For instance, the Soviet press quotes many more examples of women convicted for speculation, bribery and economic crimes than for more conventional types of crime (e.g. Cherepanov, 1980: 6; Kurasov, 1980: 6; Kapelyushny, 1983b:2; Troyan, 1983b: 6; Kazikhanov, 1983: 6; Inoveli, 1983: 4). According to Zeldes:

> in 1923, the proportion of women among those convicted for embezzlement stood at 14 percent. By 1940, it had increased to 15 percent, in 1962 it grew to 28 percent, and by 1967 it reached 36 percent. . . . For speculation and black-marketeering the percentage is almost 60 percent, and, for fraud and deception of consumers by

> sales personnel, it is greater than 70 percent. . . . Of all crimes committed by women, the one most frequently committed is that of theft of personal property (some 40 percent). Next comes theft or embezzlement of state and/or socialist property, approximately 18 percent, fraud and deception of consumers by sales personnel, 12 percent; speculating and black-marketeering, about 10 percent; vandalism and disorderly behaviour, 6 percent; murder, 4 percent; robbery, 3 percent; and others, 7 percent. It is expedient for comparison to look at the structure of male crimes. It is thus characterized: hooliganism, 38 percent; embezzlement, 27 percent; theft, robbery, and armed assault, 18 percent; crimes against persons, 10 percent; and others, 7 percent.
> (Zeldes, 1981: 78–80; see also Juviler, 1976: 151)

In Poland, 68 per cent of female convictions for economic crimes fell into the category of speculation: the accumulation of goods with the intent of resale at a profit, an offence punished by deprivation of liberty for up to 3 years. A full 60 per cent of those convicted for petty speculation in 1979 were women. To understand the nature of this kind of crime, it must be remembered that, in Poland as in the Soviet Union, there are chronic shortages of foodstuffs and consumer products. The prosperity of black markets and other forms of illegal redistribution of goods is thus an inevitable consequence of a centralized and rigidly planned state economy (see Chapter 8). As the veteran British journalist Stewart Steven undicates in his excellent book, *The Poles*:

> the black market is one of the few areas of the Polish economy which operates efficiently, which is showing record profits, and where there is genuine growth. (Steven, 1982: 50)

Another general type of economic crime for which women are often brought to court is that of causing a shortage in the state economy. According to s. 218 of the Criminal Code, 'whoever, failing to perform a duty or exceeding his authority in the field of supervision over social property, its protection or its management, creates, even unintentionally, a possibility of the occurrence of a shortage, if a significant shortage in the property ensues shall be subject to the penalty of deprivation of liberty for from six months to five years' (*The Penal Code . . .*, 1973). The percentage of women among those found guilty of these kinds of crimes totalled 66 per cent. Many of the women convicted for the crime of causing a shortage in the state economy had been employed as managers of state stores or catering establishments. Those familiar with the organization of the Polish or Soviet economy know that many disturbances and losses in production output are caused by faulty central planning and a lack of synchronization in the functioning of various economic units as well as by the existence of an inadequate system of economic incentives and criteria for promotion (see, for example, Besançon, 1981). Such aspects of the organization of the economy cannot, however, be criminalized. Blaming low-level managers or functionaries for such occurrences is part of the routine political process which promotes scapegoating and ritualistic purifi-. cations of the system.

Another previously mentioned category of crime for which women are likely to be prosecuted is that of fiscal offences. Among these, trading in foreign currency is by far the most frequently penalized. In 1979, women accounted for almost 29 per cent of these convictions. It should be noted that 'hard' currency has a special, almost magic, power within communist countries, especially since citizens are not officially allowed to purchase western currencies despite the fact that many consumers' goods (foodstuffs, cosmetics, cloth, cars, coal, building materials, apartments, etc.) which are in short supply on the open market, are readily available in 'hard currency stores' operated by the state. What has resulted, therefore, is the existence of a developed double currency system. While the state is desperate for foreign currency in order to import goods and to service foreign debts, the citizens are as desperate to obtain needed goods. As a result, the whole complex world of illegal middlemen and middlewomen (currency speculators and blackmarketeers) has emerged to service these unsatisfied needs and to facilitate the desired circulation of money. Hard currency is provided by foreign tourists, smugglers, corrupt foreign trade officials, and various other illegal deals and exchanges. Much of it ends up in the state's possession through the network of special stores, a fact which suggests that the enforcement of the law in this area may be somewhat selective and manipulative. It is widely suspected that more successful currency dealers operate with the blessing of the authorities. It is believed that they buy their immunity by 'paying off' special commissions from their spoils.

Yet another type of crime overrepresented by women is the illegal sale of alcohol, convictions for which, according to 1977 statistics, involved women in 58.7 per cent of all cases (see Łoś, 1983b: 52). Alcoholism is among the most acute social problems in Poland and the demand for alcohol is always great. This demand is easily satisfied during the day, when many grocery stores offer a large selection of vodka, beer and inexpensive wine[7] despite shortages of almost all other edible products. The purchase of spirits may be, however, more difficult at night, on Saturdays, or in cases of already intoxicated or juvenile customers since the state prohibits the sale of alcohol in all these instances. Hence, there is high enough demand for alcohol to support large-scale networks of underground dealers whose supplies come in part from illegal moonshining (which was far less prominent in 1977 than in the 1980s), in part from ordinary stores, and partially from hard currency stores where alcohol prices are relatively competitive despite the need to purchase currency on the black market. Needless to say, the state economy profits from these alcohol purchases made by traffickers in hard currency stores since they inevitably channel large amounts of black market foreign money into the state's purse. In fact, there is a clear correlation between the state's need for foreign currency and the size of its alcohol supplies to those stores which do not accept Polish money. During the early 1970s, the period of economic expansion and modernization of Polish industry which relied heavily on western imports, these sales increased by more than 24 times from 217 litres of pure alcohol in 1970 to 5278 litres in 1976. In this same period, the production of vodka rose 72.4 per cent. The increase in the rate of alcohol consumption during those six years was greater than that of any other country in Europe or North America. The number of people arrested for disorderly behaviour while intoxicated almost doubled (Wald *et al.*, 1981).

The above data indicate quite clearly that the attitude of law enforcement with respect to illegal dealing in alcohol is rather ambivalent. It is interesting to note that moonshining, on the other hand, is clearly contrary to the interest of the state since it interferes with the state's formal monopoly over the production of alcohol. It is suspected, therefore, that operators who deal in illegally distilled spirits are more diligently prosecuted than those who function as illicit middlemen within the official market-place.

This statistical picture of female convictions in both Poland and the USSR indicates that the proportion of these convictions in the global number of adult convictions is presently relatively low and especially with respect to crimes against life and health, liberty, family and private property. The following analysis will consider possible interpretations and explanations for the obvious discrepancy in officially recorded female delinquency rates in the more traditional areas of crime and for the considerably higher proportion of female convictions for those crimes related more directly to the specific features of the organization of the communist economy.

It follows logically from the earlier argument regarding the social position of women and the nature of their emancipation that they continue to be subjected to traditional controls to a much greater extent than men. The role of mother imposes upon them an exceedingly difficult task of the preservation and intergenerational transmission of the threatened values of the national cultural tradition and Christian morality. The informal infrastructure of Polish society which secures the survival of these traditions depends to a great extent upon the preservation of the traditional model of the Polish Mother. Moreover, the historical experience of Polish women who so often, in the past, successfully combined their maternal as well as external functions to carry Poland through long periods of wars, divisions, and occupations, seems to elevate and facilitate their present efforts. While these require an almost heroic attitude and perseverance, they also bring some balance to their lives; failures in one area may be compensated by successes in another, and alternative rewards derived from each activity can give them the strength needed to continue their impossible task.

The importance of the men's status, on the other hand, seems to decrease as the employment of women makes less significant their role as economic providers for the family, and their involvement in the upbringing of children still carries a stigma of femininity, a threat to their masculine egos in many social strata. In fact, while the female feeling of both economic and moral responsibility for the family grows, the male sense of responsibility and indispensability seems to dwindle. The lack of opportunities for grass roots, social and political involvement (with the exception of the period of the Solidarity movement) and the high levels of political and economic alienation in a country ruled by one party in a fully centralized manner, adds to the insecurity and relative futility of their social position. Extremely high rates of alcoholism, relatively high levels of violent crime, alarming rates of crimes against family and youth which involve child and wife battering and non-payment of alimonies, serve to reinforce the notion that the male sense of responsibility, social importance and psychological security is indeed markedly weakened.

Suicide rates, as well, seem to provide an additional indication of the remarkable level of female perseverance, selflessness and responsibility for the well-being of others which contrasts to the male feelings of relative marginality and loss of status. While male suicide rates are systematically higher in practically all countries, the disproportion between male and female suicide rates is exceptionally high in Poland, where men commit suicide five times more than women.[8] In most of the countries which publish suicide statistics, this ratio oscillates within the range of 1:2 to 1:3. Maria Jarosz, a Polish researcher of the sociological aspects of suicide, argues that the low suicide rate among Polish women is related to the relatively high birth rate in Poland[9] and, therefore, the very high involvement of women in child-rearing (Jarosz, 1980: 90). When this explanation is considered in conjunction with the cultural factors discussed above, it becomes more significant.

Interestingly, male suicide rates dropped significantly in 1980, the year full of political hopes, social solidarity and involvement. While the suicide rate in Poland rose systematically from 5 to 13 suicides per 100 000 deaths in the years from 1951 to 1979, in 1980 it dropped considerably for the first time, and this decline was most marked among industrial workers (9 suicides per 100 000 deaths of blue-collar workers in 1978 compared to 5 in 1980 – see Jarosz, 1982: 4). This clearly corroborates the earlier suggestion that men feel alienated and excluded from the political structure in contemporary Poland, and only its democratization could bring about meaningful changes in their status and self-esteem. Only then, perhaps, could there be a real chance that, through a strengthening of their self-esteem, their participation in family responsibilities would increase.

An understanding of these culturally conditioned status differences of Polish women and men helps to explain and interpret the lack of increase of female involvement in conventional criminality compared with the rates of this type of crime among men. There is no research, however, which helps to evaluate the accuracy of the official statistics in respect to this. While there is no reason to assume that the Polish police are less paternalistic towards women than their counterparts in western countries, it is impossible to conclude whether such attitude leads to any systematic bias in the law enforcement. Given the very high percentage of female judges and lay-assessors, these influences may be at least partially counter-balanced in the courts.

These arguments do not explain, however, the relatively high female conviction rates for nonconventional economic and fiscal offences. According to 1979 court statistics, only about 6 per cent of all convicted men, but approximately 26 per cent of the convicted women were found guilty of such offences (as noted in Table 10.1A). While it is possible that there does exist a systematic anti-female bias within law enforcement towards this type of crime, there are also some plausible explanations as to why these differences may, at least to some extent, reflect certain real social and cultural processes.

Radical transformations in economic organization and property relations in Poland and the USSR, with the accompaning criminalization of many new areas of economy-related activities, have not been paralleled by corresponding changes in social consciousness and these societies' informal normative culture. The economic inefficiency and corrupt political culture as well as the overtly aethist ideology of the new order have prevented a natural fusion of old and new values. It seems quite probable that, while women continue to obey the traditional mores and norms which apply to more conventional crimes, they may not feel so restrained in new areas where no authoritative guidance is provided by tradition. Moreover, these new areas are detached from the home environment and do not seem to have any immediate relevance to women's performance in their cultural role as mother. This role is regulated by the coherent and familiar morality of face-to-face relationships aimed at the protection of human life and health, family, and private property. This disjunction between the new and old morality seem to contribute to the relative lack of respect for the state property and economy among these women who carry the double burden of family and economic responsibilities.

Both economic crimes and crimes against state property are extremely widespread throughout Poland as they are in all other communist countries. Most of them are never prosecuted, either because of their uncontrollable, epidemic proportions or the perpetrator's political importance, and therefore, impunity. As indicated earlier, law enforcement in the area of economic crimes is very selective and manipulative. As well, it is subjected to much more political interference, and especially by the local party élites, than law enforcement in the area of conventional criminality.

The actual significance of the court statistics concerning economic crimes is extremely difficult to interpret. What is puzzling, for example, is the very high share of female convictions (56.9 per cent in 1977) among those found guilty of improper performance of one's functions in a unit of the state economy which considerably damages that economy. Women have also relatively high conviction rates for the illegal use of state property which they were expected to manage (32.3 per cent in 1977) and for the usurpation of state property of considerable value (20.2 per cent; see Łoś, 1983b: 60). It is apparent that people who occupy higher, managerial positions have a greater number of opportunities to cause more damage to the economy than the rank and file employees. Since, however, women are only rarely appointed to these higher positions, it seems plausible that they are more vulnerable to prosecution than more powerful male managers. Similarly, in the case of crimes committed in collusion with others, the law does not allow for any differentiation in criminal responsibility by extent of participation in conspiracy. Thus, marginal participants tend to be selected for prosecution and forced to assume full responsibility for the crimes committed by rings which often include relatively high officials (see Podemski, 1981b). Since women often work as cashiers or accountants, they are more likely to be aware of and therefore included in operations of such criminal rings, but their actual role may be relatively limited. Nevertheless, they are quite obvious targets of both suspicion and politically convenient prosecution, which generally excludes the really influential and powerful participants. This is not to say, however, that women are not able to play any significant role in such criminal gangs, but that, statistically speaking, they are rarely in a position to derive really high profits from their involvement in economic crimes.

In the case of petty speculation, which is, according to the official data, an especially feminized offence (women accounted for 60.6 per cent of convictions in 1979), it must be noted that there are various types of speculation which may involve women in rather different ways. The most common and visible type of speculation consists of buying up rare goods in state stores, from peasants, or from employees of state enterprises, and reselling them at higher prices on street corners, at private markets or through other black market channels. It does not require much organization or any special skills, and is relatively easily detected since the offender is directly involved in all the transactions (illegal purchases, illegal sales, etc.). This kind of speculation is clearly numerically dominated by women, many of whom work in the retail trade. (Some typical examples are quoted in 'Ukrywanie . . .', 1983: 47.

Women are well familiar with the operation of the market, the nature of shortages, and the mentality of buyers, because they themselves are the providers for their families and the frustrations caused by constant shortage are part of their everyday experience. Moreover, female speculators who work full time in their illicit trade have a clear advantage over men as their lack of legitimate employment does not attract as much attention or even harassment by the police.[10]

In addition to these petty speculators in everyday consumer items (food, clothing, cosmetics, flowers, etc.), there also exists a much better organized network of wholesale dealers who trade in large amounts of stolen state property (for example, with private businessmen), art (usually smuggled abroad), apartments, cars, agricultural machinery, construction materials, or any other products, whose open sales are restricted by some official regulations. In order to secure the release of large quantities of these goods to black-markets, such networks have to include very high local or even central functionaries, whose cooperation is crucial for their successful operation and relative impunity. Due to the ineffective law enforcement and assured political protection of this kind of speculation, it is difficult to determine to what extent, and in what role, women are actually involved. There can be no doubt, however, that this kind of speculation is much more detrimental to the economy and more profitable to the participants than the highly 'feminized', and criminalized, street corner speculation in stockings or flowers.

Finally, women are often prosecuted for trading in foreign currency and for the illegal sale of alcohol. As demonstrated earlier the state has a clear interest in promoting these crimes as long as it is able to control the profits and to assure the effective channelling of the bulk of the hard currency involved into its own purse. This usually requires some degree of cooperation with the police or secret agents on the part of speculators. Furthermore, since both offences are relatively socially visible, some offenders have to be singled out for prosecution to counter any public suspicion regarding the total corruption of the police or its outright indolence.

Women who deal in hard currency are often prostitutes working in expensive hotels and restaurants which attract many foreign visitors. Not only do they demand payment for their services in foreign currency, but they are also 'employed', by their pimps or currency speculators themselves, to make illegal exchanges of money for their clients. On the other hand, women involved in alcohol sales and moonshining are frequently ex-prostitutes, whose age and state of health do not allow them to continue in their trade, but who do not have any legitimate place in society, They can usually rely on their former clients and friends to spread information about their new 'business' and to secure sufficient numbers of customers. Convictions of both prostitutes and ex-prostitutes interrupt their criminal activities during the period of their imprisonment, but they usually return to their trade as soon as they can in the absence of any legal opportunities, support groups or viable economic alternatives. Thus, their occasional imprisonment does not disturb the balance of the neatly designed system of mutual services and profits in the highly integrated system of illicit and licit markets.

In sum, official statistics, which indicate the relatively high involvement of women in non-conventional, economic offences, have to be treated with caution. While there is no doubt that women do participate quite actively in various types of economic and fiscal offences, it is necessary to be aware of the highly selective and politically biased law enforcement in this area.

WOMEN, POWER AND CRIME: DISCUSSION

Polish and Soviet women are educated and work both inside and outside the home. Polish public opinion surveys show that females have a more altruistic orientation and place more value on happiness in family life than males (Reszke, 1978; Leśnicka, 1984). In addition, the educational expectations of parents are even higher in the case of daughters than in the case of sons. Occupational preferences of both girls and their parents are, however, realistically adjusted to the requirement of having a job compatible with child rearing and household duties (i.e. one which is not too physically tiring, does not involve travelling, shift work, high responsibility, etc.; see Reszke, 1978).

Women seem to be concentrated in a poorly paid, middle white-collar stratum within the Polish and Soviet occupational structures. They work as teachers and medical staff, they fill most of the rank-and-file positions in retail trade, services, financial institutions and administration. They are absent at the top of the hierarchy and their presence in skilled manual labour is far less pronounced. They fulfil, however, many extremely low-paid unskilled manual tasks and dominate the workforce in such fields as the textile industry or food processing. Although exploited and overworked, women seem, nevertheless, to be more resilient and less susceptible to the frustration engendered by the formal structure of society. Despite all the pressures and difficulties of carrying on their two master roles, women seem to be able to escape from job-related failures or disappointments to the rewards of child rearing, and vice versa.

Men do not appear to have such options. Their responsibility to their families as the providers of money has diminished markedly, while their role in child rearing remains marginal. Their educational or professional frustrations cannot be as easily compensated elsewhere and they are, therefore, more likely to either become involved in the criminal underworld or the marginal existence of alcoholics, drifters and vagrants. On the other hand, those men with entrepreneurial aspirations which cannot be fulfilled in the communist economy, are more likely to plot illegal schemes to introduce capitalist incentives and profit orientation into daring economic ventures. In contrast to women, their drive to achieve personal satisfaction, importance and economic success is not effectively restrained by mundane household chores and the responsibility for the moral development of their children.

During the years of legal operation of the Free Union Solidarity from 1980–81, Poles witnessed a massive exposure of criminal abuses of office by the communist functionaries at all levels of the economic and political hierarchy. The list of names of officials investigated or indicted for corruption and serious economic crimes confirms once more the virtual absence of women among the top level criminals. Ironically, there were also relatively few women among the political internees arrested and detained after the imposition of the state of war in Poland. As well, women were markedly under-represented among those indicted and convicted under the provisions of martial law for political offences. This seems to be consistent with the sex distribution among the Solidarity office holders[11] as well as with the official perceptions of the degree of threat posed by the defiant men and women.[12]

In conclusion, it seems clear that women constitute a tiny minority within the Communist Party apparatus, in the economic managerial élite, in the army, and indeed, in the church hierarchies. As well, their presence in the leadership of dissident movements is not very pronounced, even though they participate in these movements in many valuable roles. Consequently, since the pinnacles of power are out of the reach of these women, its criminal abuses also remain a male domain. They do fulfil, however, many important economic and administrative functions which enable them to engage in less spectacular economic and fiscal offences, which are not regulated by the traditional ethics and, therefore, do not openly conflict with their historical role as the socialization agents. While such forms of female 'deviance', as prostitution and vagrancy continue to place many women outside the traditional family ethics, the prevalent forms of women's criminal involvement often overlooked by researchers tend to challenge the rules of the 'socialist' economy rather than those of the Church and tradition.

11 Crimes of 'True Criminals' and Deviance of 'True Deviants': Conventional Crime and Deviance

PROPERTY CRIME, VIOLENT CRIME AND HOOLIGANISM

It is impossible to provide a fully reliable and precise picture of conventional crime in the Soviet Union and Poland. Some broad estimates may, however, be attempted. The available sources of information are slightly different in the case of each of the studied countries. Firstly, this account, as any other publication concerned with this subject matter, has to be read with the clear understanding that no criminal statistics are published by the Soviet authorities. Rather, the findings and data which are available come from somewhat fragmented investigative efforts by Soviet and western researchers. Additionally, while Soviet press reports serve as a good source of concrete examples of crime, they have no real value with respect to any attempts to establish the actual extent of the Soviet crime problem.

Poland, on the other hand, publishes some police and court statistics (but no data on numbers of prisoners) which, despite all the known shortcomings of this type of information, can be referred to. As well, Polish criminology and sociology of deviance have produced a number of studies which may be of interest to a student of crime in Poland. Finally, just as in the case of the Soviet press, Polish periodicals furnish numerous accounts of individual cases of crime, methods of its perception and sentences meted out. While, however, they provide some specific insights into the nature of reported offences, they are, at best, representative of crimes whose reporting is seen as being in the interests of general social policy and the political nurturing of the members of these societies, and not of the totality of crime committed or even prosecuted.

According to an estimate calculated by Zeldes, the annual number of criminal convictions by the Soviet ordinary courts in the mid-1970s was not less than 1.5 million. On the basis of his data, it may also be estimated that an overall number of criminal convictions in ordinary courts, comrades' courts, special courts and military tribunals reached approximately 3 million in the same period (Zeldes, 1981: 71–2). Hooliganism appears to be the most frequent single cause of criminal convictions by ordinary courts, accounting for up to 30 per cent of their total number. Crimes against state property account for up to 25 per cent, theft of private property up to 15 per cent and crimes against persons (i.e. violent crimes) up to 12 per cent of all convictions (Zeldes, 1981: 73; Pomorski, 1977: 239).

Juviler calculated that, on the basis of available data, in the Soviet Union in 1971, there were 163 adult convictions for crimes against persons per 100 000 inhabitants as compared to 133 in the USA; 101 Soviet convictions for crimes against property as compared to 280 American convictions, and 17 Soviet convictions for robbery as compared to 11 American convictions for the same crime (Juviler, 1976: 139). While such comparisons naturally, have to be treated with caution, they should not be totally ignored. The prominance of violent crime in the USSR has been noted by many researchers and is often linked to the 'Soviet problem with violent drinking' (Juviler, 1976: 140). The greater proportion of convictions for crimes against property in the USA, if indeed it exists, may be explained by several factors. One is simply the incomparably higher level of affluence and the abundance of goods to steal in the United States. A good example is provided by car theft, very common in the USA and definitely less prominent in the Soviet Union, where relatively few people own cars. This explanation suggests that the actual rate of crime against property, and not just the rate of its prosecution, is higher in the United States. Another possibility is that, independently of the actual extent of crime, the American conviction rate is higher due to the greater concern with property in a country where private ownership is the corner-stone of the economy and the free-market ideology which governs it. The insurance system, quite underdeveloped in the Soviet Union and extremely extensive in the USA, may also contribute to the greater tendency to report property crimes.

Another area in which American convictions seem to be much more numerous is that concerned with criminal dealing in and possession of narcotics, impaired driving, sex offences and weapons violations (Juviler, 1976: 139–40). While various aspects of drug-related offences will be discussed later, it is worthy of note that the extremely high level of latent behaviour in the area of sex offences excludes practically all comparisons. Impaired driving is definitely a grave problem in the Soviet Union, but numerically it poses a lesser threat than in western countries again due to the relatively low number of vehicles.

Official Polish court statistics for 1970–81 show that the total number of adult convictions by ordinary courts dropped from 173 000 in 1970 and 167 000 in 1975 to 155 000 in 1980 and 129 000 in 1981 (*Maly Rocznik* . . ., 1983: 288). The number of convictions increased again in the subsequent years. Moreover, petty offence boards convicted 461 000 individuals in 1970, 570 000 in 1975, 645 000 in 1980, 427 000 in 1981 and 659 000 in 1982. The decrease in court convictions in the 1980–81 period can probably be explained by the decrease in the actual extent of criminal behaviour during the period of the legal existence of the Solidarity Union (from August 1980 to December 1981). As well, according to many accounts, the consumption of alcohol, which tends to be a factor in many crimes, diminished radically during this period. The high number of convictions by petty offence boards in 1980 was probably caused by the extensive use of these panels to harass worker activists.[1] The number of crimes for which charges were laid, which is, of course, different than the number of convictions, was approximately 390 000 in 1981. Despite the strict controls of the state of war, or perhaps because of them, the number of crimes increased to 436 000 in 1982 and reached 446 000 in 1983 ('Obraz Tygodnia', 1984: 1; it must be remembered that thousands of political internees were never charged with any crimes and therefore were not included in these statistics).

The structure of criminal convictions is slightly different in Poland than in the Soviet Union. In the late 1970s, crimes against state property and the economy accounted for approximately 30 per cent of all convictions, crimes against private property for approximately 25 per cent, crimes against family and guardianship (such as non payment of alimonies, bigamy, child abduction and abuse etc.) for around 13 per cent while violent crimes against life and health (including rape) accounted for 10 per cent of all convictions[2] (for more detailed information see Table 10.1A. p. 236). Thus, it appears that the share of crimes against private property in the overall number of convictions is smaller in the Soviet Union than in Poland. This may be due to either the more limited scope of private ownership in the USSR or the lesser importance attached to such offences by Soviet prosecutors, or a combination of both. Convictions for crimes against state property, on the other hand, figure quite prominently in the total number of convictions within both countries, which is quite consistent with their dominant ideology and organization of economy. The share of convictions for violent crimes against persons is also relatively high contrary to the claims that the conditions conducive to such behaviour have long been eliminated. The most striking difference, which requires a more detailed explanation, is the huge share of convictions for hooliganism in the Soviet statistics and the absence of such a category in the Polish court data.

Hooliganism is defined in section 206 of the RSFSR Criminal Code as 'intentional actions which grossly violate public order and express an obvious disrespect towards society' (for a more detailed discussion of the legal aspects of this definition and of its transformations see *Encyclopedia of Soviet Law*, 1973: 311 and Chalidze, 1977: 73–97). Moreover, 'hooligan motives' may be treated as an aggrevating circumstance in the prosecution of several other criminal offences. The vagueness of the definition of the crime of hooliganism is quite purposeful; it allows the conviction of people who could not be so easily convicted under other charges. Additionally, once the infamous 'guilt by analogy'[3] principle was finally abandoned in the post Stalinist era, such vague criminal labels as 'hooliganism' or 'parasitism' have become even more indispensable. The variety of cases dealt with under the charges of hooliganism suggest that it may be applied to almost any type of unwelcome behaviour, ranging from bad language to murder, and from playing jazz to religious and political dissent.

The usefulness of the criminal section on hooliganism is not, however, limited to its role in 'widening the net' of criminal control; it also appears to blur successfully the usual distinctions between offences against property, violent crimes and political crimes. Therefore, even if the Soviet court statistics become somehow available despite their classified nature, the huge category of 'hooligan' offences makes it impossible to interpret them accurately and to assess the extent of criminal involvement in more familiar types of offences. For instance, violent crimes seem to be very often disguised as hooliganism which has resulted in hasty but wrong conclusions by many students of Soviet crime about the actual extent of criminal violence in that country. For example, wife-beating is apparently one of the most frequent causes for the application of the hooliganism section (Chalidze 1977: 83). Street fights, violent conflicts in communal apartments, random violent attacks in the streets, parks and trains, muggings and gang rapes or even homicide are often covered by this master label and are not, therefore, included under the rubric of 'crimes against persons'.

The Soviet law provides for three special forms of the offence of hooliganism which include petty, common and malicious hooliganism. In its petty variety, hooliganism is an administrative offence punishable by detention for from 10 to 15 months or by a fine. Petty hooliganism (e.g. the use of obscene language, offensive molestation of citizens, the violation of public order and the peace of citizens) committed by a person who has already been punished for petty hooliganism within the preceeding year is considered to be common hooliganism. The latter is a criminal, not an administrative offence, and entails the deprivation of liberty for from 6 months to 1 year. Malicious hooliganism is characterized by 'exceptional cynicism' or 'special offensiveness' or is connected with resistance to a representative of authority.[4] It is punishable by 1 to 5 years' deprivation of liberty or by 3 to 7 years when accompanied by the use or attempted use of arms or other tools adapted to inflict physical injury.

It appears, therefore, that a person charged with hooliganism may be sentenced to anything between a small fine and 7 years in prison for practically any kind of non-conformist behaviour. This is probably why hooliganism has been chosen as a convenient target for a number of anti-crime campaigns. Such campaigns can divert attention away from other problems and mobilize forces of law and order without an open admission that crime is actually on the rise. They imply only that hooliganism is a serious or even a growing problem, while crime in general is always reported to be steadily declining. The most intensive anti-hooliganism campaigns, which filled Soviet prisons with thousands of alleged hooligans, were conducted in 1926 and 1966. In the early 1980s, the USSR Prosecutor's Office turned its energies once again to the intensification of the struggle against hooliganism. The Prosecutor General, R. Rudenko, even went so far as to charge the law enforcers with attempts to cover up or misreport the omnipresence of this type of crime:

> Hooliganism is on the wane in our country, they say. But in fact, when one probes more deeply, one finds that in a great many instances these people's "benign" statistics are not borne out. Often the figures conceal a slackening in the struggle against hooliganism, if not something worse – attempts to artificially "adjust" data on the number of offences or even to create a semblance of success. . . . After a checkup conducted by the USSR Prosecutor's, the internal affairs personnel who were guilty of keeping crimes out of the record books and of failing to act upon citizen's complaints were called to strict account. (Rudenko, 1979/1980: 6)

Hooliganism was also chosen as a target of an anti-crime campaign in Poland in the 1950s. The label has been criticized, however, by many jurists ever since, and, despite its continued presence in the law, it has been rather rarely applied in practice. In fact, there is no separate offence of hooliganism in the Polish Criminal Code. A number of less-serious offences which include the intentional attack on the public security, health, liberty, personal authority, property or the public order, may be judged to have a 'hooligan character' if the perpetrator acted in public and without a clear motive, thus showing 'his flagrant disregard for the basic principles, or the legal order' (s. 120 of the Polish Criminal Code). The hooligan character of an offence is considered to be an aggravating circumstance and the court is thereby obliged to impose a penalty of deprivation of liberty not less than the minimum sanction increased by half and is not allowed to suspend the sentence (s. 59). As well, the Petty Offences Code defines hooligan offences which are within the jurisdiction of the petty crime boards. Nonetheless, both the boards and ordinary courts have been disinclined to use this concept, apparently due to the bad reputation which it has acquired (Falandysz, 1981e: 13; Kocel-Krekora, 1981).

The extent and circumstances of the application of the section on hooliganism by the petty offence boards were the subjects of an empirical study conducted in 1979 in Warsaw. It found that majority of the people charged with hooliganism or with acting under the influence of alcohol (which constitute a single offence under the petty offence law) came from the working class and were poorly educated. They were almost exclusively young males with known records of alcohol abuse. It was also established that 'hooligan motives' are rarely used as an aggravating circumstance in the prosecution of other offences. Moreover, when such circumstances are actually mentioned by the adjudicating panels, they are never precisely defined or explained and the sentences do not appear to be affected by such imputations (Kocel-Krekora, 1981: 95–7).

Both legal constructs, the offence of hooliganism and the hooligan motivation as an aggrevating factor, have been criticized by Polish and Soviet jurists as unacceptably vague (see e.g. Galchenko, *et al.*, 1973–4; Falandysz 1981e: 13). While a draft of a new criminal code proposed by a social commission under the auspices of the Solidarity Union demanded a complete removal of this concept from the Polish law, it is most unlikely that the criminal law reform which is expected to take place in the mid-1980s will follow this suggestion.

There is no evidence that violent crime has been eradicated or even significantly curbed in the two studied countries even if there has been some decline in violence in more recent periods in comparison with the turbulent early post-revolutionary years in the Soviet Union and the years immediately following the war and the Soviet take-over in Poland. The exceptionally high levels of violence in these years were caused primarily by the high intensity of political violence and the disturbances resulting from the forced movements of large ethnic and territorial groups, the disruption of families and the cultural and economic shock of early industrialization and urbanization efforts. As far as the rate of intentional homicide in the Soviet Union is concerned, it amounts, according to Van den Berg's rough estimate for the late 1970s, to 4 intentional homicides per 100 000 inhabitants per year (Van den Berg, 1983: 166). The respective rate in Poland ranged in the 1960s from 0.8 in 1961 to 1 in 1969 (Lernell, 1973: 246) and in the 1970s from 1.4 to 1.8 per 100 000 inhabitants (see official police statistics in *Rocznik* . . ., 1980: 479).[5] This rate is quite comparable to the homicide rate of 2.4 in the mid-1970s in Canada, a country with a moderate, but by no means a low rate of violent crime (approximately 2.4 – see Bayer Gammon, 1978: 181 and McGrath, 1976: 108). It is, however, considerably lower than the rate in the USA (approximately 9 homicides per 100 000 inhabitants – Reid, 1976; 50).

Several studies on homicide were conducted in the USSR and Poland in the 1960s. Generally, the Soviet studies established that the victims tended to be family members, indeed, a proportion significantly greater than that found in American studies of the same period. Acquaintances (co-workers, neighbours, etc.) appeared to be less frequently victimized, and the proportions of total strangers were similar in both countries. Another notable difference with the data from the United States was the weapon used; in Soviet homicide cases, knives and other cutting instruments were used most frequently while the use of firearms, most popular with Americans, was relatively rare. This was undoubtedly due to the very strict firearms controls and security regulations implemented in communist countries. In both Poland and the USSR, alcohol appears to be a factor in many murders and in many instances the offender as well as the victim was intoxicated. According to the existing studies, those convicted of intentional homicide tend to have exceptionally low levels of education. A Soviet study claims that a level of education beyond elementary school was attained by only 7 per cent of the offenders. A respective figure derived from Polish research is even lower (4.4 per cent). Moreover, a considerable number of Soviet offenders were found to have previous criminal records involving mainly petty crimes and hooliganism (see Connor, 1973; Ostroumov and Chugunov, 1965: 14; Holyst, 1967; Janowska, 1974).[6]

Another violent crime which appears to plague the studied societies to a similar degree as the western countries is rape. Its study has, however, been virtually prohibited in order to suppress any information about the true extent and nature of the sexual assault problem. Both Soviet and Polish sources show that the number of adult convictions for rape practically doubled during the 1960s and the increase in juvenile convictions was even greater (Van den Berg, 1983: 166–7; Lernell, 1973: 246; Glueck, 1973: 229). Given the fact that rape is one of those crimes which is most reluctantly reported by the victims[7] and very rarely committed in the presence of witnesses, an increase in official figures may signify either an actual upsurge of rape occurrences or some changes in the law enforcement and, especially, in social attitudes towards the victims. Nonetheless, given the lack of any evidence that there were any significant changes in the latter area, it is probable that the actual number of incidents of rape did increase considerably in the 1960s and early 1970s in Poland. Some decline in the official rape rates was noted in the late 1970s in Poland, however. While in 1975, the rate of solved rapes was 5.6 per 100 000 inhabitants (according to the police statistics), it dropped to 4.6 in 1978 and remained at this level in 1979 (calculated on the basis of data in *Rocznik* . . ., 1980: 479). Again, this may merely signify decreased focus on this type of crime by the police. In 1983–84, however, a number of official pronouncements expressed some anxiety about the growing rates of violent crime in general, and rape in particular (e.g. 'Przestrzeganie . . .', 1984; 'Posiedzenie . . .', 1983: 2). Moreover, according to several press reports, with the increase in the private ownership of passenger cars, a new type of dangerous rapist has emerged, a man who offers a ride to a woman who waits for a bus or walks home from work or school in deserted countryside areas. The well-known deficiencies of the public transport system in Poland force many girls and women to walk long distances often in the dark or in adverse conditions, a circumstance which creates an easy opportunity for male car-owners to pick up and sexually assault defenceless victims. According to the Polish police, an alarming number of such assaults lead eventually to the murder of the victim (Piotrowski, 1984: 2). There has also been an increase in gang rapes committed mainly by juveniles or young men. A Polish study showed the extremely high influence of the group leader in such cases and a significant over-representation of males rejected by their parents as well as of rural youths who had come alone to the cities and lost touch with their families (for horrifying descriptions of a number of gang rapes committed by very young people, see Czapów, 1974).

It appears that in a high proportion of the known cases of rape in both the USSR and Poland, the perpetrator was under the influence of alcohol (see e.g. Stern, 1980: 206; Wald *et al.*, 1981: 103).[8] The fear of being attacked by a drunken man, be it father, husband, boyfriend, acquaintance or stranger, is very real and almost omnipresent for Soviet and Polish women. Alcohol is commonly involved in the extremely widespread crime of wife battering,[9] and indeed in wife rape cases, which can, according to the law, be qualified as rape, but are not generally perceived as such. It would be erroneous, however, to claim that alcohol is solely responsible for violence against women. In fact, both alcohol abuse and victimization of women may have some common socio-cultural roots.

The weakened social and familial position of men (see Chapter 10) and their extreme political alienation leave them few avenues for their culturally promoted needs of domination and superiority. Sexual subjugation and physical abuse of women may be interpreted as cowardly, but desperate acts of men who are rendered powerless by the society or by their own dispositions or weaknesses and who try to compensate this by attacking the group which they have learned to perceive as the 'weaker sex'. They, as indeed their counterparts in many other countries, have been brought up with the belief that heterosexual conquest is very important for their status and self-worth; it naturally becomes even more central when other sources of status and self-appreciation are blocked. Under such circumstances, the traditional association of male sexuality with domination may assume even more ominous and violent expression. Moreover, the traditional male position may appear to be threatened by the massive vocational activization of women and their role as the family co-providers. Rape may, thus, serve as the ultimate means of stripping women of any power or independence they might have acquired, a way of showing them where their place is and who is still the master. While such an interpretation of the impact of some more global features of the social structure and role distribution on such individual acts like sexual assault and physical abuse of women is of course hard to prove, it may nonetheless provide viable insight into the complex issue of the persistent, and even alarming, presence of violence against women in communist societies.

According to a number of western studies, it is also known that many convicted rapists have never obtained proper, humanistically-oriented sex-education, many have witnessed the violent relationships of their parents and have never learned respect for other persons, and especially women. If these factors do, in fact, play a significant role in the aetiology of at least some proportion of rapes, then it would be rather surprising if the studied countries had low sexual assault rates. Sex education is practically non-existent in the Soviet Union (see Stern, 1980) and extremely limited in Poland, where, however, the Catholic Church makes some attempts to convey, through obligatory premarital curses, the dignity and humanity of a sexual union. Sex therapy and counselling is totally neglected and underdeveloped in these countries which may also contribute, to some degree to the aggressiveness, bitterness and insecurity with which many men approach women. Finally, the existence of a political group which is practically above the law, the omnipotent party élite, explains the extremely high involvement of the so-called 'banana youth' (i.e. the offsprings of party officials) in gang rapes and other forms of violent manifestations of superiority and overt disdain for societal values. These young people are brought up in a society of extreme inequality whose egalitarian ideology is cynically celebrated by their parents who have unlimited power over the society and who secure for their children a fully separate élite education, foreign travel opportunities and financial freedom as well as virtual impunity from criminal prosecution, all within the otherwise tightly controlled and impoverished society.

Despite the high anxiety regarding violent crime in these societies, it is property crime which sends thousands of offenders to overcrowded and overly repressive prisons. As everywhere, property crimes constitute the great majority of offences reported and processed in the USSR and Poland. A great proportion of these crimes involve state property (as discussed in detail in Chapters 8 and 9 which dealt with crimes by managers as well as workers and peasants). Yet, personal theft is also very widespread. The fear of this type of crime is very visible; practically all inhabitants of first-floor apartments install bars on their windows, car-owners remove windshield wipers when they park their vehicles in public places, vicious dogs are kept by most owners of individual houses in the suburbs and countryside. Personal property crime is usually portrayed in these countries as a lower-class phenomenon, committed by people living on the margins of society, notably alcoholics, vagrants and demoralized, anti-social individuals. And, indeed, the majority of convicted personal property offenders appear to be poorly educated, low income or unemployed people (Ostroumov and Chugunov, 1965: 17–18; Connor, 1972: 154–5, 157; Kossowska, 1978: 181). Although law enforcement tends to be biased in terms of its overconcentration on the marginal populations, it seems that very extensive opportunities for white-collar crime in the state economy and administration channel the middle-classes' criminal activities into this type of offence, leaving conventional theft and robbery to the less fortunate individuals in the 'underclass'.

Soviet criminologists have claimed for years that, not only is crime steadily declining (even if they have from time to time admitted that some specific types of crime have been increasing), but, moreover, it results from the 'lag of consciousness behind life'. Ostroumov and Chugunov, for example, give the following explanation of crime in the Soviet Union:

> Vestiges of the past are rooted in the mode of life and the minds of millions of persons long after the disappearance of the economic conditions that gave rise to them. These vestiges are responsible for the fact that the commission of crimes is an objective possibility. . . . These repulsive vestiges of the past come to the fore under the influence of particular catalysing agents, such as alcohol for example.
>
> (Ostroumov and Chugunov, 1965: 13–14)

The main forms of motivation believed to be shaped by such remnants of the capitalist past include profit orientation, greediness, disrespect for community and unconscientious attitudes towards socialist property. Despite the Soviet pressure, however, Polish criminologists explicitly rejected the 'capitalist remnants' theory. Leszek Lernell, for example, states in his authoritative criminology textbook (1973), that the thesis has been shown to be false which claims that:

> with the construction of the new socio-economic formation on the ashes of the capitalist system all crime will disappear. . . . In order to evaluate the present situation, in which crime poses a serious problem for the socialist society, it is necessary to see the reality as it really is and as it develops and to appreciate the on-going processes and the criminogenic factors which are rooted in this reality. . . . The main premises, especially, ideological ones, of the 'relic theory' are very weak; they are derived from dogmatic and apologetic and not scientific assumptions.
>
> (Lernell, 1973: 214; this author's translation from Polish)

It is impossible not to agree with Lernell, and even Soviet criminologists themselves seem to pay only lip service to the 'relic theory' while searching for other, more viable explanations for their crime rates. The hypothesis of non-antagonistic contradictions of the socialist socio-economic formation represents such an attempt to find an acceptable theoretical formula. It implies that, while the fundamental contradictions of class interests have been successfully eliminated in post-revolutionary Russia, there are still social and economic problems which need to be addressed. The process of rapid urbanization and industrialization, for example, have had some side-effects and negative repercussions for various individuals not sufficiently prepared for the change. These have led to their maladjustment and marginalization. Fast growing cities and industries furnished new jobs, but were not able to meet the new demand for housing and other services. The idea of collective dwellings, deemed progressive after the revolution, proved to be disastrous and has led to many conflicts, tragedies and generally anti-social attitudes. Moreover, the massive entrance of women into the workforce has exposed families to new pressures and problems. The state network of child-care centres has not been able to cope successfully with the task of raising the new generation; the shortcomings of collective, standardized child-rearing have become painfully obvious. Moreover, the nationalization of the economy is believed to create new opportunities for crime against state property which is not sufficiently supervised and become an easy target for vandals and thieves. Finally, many Soviet criminologists focus their attention on psychological aspects of social maladjustment in their efforts to portray a typical 'criminal personality' syndrome (for more details on Soviet criminology see, e.g. Ostroumov and Chugunov, 1965; Connor, 1972; Solomon, 1974, 1978; *Prestupnost* . . ., 1974; Djekebaer, 1975; Antonyan, 1975; Kuznetsova, 1975; *Novaya* . . ., 1979; Sieriebriakova and Syrov, 1982; *Combating* . . ., 1981).

Polish criminology, reborn after the Stalinist period, has clearly tended to focus on psychological and socio-psychological factors in crime aetiology, which are frequently studied through detailed biographical investigations of limited samples of offenders. Another, prominent, approach has focused on the socially detrimental consequences of great post-war migrations and other turbulations connected with the post-war change of borders and the intensive urbanization and industrialization. The supporters of this orientation point, for example, to the abundant evidence that the western regions of Poland, regained from the Germans after World War II, have consistently had the highest rates of crime, juvenile delinquency, alcoholism, mental hospitalizations and suicide (e.g. Maroszek, 1963, 1975, Kobus, 1975; Falewicz *et al.*, 1975). Newly created industrial centres appear also to show higher crime and general social 'pathology' rates, but these rates tend to level off once the initial period of construction and development is over and the mainly rural immigrant population settles down properly (Mościskier, 1976, 1978a, b). Mościskier's explanation of this phenomenon represents well the prevailing mode of interpretation of such temporary increases in crime rates caused by rapid population movements. His explanation includes such aspects as the weakening of social control, conflicts between indigent and immigrant groups, a cultural gap between the traditional culture and the demands of the new social environment, frustration of some people in the face of the swift promotion of selected groups and the spread of new status indicators, quite different from the traditional ones (Mościskier, 1978b, see also Kryczka, 1978).

The relationship between crime rates and the size of cities has also been given some attention by Polish criminologists. It was found that, while overall crime rates are not higher in big cities than in small ones, certain categories of offences are clearly enhanced by the size of the city. They include private property theft, breaking and entering into residential dwellings, offences against representatives of the authority and public order, and robbery. The rates of all these crimes are very considerably higher in cities with populations surpassing 200 000. These cities also tend to create special high-crime zones which can be mainly found in the central parts, where there exist high concentrations of retail trade establishments, services and entertainment. Yet, the places of residence of offenders appear to be located in quite different areas of the city, notably the poorest and most neglected areas, distant from the centre core and characterized by high alcohol abuse, inferior housing, high child mortality and the low education of its inhabitants (Kossowska, 1978).

In addition to these Polish explanations which refer to socio-psychological features of the offender and his immediate environment and those which focus on social disorganization in connection with demographic and cultural aspects of social and technological change, there have also been some attempts to look for factors contributing to crime within the criminal justice system itself. Perhaps partly influenced by the western fascination with the labelling theory, but above all concerned with the excessive repressiveness of the criminal law and its enforcement, these critics have pointed to the damaging effects of long terms of imprisonment, the brutalizing and dehumanizing impact of prison and its subculture, the dangerous aspects of the 'widening of the net' of penal repression and the myopic nature of the unqualified faith in harsh punishment (see e.g. Szerer 1964; Szelhaus, 1968; Bożyczko, 1969; Waligóra, 1970; Jasiński, 1975, 1978; Balandynowicz and Porowski, 1980; Falandysz, 1981a).

These concerns are very real given that the Polish penal system is marked by an extraordinary level of severity, which has, during the past 20 years, shown a tendency to increase steadily (see Chapter 2). The nature of punishments meted out to convicted offenders indicates that the courts choose deprivation of liberty twice as often as other options (e.g. 67 per cent of all sentences in 1979, with almost half of them being unconditional and only 3 per cent involving sentences of imprisonment less than 6 months). Two other types of punishment, the limited deprivation of freedom and the fine, are imposed with approximately the same frequency (18 per cent and 15 per cent respectively in 1979 – all data from a statistical yearbook, *Rocznik* . . ., 1980: 484). Moreover, extraordinary punishments are applied to recidivists, a response which is believed to contribute rather than limit the proportion of recidivists among convicts. The alienation of offenders from the society appears to be aggrevated by the option of placing them, upon completion of their prison sentences, in the so-called social adjustment centres for undefined periods (not less than 3 years and not exceeding 5 years). These centres have proven to be as strict, demoralizing and damaging to the chances of social rehabilitation of offenders as regular prisons (see e.g. Balandynowicz and Porowski, 1980; Urbanek, 1984).

In sum, with the exception of the 'capitalist remnants' theory, the explanations of crime offered by Soviet and Polish criminologists are not drastically different from these pronounced at various points in time by their western colleagues. Even the often ridiculed 'remnants' theory is consistent with those western publications which give a very narrow interpretation to Marx's ideas and see capitalism as the sole source of criminal behaviour. It is, of course, impossible to give a definite assessment of the accuracy of the offered explanations. Some attempts will be made in the concluding section of this chapter, however, following a brief discussion of drug and alcohol abuse and juvenile delinquency.

ALCOHOLISM AND DRUG ABUSE

There is a marked difference between the availability of information on drug abuse in Poland and the USSR. While the Polish authorities admitted in the 1980s that it was indeed a serious problem, any analysis of drug abuse in the Soviet Union has been virtually precluded by the total lack of relevant data and the persistent official denials of the existence of the problem. Some experts, however, who emigrated from the Soviet Union in the 1970s, have reported serious increases in drug addiction rates in several republics. Ilya Zemtsov, for example, reported that 18 per cent of young people in the major Soviet cities and 7 per cent in rural areas take drugs and Boris M. Segal, the ex-director of a department at the Moscow Institute of Psychiatry confirmed that drug addiction is a significant social and medical problem (Zemtsov, 1975: 10 and Segal, 1977; both sources quoted here after Barry and Barner-Barry, 1982: 311).

Several significant changes in the Soviet criminal policy concerning drugs took place during the past 20 years. The penalties for possessing and selling narcotics and for cultivating the opium poppy or hemp were increased in 1962 from 1 year to 10 years' deprivation of liberty. Three years later, a new crime was added to the criminal code which made illegal the act of inducing minors to take drugs. It was punishable by up to 5 years' deprivation of freedom. In 1966, the Supreme Court issued a directive to lower courts to pay more attention to the growing danger of drug abuse (Juviler, 1974: 37, 45–6). In 1972, compulsory treatment for narcotic addicts in treatment–labour institutions was established by the Presidium of the Supreme Soviet of the RSFSR. In 1974, the Plenum of the Supreme Court of the USSR urged the courts to give particular attention to drug-related crimes. Moreover, in 1975 and 1976, the Supreme Court issued statements in which it called for the intensification of the struggle against these types of offences (Barry and Barner-Barry, 1982: 294–5).

A number of articles appeared in the early 1980s in the Soviet press where the drug abuse problem was discussed with some alarm. For instance, the Deputy Minister of the Interior of the Abkaz Autonomous Republic stated in *Zarya Vostoka* in 1982 that the fight against drug addiction had to hold an important place in crime prevention efforts. She claimed that 'there is an obvious relationship between crime and drug addiction' for, in 'seeking money to buy narcotics, addicts frequently commit burglaries and robberies and make attempts on the life and health of citizens' (Antelava, 1982: 14). She also quoted a study, according to which:

> three major factors are conducive to drug use among young people. First, alcohol abuse and smoking by their parents. Second, when parents indulge their children's every whim and shield them from all

> difficulties, including work, teenagers become apathetic and bored, and they turn to narcotics in search of an artificial stimulant. Third, there is the bad example of friends: Youngsters who have not been given strong moral fiber by their parents and the schools often come under the influence of older comrades who use drugs.
>
> (Antelava, 1982: 14)

Moreover, the Deputy Minister underlined that many drug addicts have no jobs and lead 'the [lives] of parasites'. She went on to express a typical Soviet faith that 'stepping up the struggle against parasitism [could] be an effective preventive measure against drug addiction and other crimes' (Antelava, 1982: 15). Another press report revealed that drug abuse, especially among young people, was recognized as a serious problem in Georgia (Inoveli, 1982). Despite these signals that, contrary to the prevailing western beliefs, drug abuse is considered to be a problem by the Soviet authorities, it would be rather imprudent to try to draw any conclusions as to its actual extent or seriousness since no concrete and reliable data are available on this matter.

There is more information, however, on the drug problem in Poland where the amount of available data has rapidly increased in the early 1980s. According to the information published in a professional journal of the Canadian Addiction Research Foundation, Poland is the world's largest producer of morphine and it may have the biggest drug addiction problem of all Europe. Quoting Polish official sources, the author of the article puts the number of Poles regularly involved in the illegal production and distribution of heroin at 10 000 and the number of heroin addicts at not less than 150 000, most of them aged between 13 and 30 years (Land, 1983).

Many Polish reports indicate that there has been a rapid increase in the illegal narcotics available in that country. According to the police data, the black market has become almost totally dominated by home-grown narcotics and the number of arrested producers of narcotics has grown from 387 in 1979 to 1213 in 1982 ('Rośnie . . .', 1984: 4). At least 300 000 acres of agricultural land is devoted to opium-poppy cultivation for legitimate pharmaceutical use. It was, however, discovered around 1976 that dry poppy stalks can also be used to make high-quality heroin. Polish peasants immediately realized that they had an extremely lucrative black-market commodity available to them and quickly established networks for the illegal supply of the poppy stalks to the cities (Land, 1983: 10; see also Smożewska-Wójcikiewicz, 1984). The decree regarding the compulsory sale of poppy stalks to the state, enacted in the early 1980s, has not helped much since, according to a representative of the Polish Police Headquarters, peasants found ways to bribe sale agents and to circumvent the regulations ('Rośnie . . .', 1984: 4). Apparently, only 30 per cent of rural districts have been able to enforce the new rules ('Jak . . .', 1984). Yet, these restrictions seem to have led to a considerable rise in black market prices which, in turn, resulted in greater pressure on drug addicts to steal in order to support their habits (Lubelska, 1984a).

Thus:

> the lax anti-narcotics laws coinciding with the easy availability of heroin and the uniform drabness of life yawning at a politically-disillusioned generation of young people have combined to create a rapidly spreading drug disaster. . . . Unlike Western youngsters trying various pills as well as marijuana, giving themselves a chance to stop before they are hopelessly addicted, the East Europeans frequently begin with heroin. The under-financed health services of the region are equally unprepared for the emergency. Warsaw, for example, which has recently emerged as the heroin Mecca of Europe, has fewer than a dozen detoxification beds, all of them located at a single hospital. The entire country has only five small treatment centres.
>
> (Land, 1983: 10)

Some Polish experts claim that, around 1967–68, the drug abuse problem started to assume serious proportions and has been growing ever since. Between 1970 and 1983, there was a six-fold increase in the number of patients hospitalized for drug addiction (Lubelska, 1984a). The epidemic nature of the problem in the mid-1970s was compared, by some experts, to the spread of drug use in western countries in the 1960s, and was believed to be stimulated by the rapidly increasing popularity of the hippie-type subculture in Poland (Czapów, 1976: 383). In the mid-1970s, the problem was found to be mostly present among young and very young people and to be especially widespread in big cities and in the western regions, regained by Poland after the war (Czapów, 1976: 382–3, 385; Lubelska, 1984a; Jarosz, 1980: 328–9). It has, however, gradually reached medium cities as well ('Kolo . . .', 1984). According to the existing studies, male involvement with drugs has been approximately three times greater than that of females, and there has not been a clear monopolization of the problem by any single social stratum, although white collar milieu and the skilled working class seem to recruit by far the greatest share of addicts (Lubelska, 1984a; Jarosz, 1980: 320–7; Rogala, 1980: 88–9). In the late 1960s and the early 1970s young people experimented mainly with all kinds of home detergents, glues, foam from fire extinguishers and various mood-altering medicines since only a fraction of them had access to morphine, later on, however, hard drugs clearly dominated the scene.

Several surveys conducted in the early 1970s in elementary and secondary schools in several big cities showed that between 5 to 8 per cent of the students had tried mood-altering substances (Matalowska, 1981; Latoszek *et al.*, 1974). In a similar study conducted in the early 1980s, 11.2 per cent of first-grade high school students admitted having done so ('Jak . . .', 1984). As well, the age of youths with drug problems has decreased and includes a growing proportion of children (Jarosz, 1980: 312–13; Matalowska, 1981; 'Nastolatki . . .', 1984; Lubelska, 1984a; 'Alkohol . . .', 1983). The increased number of deaths related to drug abuse provides yet another indicator of a dangerous trend ('Kolo . . .', 1984; 'Czy . . .', 1984). While it has been estimated that 80 young people died of drug overdoses in 1982 at least 120 deaths were registered in the first 10 months of 1983 (Land, 1983).

The actual worsening of the problem and the publicity given to it led to some official steps, the most important of which was a draft of new legislation disclosed in August 1983. The current law (i.e. the 1951 law on pharmaceutical and hallucinogenic substances) criminalizes the production, treatment, transport, import, export or sale of illegal drugs, all of which are punishable by up to 5 years' deprivation of liberty and a fine. The use of narcotics is only punishable when it takes place in the company of other people, and the penalty is 1 year imprisonment or a fine, or both. The criminal code predicts 5 years' imprisonment of anyone who illegally furnishes a drug to another person or induces him to use it (s. 161). The new draft legislation proposes to increase penalties for producers and traffickers up to 15 years and allows for extremely high fines. Moreover, it proposes to decriminalize completely the use of drugs in order to encourage addicts to seek help. It imposes on the health-care administration the responsibility for the creation of sufficient treatment facilities and rules that the necessary treatment should be provided free of charge to all patients. As well it states that the Church and social organizations may also run treatment centres if they obtain special permission to do so.

The proposed law declares that treatment should not be compulsory. It recognizes, however, a need for certain exceptions from this principle, especially in cases of perpetrators of certain criminal offences. These provisions were criticized by several experts for not only being too broad, but for actually reversing the progressive principle of voluntary treatment (Tarnawski, 1983). The experts also stressed that even the best law would not solve the problem of an acute shortage of treatment facilities. Many drug addicts are motivated to seek help, but such help is simply not available. The number of beds in drug addiction rehabilitation centres was only 400 in 1983, and the number of 'detoxication beds' was 50. Approximately 2600 addicts were registered in mental health counselling centres and 2675 patients were undergoing treatment in hospitals; neither of these institutions, however, was equipped to deal with such problems ('Jak . . .', 1984; Lubelska, 1984a).

Interpretations and explanations of the causes of the drug problem in Poland range from the purely psychological, through psycho-sociological to the macro-sociological. References to the inadequate functioning of the family and school seem, however, to be most popular with experts. In fact, several studies have shown that an overwhelming proportion of young people with pronounced drug problem come from broken homes or families ridden with conflict, alcoholism and abuse (e.g. Piotrowski, 1976: 144; Rogala, 1980: 89–91). Schools and youth organizations are also frequently blamed for shortcomings ranging from the lack of individual attention and understanding of the problems of adolescence (Rogala, 1980; Lubelska, 1984b) to more political criticism like that raised in the Report on the Conditions of the Life Start of the Young Generation, prepared in 1981 by the Minister of Labour, Wages and Welfare:

> The 1970s broadened considerably the list of problems which contributed to the crisis of trust. Oversimplified curricula, many onesided textbooks, the shallowness of ideological education, the concentration by youth organizations on formal meetings, the glorification of 'success' in the mass media, the suppression of criticism, the decreasing accessibility of books . . . were especially conducive to the personality deformations among young people.
> (Quoted in Matalowska, 1981: 8; this author's translation from Polish)

Generally, most authors stress that involvement with narcotics is an escapist behaviour. Yet, as a team researching drug abuse in Gdańsk poignantly states more important from the escape itself is an answer to the question from what reality they escape (Latoszek *et al.*, 1981: 219). Several authors have argued that it is necessary to study youth subcultures or countercultures in order to grasp the underlying values, needs and protestations which lead to the adoption of a life style compatible with drug use. Yet, in their search for adequate explanations, they are rarely able to go beyond stereotypical half-truths and conventional clichés, which portray the problem in terms of fashions, experimentations, disillusionment, frustration or rejection of the societal values. The broader context in which these countercultures develop is, for the well known reasons of political censorship and control, left unstudied.

While drug addiction appears to be a growing and serious problem in Poland and, no doubt, in the Soviet Union as well, it is alcohol abuse which is definitely the greatest threat to the mental and social health of these societies. Given the extensive literature on this matter (see e.g. Connor, 1972; Powell, 1971; Roman and Gebert, 1979; Barry and Barner-Barry, 1982: 285–94; Steven, 1982: 3–21), a brief discussion should suffice as a reminder of the overwhelming importance of this problem and the total inability of the governments of these countries to deal with it. Alcoholism is openly recognized by the Soviet and Polish authorities as an acute problem, but any direct studies on its socio-political causes and actual extent are generally discouraged. The accepted explanation is a cultural one – it refers to the age-old traditions of the drinking culture in these countries and general attitudes of tolerance or even approval of drunkenness. This tolerance is believed to be practised even by the law enforcers and, according to the Soviet Prosecutor General:

> there are still a good many officials who take a lenient attitude toward drunkards and do a poor job of fulfilling their obligations stemming from the laws on intensifying the struggle against drunkenness and alcoholism. (Rudenko, 1979/80: 6)

Moreover, workers are blamed for 'covering' for their drunken comrades 'in order to win top ranking [in socialist competitions], to get bonuses, and out of pity – after all, when he's not drinking he's a fine worker. They cover for such a person today, without thinking about the future' ('Rehabilitate . . .', 1983: 2).

There are also Soviet experts who claim that Soviet people drink due to 'emptiness', spiritual poverty, and a lack of higher interests and values (Losoto, 1980). Yet, they inevitably fail to explore the conditions responsible for such a spiritual crisis. The capitalist remnants theory is still alive, but more contemporary and concrete roots of the drinking problem are not totally overlooked. Both points of view were, for example, demonstrated during an interesting exchange which took place during a round table discussion organized by the editorial board of a leading Soviet legal journal:

> *Candidate of Jurisprudence F.M. Rudinsky*: Drunkenness is a complex social phenomenon with a long history. It is alien to socialism and reflects vestiges of the past in people's attitudes and behavior . . . *M.I. Piskotin*: I think that putting sole, or even primary, blame on 'vestiges of the past' for the spread of drunkenness and alcoholism in our country oversimplifies the problem . . . We cannot change those causes of alcohol abuse that are rooted in the past, but there are other contributing factors that we can and must change. These include the insufficient development of people's interests, perceived needs and self-respect; the lack of sufficient opportunity for people to use their abilities and talents, become socially active, and spend their leisure time intelligently; the lag in the development of the services sphere; the shortage of consumer goods; the arduous working and living conditions that still exist in some places; shortcomings in enforcing discipline, etc. ('Sovetskoye . . .', 1980/81: 2–3)

Yet, typically, the list of practical conclusions, prepared by the editor of the journal, presents an eclectic mixture of wishful thinking ('eliminating drinking among children and adolescents under the age of 18'), totally impractical resolutions ('promulgating health regulations prohibiting the conception of children by persons in a state of intoxication'), half-measures ('improving the conditions in which people spend their free time and drink alcoholic beverages') and coercive steps ('providing various forms of mandatory treatment').

It was revealed during the short period of Andropov's rule that almost 10 million people in the USSR were officially registered alcoholics and that tens of millions were abusing alcohol on a scale that prevents them from working productively. The work discipline appears to be drastically undermined by these facts; for example, according to *Komsomolskaya Pravda*, 6 out of 10 industrial workers do not show up for work on Mondays and half of those who do show up cannot work because of hangovers (Gerol, 1983). These are rather fragmented data of course. More elaborate statistical information is available, however, concerning alcohol consumption and alcoholism in Poland.

According to a public opinion survey conducted in 1983 on a representative sample of the adult Polish population, alcoholism was seen by the greatest number of respondents as a serious threat to Poland even before such phenomena as a world war, pollution, moral decadence, narcotics, civil war, anarchy, poverty and hunger (Goban-Klas, 1984). Such a hierarchy of fears is not surprising, given that there has been at least a six-fold increase in the consumption of pure alcohol since the pre-war period, and the rate of increase has been considerably precipitated in the 1970s (Falewicz *et al.*, 1975; Wald *et al.*, 1981). While a statistical Pole drank 1.5 litres of pure alcohol in 1938, the respective figure for 1976 was 7.8 litres, and it reached 8.4 litres in 1980 (Wald *et al.*, 1981: 89; Wieczorkowska-Bednarek, 1982). The 1976 estimate of 7.8 litres of pure alcohol was calculated on the basis of an average consumption of 13.4 litres of vodka, 8.5 litres of wine and 34.9 of beer. This estimate did not include moonshine, however, whose inclusion would bring this figure to a much higher level. (According to official estimates, 30 per cent of the alcohol consumed in Poland is produced illegally, see Wieczorkowska-Bednarek, 1982: 5). The rate of increase of alcohol consumption in the period between 1970–75, as well as the share of hard spirits (vodka) in the overall alcohol consumption, were the highest among all the countries which publish relevant statistics. For example, those countries with very high levels of alcohol consumption such as France and Italy, consume approximately 50 per cent less hard liquor per capita than Poland. Moreover, the production of vodka, over 90 per cent of which is destined for the home market, increased in Poland in the 1970–76 period by 72.4 per cent. In the same period, the number of people brought by the police to the sobering up stations increased by approximately 44 per cent. The number of patients with alcoholic psychosis hospitalized for the first time went up as well. While the rate of male hospitalization was 3.4 per 100 000 male population in 1957, it rose to 13.9 in 1975. Moreover, the number of people killed in traffic accidents caused by impaired drivers more than doubled in the period between 1972 and 1976 (all the quoted data come from Wald *et al.*, 1981). It is also worth noting that numerous studies show that the rate of increase in alcohol consumption among juveniles has been much greater than that noted for the adult population (Falewicz *et al.*, 1975; Falewicz 1976; Swiecicki, 1977: 46–58; Jarosz, 1980: 263–6).

While more recent statistics are not available, various official and unofficial pronouncements indicate that the alcohol problem continues to grow. It has been estimated, for example, that, in 1983, there were approximately 4.5 million problem drinkers as compared to 1.5 to 2 million in the early 1970s (Falewicz, 1973: 87; Dux, 1983: 3). This is a frighteningly high proportion of the total population which numbers approximately 36 million. Yet, the treatment and rehabilitation facilities are drastically inadequate; even those alcoholics who, according to the law, should obtain compulsory treatment cannot be accommodated due to the extremely limited resources and the miniscule number of specialized staff (see e.g. Wieczorkowa-Bednarek, 1982).

The Polish authorities' faith in the criminal law as the main instrument of anti-alcoholic policy has led to the introduction of repressive laws (especially important was the 1959 law) which allow for coercive treatment and imprisonment of alcoholics without much consideration for the development of necessary treatment methods and facilities. The law, with its high penalties for moonshining, seems to be more concerned with the protection of the state's monopoly of alcohol production than with any real prevention measures. The revenues from alcohol sales accounted for 16 per cent of the total state budget in 1980 (Zukowska, 1981). The situation is not different in the USSR, where alcohol plays a very important economic role and where, in the 1970s, 'turnover taxes collected on sales of alcoholic beverages in retail trade and in dining and drinking establishments comprised some ten to twelve per cent of all state revenues and more than one-third of all taxes paid by the population' (Treml, 1975: 163). Alcohol is undoubtedly a very profitable business since the prices of alcohol do not have to bear any relation to the costs of production which are, in fact, minimal. Alcohol sales also bring desperately needed foreign currency as a significant proportion of the state-produced alcohol in both countries is sold through the chains of 'hard' currency stores. The volume of alcohol sold by these stores in Poland increased 24 times in the years 1970–76, the period of intensive modernization of industry, whereby the massive imports of modern western technology considerably increased the state demand for foreign currency (Wald *et al.*, 1981: 99).

These economic considerations and the tendency to rely on legal controls are very apparent in a new law passed in Poland in November 1982. This law attempts to reorganize completely the retail trade in alcoholic beverages, including changes in the institutional structure, sales hours, prices, structure of profits, etc. without even touching other aspects of socio-political reality which contribute to the problem. The new legislation disregards the voices of experts who, in the relatively free period of 1980–81, spoke against repressive measures and spurious reforms of retail policies and prices and who criticized the prevailing approach which saw alcoholism as a problem in itself, an isolated social illness, unrelated to the ailing of the whole society (e.g. Falewicz, 1981; Zukowska, 1981; Kapuściński, 1981).

In sum, while the alcohol problem receives much attention in both studied countries, the recommended and implemented measures appear to be totally ineffective. They are restricted to individual therapy (on a limited scale due to the lack of resources), pricing and trade regulations, criminal repression and, above all, anti-alcohol propaganda.

JUVENILE DELINQUENCY

Both the Soviet Union and Poland have separate legislations and institutional arrangements for juvenile delinquents. The Soviet Commissions for Minors' Affairs which deal with child-welfare cases also act as juvenile courts. They are established by the local executive committees of the Soviets and include representatives of trade unions, party and youth organizations, teachers and law-enforcement agents. The Commissions have exclusive jurisdiction over children under 14 and limited jurisdiction for the 14–15 age group in cases which involve lesser offences. Criminal responsibility starts at the age of 14 for more serious offences and at 16 for all offences listed in the criminal code. The Commissions consider both cases which involve violations of the law and those which are believed to infringe on general social norms (i.e. 'status offences'). The Commissions may send children to rehabilitative work colonies, approved schools or other institutions, place them on probation or subject them to other educational disciplinary or medical measures. They may also fine the parents of unruly children or request the court to deprive such parents of the custody of their children. In the criminal prosecution of young offenders over 14, the ordinary courts are instructed to limit the punitive aspects of penalties and to stress re-education. Moreover, persons under 18 cannot be sentenced to death, exile or banishment. Their deprivation of liberty cannot exceed a period of 10 years (see e.g. Beermann, 1973: 352–5; Zeldes, 1981: 108–12; Connor, 1972: 85; Kiralfy, 1976).

The Polish juvenile law was revised in 1982, during the state of war. Contrary to the prevailing trends in western countries, the change has involved a shift towards a more paternalistic, 'rehabilitative' model, which, in turn, has broadened the definition of the delinquent and delinquency and expanded the system of the existing controls over juveniles. Unlike the previous legislation, the law of 26 October 1982 includes so-called 'status offences' as a sufficient basis for juvenile court proceedings (see Giżycka-Koprowska, 1982). Before 1956, the nature of the offence had been of major importance for the court, but afterwards, much more attention was given to the level and nature of the juvenile's demoralization or maladjustment. The law of 1982 went even further by accepting 'demoralization' as sufficient grounds for prosecution. Thus, 'demoralized' juveniles under the age of 18 may be subject to 'educational' measures even if they do not violate the criminal law.

Juveniles in the 13–16 age group are subject to correctional measures if they violate the criminal law. Cases of youths 17 years of age and older fall within the jurisdiction of ordinary criminal courts. Nevertheless, courts may also apply educational or correctional means generally reserved for juveniles to offenders in the 17–18 age bracket and they may not be sentenced to death. Moreover, persons between 17 and 21 years of age are treated as young offenders and the law stipulates that, in their cases, the re-educative aspects of the sentence should be given priority over general prevention and retribution. As well, they can be parolled from prison after serving half of the sentence while adult prisoners become eligible for parole only after having served two-thirds of their sentences. On the other hand, young offenders are subject to mandatory supervision by probation or parole officers whenever they receive a suspended sentence or are parolled from prison, while the supervision of adult convicts is facultative and depends on the specific circumstances of each case.

The inclusion of demoralization as the sufficient ground for prosecution by a juvenile court is especially controversial and has been criticized by some experts in Poland as vague and grossly unfair. They have also warned that such a solution will lead to stigmatization of greater numbers of youths and may be counter-productive. Such, critics also challenge the definition of 'demoralization' provided by the law which lists several very broad indicators of demoralization including encroachment upon the rules of social coexistence, the commission of a forbidden act, avoidance of school, drinking or using other substances, prostitution, vagrancy or membership in delinquent groups (see e.g. Kowalska-Ehrlich, 1983: 283–5; Tuhan-Mirza-Baranowska *et al.*, 1971; for the text of the law see *Acts* . . ., 1984).

There are two major types of juvenile institutions: more liberal, educational homes and more security-oriented correctional institutions. Juveniles under 13 years of age cannot be sent to correctional institutions, nor can status offences be sufficient grounds for a correctional sentence. These restrictions do not apply, however, to educational institutions, where children can be placed even without a court disposition. Custodial sentences meted out to juveniles in Poland are indeterminate and, at least in theory, depend on the progress in their rehabilitation and their family situation. The stay in an educational home must be terminated upon the inmate's eighteenth birthday and the confinement in a correctional institution must not be continued beyond the twenty-first birthday. Such release is usually conditional and involves supervision by a probation officer.

It appears that, once caught in the educational–correctional net, juveniles have a few chances to become totally freed from its control and associated stigma. According to a press article published in Poland, more than 3000 juveniles were confined in 34 correctional institutions in 1981 in Poland (Jakubiec, 1981). The Polish court statistics for 1979 reveal that approximately one-third of delinquent juveniles received custodial sentences involving terms in educational homes or correctional institutions and almost half of the remaining sentences involved the supervision by a probation officer. It has also been disclosed that the total number of juveniles confined in juvenile institutions in December 1979 was 7858. Correctional institutions housed 37 per cent and educational homes 50 per cent of all juvenile inmates. Ten per cent stayed in temporary detention centres while the remaining 3 per cent resided in half-way houses (*Rocznik* . . ., 1980: 482).

Correctional institutions have been known for their very high degree of punitiveness and arbitrariness. They are usually located in grossly inadequate, overcrowded buildings, often with no hot water, with defective heating and sewage and very unhygienic kitchens and other facilities. Extremely heavy and demanding work is often performed by male inmates in conditions of hunger or near-hunger. An enquiry into the predicament of the inmates of one such institution, conducted during the Solidarity period, found that the youths were forced to work 16 hours or more per day, they worked in conditions detrimental to their health, frequent work-related accidents were covered up and no compensations were ever paid. As well, they were forced to work on private projects without remuneration. The water available in the building was contaminated, cockroaches, fleas and lice were omnipresent. Physical and sexual abuse by guards and fellow inmates was common place. Beatings, torture and various other humiliating, painful or even crippling practices were found to be a part of the daily routine. The inmate leaders were given a free hand in their violent exercise of control over weaker juveniles (Jakubiec, 1981). Another publication presents a vivid description of unimaginable cruelty by guards and educational workers and indicates clearly the total defencelessness of juvenile inmates ('Dziekuje . . .', 1981).

A number of studies initiated by Adam Podgórecki in the 1970s inquired into the inmate subculture in correctional institutions.[10] It was found that there existed a very sharp division of inmates into two basic cast-like groups, known in the subcultural argot as *ludzie* (people) and *frajerzy* (suckers). There was very little mobility between the two and promotion from the lower to the higher cast was practically impossible. The 'people' were found to have their special language and a highly developed set of magic customs and taboos. They formed a very cohesive group and had their own normative code which applied only to themselves. 'Suckers' were not permitted to communicate with the 'people' in the normal course of daily events and were forbidden to use the code of the 'people' among themselves. They were regarded by the 'people' as dirty and were not allowed to touch their property. It was the role of the 'sucker' to serve the 'man' in any way requested and to obey his orders. The principal role of a 'sucker' was to serve as an object for the 'man's' sexual gratification. 'Suckers' were also subject to endless violence and abuse by both the 'people' and the guards.

It appears that in the situation of a total lack of rewards and genuine competition within the institutional setting, the boys' needs for self esteem, personal integrity and social importance can only be satisfied through rewards derived from the negative phenomenon of the degradation of others. While the 'people' know that their social position is low, they appreciate that there is a category of non-people who are inferior and, thus, compared to them, they can see themselves as real men. The brutality and mysteriousness with which 'people' guard their position against the 'suckers' can be explained by the fact that this hierarchy is the only dimension and source of social status available to them, and that it lacks any rational basis. In this kind of 'negative' structure, the only source of rewards lies in administering punishment to the weak, and the sole possibility of advancement is found in pushing down other individuals. Moreover, the only possible justification of this structure must come in the form of a doctrinaire, rigid and fatalistic ideology, guarded by magical principles and rituals (Łoś and Anderson, 1981: 201–17).

It may be suggested that the temporarily isolated populations tend to reproduce the structural principles of the broader society. Indeed, some aspects of the unique Polish inmate subculture seem to bear a striking resemblance to the artificial dichotomy of a communist society, where membership in the party 'nomenklatura' separates the 'men' from the suppressed masses. It appears that both inside and outside prison walls, the cast-like structures are secured by highly irrational and dogmatic ideologies used by the respective élites.

Despite all the well-known negative consequences of imprisonment, both Polish and Soviet courts tend to favour deprivation of liberty in their dealing with juveniles. Approximately 60 to 70 per cent of adjudicated juveniles in the USSR are sentenced to terms in juvenile labour colonies ('standard' or 'intensified' regime). The average sentence is 3 years, but the average period of time actually spent in a colony is about 9 months. This is partly due to the mandatory transfer to adult institutions when the inmate reaches 18 years of age (Barry and Barner-Barry, 1982: 301; see also The Statute of the Labour Colonies for Minors, 1968/1969).

Soviet juvenile institutions appear to share many features with their Polish counterparts, but they probably surpass them in the degree of cruelty, punitiveness and harshness of conditions, especially when their location in the Siberian wilderness allows totally uncontrolled abuse and exposure to the merciless climate. An eyewitness account of the situation in a number of camps in Novosibirsk illustrates well the plight of juvenile inmates:

> clubcarrying supervisors (officially called 'educators') roaming about the camp grounds subject the young prisoners (aged 10 to 18) to merciless beatings. In addition, the younger boys must also suffer the harassments of the older inmates – stolen food rations, sexual abuses (homosexuality is rampant), pressures to perform involuntary favors. Those who resist are beaten. Otherwise, the boys are assigned to hard labour projects – in construction, for example – or to dangerous duties in industrial plants, such as in iron foundries . . . [C]onditions in the intensified-regime children's camp in Gornyi (Toguchin District, Novosibirsk Region) are even more horrifying. The children are assigned backbreaking duties, despite the prevalence of hunger in the camp. Those who fall ill and request transfer to hospital are beaten. (Shifrin, 1982: 17–18)

Subcultural stratification and the exploitation of the weaker group by the élite seem to exist in the Soviet juvenile colonies as well. And, not unlike Poland, the guards and 'educators' exploit the subcultural divisions in their efforts to keep order inside the institution. According to an account given by a young inmate placed in a labour colony after the family had applied for permission to emigrate to Israel:

> there were regular criminals among the children in the camp and . . . they exercised control over all the others. They forced the younger inmates to perform services for them. Those who refused were beaten. The older boys often mishandled the younger ones and sexually assaulted them. The 'tutors' – that is, guardians – wandered about the place in a drunken state instead of attempting to put a stop to the abuses on the part of the thugs. On the contrary, the thugs were appointed as brigade leaders and told to push the others to fulfill their work quotas. (Shifrin, 1982: 112–13)

There are, however some critics of the extensive use of

correctional labour colonies as an article in the *Literaturnaya Gazeta* indicates. It points out that:

> teenagers who have learned to curb their instincts under strict supervision by older people are lost when this constant supervision ends and other forces – both external and internal – begin to have an effect on their actions. The transition is too sharp. . . . To the children in this neighborhood, a returnee is just as attractive as a hockey star. . . . In this way, many teenagers who return from sentences in colonies become (even if they don't intend to) criminogenic centers – as jurists put it – for other youngsters. (Shchekochikhin, 1983: 16)

It is impossible to estimate the true extent of juvenile delinquency in these countries, but numerous journalistic, academic and governmental publications clearly treat it as a very serious and widespread problem. While very different legal definitions of juvenile delinquency and of juvenile courts' jurisdiction also make impossible any comparisons between the extent of youth criminalization and institutionalization in communist and capitalist countries, it seems that the tendency to utilize custodial sentences is more pronounced in the former.

According to Polish statistics, in 1979, there were 153 557 juveniles found by Polish juvenile courts to be in need of care and supervision and another 15 220 were judged to be delinquent, as compared to 153 026 adults sentenced by ordinary courts in the same year. Approximately 55 per cent of juveniles were convicted for offences against individual property and 36 per cent for theft of state property. Around 5 per cent of juveniles were convicted for violent crimes, notably crimes against life and health, rape, and crimes against the physical integrity of the person. (The proportion of violent crimes by juveniles in the USSR seems to be closer to 20 per cent – Connor, 1972: 285; Zeldes, 1981: 99). Female delinquents constituted only 6.8 per cent of all convicted juveniles in Poland. Since no statistics on juvenile convictions are published in the Soviet Union and the existing estimates are rather outdated, it is necessary to base this comparative analysis on mainly qualitative and incomplete data.

While property is the most popular target of juvenile offences in both countries, violent crime is increasingly portrayed as a cause for a great concern. It is usually linked to the growing rate of alcohol abuse by teenagers. Senseless attacks on randomly selected individuals, violent gang robberies, muggings, rapes and fights are among the most common forms of violence. Soviet newspapers are full of cases such as those of a young hooligan who savagely beat a boy who, in his opinion, looked 'too cultured' (Kondratov, 1983: 21), a group of thugs in Kiev who beat an engineer to death to steal his western-style jeans, the incident in which drunken youths climbed into an open-air cage at the Moscow Zoo and killed five wallabies (Daniloff, 1982), or the case in Gorno-Altaisk, in which a passer-by who later proved to be a writer, was murdered by serveral students of a medical school who had had too much to drink and little to do:

> They were looking for adventures and they found them. Kokyshev didn't suspect anything was wrong until three of them, without a word, sat down beside him on the bench. Then he stood up. But Krechetov grabbed him by the arm and, putting the knife to his chest, demanded money. Lazar [Kokyshev] offered him everything he could find in his pockets – 32 kopeks. Krechetov considered such a trifling sum an insult. He didn't take the money, but with two blows to the face knocked Kokyshev to the ground. They began to beat him as he lay there. Three against one . . . [Later during the trial:] 'Did Kokyshev put up any resistance?' the judge kept asking. 'Did he insult you? Did he say anything at all? Perhaps you had met him before and he had offended you in some way? . . .' 'No. No. No.' 'Then why did you beat him up?' 'I don't know'. 'The fellows were kicking him, so I kicked him too'. 'The others were beating him, and I joined in'. (Samokhin, 1975: 7)

The report in *Literaturnaya Gazeta* ends with an interesting comment on middle-class delinquency:

> It is possible to build a hydroelectric station, to overfulfill the plan in ton-kilometers, to give everyone a motorcycle and a television set, but not to notice that a new Pithecanthropus, something in bell-bottom trousers and an expensive leather jacket bought with Papa's hard-earned money, is growing up next to us. (Samokhin, 1975: 8)

Most violent crime is committed by youth gangs and their behaviour has increasingly been portrayed as 'mindless' aggression, not connected with any tangible advantages, economic or otherwise (Voronitsyn, 1974: Barry and Barner-Barry, 1982: 299; Baniloff, 1982; Zeldes, 1981: 89); Mościskier and Szelhaus, 1979: 507). Much of this aggression is directed against female victims. Gang rapes are among the favoured pass-times of some, both underprivileged and affluent, juvenile groups in the cities and in the countryside. Gang rapes often occur during or in the aftermath of drinking parties (see Czapów, 1976; Zeldes, 1981: 56; Stern, 1980: 204, 206), but more premeditated schemes are also employed whereby totally unsuspecting females are often brutally abused. A typical example of the latter situation is a case quoted by Czeslaw Czapów who studied gang rapes in Poland in the early 1970s:

> Around 8 a.m. Teresa K. (13 years old) walks to school with a briefcase. A boy blocks her way, pulls the briefcase out from her hands and runs away. The girl runs after him shouting 'Give back my briefcase'. Once she runs into the entrance of an apartment house, several boys jump on her, drag her to the basement and rape her.
>
> (Czapów, 1974: 394; this author's translation from Polish)

One of the major conclusions of Czapów's research points to an important feature of the male gang subculture:

> [Sexual assault] results also from the acceptance of the typical for hooligan subcultures attitudes toward women. . . . The language referring to sexual matters . . . is not only based on vocabulary which in our culture is used to express hostility, a desire to humiliate, to degrade; it is also a language which accentuates instrumental aspects of sexual contacts and expresses the perception of the woman as an 'object' not a person. A girl is treated as bottle of wine or a 'snack' to accompany it. If no one takes care of her, if she is 'nobody's' than one can grab her, and since it is not a valuable object and is meant for immediate consumption, the event is not seen as a crime.
>
> (Czapów, 1974: 408–9)

Juvenile subcultures tend, to some extent, to be influenced by western patterns of youth rebellion. Yet despite superficial similarities, these foreign counter-cultures appear to be adopted to express or symbolically overcome problems with their own socio-economic status. The 'hippie' values and symbolism played an important role in the counter-cultures of the studied countries in the 1970s (for an analysis of the Soviet 'jazz' counter-culture in the 1945–56 period, see Starr, 1981). The 1980s ushered in a fascination with a more violent expression of the rejection of the conventional order modelled on the 'punk' movement. Reports in the Soviet and Polish press tend to dismiss them as lamentable imitations of decadent western fashions and usually recommend that better police surveillance be implemented and more attention be paid by the school and parents to teenage leisure habits.

The most visible presence of the punk counterculture has been noted in 1984 in the Polish industrial city of Nowa Huta, which has always been glorified as a symbol of the communist industrialization of Poland. A blue-collar city, exposed constantly to the double pressure of the ideology of working-class supremacy and the reality of acute hardship and suppression, Nowa Huta has also become a symbol of the stubborn struggle for religious freedom and an important centre of the Solidarity movement in the South of Poland. It was also the scene of extremely violent and bloody police actions in the aftermath of the imposition of the state of war in 1981. A couple of years later, the city became the terrain of a war between two youths' subcultures: the 'popers' and the 'punks'. According to Polish press reports, groups consisting of dozens of followers of each persuasion fight regularly in the streets using sharp instruments against each other. The aim of their efforts appears to be a desire to cut the hair of the members of the opposite gang. Both groups sport very distinctive hairstyles and are generally distinguished by very contrasting appearances. While the popers are elegant and clean and adore western clothes, the punks are dirty to the point of stinking and have their hair treated with a sugar solution in order to make it rigid. The popers are confident, arrogant and convinced of their own superiority. They are ashamed of being workers' sons. The punks, on the other hand, see themselves as inferior, they do not want anything from anybody, they wish to be left alone and accept their own uselessness, poverty and failure (Wilk, 1984b: 3; 'Porachunki . . .', 1984: 6, 'Kroki . . .', 1984: 6; Moda, 1984: 3).

Clearly, these two working class groups have found two different expressions of their experiences with the complex problems related to their class identity and their disadvantaged position within the grossly unfair social structure. It has to be kept in mind that what these youths witnessed in their adolescence was not only a violent suppression of their parents' efforts to regain dignity and secure some control over the industry to which they give their lives, but also a suppression of working people by the clubs and firearms put in the hands of the sons of workers and peasants hoping for economic advancement through careers in the police forces. It is important to note that this is not the first time that conflicting and highly ritualistic youth subcultures have symbolized the grave dilemmas experienced by the children of suppressed or underprivileged classes faced with certain new pressures or disruptions in their communities (see e.g. Hall and Jefferson, 1976; Mungham and Pearson, 1976).

Some Soviet newspapers also make passing remarks about the existence of a 'punk' subculture as illustrated by the following passage from *Izvestia*:

> Valera Mashkov, a third-year student at the railroad-transport technicum, was known around town as a punk. He and his friends had

> a special style: They sported trousers that were ridiculously tight around the ankles, wore cloth caps pushed back on their heads and cut their hair so short that they were almost bald. But the chief distinguishing feature of these rowdies was their belligerent behaviour toward others. They used foul language, drank bottles of 'stunner' . . . and then roamed about the city's parks and courtyards in hopes of meeting and then thrashing boys who weren't members of their gang.
> (Kondratov, 1983: 21)

Yet, the most frequently mentioned aspect of juvenile delinquency appears to be the perennial, and ever worsening, problem of alcohol abuse. Many Polish and Soviet studies quote very high percentages of crimes committed under the influence of alcohol or motivated by the desire to secure funds to purchase it. Children learn to drink early, often at home and their patterns of drinking resemble those of the adult population: not only do they drink far too much, but they also tend to prefer vodka over beer and wine, they drink without food and drink to get drunk. A report published in Poland in 1978 indicated that half of the 14-year-old population drank alcohol from time to time as did virtually all boys in the 15–18 age group (quoted in Markiewicz, 1984). According to a number of sources, approximately half of the Soviet and Polish juvenile delinquents identified by the police come from homes where alcohol abuse is a serious problem (Mościskier and Szelhaus, 1976: 498; Kryczka, 1978: 106; 'Alkohol . . .', 1983; Lubelska, 1984b: 2; Kolakowska-Przelomiec, 1975: 171–2; Zeldes 1981: 92). Moreover, many researchers report that the drinking age has been declining systematically. Statistics quoted in a Soviet youth magazine show how dramatic these changes are:

> The percentage of people who begin drinking prior to age 18 has jumped from 16.6% in 1925 to 90%–95% at present. . . . one survey of 27 preschoolers found 20 who had already tried beer, 7 who tried wine, and one who had drunk vodka with his father.
> (Lirmyan, 1982: 15)

The drinking subculture at workplaces is also cited by many authors as the cause of the formation of bad habits in young employees. The prevailing pattern of drinking during working hours and paydays drinking bouts is believed to lead to alcohol problems in young males (see e.g. Barry and Barner-Barry, 1982: 298; Labudzka, 1974: 150–60; Connor, 1970: 292–3). Trade schools, where the majority of working-class children tends to end up, are also often described as major breeding grounds of delinquency and alcoholism (Connor, 1972: 102; Swiecicki,

1977: 48–9). According to one Soviet source, criminality among trade school students is five times higher than that of high school students (see Zeldes, 1981: 98). It is common knowledge in these countries that many trade school teachers, who rarely have any pedagogical training, do not treat their duties very seriously, come to school drunk, drink with students and are frequently involved in various criminal schemes.

In addition to the alcoholic or criminal environment, the major causes of juvenile delinquency identified by Soviet and Polish authors include the malfunctioning of the family (its breakdown, single parenthood, child-beating and abuse, low education levels of the parents and employment of mothers), the poor quality and other shortcomings of schools, the inactivity of youth organizations and boredom, migrations from the countryside to the cities, substandard and overcrowded housing, poor economic conditions (the latter more frequently mentioned in Polish publications), low IQ levels., unstable or immature personalities, learning disabilities, absences from school, peer pressure and the fascination with western fashions. Some publications, however, make more daring references to the lack of perspectives, the emptiness of life, general social corruption, the inefficiency of the economy and persistent shortages of basic goods, the monotony and hypocrisy, of the official propaganda. A Soviet author cites, for example, the following causes of delinquency:

> the rejection by young people of moral guidance from mentors whose smugness, self-seeking and pompous hypocrisy they sense keenly, dislocations due to frequent changes in educational policy . . ., the inability or unwillingness of many educationists, officials and judges to think of pupils or offenders as individuals, and the general attitude of high-minded severity.
>
> (Beermann, 1960a: 452, a review of a publication by a Grigori Medynski in *Moskva*, Nos 4, 5, 10 and 11, 1959)

A Polish author writing in the 1970s notes the omnipresent hypocrisy evident in 'the gap between the principles declared by the adults and their actual behaviour, uselessness of many behavioural norms . . ., [the presence of] diverse influences and pressures coming through different channels, often equally categorical as contradictory . . .' (Glueck, 1973: 251; this author's translation from Polish). Similar observations were made during the Solidarity period by numerous writers. One of them, a sociologist, wrote, for example, of 'an essential dissonance between the 'festive' values of the socialist ideology proclaimed in political programmes and in the propaganda subordinated to them, on the one hand, and the real, empirically observable values on the basis of which real socialism . . . functions, on the other' (Wnuk-Lipiński, 1982: 85; this author's translation from Polish). The same author emphasised the presence of the 'social schizophrenia' or 'dimorphism of values' which is expressed in the existence of two totally separate systems of values and social activities: the official, communist one and the private world permeated by traditional patriotic values and individual loyalties. He suggests that 'the less democratic a given society, the stronger the division into the private and the public sphere and the more acute the manifestations of dimorphism of values. . . . This probably accounts for aggression observable in human relations in everyday life [in Poland]' (Wnuk-Lipiński, 1982: 87, 88).

More recent Polish comments refer to the disastrous political and economic crisis in the aftermath of the suppression of Solidarity. A researcher, interviewed by a daily newspaper states, for example, that:

> for years, the state's pedagogic policy in relation to the young generation was based above all on declarations, promises of work, wages, apartments. But these promises proved to be false. The lack of economic perspectives has been accompanied by a complicated social situation, disorientation and doubts as to what really counts and what one lives for . . . [Apparently motiveless, destructive delinquency] results from [these youths'] perception of the inequality of opportunities and the lack of faith in their ability to achieve higher standards through their own work.
>
> (Lubelska, 1984b: 1; this author's translation from Polish)

Another researcher notes that 'the loss of credibility of the adult world produces disoriented, lost individuals' (Wilk, 1984a: 3; this author's translation from Polish). A high-school director states in a newspaper interview that 'the lack of consistency in the implementation of economic reforms and the lack of a clear, precise vision of the future have a very bad impact on young people. What is more, the mass media glorify violence and aggression' (Wilk, 1984b: 3; this author's translation from Polish). In the same article, based on a series of interviews, several high-school students complain about the imposed uniformity of the environment in which they grow up: 'We live in identical apartment houses, we have identical parents, we go to identical grey-walled schools. Green hair is not compatible with this pattern' (Wilk, 1984b: 3; this author's translation from Polish). They accuse social control agents with an overconcern for harmless signs of non-conformity and the zealous suppression of efforts by youth to protect their identity as individuals.

It appears that these scattered voices point to an interpretation of the youth rebellion and delinquency as, not always a conscious, but often violent, reaction against hypocrisy, the falseness of ideology, extreme injustices and inequality, the 'drabness' of life, the sterility of mass culture and education, the harshness of living and working conditions, the brutality of the suppression of any democratic tendencies, the omnipresence of social schizophrenia and alienation. The same factors undoubtedly contribute to other troublesome developments which, in turn, are themselves conducive to youth alienation and criminal involvement. They include such frequently emphasized problems as alcoholism and the continuous deterioration of family life. Not only did the divorce rate double in Poland in the period from 1960 to 1979 (*Rocznik* . . ., 1980: 46), but, as well, the number of parents whose parental rights were taken away by the courts[11] has increased at an alarming rate; in the period form 1966 to 1972 there was an increase of 40 per cent in such cases (Lipka, 1975: 36). Between 1972 and 1982, the number of children in the care of family courts practically doubled, from 107 000 in 1972 to 200 000 in 1982 (Lipka, 1975: 36; 'Alkohol . . .', 1983: 6). While similar manyfold increases in cases of parental rights' deprivation were found by Soviet researchers, no global statistics are made available to the citizens (Zeldes, 1981: 92).

Finally, political mismanagement of the economy, unfavourable social conditions and the resulting high rates of alcoholism contribute to the elevated numbers of children with developmental problems and learning disabilities. A 1983 press report in a Polish daily reveals, for example, that 30 per cent of the young men examined by the army draft commissions are exempted from compulsory service as a result of serious physical or psychological defects. Moreover, only 30 per cent of six-year-olds are qualified as sufficiently developed to start school. Around 40 per cent of six-year-olds are found to have serious developmental problems. As well, around 40 per cent of schoolchildren are qualified by schools as socially maladjusted or 'predelinquent' ('Alkohol . . .', 1983: 6). Last, but not least, juvenile suicide and attempted suicide rates have been increasing much faster than these of any other age group ('Alkohol . . .', 1983: 6; Jarosz, 1978, 1980).

There is no doubt that the overall conditions in which both the Soviet and Polish young generations grow up are not favourable. These young people appear to be unfit physically and psychologically, often abused at home or institutionalized by the state, quite heavily involved in delinquency and punished for it severely, disoriented ideologically and frustrated by the persistent incompatibility of the words and the deeds of the rulers. Their state-dominated upbringing tends to assault their desire for individuality, truth and achievement, and random aggression or self-destruction are not an uncommon outcome. The alarming increase in drug abuse by Polish adolescents in the 1980s, which caught the authorities by surprise, only confirms the often questioned hypothesis that there is a relationship between the political situation and the juvenile unwillingness to 'adjust' to the societal norms.

DISCUSSION

The repeated claim made by various western and eastern authors that there is less crime in communist countries than in capitalist nations does not appear to be particularly well founded, even in light of the data reported within the communist countries themselves. Such a claim tends to be based on a variety of arguments ranging from those referring to the superiority of the communist socio-political organization, through the more neutral claims of greater community involvement in the control and protection of its members, to the rather negative comments on stricter and all-encompassing, totalitarian controls or the total uniformization of an over-disciplined society. The arguments concerning the superiority of the political system may include claims that the profit orientation has been successfully eliminated in these countries, that typical capitalist competitiveness and consumerism have lost their meaning, that the anomie syndrome characterized by the unrealistic obsession with success at any price has vanished, that poverty has been eradicated, that racial prejudice and discrimination have disappeared without a trace and, finally, that a better, more conscientious and pro-social type of citizen has been moulded.

There is very little hard evidence, however, to support these general claims. The flourishing of the so-called 'second economy' and the omnipresence of black-markets indicate clearly that profit orientation is not only alive but pursued with great vigour under communist conditions. Competitiveness, consumerism and related to it, anomie, seem to flourish as the promise of communist affluence and equality prompts aspirations which the reality of scarcity and extreme economic and political disparities can hardly match. While the dispair and poverty of kolkhoz peasants, city slum-dwellers and thousands of disabled, old and unemployed are definitely not less acute than those of the western poor, they may not hope for unemployment benefits or welfare payments. The absurdity of the claim that racial discrimination has been abolished is clear to any student of the plight of ethnic minorities in the Soviet Union and Poland.

Finally, while, the new 'socialist man' has indeed emerged, he is not what Marx had hoped for or the communist leaders claim him to be. He is a frightened, corrupt, politically and economically exploited individual, deprived of basic freedoms, kept in the dark about the most vital developments and facts in his own country and in the world, indeed, inevitable product of a monopolistic party rule bent on the eradication of individuality, spontaneity and participation. Moreover, he is a hypocritical being, a chameleon, able to demonstrate on the surface his unconditional obedience and orthodoxy while tirelessly planning his tenuous 'capitalist' plots to acquire needed goods, secure promotions or manifest his true attitudes. Of course, 'he' may be either male or female, but he is nevertheless brought up in a male-dominated culture with a preponderance of military symbols and all-male power machinery.

The claim that crime and deviance have been significantly reduced due to the party efforts to exercise total control over the society is also rather unconvincing. It is true that these societies are subject to a massive control apparatus, that the pressure on people to inform on their fellow citizens is quite extraordinary, and that deviations are punished with exceptional harshness, however, these realities, do not necessarily result in less crime. First of all, the efforts to establish total control over the behaviour and life styles of citizens lead to broader, more flexible definitions of deviance and crime (e.g. hooliganism, parasitism, membership in unregistered associations etc.). These must logically lead to greater rates of officially registered crimes. Yet, even if western definitions of crime are applied, it seems that there are no drastic quantitative differences between the studied countries and the western world. While it would be futile to make precise comparisons between individual countries in Eastern Europe on the one hand, and those in Western Europe and North America, on the other, due to the questionable value of the available crime statistics, it may be safely stated that, on the basis of a variety of sources, communist countries are at least as unsuccessful in their efforts to control crime as are their capitalist counterparts.

Undoubtedly, some causes of crime may be similar in both types of countries, however, their actual expressions do differ significantly. Moreover, various specific features characteristic of each of the political and economic systems are conducive to crime in unique ways. Conventional crime must be seen as an outcome of the global social, political and economic conditions and values, specific environmental situations and factors, and individual dispositions. As noted earlier, the global system of communist societies appears to have many criminogenic ingredients. Most notable among these are: injustice, overcentralization, drastic limitations of individual freedoms, frustrating economic inefficiency and scarcity of basic goods, all-pervasive corruption and illegality within the ruling élite, the falseness of ideological rhetoric, and constant efforts to break non-party solidarity among people and stifle informal communication and social exchange. Crime may appear to be an understandable reaction to such an accumulation of pressure on individuals who are forbidden to cooperate with others, form associations or even express their views.

Anomie theory (see, e.g. Durkheim, 1963: 69–84: Merton, 1938) which is believed to explain at least some criminal behaviour in capitalist countries, seems to apply to communist societies as well. The glorification of success and optimistic forecasts of constant progress as well as the egalitarian ideology and slogans about workers', or people's, ownership of the economy contrast sharply with the reality of impoverished, stagnant societies, ridden with alienation and feelings of hopelessness and fear. In addition to these general, persistent features, specific periods, such as the early years of the intensive industrialization of these countries and the Polish economic modernization and expansion in the 1970s, promoted new hopes and material aspirations which were bound to be disappointed by the actual opportunities created by these developments. The persistent overconcentration on heavy industry by both these countries, as well as the short-sighted Polish industrial modernization financed by foreign money borrowed by Edward Gierek, have led to the conspicuous disparity between the grandiose industrial projects on the one hand, and the drastic deprivations suffered by individuals, on the other. There is something humiliating and disgruntling about a situation where workers in such glorified heavy industries are unable to secure basic foodstuffs for their families and shortages in consumer goods make it almost impossible to obtain the most mundane items, including underwear or furniture.

Anomie theory, when adjusted to communist conditions, may, therefore, explain the temptation on the part of members of these societies to use illegal means to achieve their basic, legitimate goals. The constant official laudations of great national achievements and the concentration on visible and monumental industrial and military projects, leave individuals in a limbo of unfulfilled promises. If their societies are so great and successful, why is it that their pots and pockets are empty and stores offer little food but a lot of vodka? If their societies are indeed workers' promised lands, why is it that workers do not have any say, even at the shopfloor level, why is it that their children go to second-rate schools and live in inferior, overcrowed quarters? Since there are no satisfactory answers to these obvious questions, the norms of such societies may also be questioned. If double-standards prevail within the ideology and official life, and the individual represents no value to the rulers, then the individual does not feel bound by their norms and he may, therefore, try to achieve what he perceives as his legitimate right by illegitimate means.

The types of illegitimate means available depend, of course, on the individual's position within the societal organization. Those with white-collar jobs may have greater occupational opportunities to commit fraud or other economic malversations, blue collar workers may have some opportunities to steal and deal in state property. There are also those, however, who, for various reasons, are unable or unwilling to participate in these occupational criminal activities, and for whom more conventional property crime may become a viable option. As Cloward and Ohlin (1960) suggested in their sociological comments on American criminal subcultures, it is not just blocked legitimate opportunties which produce illegal involvement, but also the presence and availability of specific types of criminal opportunities. This comment applies equally to communist societies. Those with the most limited occupational criminal avenues are most likely to be caught committing typical 'street crimes', alone or in collaboration with other 'underclass', 'underworld' individuals.

While property crimes seem to be the dominant form of criminal involvement in these countries, their violent crime problem is probably more serious than in many Western European societies. The Soviet rates of violence are probably comparable to the American ones, with the exception of the common homicide rate (as opposed to homicides by the state), which is most probably lower in the Soviet Union due to the unavailability of firearms. If there is any truth to the theory that frustration produced by blocked opportunities may lead to aggression, the sources of violence in communist countries are not difficult to identify. In addition to the economic and political frustrations already discussed, there also exist more existential problems resulting from the official denial of the importance of the individual in the historic mission of these societies. All the institutional arrangements, from child centres and schools to workplaces and the state administration, are based on the principle of the insignificance of the individual will and preferences.

Human dignity, self-worth and identity are, therefore, constantly threatened which, in turn, results in feelings which may range from aggression, anger and bitterness to self-abasement and resignation.

Ready supply of alcohol, sold in most grocery stores and eating establishments, provides a remedy with which people try to rebuild their self-importance and image or try to simply forget their humiliations. Since the individual ability to cope and to control one's bitterness and aggression is lowered by alcohol, the connection between high alcohol consumption and violence is understandable. It is necessary, however, to remember that violence is not produced by alcoholism, but rather that both drunkenness and aggression have some common structural causes.

The widespread alcohol abuse cannot be, however, fully explained by anomie, alienation and blocked opportunities for expression. It may also be argued that the state promotes high alcohol consumption in order to increase its revenues in both domestic and foreign currencies. The high volume of alcohol sold in 'hard currency' stores and the availability of alcoholic beverages in otherwise empty grocery stores suggest that the authorities are quite interested in the maximization of alcohol sales. It has also been documented in the USSR that factory management frequently provides vodka to workers to induce higher productivity, and that enterprises, which utilize alcohol for technical purposes, often use it as payment-in-kind for various minor jobs or overtime (Treml, 1981: 35–6).

Finally, in these countries, where domestic currency has little purchasing power and dollars are hard to obtain, alcohol has become an unofficial second currency in which bribes and tips are paid, deals are sealed and goods purchased. It is well known that, in Poland, 'almost everything can be arranged in a barroom' (Dux, 1983: 3). Similarly, in the Soviet Union, in many transactions:

> a bottle of vodka becomes almost a token payment without regard to the value of the transaction. . . . Equally frequent is the use of vodka as a supplementary payment or as an inducement within the state sector, when employees agree to perform the task for which they are responsible by the terms of their jobs only upon the gift of a bottle. . . . In rural areas samogon is used to reward the peasants . . . [Moreover,] the use of vodka as money is particularly widespread in second economy markets and in the criminal underworld.
>
> (Treml, 1981: 35–6)

Yet, the use of vodka is most strongly associated with corruption, practised on such a large scale in the studied societies. It does not necessarily serve as a bribe in itself, but it is routinely used to facilitate corrupt exchanges:

> It is quite clear that very often the bottle of vodka plays only a symbolic role in that its value is insignificant compared with the overall magnitude of the bribe. But the act of passing this bottle from the person seeking the favour to the person providing it establishes some bond of trust between the parties to the illegal transactions. (Treml, 1981: 37)

In sum:

> the use of vodka as the second currency clearly facilitates small transactions in the second economy, attracts labour to the sphere of illegal activities and generally leads to expansion of corruption and graff. It [also] leads to increasing alcohol abuse and heavy drinking. (Treml, 1981: 38)

The dependance on alcohol has thus become an essential element of the politico-economic reality of these countries, not just an individual vice or a subcultural deviation.

The young generations of the studied countries may be more controlled than their western counterparts due to longer hours spent in school, more homework, the compulsory or at least expected, involvement in youth organizations, longer economic dependence on parents and, finally, the two to four years' compulsory army service for all young males. And yet, there seem to exist sufficient reasons for their heavy involvement in diverse forms of delinquency and crime. It is especially the young people who want to have hopes and find a meaning in their lives and who are most sensitive to any signs of hypocrisy, double-morality and false ideological rhetoric. It is also young people who are most vulnerable to fashionable trends in clothes and music and who are overwhelmed by the free, colourful, and provocative western innovations. It explains the willingness of some of them to resort to theft or violence in order to acquire a pair of western jeans, a T-shirt, or a recent pop-record. The uniformity and greyness of the goods legally available to them explains their frantic search for more diverse and glamorous western gadgets, or just for any goods which have not received the stamp of approval from the monopolistic state. It seems that young people feel especially insecure about their identity and social status and, thus, the overwhelming pressure towards obedience and standardized appearance is more threatening to their selves and their needs for recognition as individuals. It is possible that drugs have provided, for some of these youths, especially in Poland, an avenue for a more unique, private, nonconformistic expression of their threatened individuality. As well, drugs have helped to repress feelings of emptiness, fear and lack of hope for the post-Solidarity generation, those same adolescents who experienced the enthusiasm of a democratic movement only to witness its violent suppression and the strengthening of the authoritarian rule.

Part Three: Withering Away of the Law and Crime?

12 Conclusion

WITHERING AWAY OF THE STATE AND LAW?

Despite the fact that the origins of communist order are rather different in the Soviet Union and Poland, the similarities of their politico-economic structures are striking. Even though Soviet communism originated from a revolution, it was an élitist revolt, lacking support from any socialist proletarian movement. Just like the earlier tsarist rule and the subsequent Stalinist terror, the Bolshevik revolution came from above. In Poland, on the other hand, there was neither a grass-roots socialist movement nor a revolution. The imposition of communism was achieved by a masterful Soviet deception, backed by the Red Army tanks and the reluctant, but nevertheless fateful, consent of the greatest world leaders.

Unlike Russia, Poland has had a long tradition of democratic thought. While prolonged periods of foreign occupations and divisions made its actual, institutional application rather difficult, it was the Catholic Church which helped the Polish people to survive as a nation, to nurture their democratic ethos and to continue their struggle for liberation and self-rule. The Russian Orthodox Church's influence on the Russian masses was clearly very different, for, far from encouraging any liberation tendencies, it was inclined to represent the tsarist rule and teach obedience, patience and passivity. The ruthless Stalinist repressions led to the distruction of the Orthodox Church through the annihilation of the majority of churchmen and the forceful subjugation of the survivors. The ideological and moral monopoly of the Soviet Communist Party has thus been established on the ashes of the tsarist and religious orders. Despite its strenuous efforts, the Polish communists have not been able to eliminate or even weaken the Catholic Church's moral authority, and the party's monopoly over the people's lives has never been extended over their souls as well.

These differences notwithstanding, the legal orders of the studied countries show remarkable similarities. Each major Soviet legal enactment has been closely followed by Polish legislators with little respect for the unique features of the Polish moral and legal traditions. All stages of the Soviet legal history including the lawlessness of the Stalinist years, the 'popular justice' rhetoric of the early Khrushchev's rule, the strengthening of the rule of law and the introduction of the draconian penalties of his later years, the scapegoating tactics of periodical anti-crime campaigns related to domestic economic and political crises can be found faithfully copied in Poland.

One of the rare examples of Polish legislative non-conformity was the prolonged resistance against the replication of the Soviet anti-parasite legislation, which nevertheless ended, in 1982 under the military rule of General Jaruzelski. Another, however weak, sign of legislative deviation from the line imposed by Poland's powerful neighbour is the absence in the Polish Criminal Code of the crime of hooliganism, one of the most used criminal labels under the Soviet law. The Polish law provides a special legal formula, however, which allows for especially harsh punishment for a variety of crimes when committed for hooligan motives.

Thus, starting with the infamous analogy rule, exercised liberally during the Stalinist years in both countries, through the legal concept of hooliganism and hooligan motivation, to the offence of a parasitic style of life, all the major Soviet legal devices aimed at expanding the flexibility of legal definitions have been eventually incorporated into the Polish law. Their importance should not be underestimated for it is their ability to provide a criminal label for almost any kind of behaviour which appears to be especially exploited by the communist rulers. Not only do vague labels of this kind facilitate political control over the society, but they may also fulfil a multitude of other functions.

They are, for example, good reference points for anti-crime campaigns which serve to divert the population's attention from the deteriorating economic or political situation while emphasizing the benevolent role of the state as the protector of its citizens. These labels no only appear to be specific enough to avoid any generalized impression that the overall rate of crime is increasing, but they are also general enough to allow for the free adjustment of the numbers of arrests in accordance with the current needs.

These flexible criminal labels are also most functional in various 'cleaning up' operations, in which people who should be offered treatment, housing or welfare assistance can be removed from the streets and placed in correctional institutions. As a result, not only can the existence of destitution and homelessness be denied, but the absence of adequate health care and welfare provisions can also be successfully covered up (see Chapter 4). Finally, such criminal offences as hooliganism make impossible any legible interpretation of the crime rates within these societies since they can be applied to behaviours ranging from public drunkenness or swearing to political dissent, and even to a variety of violent crimes, including wife battering, rape and murder.

The definitions of the law have changed in the studied countries through several stages. The revolutionary *ad hoc* justice was followed by rather orthodox Soviet attempts to develop a 'new socialist law' based on Marxist dialectics, followed by the total subordination of the law to the will of the despotic leader, succeeded eventually by attempts at a symbolic popularization of the law and, finally, replaced by the pragmatic and exceptionally harsh rule of law, whereby the law could be altered or given vague wording in order to accommodate the dominant political and economic interests. The ease with which the law can be substantially revised to enhance its political functions was clearly demonstrated in the Polish Diet's consent to incorporate most of the provisions of the military regulations of the state of war into the criminal law and even the Constitution of that country (see Chapter 2).

The close functional relationship between the law and the changing politico-economic needs is also demonstrated in the patterns of the utilization of prisons and labour camps throughout the recent histories of those countries. Their extensive use to control political, religious and ethnic dissent has been well documented. It is less known, however, that those countries' penal networks have been fulfilling economic tasks of an extraordinary magnitude. They have actually constituted an indispensable part of the global production output projected by the Central Economic Plans in both the USSR and Poland.

As demonstrated in Chapter 5, the size, distribution and forms of employment of the Soviet prison population have been clearly correlated with the needs of the labour market and other economic developments. In the period of intensive industrialization under Stalin, there even existed a quota system which determined the number and length of prison sentences to be meted out in accordance with the shifting needs of the economy. All major industrial projects built in the hinterlands of Siberia and other hostile regions and glorified by the Soviet and western media of the period, were actually mass graves of famished and frost-bitten prison labourers forced to toil under totally unrealistic work quota systems.

Since that time, convicts have continued to be transported to work in most unhospitable climates, in unsafe and unhealthy industries and military projects and, indeed, anywhere where their participation has been deemed to be economically profitable. This high economic utility of both Soviet and Polish prisoners has removed any restraints which might limit the size of the prison population on the grounds of high maintenance costs. On the contrary, its growth is encouraged as it serves a unique and valuable function within the economies of these countries. As argued earlier in this book, the slave labour which has long lost its utility under capitalist conditions, appears to be well suited for the needs of communist labour markets. Under the conditions of the state monopoly over economic production and the exclusion of the principle of free competition, work processes must be strictly controlled by the state. Both the work output and the manpower must, therefore, be subordinated to tight regulations, and the meagre incentives offered by the state have to be supplemented by strong coercive measures to secure the fulfilment of the plan and preclude any efforts on the part of the workers to organize. Thus, the productive involvement of free and convicted labourers is not dramatically different. Nor is the quality of their labour output which tends, in both cases, to be rather shoddy due to poor work organization, lack of interest from management and the predominant lack of concern for the well being of the nationalized economy.

The Polish prison network has served a function very similar to that of its Soviet counterpart. Despite the absence of Siberia-like territories where the use of slave labour appears almost indispensable, many dangerous and exceptionally heavy industries in Poland have extensively utilized both adult and juvenile convicts. While they have clearly fulfilled considerable economic tasks, their forced labour has also served as an ultimate means of their control and subjugation to the anonymous, inhuman state economic machinery which constitutes the essence of the Soviet-style communist system. The full alienation and destruction of their individuality, achieved through such dehumanizing labour, could not be achieved by any other means.

The answer to the question regarding the likelihood of the gradual withering away of the state and law in these countries is not difficult to provide. The state and the law have become synonymous with the party and, therefore, their existence, expansion or diminution may only be triggered by similar transformations in the status of the Communist Party itself. There were some forecasts made in the early 1980s that the party may be eventually replaced in both countries by the army apparatus but this seems extremely unlikely. The party monopoly over all vital processes of these societies is crucial to the ideological survival of the real life communism as a distinctive formation. The law provides the party with the coercive force not only needed but absolutely essential to the continuation of its monopolistic rule. Since the party is not given legitimacy through general elections or other expressions of popular will, it is bound to rely on the criminal law in its efforts to stifle opposition. The act of outlawing all opposition parties, undertaken by Lenin at the outset of his rule and consistent with Marx's ideas, has created the necessity for the continuous suppression of any dissenting opinions.

In a similar manner, the creation of the communist economy, which has closely followed the formal ideological prescriptions, has run counter to many economic habits and aspirations of the people. Moreover, it contradicts the economic logic of complex industrial production itself. It is worthy of note that industrial production not only has its roots in capitalism but has been moulded in agreement with capitalist principles. It seems quite logical, therefore, that efforts to recreate western industrialization patterns under different general principles are unlikely to work. The communist economic conventions of full étatization, centralization, planification and rejection of the relevance of consumers' demands are cases in point. It appears that such an artificially constructed economy will always require the rather massive intervention of the criminal law not only to coerce the population to accept it, but also, quite simply, to induce it to function at all.

THE WITHERING AWAY OF CRIME?

Crime adopts many forms in communist countries, some of which are quite different, or at least differently patterned, than those found in western countries. In addition, the distribution of crime appears to be neatly organized in accordance with the distinctive stratification patterns of these societies. By studying the nature of typical crimes committed by various strata or classes, it is possible to acquire interesting insights into their actual structural positions. Their crimes cannot be adequately explained, however, without thorough knowledge of their political, economic and cultural placement within the social structure.

The crimes of the top party élite, structured into the nomenklatura networks, are only possible under the conditions of almost unlimited power and the absence of any mechanism of political accountability by this élite. Crimes typical to this group consist of all-pervading graft and corruption, and the free use of public wealth to satisfy their individual needs. These types of illicit behaviour are actually explicitly forbidden by the criminal laws of these countries and were analysed in detail, therefore, in Chapter 6 on 'red-collar crime'. Yet, the greatest crimes are perhaps these directed against humanity, justice, morality and the natural environment which are a direct result of this group's political mandate and are not criminalized under the existing laws. Yet, even if these actions are disregarded and only those which are actually criminal under the laws of these countries are strictly prosecuted, it is most likely that not a single member of the nomenklatura would remain at liberty, and many would inevitably be subject to capital punishment. Clearly, their confidence in their own unlimited power and impunity is so great that they do not hesitate to pass extremely harsh laws against themselves in order to achieve some purely symbolic gains.

It is often argued that tsarist Russia achieved unparalleled levels of corruption and the contemporary Soviet patterns of élite crime are merely a perpetuation of these old traditions and not an inevitable outcome of the communist order. It must be noted, however, that the Polish communist élite has achieved similar levels of involvement in corrupt practices despite the lack of the strong historical traditions of the Soviet Union. Therefore, even if tsarist habits have survived in Russia, there must exist some additional mechanisms, specific to the Soviet-style communist regime, which generate powerful incentives and opportunities for large-scale graft and bribery. Among such mechanisms are undoubtedly these political factors already mentioned as well as the dangerous illusion, enhanced by the prevailing economic arrangements and shared by the powerful functionaries, that they are the actual, even if only the temporary, owners of the state's wealth. Due to the inevitably temporary nature of this ownership, they do not implement any long-term policies of the rational maximization of profits, but rather concentrate on immediate private gains irrespective of any lasting damage they may cause to the economy. Since they cannot reinvest their profits, as they would undoubtedly do under capitalist conditions, they establish rather extravagant spending patterns for themselves and their families and engage in life styles of conspicuous consumption and luxury. This has resulted in the emergence of purely material status indicators which members of the élite are under pressure to achieve. These patterns are facilitated by the double monopoly of the élite, over both the political and economic spheres, control which in effect frees them from the constraints which the relative autonomy of these two spheres might have imposed.

These patterns of corruption, extortion and favouritism extend far beyond the strict circles of nomenklatura, however. The employees of the state bureaucracy, services, trade and even criminal justice system seem to succumb to the temptations created by the situation in which citizens' lives depend on discretional decisions over which they, the state bureaucrats, have an exclusive monopoly. The strict controls and bureaucratization of life make it necessary for the citizens of these countries to obtain permits, authorizations, or registrations in most spheres of their everyday activities. For example, they need special permits to reside in given areas, they have to obtain permissions if they want to travel, to change jobs, to buy cars or washing machines or to have telephones connected. Many of these permits can be given to a very restricted number of people and those who make such decisions are faced with almost unlimited opportunities for extra income through extortion or the acceptance of bribes. Similarly, store clerks and other employees of the retail trade deal constantly with goods in short supply, for which there are always more eager buyers than can be satisfied. This naturally creates great temptations for the illicit inflation of prices adjusted to the actual consumer demand, with the difference being privately appropriated by the sales staff themselves. The chronic shortages and regimentation of life thereby provide to even relatively minor functionaries the extraordinary power to make vital decisions about the distribution of scarce goods, services, and administrative permits. This must inevitably result in corruption.

The criminal justice system, as well, appears to be very vulnerable to corrupt practices, since the over-regulation of all aspects of life forces virtually all citizens to violate at least some of the numerous restrictions. This gives the police and other law enforcers an enormous scope of discretion in their decisions regarding arrest and prosecution. Both political position and the ability to bribe appear to be crucially important in many such cases. Furthermore, the party's pressure and control over judges excludes any reasonable assumption of their independence. Their integrity is compromised by the clearly political structure of the court systems within these countries. The bribes they occasionally take and the illegal schemes they participate in may not be so morally different from the perks, promotions and renewed contracts they secure through their obedience in court.

The communist economy also presents almost unlimited criminal opportunities. With no private ownership and, therefore no private interests vested in the long term economic performance of communist enterprises, the immediate concern of all groups involved in the production processes lies, above all, with their own, individual short-term gains. Those control mechanisms which do exist are also in the hands of people whose main interest is the maximization of their incomes and the minimization of trouble. They tend to be, therefore, heavily involved in the corrupt cover up of illegal economic conduct. The overall inefficiency and irrationality of the economic structure contributes to the prevailing belief that these illegal machinations, even if they result in huge profits to the individuals involved, are not actively harming anyone and definitely not the state economy, which is perceived as being in permanent disarray. Any actions taken against such criminal entrepreneurs tend to be motivated more by envy, political competition or the need for scapegoats than by a genuine concern for the state of the national economy.

As with other areas of life, the economic sphere tends to be highly centralized and regulated resulting in a maze of norms, prohibitions and quotas which have to be constantly bent or violated. Given their virtual lack of economic functionality, pro-legal attitudes within the state economy do not have much support, credibility or, indeed, utility. A certain proportion of economic crimes is, therefore, inevitably committed in the course of genuine efforts to make the economy work and to fulfil the centrally planned objectives. These activities, however, co-exist with much more particularistic attempts to reorganize the processes of production and distribution along more capitalist lines in order to achieve ideologically 'tainted', but privately welcomed, extra income.

Economic crimes, like the general phenomena of graft and corruption, assume very similar forms and proportions in both the Soviet Union and Poland. While the different ethnic compositions and cultural traditions of the various Soviet republics contribute to a greater diversity of criminal patterns and the greater autonomy of criminal gangs from the 'centre', these differences do not normally involve any dramatic deviations from the basic archetypes depicted in more detail in Chapter 8. The methods of dealing with them are slightly different, however, in both studied countries to the extent that capital punishment, relatively frequently meted out to Soviet perpetrators of economic crimes and corruption, is clearly avoided by the Polish courts. Executions of highly placed individuals have constituted one of the major Soviet methods of dealing with economic problems since Lenin, developed to truly monstrous proportions by Stalin and continued under more careful legal safeguards by his successors. This appears to be a spectacular way of both removing inconvenient co-players in the on-going power struggle and creating appearances of an egalitarian and impartial legal system. Generally less ruthless methods governing power struggles among Polish communists, who seem to create a more cohesive and inter-dependent stratum, have clearly resulted in a greater reluctance to rely on the criminal law for solving internal conflicts. For example, these solemn promises given to the Polish people that the top leaders responsible for the scandalous proportions of political and economic corruption in the 1970s would be duly punished, have not been fulfilled. While many lower level functionaries were sent to serve long prison sentences, the top office holders have been quietly discharged after prolonged investigations.

The very nature of the economic organization of communist societies is also conducive to the wide-spread criminal involvement of rank-and-file employees, industrial workers and peasants. Their alienation from the political organization of the society and the ban on free unions, meetings and strikes, prevent them from developing any loyalty to the state economy. Exploited and manipulated by both the party-assigned management and the criminal entrepreneurs, they react by becoming heavily involved in employee theft and fraud and less than conscientious attitudes towards work. In the absence of avenues for meaningful involvement or fair rewards for their efforts, they turn to alcohol, petty crime and sabotage. The cultural explanations of wide-spread alcohol abuse, which refer to deeply-rooted drinking traditions within these societies serve as a smokescreen, allowing the communist rulers to admit the existence of the problem without taking the blame for it.

Both the Soviet Union and Poland have experienced free trade union movements, and both states have suppressed them brutally. The developments in Poland in 1980, however, reached much greater proportions than has ever been possible in the USSR. The periodic outbursts of popular discontent and the subsequent periods of the relaxation of political controls, have strengthened the faith of the Poles in their ability to attain some change and their will to try. A more compact geographical territory with a denser and more evenly distributed population, coupled with a long tradition of underground resistance against occupying forces, have allowed for greater communication and easier organization among Poles. The vastness of Soviet lands, the internal passport system, ethnic differences, the total isolation from the West, the memories of the Stalinist horrors and the ruthlessness of the present controls seem to have jointly contributed to a breakdown in the social communication lines and the abilities to self-organize within the Soviet society. Yet, brave individuals do continue their doomed attempts to form political, social and religious networks only to find themselves in prison camps among common criminals or in metal hospitals among psychiatric patients.

The socio-economic organization within the studied communist countries reflects upon the roles of their citizens and women in particular. Even though women cannot be treated as a separate socio-economic stratum, their social position continues to be distinctly different from the male status. As well, their criminal involvement has remained quite dissimilar to that typical for men. Despite radical social change, Polish and Soviet women continue to be grossly under-represented in convictions for so-called conventional crime; their share of convictions of non-conventional, economic crime, however, appears to be unusally high. While occupationally and educationally very active, women still remain as the main socialization agents and homemakers. It is this double burden of their family and occupational roles as well as the responsibility for the transmission of moral and patriotic traditions which make them less susceptible to the temptations to violate traditional ethical codes and religion-based mores. Not only are they too involved in life's responsibilities but, as well, social controls, such as the Church and informal control systems, monitor them too closely to allow for their overt involvement in criminal life styles. Yet, unconventional, economic crime presents women with new criminal opportunities, free of conventional criminal stigma and consistent with their occupational roles. Their employment enables them to engage in economic and fiscal offences which are not regulated by the traditional ethics and, therefore, do not openly conflict with their historical role as socialization agents.

Conventional crime, in which men play the dominant role, appears to be not less wide-spread and diverse, and perhaps even more violent, than that in the countries of the West. The detailed analysis of these crimes presented in the preceding chapter, which also contains a rather comprehensive concluding section, makes redundant any further discussion of the findings here. It should only be added that, while these countries have consistently claimed to have overcome the traditional correlation between industrialization and urbanization, on the one hand, and crime and social disorganization, on the other, these claims cannot be substantiated. While, indeed, urban patterns of crime appear to be different in communist and capitalist countries, they do not necessarily prove the superiority of the Soviet style modernization. This modernization is achieved under the conditions of strict administrative controls and planning, that not only affect the impact of urban growth on crime, but also severely limit the freedom of choice and movement of the citizens (Shelley, 1981). The Soviet internal passport system, for example, has restricted the population movement to the point where their access to larger urban centres is fully controlled. Moreover, both Soviet and Polish cities have strict residential rules and special permission must be obtained by any potential settler. These permissions are extremely difficult to obtain and are conditional on a permanent job offer, a clean criminal record, a good political reputation and many other factors. Furthermore, convicts are not permitted to return to big cities after having served long sentences and people with criminal records or reputations can be simply evicted and deported. Thus, in contradistinction to western patterns, the communist suburbs tend to be inhabited by those who were refused residential permits or were forced to leave the city. Clearly over-represented among these are poor, unemployed, and criminally active individuals. They suffer acute deprivations, commute long hours to work or shop and tend to have a very high rate of criminal conviction for conventional crimes. Additionally, as a result of the residential restrictions in big cities, many rural youths who dream about city life move from the countryside to smaller urban and industrial centres and especially new ones, where there may be greater demand for manual labour. Thus, criminality is being partially shifted away from the larger and into the smaller centres, where there are exceptionally high proportions of young males, the social category known to be most prone to conventional crime. Luise Shelley's extensive research on the geography of Soviet crime (1980a, b; 1981) confirms this trend and emphasizes the exceptionally high crime rates in the Far East and the Far North areas where young people are encouraged to take up employment. While the remoteness of these industrial centres reduces the visibility of the problem, its existence testifies to the inability of the communist governments to cope with industrialization-related social problems. Moreover, despite vigorous attempts to control crime in big cities, it is very clear that their crime rates are quite elevated. It is interesting to note that those statistics which rely on the offender's place of residence persistently misrepresent the volume of urban crime since many individuals known to be involved in conventional crime live outside the city limits, but commit their crimes in the cities. In sum, the drastic restrictions on personal freedom and the coercive employment and settlement policies have not reduced, but merely altered, the manifestations of the crime problem in these societies (see also Connor, 1976).

The task undertaken in this book focused on the impact of the dominant ideology and politico-economic organization on the nature of crime and crime control in communist countries. The selection of two rather different communist countries was guided by a desire to identify both universal and more specific relationships in the studied area. It has been found, after arduous and painstaking research, that the major forms and mechanisms of crime and the criminal justice system are strikingly similar in both countries. Furthermore, a clear Soviet influence has been noted in the criminal law and criminal policy solutions adopted in Poland. Both the time sequence and the mechanisms involved clearly indicate that these similarities are not incidental and that there has not been a reverse effect of the Polish law on the Soviet legal institutions. It has also been found that crime, in both the USSR and Poland, tends to be stratified and directly influenced by the ideological, political, economic and legal forces which operate similarly in both these societies.

Notes

Chapter 1: THE STATE AND LAW IN THE SOVIET UNION

1. For example, the American Marxist criminologists, Herman and Julia Schwendinger, wrote recently that Western radical criminologists generally agreed 'that socialist societies have enormously reduced ordinary crimes. . . . For radical criminologists such reductions are due mainly to the development of economic security for working people and to the state planning that is genuinely regulated by social needs. Doubtless, such reductions are also due to the stable collective relations at the workplace and in the community that support social solidarity and moral obligations' (Schwendinger and Schwendinger, 1979: 248). It seems, however, that such views are now questioned by increasing numbers of radical criminologists themselves.
2. Although Lenin denied receiving any money from the Germans, this accusation has been substantiated by the evidence of the archives of the German Foreign Office which fell into Allied hands during World War I (see Schapiro, 1977: 33).
3. Lublyanka – the secret police headquarters and prison in central Moscow.
4. Gulag – an acronym for Chief Administration of Corrective Labour Camps.
5. The idea of the 'new class' was earlier elaborated in 1953 by a Polish underground group called the Neo-Pickwicks Club (Lipski, 1983: 16).

Chapter 2: THE STATE AND LAW IN POLAND

1. Of 14 500–14 800 officers and intellectuals captured by the Soviets, only 449 people survived. Mass graves of 4400 Polish officers in the Katyń Forest were unearthed by the Germans in 1943. The graves of the remaining victims have never been found. The Soviet Union has never accepted the responsibility for these mass killings and the Polish authorities banned any information about the Katyń massacre (Zawodny, 1962; Fitzgibbon, 1971, 1972; Jerzewski, 1980; *Zbrodnia . . .*, 1982; Montfort, 1966).
2. The fact that the PKWN, as well as its manifesto, originated in Moscow has been carefully omitted in the official history books in Poland and publicly revealed only during the Solidarity period, at the beginning of 1980s (see, for example, Kersten, 1981).
3. The official figures given by the Prosecutor-General were 53 people killed, 300 injured and 323 arrested (Karpiński, 1982: 51).
4. The Warsaw Pact was signed in 1955 and aimed at legitimizing the dominant role of the Soviet Union and its rights to interfere in the internal affairs of subjugated countries.

5. Imre Nagy and several of his associates were executed in 1958.
6. In Poland, citizens do not have access to copying equipment and only censored material may be reproduced on highly-controlled machines in workplaces.
7. The pressure exercised by KOR and other groups in and outside Poland proved to be effective and, in July 1977, an amnesty was announced which freed most of the workers convicted in the infamous trials of 1976.
8. Forms of harassment included dismissals from work, searches, interrogations, frequent detentions, blackmail tactics and beatings (also of activists' children). In some cases, these brutal beatings lead to the death of the victim but the police denied all responsibility for them (for details, see *Prologue*, 1980). In May 1977, for example, a student (S. Pyjas) died of injuries inflicted by police. The only witness able to recognize one of the policemen involved was found dead soon after he expressed his willingness to testify (Lipski, 1983: 124–7).
9. Many informal discussion groups were formed and the so-called Flying University was organized, which offered lectures by distinguished scholars and intellectuals in private apartments and other 'safe' accommodations.
10. In 1981, the Communist Party membership totalled approximately 2.5 million, while the membership of all independent unions (including those of urban employees, farmers and students' unions) reached at least 13 million.
11. At the time, an overwhelming majority of the working population belonged to the Solidarity Union.
12. Seven top elected executives of the Union were charged with anti-state activity. Yet, since all of them were arrested immediately after the imposition of the state of war, it is clear that they were being held criminally responsible for their union activities performed during the legal operation of the Solidarity Union, and not after it was banned.
13. Seven KOR members were charged with 'aiming to overthrow the political system', the minimum penalty for which is five years imprisonment and the maximum is death.
14. Ten alleged workers of the Radio were sentenced early in 1983 for 'continuing union activities after 13 December 1981' to prison sentences ranging from one to 4.5 years.
15. Usually mentioned among the unique features of the communist state in Poland are: the importance of the Catholic Church, the private ownership of farms and the lively cultural links with the West.
16. Before the passage of this and several other amendments, numerous intellectuals, artists and other individuals and groups sent letters of protest to the Diet demanding the relinquishment of the incorporation of such changes as well as a general national referendum on the key issues of the constitutional reform. As a result, hundreds of people lost their jobs, were expelled from universities, banned from publishing or performing, forbidden to travel abroad, and so forth (Raina, 1978: 210–28; Lipski, 1983: 24–9).
17. The draft of a new penal code prepared in 1981 under the auspices of the Solidarity Union proposed the elimination of capital punishment and the

retention of the 25-year imprisonment term as the maximum sentence (Kubiak, 1981: 13).

18. In the five years of the Stalinist rule from 1949–54, there were approximately 948 death sentences adjudicated by the courts and a still unknown number of death sentences and executions carried out by special courts and secret police (Kubiak, 1981: 13).
19. The Polish authorities do not recognize the status of the political prisoner. For an interesting documentation regarding the situation of political prisoners and their struggle for the recognition of their status see *Les Droits* . . ., 1983; 161–92).
20. In the months prior to the imposition of the state of war, many criminals were given the option of joining the anti-riot police forces (ZOMO) instead of going to or staying in prison. In this way, they vacated needed prison space for the political internees and strengthened the ranks of the police (see e.g. 'In Katowice', 1982: 14).

Chapter 3: STATE AND POPULAR JUSTICE IN USSR AND POLAND

1. This finding is quite easily explained given the fact that women have far less spare time than men acting simultaneously as full-time employees, mothers and housekeepers.
2. See note 1.
3. A more detailed analysis of the concept of the reference group and its evolution can be found in Łoś, 1979b.
4. The most reliable among these are Podgórecki, 1969: 142–9; 1971: 306–28; 1974: 149–61; Górski, 1967; Jasiński, 1966; Kurczewski and Frieske, 1978; Wasilewski, 1970).
5. Before the revolution, the '*volost*' courts, based on the principle of peer mediation and conflict resolution, enjoyed considerable popularity among the peasants (Solomon, 1981–82: 19).

Chapter 4: LAW, IDEOLOGY AND ECONOMY

1. For example, the official weekly *Polityka* reported in 1984 that two Jehovah's Witness preachers were registered as 'people persistently avoiding employment' (Podemski, 1984a). A subsequent report informed, however, that this decision was reversed by the Superior Administrative Court (Podemski, 1984b).

Chapter 5: PRISONS, POLITICS AND ECONOMY

1. This number does not include inmates in regular prisons, whose total population reached approximately 198 thousand by 1927 (Juviler, 1976: 33).

2. It is estimated, for example, that of the more than 200 000 inmates who worked on the 142-mile long White Sea Canal, over 50 000 died in a year and a half (Dallin, 1947: 241).
3. The largest prison population in tsarist Russia was about 184 000 registered in 1912 (Juviler, 1976: 33).
4. For example, according to the sources reviewed by Sellin, after the 1953 amnesty the population of Norilsk city and the surrounding county consisted of 45 000 prisoners, 225 000 discharged prisoners, 15 000 functionaries and 60 000 immigrants. The population of the Vorkuta region was composed of 105 000 prisoners, 120 000 discharged convicts, and 12 000 guards, administrators and technicians. This research led Sellin to conclude that 'the present population of distant, inhospitable regions of Siberia consists largely of prisoners, mostly politicals, and their families' (Sellin, 1976: 132).
5. Exile outside the Soviet Union is also practised, although it is not legally recognized. This practice, initiated with the exile of Trotsky in 1929, has been revived in the 1970s through the forcible exile of a number of dissidents (including Alexander Solzhenitsyn) from the Soviet Union.
6. Under Lenin and Stalin, the application of the death penalty was totally subordinated to political and economic interests. The 1926 penal code reflects well this tendency: it reserved the most severe punishments for crimes against the Soviet regime, while aggravated murder was not qualified as a dangerous crime and was punishable by a maximum of 10 years (Sellin, 1976: 128). It was not until 1954 that first-degree murder became a capital offence (Van den Berg, 1983: 159). In recent years, most of those known to have been sentenced to death had been convicted of violent crimes, but a number of executions of those convicted of economic crimes were also carried out in the 1960s and 1970s (see, e.g. *Prisoners* . . , 1980:87).
7. The total population of Poland was approximately 34.4 million at that time.
8. In 1981, prisons were allowed to spend 10.80 zlotych daily on food per prisoner (9 zlotych in the case of an unemployed prisoner) while the allowance per day for each prison dog was 28 zlotych (Wróblewski W., 1981: 30).

Chapter 6: CRIMES OF THE POLITICAL ELITE

1. The term 'red-collar crime' was coined by a graduate student at the University of Ottawa, Ms Ellen Gottheil in 1983.
2. Some other aspects of corruption in communist countries have been analyzed in Chapter 7 and in Łoś, 1980 and Łoś, 1982a.
3. Included in this research were: the national weekly magazine *Polityka* (all issues printed between mid-August 1980 and June 1981), the national weekly *Kultura* (most of the issues published in the above mentioned period), selected issues of weekly magazines including: *Zycie Literackie, Literatura* and *Tygodnik Powszechny* as well as of the daily papers from Warsaw, Cracow and other cities. Moreover, the present analysis also

included all the issues of *Solidarność*, the weekly magazine published between April and December 1981 (it was a regular publication of the free trade-union Solidarity, submitted to the censor's approval just like the other periodicals mentioned above). Twenty articles dealing directly with corruption of the privileged individuals and groups, and around 10 short reports in daily papers concerning many legal or disciplinary actions against corrupt officials were found in the reviewed periodicals. This material is supplemented in the present chapter by press articles published after the imposition of the state of war.

4. In the Soviet Union, serious bribery is subject to prison terms of 8–15 years of deprivation of liberty or death penalty. In Poland it is punishable by deprivation of liberty for up to 10 years.
5. According to another similar report, a deputy-head of a region and his colleagues had their mansions financed by state-owned companies and had the introduction of electricity to their properties covered by the funds assigned for the supply of electricity to the neighbouring village (Indelak, 1981).
6. Villas and mansions were only a small part of the private empire which the top officials have built for themselves. For instance, the French journal *Le Point* lists some of the possessions of the director of the Polish television network who was eventually sentenced to eight years of deprivation of liberty for his criminal involvement: 2 yachts, 3 aeroplanes, 7 cars, 1 stable with 7 horses on a farm of 16 hectares, 1 mansion near Warsaw, one 25-room house in the south-east of Poland and a villa near Warsaw. His villa was equipped with a swimming pool, a sauna and 4 prostitutes at his disposal. He also had a residence in Nairobi because he was fond of safaris. He owned an elegant apartment house in central Warsaw. Next to his office, where he worked as the television chief, he had a private swimming pool, sauna, beauty parlour with special masseurs, a small cinema and 900 video-cassettes with pornographic films (Christitch, 1980).
7. It was estimated in the early 1980s that party apparatus consisted of around 160 000 functionaries. Together with top echelons of the army, police and security forces and the holders of the managerial positions within the economy and state administration, the membership of this élite amounts to approximately 1 million people ('Sytuacja . . .', 1983: 44).
8. The official exchange rate was at that time between $50 to $70 for one zloty.

Chapter 7: CRIMES BY THE FUNCTIONARIES

1. The KGB and the Ministry of the Interior, which has been one ministry under Josef Stalin, were separated by his successor Nikita Krushchev.
2. In the USSR, such an individual is given full immunity; the Polish Penal Code of 1969 left the application of extraordinary mitigation of the penalty or even the waiving of its imposition to the discretion of the court. An amendment introduced in July 1983 made mandatory the use of such

extraordinary measures in certain cases of voluntary informers ('Analiza . . .', 1983: 53).

Chapter 8: CRIMES OF MANAGERS AND ENTREPRENEURS

1. For example, s. 246(1) states that a public functionary who, exceeding his authority or failing to perform a duty, acts to the damage of a social or individual good shall be subject to the penalty of deprivation of liberty for a period from 6 months to 5 years. Subsection 2 increases the maximum penalty to 10 years for cases where the perpetrator commits the act with the purpose of obtaining a material or a personal benefit (*The Penal Code* . . ., 1973: 102). This article of the Penal Code, however, is very rarely used by Polish judges (Spotowski, 1981: 10).
2. The following excerpt from a recent report by Weschler illustrates well the disastrous consequences of the neglect of safety standards in a Polish mine:

   > On 18 June 1982 ten miners were killed in an explosion at the Dymitrow mine, in Bytom, Silesia. Less than a month later, on 8 July, at the same mine, two more died in another accident; on 6 October, six more died, and then on 28 November, still at the same mine, eighteen miners were killed and ten seriously wounded. . . . Following that first accident experts estimated that the mine should have been closed for safety reasons at least six months earlier, but the commissars, under tremendous pressure to produce coal for hard-currency export, ignored advice that this be done. (Weschler, 1983: 112)
3. Some information about the Polish 'ecological disaster' was, for the first time, disclosed in the early 1980s. In 1980, a bill concerning the Protection and Development of the Environment was passed. In the years following the imposition of the state of war in 1981, the issue was only partially suppressed. The urgency and visibility of the problem could no longer be neglected. Nonetheless, the bill has remained unenforced due to the lack of resources and, above all, the persistent disregard for this problem by the political authorities (see, e.g. Walczak, 1984: 6; Jacyna, 1984: 12–17).

Chapter 9: CRIMES OF WORKERS AND PEASANTS

1. Pomorski's analysis includes the following explanations of this penomenon: the contradiction between the low living standards of large segments of the Soviet population and the ideology of affluence and success; the non-egalitarian system of wages and 'material incentives' and the widespread sense of economic injustice; relative accessibility of state property (as compared to private property); general feelings of dissatisfaction; the clear contradiction between the ideology of participation and the social experience of the total control by the party/state apparatus as well as acute workers' alienation; and, finally, the fact that state property is systematically wasted by incompetent decision-makers at all levels (Pomorski, 1977: 223–45).

2. See sections 10 and 11 of the Constitution of the Union of Soviet Socialist Republics adopted by the Supreme Soviet of the USSR on 7 October 1977 (reprinted in Barry and Barner-Barry, 1982: Appendix A). Section 10 states that 'The foundation of the economic system of the USSR is socialist ownership of the means of production in the form of state property (belonging to all the people) and collective-farm and cooperative property.' Section 11 emphasizes that 'State property, that is, the common property of the Soviet people, is the principal form of the socialist property.' In the Polish Constitution it is labelled 'social property' and is described as the foundation of the economic strengths and the welfare of the nation (*Konstytucja* . . ., 1952:s.5(4)).
3. In a public opinion survey conducted in the early 1980s in Poland it was found that 44.8 per cent of the farmers thought that the 'purchase of agricultural machines and spare parts' was the most important problem to be solved. The second most important problem was the 'purchase of building materials' (21.1 per cent). While the third was the 'increasing of one's farm' (9.1 per cent) (Bialecki and Sikorska, 1982:195).

Chapter 10: CRIMES OF WOMEN

1. In my search for materials for this chapter I read virtually every issue of the women's magazine *Kobieta i Zycie* (Woman and Life) for the period between April 1981 and January 1983. Female involvement in crime, however, was not mentioned even once. In fact, only one short story was related to female alcoholism while one report discussed (in very idealized terms) the situation in a detention centre for delinquent girls. Yet there were a fair number of articles which portrayed women as victims of men, either as economically exploited, battered or deserted wives of alcoholics or as mothers tormented and abused by their drug- or alcohol- addicted sons. Women's involvement in economic crimes, prostitution, abuse of alcohol and drugs and other forms of delinquency were never recognized as problems deserving attention.
2. The same journalist suggests elsewhere that child care facilities have been recently further limited in order to force mothers to stay at home, an act which is expected to help alleviate the problem of surplus manpower (Mankiewicz, 1981b: 4).
3. Other pages contain a curious mixture of ideological communist slogans and the hottest gossip about Princess Diana, Sophia Loren, and other publicly recognized women.
4. In the period between 1946 and 1975, 3.5 million people moved from the countryside to the cities (Dyoniziak *et al.*, 1978: 57).
5. According to the official statistics, 4.5 million people had settled in the western territories by 1950. Almost 3 million came from other parts of Poland while 1.5 million were repatriated from the Soviet Union (Dyoniziak *et al.*, 1978: 55).
6. More specific data available for 1977 show that convictions of women constituted as much as 32.3 per cent (1970 cases) of all convictions in 1977 for illegal use of state property which they were employed to manage,

protect or supervise. (This crime is punishable by deprivation of liberty for one to ten years.) Additionally, women accounted for 20.2 per cent (82 cases) of all convictions for the usurpation of social property of considerable value. This is considered a very serious crime and carries a penalty of five to 25 years of deprivation of liberty. Moreover, female convictions constituted 18.6 per cent (283 cases) of convictions for the usurpation of state property committed in agreement with another person(s), an offence involving penalties for one to 25 years of deprivation of freedom.

7. While this was at least true in the 1970s, in the early 1980s, the rationing of alcohol was introduced. This has caused tremendous increases in the illegal production and trading of alcohol along with increased reliance on the hard currency stores, where rationing does not apply.
8. For example, while suicide rates in Poland and Canada are rather similar, Canadian women are twice as likely to take their lives as Polish women (see Jarosz, 1978; 1980).
9. Countries with similarly low rates of female suicide such as Greece, Portugal and Spain, also all have relatively high birth rates (Jarosz, 1980).
10. It is worth noting that a new 'anti-parasite' law in Poland, passed in October 1982, makes it a criminal offence for a man to remain persistently without socially useful employment. The law does not, however, apply to women.
11. Women constituted a small minority among the delegates to the Solidarity National Congress in 1981 and held very few elected offices. In an interesting, although not exhaustive, publication on the Solidarity Union entitled *Who's Who, What's What* (1981), biographies of 49 men, but only four women are presented. This disproportion became a theme of many open discussions and controversies within the Solidarity ranks and has contributed to a sharp increase in social awareness of the unequal status of women in society.
12. A good indication that such differentiated perceptions may in fact exist is the recent 'anti-parasite' law, which, as mentioned in note 10 above, applies only to men. In its general interpretation, this new law has been introduced to facilitate the removal or harassment of dissidents and political nonconformists dismissed from work for their political convictions. Many examples of this type of application of the 'anti-parasite' legislation are provided by the Soviet experience where such laws have existed since the 1950s (see Chapter 4).

Chapter 11: CRIMES OF 'TRUE CRIMINALS' . . .

1. Penalties at the disposal of petty offence boards include fines and terms of up to 3 months of absolute or limited deprivation of liberty. They deal with cases of petty theft, small scale speculation, disturbance of public order, hooliganism, public drunkenness, indecency, and so on. These lay boards (or tribunals as they are also referred to in the English language literature) usually consist of three members, chairman always being an official of the local administration. They are subordinated to local

administration and supervised by the Minister of the Interior, to whom the police are also subordinated. Appeals from their decisions can be lodged to ordinary courts only when the penalty involves the deprivation or limitation of freedom. In certain, not infrequent cases, these tribunals are allowed to use the so-called 'summary procedure' which deprives the accused to the right counsel, to call witnesses, communicate with families, and so on. Petty offence boards are extensively utilized against lower class petty offenders, drunks and prostitutes, as well as against participants of strikes, demonstrations, informal discussion meetings, etc. (see, for example, *Prologue* . . ., 1980: 86–91).

2. Crimes of violence accounted for 7.6 per cent of all criminal code offences in Canada, a western country with 'medium' level of violence.
3. This principle was explicitly defined in the 1926 Criminal Code: 'Where a socially dangerous act has not been expressly dealt with in the Present Code, the basis and limits of responsibility for it shall be determined in conformity with those Articles of the Code which deal with the crimes most closely resembling it' (quoted here after Chalidze, 1977: 92).
4. It was estimated in the 1960s that more than 40 per cent of the cases of malicious hooliganism involved serious violence and bodily injuries, while most of remaining cases involved abuse and insults without serious violence (Gertsenzon, 1970). There is no reliable information, however, on the share of malicious hooliganism in the total number of all the convictions for hooliganism.
5. According to an official press release in Poland the rate of death resulting from crime amounted in 1981 to approximately 3 occurrences per 100 000 (Markiewicz, 1981: 4).
6. See also examples of homicides cited in the Soviet press: Samokhin, 1975; 'From the Courtroom', 1980 and Kapelyushny, 1983b. Numerous examples can also be found in Polish periodicals and show that the forms and circumstances of homicides are as diverse in Poland as they are in western countries. The press cites examples of homicides during robberies (e.g. 'Ujecie sprawców wlamania . . .' 1984; 'Kara . . .', 1984; 'Ujecie sprawców bestialskiego . . .', 1984), murders of taxi-drivers ('Wykonanie . . .', 1983; 'Zabójstwo . . .', 1983; 'Aresztowanie . . .', 1983; 'Wyrok . . .', 1984), murders of policemen ('Kara śmierci i dożywocie . . .' 1983; 'Wyroki . . .', 1984), murders by hired killers ('Zbrodnia . . .', 1983), murders by jealous lovers ('Kronika . . .', 1983; 'Zabil . . .', 1984), murders by alcoholics ('Syn . . .', 1984), and finally murder-rapes, involving victims ranging from young children to old women ('Wykonano wyrok . . .', 1983; 'Kara śmierci dla gwalciciela . . .', 1983; 'Dwadzieścia . . .', 1983; 'Twelve . . .', 1984; 'Kara śmierci dla mordercy . . .', 1983; 'Ujeto . . .', 1983; Piotrowski, 1984; Pruski and Zukowski, 1983). (Each of the publications quoted above refers to different cases of murder.)
7. Many western studies indicate that rape victims often choose not to report the incident because of the fear of stigmatization and the degrading ordeal of investigation and trial. The same factor operates undoubtedly in the studied communist countries. The stigma and the stereotype of the victim provoking the assault are still quite powerful there (see a public opinion

survey to Wódz, 1981: 163–6). A study by the Police Headquarters in Poland showed that in 50 per cent of studied cases, the reluctance of rape victims to report was caused by the fear of revenge by the offender, in 30 per cent by the shame of being a rape victim, in 10 per cent by the lack of faith in the efficiency of the police and in 5 per cent by the unwillingness to be subjected to examination and cross-investigation (Holyst, 1977: 89). These findings may be compared, for example, with the results of a Canadian study where 52 per cent of sexual assault victims explained that their failure to report was due to a lack of faith in the efficiency of the police while 43 per cent were concerned about the attitude of the police or courts towards this type of incident. Moreover, one-third cited a fear of revenge by the offender (in this study, respondents could give more than one answer; *Victims of Crime*, 1983: 5).

8. According to the police statistics for 1975, 72 per cent of the individuals suspected of rape were intoxicated during the commission of the crime (quoted in Wald *et al.*, 1981: 103).
9. According to police statistics, 23 154 investigations of crimes against family, guardianship and youth were concluded in Poland in 1975 and 24 664 in 1979 (*Rocznik* . . ., 1980: 479; see also Jarosz, 1979: 78). While approximately half of these offences involved the failure to make child maintenance payments, almost all the remaining cases had to do with the physical abuse of family members, mainly wives and children, a crime notoriously underreported and processed by the police only in the most extreme cases. According to the police statistics for 1975, 85 per cent of the suspects in family violence cases were under the influence of alcohol (quoted in Vald *et al.*, 1981: 103).
10. The studies initiated and supervised by A. Podgórecki were carried out in 1969–71 in several Polish correctional institutions and prisons. The members of the research team were: S. Malkowski, A. Pilinow, M. Rydz, J. Wasilewski, B. Zielińska and the consultants M. Łoś and J. Kurczewski. The publications which resulted from this project include a series of articles in *Etyka*, no. 8, 1971 and publications by Podgórecki (1971: 281–303; 1974: 137–48, 269–70), Łoś and Anderson (1976, 1981) and others. These initial studies were later continued by other researchers whose findings were basically consistent with earlier observations (see, e.g. Górska, 1975, 1979).
11. The reasons for the removal of parental rights include parents' alcoholism, imprisonment, incapacitation by mental illness and child abuse. In exceptional cases, a political motive may also be involved.

References

(The abbreviation *CDSP* stands for *The Current Digest of the Soviet Press*).

Acts of 26 October 1982 (1984) Warsaw: Wydawnictwo Prawnicze.

Adler, F. (1977), 'The Interaction Between Women's Emancipation and Female Criminality', *International Journal of Criminology and Penology*, 5(2): 101–12.

'After the Trial: in the Name of the Republic' (1980), *Zarya Vostoka*, 13 Aug.: 4, condensed in *CDSP*, 32(37), 15 Oct.: 14 ('Tbilisi Borough Official Shot for Bribe Taking').

'Alkohol, narkotyki, przestepczość: Patologia spoleczna wśród mlodzieży' (1983), (Alcohol, Narcotics, Crime: Social Pathology Among Youth), Zycie Warszawy, 7 Dec.: 6.

L'Alternative: Pour les droits et les libertés démocratiques en Europe de l'Est, bi-monthly magazine, Paris.

Ambroziak, J. (1981), 'Dyspozycyjni sedziowie' (Obedient Judges), *Solidarność* (Warsaw), no. 20 (14 Aug.): 13.

'Amnesty for "those led astray": Tough Curbs Replace Polish Martial Law' (1983), *Globe and Mail* (Toronto), 22 July: 1.

'Analiza prawna sytuacji po zniesieniu stanu wojennego' (1983), (Analysis of the legal situation after the state of war), *Kontakt* (Paris), no. 12, Dec.: 51–7.

Anashkin, G. (1982), 'The Citizen, Society and the Law: Personally Responsible', *Pravda*, 16 Apr.: 3, condensed in *CDSP*, 32(15), 14 May: 20–1 ('State of Law').

Andrejew, I. (1975), *Zarys Prawa Karnego Państw Socjalistycznych* (Outline of the Criminal Law of Socialist States), Warsaw.

Antelava, A. (1982), 'Law Enforcement Agencies Must Improve Their Work Style: Socially Dangerous', *Zarya Vostoka*, 17 Feb.: 4, condensed in *CDSP*, 34(12), 21 Apr.: 14–15 ('Can Toughness on "Parasitism" Help Prevent Drug Addiction?').

Antonyan, Yu, M. (1975), 'The Social–Psychological Consequences of Urbanization and Their Effect on Crime', *Sovetskoye Gosudarstvo i Pravo*, no. 8 (Aug.): 67–73, condensed in *CDSP*, 27(49), 31 Dec.: 1–4 ('Factors in Urban Crime Analysed').

'Aresztowanie dwóch funkcjonariuszy MO w Bielsku Bialej' (1983), (Arrest of Two Policemen in Bielsko Biala), *Zycie Warszawy*, 12–13 Nov.: 6.

'Aresztowanie podejrzanych o zabójstwo taksówkarza' (1983), (Arrest of the Suspects in a Case of a Taxi-Driver Murder), *Zycie Warszawy*, 28 Dec.: 2.

Armstrong, M. (1967), 'The Campaign Against Parasites', pp. 163–82 in P. H. Juviler, and H. W. Morton (eds), *Soviet Policy-Making: Studies of Communism in Transition*, London: Pall Mall Press.

AS (1981), Biuletyn Pism Zwiazkowych i Zakladowych, (Bulletin of Union Press), 7–9 Dec.: 201–2, Warsaw: Agencja Prasowa Solidarność.

Astafyev, I. (1983), 'Called to Account: Zigzag to Dacha', *Pravda*, 11 Feb.: 3, condensed in *CDSP*, 35(6), 9 Mar.: 22 ('State of Law').

Bablumyan, S. (1982), 'Face to Face with the Law: Flowers of Evil', *Izvestia*, 11 Mar. condensed in *CDSP*, 34(10), 7 Apr.: 19.

Bablumyan, S. (1983), 'From the Courtroom: Speculators in Books', *Izvestia*, 27 Jan.: 6, condensed in *CDSP*, 35(4), 23 Feb.: 25.

Balandynowicz, A. and Porowski, M. (1980), 'Srodki przymusowej opieki postpenitencjarnej w systemie polskiego prawa karnego' (Means of compulsory after-prison care in the system of the Polish penal law), pp. 145–70 in *Przejawy Dewiacji Spolecznej i Postepowanie z Dewiantami*, Warsaw: Wydawnictwa Uniwersytetu Warszawskiego (IPSiR, vol. 6).

Barghoorn, F. C. (1972), *Politics in the USSR*, Boston: Little Brown & Co. Inc. (2nd edn).

Barron, J. (1974), *The Secret Work of Soviet Agents*; New York: Reader's Digest Press.

Barron, J. (1983), *K.G.B. Today: the Hidden Hand*, New York: Reader's Digest Press.

Barry, D. D. and Barner-Barry, C. (1982), *Contemporary Soviet Politics*, Englewood Cliffs, N.J.: Prentice Hall.

Basic Facts about Corrections in Canada (1982), Ottawa: Correctional Service of Canada.

Beermann, R. (1957), 'From Soviet Publications. Reports and Commentaries: a Discussion on the Draft Law against Parasites, Tramps and Beggars', *Soviet Studies*, 9: 214–22.

—— (1960a), 'Criminology and Juvenile Delinquency Reconsidered', *Soviet Studies*, 11: 451–52.

—— (1960b), 'The Law Against Parasites, Tramps and Beggars', *Soviet Studies*, 11: 453–55.

—— (1962), 'The Parasites Law', *Soviet Studies*, 13: 191–205.

—— (1964), 'Soviet and Russian Anti-Parasite Laws', *Soviet Studies*, 15: 420–9.

—— (1966), 'The Anti-Parasite Law of the RSFSR Modified', *Soviet Studies*, 17: 387–8.

—— (1973), 'Juvenile Delinquency', pp. 352–5 in F. J. M. Feldbrugge (ed.), *Encyclopedia of Soviet Law*, Leiden: Sijthoff (vol. 1).

Berman, H. J. (1957), 'Soviet Legal Reform – Dateline Moscow 1957', *Yale Law Journal*, 66.

Berman, H. J. (1973), 'Justice in the USSR', pp. 202–10 in S. Hendel (ed.), *The Soviet Crucible*, North Scituate, Mass.: Duxbury Press.

Bertrand, M.-A. (1979), *La femme et le crime*, Montréal: L'Aurore.

Besançon, A. (1981), *Anatomie d'un Spectre: L'Économie Politique du Socialisme Reel*, France: Calmann-Levey.

Bethell, N. (1969), *Gomulka: His Poland and His Communism*, London: The Camelot Press.

Beyer Gammon, M. A. (1978), *Violence in Canada*, Toronto/New York: Methuen.

Bialecki, I. and Sikorska, J. (1982), 'In the Sphere of Human Needs and Aspirations', pp. 188–205 in *Sisyphus, Sociological Studies* (vol. III: *Crisis and Conflicts: the Case of Poland 1980–81*), Warsaw: PWN (Polish Scientific Publishers).

Biddle, W. and Slade, M. (1983), 'Soviet Symptoms of Withdrawal', *New York Times*, 13 Feb.

Biedzki, T. (1981), 'Rachunek dla bezkarnych' (A Bill for the Impunity), *Gazeta Krakowska* (Cracow), 1–3 May.

Bloch, S. and Reddaway, P. (1977), *Russia's Political Hospitals: the Abuse of Psychiatry in the Soviet Union*, London: Gollancz. Published also as *Psychiatric Terror*, New York: Basic Books.

'Blocking the Way to Easy Money' (1981), *Sovetskaya Rossia*, 18 Oct.: 3, condensed in *CDSP*, 33(49), 6 Jan.: 13 and 23 ('Service-Sector Bribery: New Penalty Set').

Boiter, A. (1973), 'Comrades' Courts', pp. 145–8 in *F. J. M. Feldbrugge (ed.), Encyclopedia of Soviet Law*, vol. I, Leiden: Sijthoff.

Bottomore, T. B. and Rubel, M. (eds) (1963), *Karl Marx: Selected Writings in Sociology and Social Philosophy*, Harmondsworth, Middlesex: Penguin Books.

Boukovsky, V. (1971), *Une nouvelle maladie mentale en URSS: L'opposition*, Paris: Editions du Seuil.

Bożyczko, Z. (1969), 'Niektóre aspekty spolecznego wykolejania sie w toku pozbawienia wolności na przykladzie wlamywaczy' (Certain aspects of social degradation in prison in case of burglars), *Ruch Prawniczy, Ekonomiczny i Socjologiczny*, no. 2: 55–75.

Bragin, Yu. (1982), 'From the Courtroom: Trip "on the Side"', *Nedelya*, 31 May–6 June, no. 22: 5, condensed in *CDSP*, 34(22), 30 June: 24.

Bukovsky, V. and Gluzman, S. (1975), 'A Dissident's Guide to Psychiatry', *A Chronicle of Human Rights in the USSR*, Jan.–Feb.

'Bunt wieźniów w Kamińsku' (1981), (Prison Rebellion in Kaminsk), *Solidarność*, no. 33, 13 Nov.: 2.

Burns, J. F. (1981), 'Moscow Silencing Psychiatry Critics', *The New York Times*, 26 July.

—— (1983a), 'Confessions of a Sluggard', *The Globe and Mail*, 10 Jan.: 1 and 2.

—— (1983b), 'Under Adropov, Policeman's Lot Isn't Happy One', *The New York Times*, 14 Aug.

Butler, W. E. (1977), 'Comradely Justice Revised', *Review of Socialist Law*, 3: 325–31.

Chalidze, V. (1977), *Criminal Russia: Crime in the Soviet Union*, New York: Random House.

Chambliss, W. J. (1964), 'A Sociological Analysis of the Law of Vagrancy', *Social Problems*, 12(1), Summer: 67–77.

Chambliss. W. J. (1971), 'A Sociological Analysis of the Law of Vagrancy', pp. 237–51 in W. G. Carson and P. Wiles (eds), *The Sociology of Crime and Delinquency in Britain* (vol. 1, *The British Tradition*), London: Martin Robertson.

'Changes in Security Positions Meant to Root Out Corruption' (1982), *The Citizen* (Ottawa), 18 Dec.

'Charades in Poland' (1983), *The Citizen* (Ottawa), 23 July: 16.

Cherepanov, V. (1980), 'A Case is Heard: Benefactress', *Pravda*, 11 Apr.: 6, condensed in *CDSP*, 32(15), 14 May: 20.

Chlopecki, J. (1980), 'Niesprawność systemu' (Inefficiency of the System), *Literatura*, no. 457, 20 Nov.: 4.

Chorover, S. L. (1973), 'Big Brother and Psychotechnology', *Psychology Today* 7(5), Oct.: 43–54.

Christie, N. (1976), 'Conflicts as Property'. Foundation Lecture to mark the opening of the Centre for Criminological Studies, University of Sheffield, 31 Mar. 1976. Also published in *British Journal of Criminology*, 1977, no. 17: 1–19.

Christitch, K. (1980), 'Des privilèges héréditaires', *Le Point*, 15 Sept.: 54–5.

'C.I.A. Says 4 Million in Soviet Union Are Doing Penal Labour' (1982), *The New York Times*, 7 Nov.: 3.

Circular letter of the Minister of Justice of 8 Dec. 1967, *Dziennik Urzedowy Ministerstwa Sprawiedliwości*, item 66.

Cliff, T. (1974), *State Capitalism in Russia*, London: Pluto Press.

Cloward, R. A. and Ohlin, L. E. (1960), *Delinquency and Opportunity*, New York: Free Press.

Combating Crime in Towns (1981), Moscow: USSR Academy of Sciences.

Committee in Support of Solidarity Reports, published periodically since Dec. 1981 by the Committee in Support of Solidarity in New York.

Connor, W. D. (1970), 'Juvenile Delinquency in the USSR: Some Quantitative and Qualitative Indicators', *American Sociological Review*, 35(2), Apr.: 283–97.

—— (1972), *Deviance in Soviet Society: Crime, Delinquency and Alcoholism*, New York and London: Columbia University Press.

—— (1973), 'Criminal Homicide: USSR/USA: Reflections on Soviet Data in a Comparative Framework', *Journal of Criminal Law and Criminology*, 64(1), Mar.: 111–17.

—— (1976), 'Deviance, Stress and Modernization in Eastern Europe', pp. 181–203, in M. G. Field (ed.), *Social Consequences of Modernization in Communist Societies*, Baltimore & London: The John Hopkins University Press.

Conquest, R. (ed.) (1968), *The Soviet Police System*, New York: Praeger.

—— (1973), *The Great Terror: Stalin's Purge of the Thirties*, New York: Macmillan.

—— (1982), 'Forced Labor Statistics: Some Comments', *Soviet Studies* 34(3), Jul.: 434–9.

Constitution (Fundamental Law) of the Union of Soviet Socialist Republics (1977), reprinted in D. D. Barry and C. Barner-Barry (eds), (1982) *Contemporary Soviet Politics*, Englewood Cliffs, N.J.: Prentice-Hall Inc.

Coser, R. L. (1980), 'Women at Work', *Dissent*, 27(1), Winter: 51–5.

'Cuba jails trade unionists' (1984), *Canadian Labour* (Monthly publication of the Canadian Labour Congress), 28(8), Sept.: 9.

Cullen, R. B. (1983), 'Corrupt Practices Cut to Core of Soviet Society', *The Citizen* (Ottawa), 2 Apr.: 23.

Curtiss, J. S. (1973), *The Russian Revolutions of 1917*, pp. 84–101 in S. Hendel (ed.), *The Soviet Crucible*, North Scituate, Mass.: Duxbury Press.

Czabański, K. (1981a), 'Przeglad wstepny' (Initial overview), *Literatura* (Warszaw), 22 Jan., no. 466: 2.

Czabański, K. (1981b), 'Przywileje', *Solidarność* (Warsaw), no. 34, 20 Nov.: 8.

Czapów, Cz. (1974), 'O niektórych skutkach patologii instytucji socjalizujacych' (On some consequences of the pathology of socialization agencies), pp. 385–436 in A. Podgórecki (ed.), *Socjotechnika*, Warsaw: KiW.

Czapów, Cz. (1976), 'Narkomania' (Drug Abuse), pp. 371–85 in A. Podgórecki (ed.), *Zagadnienia Patologii Spolecznej*, Warsaw: PWN (Polish Scientific Publishers).

'Czy ktoś widzial starego narkomana?' (1984), (Has Anyone Seen an Old Drug Addict?), *Zycie Warszawy*, 6 Feb.: 8.

Dallin, D. J. (1947), *The Real Soviet Russia*, New Haven: Yale University Press.

Dallin, D. J. and Nicolaevsky, B. I. (1947), *Forced Labor in Soviet Russia*, New Haven: Yale University Press.

Daniels, R. V. (1973), 'The Stalin Revolution and its Aftermath', pp. 153–61 in S. Hendel (ed.), *The Soviet Crucible: the Soviet System in Theory and Practice*, North Scituate, Mass.: Duxbury Press.

Daniloff, N. (1982), 'Drugs, Discos, Denim Overtake Russia's Youth', *The Citizen* (Ottawa), 20 Nov.: 21.

Dankowski, J. (1981), 'Jakie sa gwarancje sedziowskiej niezawislości' (What Are the Guarantees of the Judicial Independence), *Solidarność*, (Warsaw), no. 4, 24 Apr. 13–14.

Daszkiewicz, K. (1971), *Klimaty Bezprawia* (Realms of Lawlessness), Warszawa: KiW.

David, R. (1954), *Les données fondamentales du droit soviétique* (vol. II of David, R. and Hazard, J. N., *Le Droit Soviétique*), Paris: R. Pichon et R. Durand-Auzias.

Decree of the Presidium of the Supreme Soviet of the RSFSR, 25 Feb. 1970, reprinted in L. Lipson and V. Chalidze (eds), (1977) *Papers on Soviet Law* (no. 1), New York: Institute on Socialist Law: 195–6.

Demichev, M. (1982), 'What's New in Legislation: Strict and Inevitable', *Sovetskaya Kirgizia*, 22 Jan.: 4, condensed in*CDSP* , 34(8), 24 Mar.: 14, ('Kirgizia Toughens Its Laws on Theft, Robbery, Assault').

Deutscher, I. (1973), 'Defeat in Victory', pp. 103–11 in S. Hendel (ed.), *The Soviet Crucible*, North Scituate, Mass.: Duxbury Press.

Djekebaer, U. S. (1975), 'Crime in Socialist Society and its Principle Features', *Soviet Sociology*, 14(1), Summer: 62–85.

Djilas, M. (1957), *The New Class*, New York: Frederick A. Praeger Inc.

Les Droits de l'homme et du citoyen en République Populaire de Pologne pendant l'état de guerre (1983), Texte élaboré par le Comité Helsinki en Pologne, Bruxelles: Bureau de Coordination à la l'Étranger NSZZ 'Solidarność'.

Durkheim, E. (1963), *Selections from his work*, New York: Thomas Y. Crowell Co.

Dux, E. (1983) 'Zaczac od siebie' (Let Us Start with Ourselves), *Zycie Warszawy*, 8 Nov.: 1 and 3.

'Dwadzieścia pieć lat wiezienia za gwalt i zabójstwo' (1983), (Twenty-Five Years in Prison for Rape and Murder), *Zycie Warszawy*, 9 Dec.: 6.

'Dwanaście lat pozbawienia wolności dla zabójcy' (1984), (Twelve years imprisonment for a murder), *Zycie Warszawy*, 18 Jan.: 6.

Dyoniziak, R., Mikulowski-Pomorski, J. and Pucek, Z. (1978), *Wspólczesne Spoleczeństwo Polskie* (Contemporary Polish Society), Warszawa: PWN (Polish Scientific Publishers).

'Dzialalność WKKP, NIK i prokuratury' (1981), (Activity of Warsaw Party Control Commission, NIK and Public Prosecutor's Office), *Zycie Warszawy*, 31 Mar.: 8.

'Dziekuje za bardzo dobre wychowanie' (1981) (Thanks for the Excellent Education), *Solidarność* (Warsaw), no. 14, 3 Aug.: 12–14.

Eberstadt, N. (1981), 'The Health Crisis in the USSR', *The New York Review of Books*, 19 Feb.: 24.

'Echa Ulicy Wiejskiej' (1982), (News from Wiejska Street), Polskie Wiadomości (Vienna), no. 60, 2 Nov.: 13–15.

Edict of the Presidium of the Supreme Soviet of the RSFSR of 4, May 1961: 'On Strengthening the Struggle Against Persons Who Avoid Socially Useful Work and Lead an Antisocial Parasitic Way of Life', reprinted in L. Lipson and V. Chalidze (eds), (1977) *Papers on Soviet Law*, no. 1, New York: Institute on Socialist Law: 188–90.

Edict of the Presidium of the Supreme Soviet of the RSFSR of 7 Aug., 1975, reprinted in L. Lipson and V. Chalidze, (eds), (1977) *Papers on Soviet Law*, no. 1, New York: Institute on Socialist Law: 196–7.

Encyclopaedia Britannica (1972), 'Poland', vol. 18: 111–47.

Encyclopedia of Soviet Law (1973), (ed. by Feldbrugge, F. J. M.), Leiden: Sijthoff.

'Ex-Official is Reported Jailed in Soviet Georgia' (1982) *International Herald Tribune*, 10 May: 7.

Fainsod, M. (1973), 'Terror as a System of Power', pp. 139–45 in S. Hendel (ed.), *The Soviet Crucible*, North Scituate, Mass.: Duxbury Press.

Falandysz, L. (1981a), 'Kilka uwag o prawie karnym i wymiarze sprawiedliwości (Some Remarks About the Penal Law and the Criminal Justice System), pp. 29–39 in K. Frieske (ed), *Dewiacja i Kontrola Spoleczna*, Warsaw: PTS (Polish Sociological Association).

—— (1981b), 'Przedstawiciel spoleczny' (Social representative), *Solidarność* (Warsaw), no. 9, 29 May: 11.

—— (1981c), 'Projekty zmian w kodeksie karnym' (New drafts of penal codes), *Solidarność* (Warsaw), no. 35, 27 Nov.: 11.

—— (1981d), 'Kodeks karny i matematyka' (Penal code and mathematics), *Solidarność* (Warsaw), no. 13, 26 June: 13.

—— (1981e), 'Chuligaństwo i prawnicy' (Hooliganism and Lawyers), *Solidarność* (Warsaw), no. 14, 2 July: 13.

Falewicz, J. K. (1973), 'Szkic ekspertyzy na temat alkoholizmu' (An outline of a report on alcoholism), pp. 85–97 in *Diagnostyczny Obraz Niektórych Trudnych Problemow Spoleczeństwa Polskiego*, Warsaw: Uniwersytet Warszawski, IPSiR.

—— (1976), 'Spoleczne uwarunkowania alkoholizmu w Polsce' (Social Conditions and Alcoholism in Poland), pp. 347–70 in A. Podgórecki (ed.), *Zagadnienia Patologii Spolecznej*, Warsaw: PWN (Polish Scientific Publishers).

—— (1981), 'Czego trzeba polityce trzeźwości (Shortcomings of the 'Sobering Up' Policy), *Problemy Alkoholizmu*, no. 2: 12–15.

Falewicz, J. K., Jasiński, J., Rażniewski, A. (1975), *Elementy Patologii Spolecznej w Polsce* (Elements of Social Pathology in Poland), Warsaw: Komitert Badań i Prognoz 'Polska 2000', The Polish Academy of Sciences.

Falkowska, W. (1981a), 'Votum nieufności' (The Vote of Non-confidence), *Solidarność* (Warsaw), no. 33, 13 Nov.: 12.

—— (1981b), 'Kraty i ciernie' (Bars and Thorns), *Solidarność* (Warsaw), no. 9, 29 May: 5 and 15.

——(1981c) 'Czekajac na amnestie' (Waiting for an Amnesty), *Solidarność* (Warsaw), no. 12, 19 June: 13.
Feldbrugge, F. J. M. (1973), 'Parasities' in F. J. M. Feldbrugge *Encyclopedia of Soviet Law*, vol. II, Leiden: Sijhoff, p. 484.
——(1974), 'Law and Political Dissent in the Soviet Union', pp. 55–69 in D. D. Barry *et al.* (eds), *Contemporary Soviet Law*, The Hague: Martinus Nijhoff.
——(1975), 'Soviet Penitentiary Law', *Review of Socialist Law*, 1(1): 123–39.
——(1977), 'Correction Through Labour: New Criminal Legislation in the USSR', *Review of Socialist Law*, 3(3): 345–50.
Fireside, H. (1979), *Soviet Psychoprisons*, New York, London: W. W. Norton and Co.
Fitzgibbon, L. (1971), *Katyń: a Crime without Parallel*, vols I and II, London: Tom Stacey.
Fitzgibbon, L. (1972), *The Katyń Cover Up*, London: Tom Stacey.
Foucault, M. (1977) *Discipline and Punish: the Birth of the Prison*, New York: Vintage Books, a Division of Random House.
'Frasyniuk on Trial' (1983), *Committee in Support of Solidarity Reports*, Issue 10/11, 24 Jan.: 14–16.
'From the Courtroom: the Extortionist Auditor' (1975), *Bakinsky Rabochy*, 28 Feb.: 4, condensed in *CDSP*, 27(30), 20 Aug.: 16 ('Auditor Convicted of Bribery Gets 12 Years at Hard Labour').
'From the Courtroom: Sentence Has Been Carried Out' (1980), *Zarya Vostoka*, 11 Sept.: 4, condensed in *CDSP*, 32(37), 15 Oct. 15 ('Firing Squad Ends Armed-Robbery Spree').
'From the Courtroom: in a Situation of Connivance and Lack of Oversight' (1981–82) *Bakinsky Rabochy*, 21 Nov. 1981: 4, condensed in *CDSP*, 34(8), 24 Mar. 1982: 15 ('Azerbaidzhan Authorities Crack Major Crime Ring').
Gaberle, A. (1978), 'Poglady na dzialalność organów wymiaru sprawiedliwości skierowana na zwalczanie przestepstw przeciwko mieniu oraz stosunek do naruszeń mienia' (Opinions on criminal justice agencies' activities directed against property crimes) pp. 153–207 in M. Borucka-Arctowa (ed.), *Poglady Spoleczeństwa Polskiego na Stosowanie Prawa*, Wroclaw: Ossolineum.
Gal'chenko, F., Matyshevskii, P. and Iatsenko, S. (1973–74), 'The Charge of Hooliganism', *Soviet Law and Government*, 12(2): 99–101.
Garfinkel, H. (1956), 'Conditions of Successful Degradation Ceremonies', *The American Journal of Sociology*, 61, Mar.: 420–4.
Gerol, I. (1983), 'Police Crackdown not the Cure for Soviet Alcoholism', *The Citizen* (Ottawa), 19 Feb.: 22.
Gertsenzon, A. A. (1970), *Ugolovnoye pravo i sotsiologiya* (Criminal Law and Sociology), Moscow.
Gidwitz, B. (1982), 'Labor Unrest in the Soviet Union', *Problems of Communism*, 21, Nov.–Dec.: 25–42.
Gidyński, J. (1976), 'The Relations of the Polish Communist Party to the Constitution of the Polish People's Republic, *The Polish Review*, 21(1–2): 41–53.
Giżycka-Koprowska, J. (1982), 'Plenarne Obrady Sejmu PRL: Projekt Ustawy o Postepowaniu w Sprawach Nieletnich' (Plenary Session of the Polish Diet: a Proposal of the Law on Proceedings in Juvenile Cases), *Trybuna Ludu* (Warsaw), 25(255), 27 Oct.: 3.

Gluck, L. (1973), 'Propozycja interpretacji calościowej' (An attempt at a comprehensive interpretation), pp. 198–275 in *Diagnostyczny Obraz Niektórych Trudnych Problemów Spoleczeństwa Polskiego*, Warsaw: Uniwersytet Warszawski, IPSiR.

Goban-Klas, T. (1984), 'Leki i nadzieje Polaków' (Fears and Hopes of Poles), *Polityka* (Warsaw), 28(2), 14 Jan.: 3.

Goffman, E. (1961), *Asylums*, Garden City, N.J.: Achor Books.

Goffman, E. (1963) *Stigma: Notes on the Management of Spoiled Identity*, Englewood Cliffs, N.J.: Prentice-Hall, Inc.

Golodniuk, M. N. (1975), 'A Criminological Characterization of Female Recidivists', *Soviet Law and Government*, 14(2): 68–78.

Golodniuk, M. N. (1980), 'Questions of Prevention of Crime by Women', *Soviet Law and Government*, 19(2), Autumn: 41–52.

Górska, K. (1975), 'Nieformalna stratyfikacja skazanych' (Informal stratification of inmates). Unpublished doctoral dissertation, Warsaw: Uniwersytet Warszawski.

Górska, K. (1979), 'Podkulturowe czynniki różnicujace pozycje w nieformalnej strukturze zakladu karnego' (Subcultural Factors Which Shape Informal Structure of the Penal Institution), pp. 3–25 in *Zachowania Dewiacyjne i Kierunki Oddzialywania*, Warsaw: Uniwersytet Warszawski (Prace IPSiR, vol. 3).

Górski, J. (1967), *Doświadczenia i Perspektywy Sadów Robotniczych w Polsce (1960–1965)* (Experience and Prospects of Workers' Courts in Poland in 1960–65), Warsaw.

Górski, K. (1981), 'Adwokaci o walce ze spekulacja' (Lawyers on struggle against speculation), *Zycie Warszawy*, 22 Sept.: 2.

Grajewski, J. and Lammich, S. (1981), 'Criminal Policy in Poland in Light of the Criminal Code of 1969', *Review of Socialist Law*, 7(3): 407–23.

Gramsci, A. (1971), *Selection from the Prison Notebooks*, London: Lawrence & Wishart.

The Great Soviet Encyclopedia (1973), New York: Macmillan; London: Collier Macmillan Publishers.

Gross, J. T. (1979), *Polish Society Under German Occupation: The General Government 1939–1944*, Princeton University Press.

Grossman, G. (1977), 'The Second Economy of the USSR', *Problems of Communism*, 26(5), Sept.–Oct.: 25–40.

Guzowska, M. (1981), 'Z Leszna do Warszawy' (From Leszno to Warsaw), *Express Wieczorny*, 10 Aug.: 3.

Hagan, J., Simpson, J. H. and Gills, A. R. (1979), 'The Sexual Stratification of Social Control: a Gender-Based Perspective on Crime and Delinquency', *British Journal of Sociology*, 30(1), Mar.: 25–38.

Hall, S. and Jefferson, T., (eds.), (1976), *Resistance Through Rituals: Youth Subcultures in Post-War Britain*, London: Hutchinson.

'Handel i Etyka' (1980) (Trade and Ethics), *Polityka* (Warsaw), 24(45), 8 Nov.: 17–18.

Haynes, V. and Semyonova, O., (eds.), (1979) *Workers Against the Gulag*, London: Pluto Press.

Hazard, J. N. (1968), *The Soviet System of Government*, 4th edn rev., Chicago & London: The University of Chicago Press.

Hazard, J. N. (1978) 'Development and "New Law"', *The University of Chicago Law Review*, 45(3), Spring: 637–52.
Heller, M. (1979), 'Lenin and the Cheka: The Real Lenin', *Survey* 24(2): 175–92.
Holwiński, J. (1981), 'O legalnym bezprawiu' (On Legal Lawlessness), *Solidarność* (Warsaw), no. 9, 29 May: 10.
Holyst, B. (1967), *Wykrywalność Sprawców Zabójstw* (Detectability in Homicide Cases), Warsaw.
Holyst, B. (1977), *Przestepczość w Polsce. Studium kryminologiczne* (Crime in Poland: a Criminological Study), Warsaw.
Hutchings, R. (1971), *Soviet Economic Development*, Oxford: Basil Blackwell.
'In Katowice' (1982), *Press Advisory*, Special edn, 10 Jan.: 1–4, New York: Committee in Support of Solidarity.
'In the Azerbaidzhan Communist Party Central Committee' (1979), *Bakinsky Rabochy*, 16 June: 2, excerpted in *CDSP*, 31(31), 29 Aug.: 9–10 ('Defects in Health Ministry Detailed').
'In the Azerbaidzhan Communist Party Central Committee' (1982), *Bakinsky Rabochy*, 6 Feb.: 3, condensed in *CDSP*, 34(11), 14 Apr.: 14 ('Corruption, Nepotism Topple Azerbaidzhan District Officials').
Indelak, J. (1981), 'W strone drugiej Polski' (Towards a Second Poland), *Odglosy*, (Lodz), 8 Feb., 24(6): 1, 4 and 5.
Inoveli, I. (1980), 'Courtroom Sketch: Carrying Out the Will of the People', *Zarya Vostoka*, 31 May: 4, condensed in *CDSP*, 32(24), 16 July: 12 ('Georgian Kidnappers Draw Stiff Sentences').
—— (1982), 'Over the Abyss', *Zarya Vostoka*, 31 Mar.: 4, condensed in *CDSP*, 34(6), 19 May: 16 ('Georgia's "Well-Off" Drug Users Are the Toughest to Cure').
—— (1983), 'After the Trial: The Swindler and Her "Clientele"', *Zarya Vostoka*, 24 Mar.: 4, condensed in *CDSP*, 35(13), 27 Apr.: 13 ('Fixer of University Admissions Gets 10 years for Bribetaking').
'The Institutionalization of Martial Law' (1982), *Tygodnik Mazowsze*, no. 36, 1 Dec., reprinted in *Survey*, 26(4), Autumn: 60–7.
'The Institutionalization of Martial Law' (1983), Committee in Support of Solidarity Reports(New York), no. 10–11, 24 Jan.: 3–8.
'Instrukcje' (1982) (Instructions), *Kontakt* (Paris), Apr.: 36.
'Investigations against Persons Accused of Abuse of Office' (1982) *Uncensored Poland News Bulletin*, Information Centre for Polish Affairs, London, no. 1, 10 Jan.: 11.
'It was premeditated murder coldly calculated . . .' (1982), *Committee in Support of Solidarity Reports* (New York), no. 8, 22 Oct.: 3–16.
Jacoby, N. H., Nehemkis, P., and Eells, R. (1977), *Bribery and Extortion in World Business: a Study of Corporate Political Payments Abroad*, New York: Macmillan.
Jacyna, I. (1984), 'Margines bezpieczeństwa', (Safety Margin), *Odra* (Wroclaw), 24: 2, Feb.: 12–17.
Jain, A., (ed.), (1983), *Solidarity: the Origins and Implications of Polish Trade Unions*, Baton Rouge, La.: Oracle Press.
'Jak ukrócić spekulacje ksiaźkami?' (1983), (How To Curb Speculation in Books?), *Zycie Warszawy*, 11 Nov.: 2.
'Jak walczyć z narkomania?' (1984), (How To Fight Drug Addiction?), *Zycie Warszawy*, 29 Mar.: 6.

Jakubiec, Z. (1981), 'Zaklady poprawcze: Resocjalizacja czy demoralizacja?', (Correctional Institutions: Rehabilitation or Demoralization?), *Solidarność* (Warsaw), no. 27, 2 Oct.: 13.

Jakubowska, A. (1981), 'Fikcyjne równouprawnienie' (Fictitious Equality), *Sztandar Mlodych* (Warsaw), Apr.: 8.

Janowska, H. (1974), *Zabójstwa i Ich Sprawcy. Analiza Socjologiczna* (Homicides and Their Perpertrators: a Sociological Analysis), Warsaw: PWN (Polish Scientific Publishers).

Jarecki, P. (1982), 'Ustawa pasożytów o . . . pasożytnictlwie' (Parasites' Law Against . . . Parasites), *Orzel Bialy* (London), no. 1367/XLII, Dec.: 37–39.

Jarosz, M. (1978), 'Le Suicide en Pologne', *Revue d'Études Comparatives Est-Ouest*, 9(4): 65–101.

——(1979), *Problemy Dezorganizacji Rodziny* (Problems of Family Dezorganization), Warsaw: PWN (Polish Scientific Publishers).

——(1980), *Samoniszczenie* (Self-Destruction), Wroclaw: Ossolineum.

——(1982), 'Zostawić i odejść', (Abandon and Leave), *Kobieta i Zycie* (Warsaw), no 34, 24 Nov.: 4.

Jasińska, M. (1967), *Proces Spolecznego Wykolejenia Mlodocianych Dziewczat* (A Process of Social Demoralization of Girls), Warszawa: Wydawnictwo Prawnicze.

——(1976), 'Problematyka prostytucji w Polsce' (Problems of Prostitution in Poland), pp. 435–56 in A. Podgórecki (ed.), *Zagadnienia Patologii Spolecznej*, Warsaw: PWN (Polish Scientific Publishers).

——(1982), 'Prostytucja mlodocianych w Warszawie na przelomie lat 1970–80', (Young Prostitutes in Warsaw at the End of the 1970s and Beginning of the 1980s), pp. 81–96 in A. Krukowski (ed.), *Praktyczne Implikacje Badań nad Patologia Spoleczna*, Warsaw: University of Warsaw, IPSiR.

Jasiński, J. (1966), *Sady Spoleczne* (Social Courts), Warszawa.

——(1975a), 'Charakterystyka przestepczości (Characterising Criminality), pp. 50–90 in J. Jasiński (ed.), *Zagadnienia Przestepczości w Polsce*, Warsaw: Wydawnictwo Prawnicze.

——(1975b), 'Punitywność systemów prawnych' (Punitiveness of Legal Systems), *Studia Prawnicze*, no. 35.

——(1978), 'Kształtowanie sie polityki karnej sadów w latach 1972–76' (Sentencing Policy in 1972–76), *Państwo i Prawo* (Warsaw), no. 2, Feb.: 42–55.

Jaśkiewicz, W., Jackowiak, C. and Piotrowski, W. (1970), *Prawo Pracy: Zarys Wykladu* (Labour Law: an Outline), Warsaw: Wydawnictwo Prawnicze.

Jerzewski, L. (1980), *Dzieje Sprawy Katynia* (The History of Katyń), Warsaw: Wydawnictwo Glos (reprinted by Glos Publishing, New York, 1983).

Jerzewski, L., ed. (1982), *Relacja z Gdańska 1970* (A Report from Gdańsk 1970), New York: Glos Publishing.

'Jeszcze raz Bydgoszcz' (1981), (Once Again Bydgoszcz), *Solidarność* (Warsaw), no. 25, 18 Sept.: 2.

Jotecka, Z. (1981), 'Jest dobrze (w wiezieniu)' (It's O.K./in prison/), *Solidarność* (Warsaw), no. 12, 19 June: 10–11.

Jowitt, K. (1983), 'Soviet Neotraditionalism: the Political Corruption of Leninist Regime', *Soviet Studies*, 35(3): 275–97.

Juviler, P. H. (1974), 'Criminal Law and Social Control' pp. 17–54 in B. Barry, W. E. Butler and G. Ginsburgs (eds), *Contemporary Soviet Law: Essays in Honor of John N. Hazard*, The Hague: Martinus Nijhoff.

Juviler, P. H. (1976), *Revolutionary Law and Order*, New York: Free Press.

Kamenka, E. (1970), 'The Soviet View of Law', pp. 313–22 in R. Cornell (ed.), *The Soviet Political System*, Englewood Cliffs, N.Y.: Prentice-Hall.

Kapelyushny, L. (1983a), 'Face to Face with the Law: Retribution', *Izvestia*, 8 Jan.: 6, condensed in *CDSP*, 35(1), 2 Feb.: 19.

Kapelyushny, L. (1983b), 'Face to Face with the Law: Beware of Greeks Bearing Gifts', *Izvestia*, 28 Feb.: 2, condensed in *CDSP*, 35(9), 30 Mar.: 19 ('State of Law').

Karpiński, J. (1982) *Count-Down: the Polish Upheavals of 1956, 1968, 1970, 1976, 1980 . . .*, New York: Karz-Cohl Publishers Inc.

'Kara śmierci dla gwalciciela i mordercy' (1983), (Death Penalty for a rapist–murderer), *Zycie Warszawy*, 15 Dec.: 4.

'Kara śmierci dla mordercy staruszki i chlopca' (1983), (Death Penalty for the Murderer of an Elderly Woman and a Boy), *Zycie Warszawy*, 29–30 Oct.: 6.

'Kara śmierci dla zabójcy kobiety' (1984), (Death Penalty for the Murderer of a Woman), *Zycie Warszawy*, 2 Feb.: 6.

'Kara śmierci i dożywocie dla zabójców milicjanta ze Slawna' (1983), (Death Penalty and Life Sentence for the Murderers of a Policeman in Slawno), *Zycie Warszawy*, 17–18 Dec.: 6.

Katsenelinboigen, A. (1977), 'Coloured Markets in the Soviet Union', *Soviet Studies*, 29: 62–85.

—— (1978a), 'Quelques commentaires sur les mécanismes verticaux et horizontaux dans l'économie soviétique', *Revue d'études comparatives est-ouest*, 9(4), Dec.: 7–19.

—— (1978b), *Studies in Soviet Economic Planning*, White Plains, N.Y.: M.E. Sharpe.

Kazikhanov, A. (1983) 'Face to Face with the Law: Bribe-takers' *Izvestia*, 20 Jan.: 6, condensed in *CDSP*, 35(3), 16 Feb. 21 ('State of Law').

Kazmierczak, A. (1981), 'Dziekuje za bardzo dobre wychowanie' (Thanks for the Excellent Education), *Solidarność* (Warsaw), no. 14, 3 Aug.: 12–14.

Kedzierska, D. (1982), 'Poniżej 5 tysiecy nie budzić' (Below Five Thousand Don't Wake Them Up), *Polityka* (Warsaw), 26(6), 27 Mar.: 7.

Kersten, K. (1981), 'Powstanie PKWN – mówia dokumenty' (The Origins of the PKWN – the Documents Speak), *Solidarność* (Warsaw), no. 17, 24 July: 4 and 6.

Khrushchev, N. S. (1973), 'Stalin and the Cult of the Individual', pp. 145–52 in S. Hendel (ed.), *The Soviet Crucible*, North Scituate, Mass.: Duxbury Press.

Kiciński, K. (1982), 'Systemy wartości i struktury postaw moralnych spoleczeństwa polskiego jako mechanizmy przeciwdzialania zachowaniom dysfunkcjonalnym spolecznie – wnioski praktyczne z badań' (Value Systems and Moral Attitudes of Polish Society as Mechanisms of Deviance Prevention – Practical Interpretations of Empirical Studies), pp. 8–17 in A. Krukowski (ed.), *Praktyczne Implikacje Badan nad Patologia Spoleczna*, Warsaw: University of Warsaw, IPSiR.

Kiralfy, A. R. (1976), 'The Child in Soviet Law: the Juvenile Delinquent', *Review of Socialist Law*, 2(1): 67–77.

Kobieta i Zycie, an official Polish weekly magazine for women.

Kobus, A. (1975), 'Niektóre zagadnienia przestepczości nieletnich w Polsce w latach 1958–1973' (Some Aspects of Juvenile Delinquency in Poland in 1958–1973), pp. 103–22 in M. Jarosz (ed.), *Wybrane Zagadnienia Patologii Spolecznej*, Warsaw: GUS.

Kocel-Krekora, Z. (1981), 'Problematyka chuligaństwa w kodeksie wykroczeń' (Hooliganism in the Petty Offences Code), *Państwo I Prawo*, no. 6, June: 91–8.

Kojder, A. and Kwaśniewski, J. (1981), 'Stosunek spoleczeústwa polskiego do zjawisk i zachowań dewiacyjnych' (Polish Society's Attitudes Towards Deviance), pp. 85–106 in B. Holyst (ed.), *Opinia Publiczna i Srodki Masowego Przekazk a Ujemne Zjawiska Spoleczne*, Warsaw: Wydawnictwo Prawniczeo

Kolakowska-Przelomiec, H. (1975), 'Srodowisko rodzinne w swietle badań kryminologicznych' (Family Environment in Light of Criminological Research), pp. 159–205 in J. Jasiński (ed.), *Zagadnienia Przestepczości w Polsce*, Warsaw: Wydawnictwo Prawnicze.

'Kolo Koszalina powstal ośrodek rehabilitacji narkomanów' (1984), (A Rehabilitation Centre for Drug-Addicts Has Been Established near Koszalin), *Zycie Warszawy*, 9 Feb.: 6.

Komarov, B. (1980), *The Destruction of Nature in the Soviet Union*, White Planes, N.Y.: M.E. Sharpe Inc.

Komarov, B. (1981) *Le Rouge et la Vert*, Paris: Editions du Seuil.

'Komunikat Prokuratury Generalnej o Sledztwach Przeciwko Bylym Prominentom' (1981), (A Communique of the Prosecutor General on Proceedings Against Ex-executives), *Zycie Warszawy*, 3 Nov.: 2.

Kondratov, E. (1983), 'Cruel Blindness', *Izvestia*, 18 Mar.: 6, condensed in *CDSP*, 35(11), 13 Apr.: 21–2 (State and Law).

Konstytucja Polskiej Rzeczypospolitej Ludowej (1952, with the 1976 amendments) (The Constitution of the Polish People's Republic).

Kontakt, a Polish language monthly magazine published since Apr. 1982 in Paris by members and collaborators of the Solidarity Union.

'Kontrola rynku' (1981), (Market Control), *Zycie Warszawy*, 12 Aug.: 3.

Kos-Rabcewicz-Zubkowski, L. (1976), 'Conciliation Commissions in Poland', *The American Journal of Comparative Law*, 24.

Kossawska, A. (1978), 'Przestepczość na terenie wielkiego miasta' (Big City Crime), pp. 165–83 in J. Jasiński (ed.), *Zagadnienia Nieprzystosowania Spolecznego i Przestepczości w Polsce*, Wroclaw: Ossolineum.

Kowalska-Ehrlich, B. (1983), 'Zasady postepowania z nieletnimi i mlodocianymi' (The Principles of Treatment of Juvenile Delinquents and Young Offenders), pp. 265–321 in A. Krukowski (ed.), *Prawne Podstawy Resocjalizacji i Zapobiegania Przestepczości*, Warsaw: PWN (Polish Scientific Publishers).

Krakowski, L. (1970), 'Sady Spoleczne w Zakladzie Pracy' (Social Courts in the Workplace), Warsaw: CRZZ.

Kramer, J. M. (1977), 'Political Corruption in the USSR', *Western Political Quarterly*, 30(2): 213–24.

'Kroki zaradcze po burdach zwalczajacych sie gangów mlodzieżowych w Nowej Hucie' (1984), (Remedial Steps After the Youth Gangs Clashes in Nowa Huta), *Zycie Warszawy*, 8 Mar.: 6.

'Kronika sadowa: Dwadzieścia pieć lat pozbawienia wolności za morderstwo na oczach dzieci' (1983), (Court Chronicle: Twenty Five Year's Imprisonment for a Murder in Presence of Children), *Zycie Warszawy*, 8 Dec.: 6.

Kryczka, P. (1978), 'Some Phenomena of Social Pathology in Poland', *The Polish Sociological Bulletin*, no. 2: 101–9.

Kubiak, J. R. (1981), 'Kara śmierci' (Death Penalty), *Polityka* (Warsaw), no. 40, 4 Oct.: 13.

Kucharski, T. (1983), 'Pierwsza potrzeba: sprawiedliwość (Primary Need: Justice: an Interview with the Minister of Justice, Lech Domeracki), *Tu i Teraz* (Warsaw), 2(52), 28 Dec.: 1 and 5.

Kucherenko, A. (1981–82), 'With Satirical Pen: Miracle Conveyor', *Pravda*, 15 Dec. 1981: 6, condensed in *CDSP*, 33(50), 13 Jan.: 20–1 ('State and Law').

Kulagiu, V. (1983), Villagers Take Tough Stance on Crime', Izvestia, 20 Jan.: 2, condensed in *CDSP*, 35(3), 16 Feb.: 9–10.

Kultura, an official Polish weekly magazine.

Kurasov, V. (1980), 'Face to Face with the Law: Surcharge for a Mark', *Izvestia*, 2 Apr.: 6, condensed in *CDSP*, 35(13), 30 Apr.: 13 ('State and Law').

Kurczewski, J. (1982), 'The Old System and the Revolution', pp. 21–32 in *Sisyphus: Sociological Studies*, (vol. III: *Crises and Conflicts: the Case of Poland 1980–81*), Warsaw: PWN (Polish Scientific Publishers).

Kurczewski, J. and Frieske, K. (1977) 'Some Problems in the Legal Regulation of the Activities of Economic Institutions', *Law and Society Review*, 11(Winter): 489–505.

Kurczewski, J. and Frieske, K. (1978), 'The Social Conciliatory Commissions in Poland', pp. 153–427 in M. Cappelletti and J. Weisner (eds), *Access to Justice*, (vol. II, *Promising Institutions*), Leyden: A. W. Sijthoff International Publishing Co.; Milan: Dott, A., Giuffrè Editore.

Kurczewski, J. and Frieske, K. (1979), 'Dzialalność spolecznych komisji pojednawczych' (The Functioning of the Social Conciliatory Commissions), pp. 34–58 in *Konflikt i Przystosowanie*, Warsaw: University of Warsaw (Prace IPSiR, vol. 4).

Kurowski, S. (1980), 'Doktrynalne uwarunkowania obecnego kryzysu gospodarczego PRL' (Doctrinal Determinants of the Present Economic Crisis in Poland). Paper to a conference of the Polish Sociological Association (12 May 1979). Published in: *Raport o Stanie Narodu i PRL*, Paris: Instytut Literacki/Institut Litteraire.

Kuzentsova, N. F. (1975), 'The Strengthening of Socialist Legality and the Organization of the Struggle Against Crime in the Light of the Decisions of the 24th the CPSU Congress', Sovetskoye Gosudarstvo i Pravo, no. 3, Mar.: 122–30, condensed in *CDSP*, 27(26), 23 July: 6–7, ('Crime: Its Causes and Their Eradication').

Kwaśniewski, J. (1981), 'Sprawozdanie z zebrania naukowego na temat lapownictwa' (A Resumé of a Conference on Bribery), pp. 111–15 in K. Frieske (ed.), *Dewiacja i Kontrola Spoleczna*, Warsaw: PTS (Polish Sociological Association).

—— (1984), *Society and Deviance in Communist Poland*, Leamington Spa: Berg Publications.

Kwaśniewski, J. and Kojder, A. (1979), 'Postawy mieszkańcow Warszawy wobec zjawisk i zachowań dewiacyjnych' (Attitudes of Warsaw Inhabitants

Towards Deviant Behaviour and Phenomena), *Studia Socjologiczne* (Warsaw), no. 1: 158–79.

Labudzka, I. (1974), *Zjawisko Alkoholizmu na Tle Procesu Urbanizacji* (Alcoholism in Relation to Urbanization Processes), Wroclaw: Ossolineum.

Land, T. (1983), 'Poland Ends Pretence, Clamps Down on Heroin', *The Journal*, 12(11), 1 Nov.: 10, Toronto: The Addiction Research Foundation.

Lapenna, I. (1975), 'The Contemporary Crisis of Legality in the Soviet Union Substantive Criminal Law', *Review of Socialist Law*, 1(1): 73–95.

Latoszek, M., Lemska, A. and Sieliwończyk, P. (1974), 'Badania socjologiczne nad narkomania wsród mlodzieży szkól średnich Trójmiasta' (Sociological Research on Drug-Addiction Among High-School Students in Trójmiasto), *Studia Socjologiczne* (Warsaw), no. 4: 243–62.

Latoszek, M., Ochman, P., Koziol-Bielska, I. (1981), 'Socjologiczne aspekty narkomanii' (Sociological Aspects of Drug Abuse), *Studia Socjologiczne* (Warsaw), no. 3: 211–21.

Leggett, G. H. (1975), 'Lenin, Terror, and the Political Police', *Survey* 21(4): 157–87.

Leggett, G. H. (1981), *The Cheka: Lenin's Political Police*, Oxford: Clarendon Press.

Lenin, V. I. (1973a), 'Communist Ethics'. From a speech delivered at the Third All-Russian Congress of the Young Communist League of the Soviet Union on 2 Oct.: 1920, p. 66 in S. Hendel (ed.), *The Soviet Crucible*, North Scituate, Mass.: Duxbury Press.

Lenin, V. I. (1973b, first published in 1917), 'State and Revolution', pp. 61–6 in S. Hendel (ed.), *The Soviet Crucible*, North Scituate, Mass.: Duxbury Press.

Lenin, V. I. (1973c, first published in 1902), 'What Is To Be Done?', pp. 57–60 in S. Hendel (ed.), *The Soviet Crucible*, North Scituate, Mass.: Duxbury Press.

Lernell, L. (1973), *Zarys Kryminologii Ogolnej* (An Outline of General Criminology), Warsaw: PWN (Polish Scientific Publishers).

Leśnicka, H. (1984), 'Portret zbiorowy Polek' (Collective Portrait of Polish Women), *Zycie Warszawy*, 3–4 Mar.: 3.

Levin, B. (1982), '*Will Arthur Scargill Face the Truth that Joe Gormley Dodged?*', *The Times*, 6 May: 12.

Lipka, M. (1975), 'Zapobieganie przestepczości wśród mlodzieży' (Juvenile Delinquency Prevention), pp. 34–45 in *Patologica Spoleczna – Zapobieganie*, (vol. 1), Warsaw: Wydawnictwo Prawnicze.

Lipski, J. J. (1983), *KOR* (The Committee of Workers' Defense), London: Aneks.

Lipson, L. (1970), 'Hosts and Pests: the Fight Against Parasites', pp. 323–32 in R. Cornell (ed.), *The Soviet Political System*, Englewood Cliffs, N.J.: Prentice Hall Inc.

Lirmyan, R. and Sheverdin, S. (1982), 'Alcoholic Beverage Sales and the Temperance Campaign', *Molodoi Kommunist*, no. 2, Feb.: 64–70, condensed in *CDSP*, 32(15) ('Studies Show Drinking Age Is Down, Alcoholism Up').

'Listy z wiezienia' (1981), (Letters from Prison), *Solidarność* (Warsaw), no. 8, 22 May: 8.

Literatura, an official Polish weekly magazine.

Loch, J. (1980) 'W szarym tloku' (In the grey crowd), *Polityka* (Warsaw), 24(42), 18 Oct.: 3.

Loch, J. (1981), 'W strone drugiej Polski' (Towards a Second Poland, *Odglosy* (Lódź), 24(6), 8 Feb.: 1, 4 and 5.

Lorimer, F. (1946) *The Population of the Soviet Union: History and Prospects*, Geneva: League of Nations.

Łoś, M. (1978), 'Access to the Civil Justice System in Poland', pp. 785–815 in M. Cappelletti and B. Garth, *Access to Justice*, (vol. 1, *A World Survey*), Leyden, London and Boston: A. W. Sijthoff Int.

——(1979a), 'Multi-Dimensional Sociology', pp. 118–137 in A. Podgórecki and M. Łoś (eds), *Multi-Dimensional Sociology*, London: Routledge & Kegan Paul.

——(1979b), 'Theoretical Background of Reference-Group Concept and Its Evolution', pp. 182–93, in A. Podgórecki and M. Łoś, *Multi-Dimensional Sociology*, London: Routledge & Kegan Paul.

——(1980), 'Economic Crimes from a Comparative Perspective', pp. 251–93 in G. R. Newman (ed.), *Crime and Deviance: a Comparative Perspective*, Beverly Hills, Calif.: Sage Publications.

——(1982a), 'Crime and the Economy in the Communist Countries', pp. 121–37 in P. Wickman, and T. Dailey (eds), *White-Collar and Economic-Crime*, Lexington, Mass.: Lexington Books.

——(1982b), *Welfare and Justice*, University of Sheffield (Centre for Criminological and Socio-legal Studies).

——(1983a), 'Economic Crimes in Communist Countries', pp. 39–57 in I. L. Barak-Glantz and E. H. Johnson (eds), *Comparative Criminology*, Beverly Hills, Calif.: Sage Publications.

——(1983b), 'Les femmes, les pouvoirs et le crime en Pologne', *Criminologie*, 16(2): 47–66, Les Presses de l'Université de Montréal.

——(1983c), 'Poverty, Welfare Rights and the Solidarity Movement in Poland', pp. 94–114 in A. Jain (ed.), *Solidarity: the Origins and Implications of Polish Trade Unions*, Baton Rouge, La.: Oracle Press.

——(1983d) 'Law and Order in Contemporary Poland', *Canadian Slavonic Papers*, 25(3), (Sept.): 392–410.

—— (1984) 'Corruption in a Communist Country: A Case Study of Poland', *International Annals of Criminology*, 22(1 & 2): 194–206.

——and Anderson, P. (1976), 'The "Second Life": a Cross-Cultural View of Peer Subcultures in Correctional Institutions in Poland and the United States', *The Polish Sociological Bulletin*, no. 4: 47–61.

——and Anderson, P. (1981), 'The "Second Life": a Cross-Cultural View of Peer Subcultures in Correctional Institutions in Poland and the United States', pp. 201–17 in L. Shelley (ed.), *Readings in Comparative Criminology*, Carbondale: Southern Illinois University Press.

Losoto, Ye, (1980), 'Come to Your Own Rescue!', *Nauka i Religia*, no. 2, Feb.: 42–4, condensed in *CDSP*, 32(17), 28 May: 17 ('Do People Drink Out of "Emptiness"?').

Lubelska, K. (1983), 'Narkoman – podejrzenie czy fakt?' (A Drug-Addict: a Suspicion or Fact?'), *Zycie Warszawy*, 20 Oct.: 3.

——(1984a), 'Czy narkoman chce sie leczyć?' (Does the Drug-Addict Want to Be Treated?), *Zycie Warszawy*, 30 Jan.: 3.

——(1984b), 'Indywidualnie – nie zbiorowo' (Individually – not Collectively), *Zycie Warszawy*, 11 Jan.: 1.

'Ludzie pisza do Sejmu, NIK, prokuratury' (1981), (People Write to the Diet, NIK, Public Prosecutor's Office), *Zycie Warszawy*, 18 Mar.: 6.

Luryi, Y. (ed.), (1978), *Soviet Law and Legal System*, York University, Osgoode Hall Law School (xeroxed materials).

Łyczywek, R. (1981), 'Kara śmierci' (Death Penalty), *Kultura* (Warsaw), no. 32, 9 Aug.: 9.

Madison, B. Q. (1968), *Social Welfare in the Soviet Union*, Stanford, Calif.: Stanford University Press.

Majchrzak, I. (1965), *Pracownicze Przestepstwo i Jego Sprawca* (White-Collar Crime and White-Collar Criminal), Warsaw: KiW.

"Mala Encyklopedia ZOMO, ROMO, MO" (1983), (Small Encyclopedia of ZOMO, ROMO, MO), *Biuletyn Informacyjny*, no. 71, 28 Feb.: 9–10, New York: Committee in Support of Solidarity.

Maly Rocznik Statystyczny (1983) (Small Statistical Yearbook), Warsaw: GUS (The Main Statistical Office).

Mandel, W. M. (1975), *Soviet Women*, New York: Anchor Books.

Mankiewicz, M. (1981a), 'Dużo sie teraz robi dla dobra dziecka' (Much Is Being Done Now for Children), *Kobieta i Zycie*, (Warsaw), no. 36, 6 Sept.: 23.

Mankiewicz, M. (1981b), 'Tajemnica cudownego rozmnożenia po polsku' (The Secret of Miraculous Multiplication *à la polonaise*), *Kobieta i Zycie* (Warsaw), no. 40, Oct.: 4–5.

Markiewicz, W. (1981), 'Czy obywatel może czuć sie bezpieczny?' (Is Citizen Safe?), *Zycie Warszawy*, 9 Apr.: 1 and 4.

Markiewicz, W. (1984), 'Cnota albo przyjemność (Virtue or Fun), *Polityka* (Warsaw), no. 6, 11 Feb.: 5.

Markovits, I. (1978), 'Socialist vs. Bourgeois Rights: an East–West German Comparison', *The University of Chicago Law Review*, 45(3), (Spring): 612–36.

Maroszek, B. (1963), *Wieź Spoleczna a Przestepczość Mlodzieży*, Gdańsk.

Maroszek, B. (1975), 'Délinquance juvénile et développement socio-économique en Pologne', in I. Chirol, Marszek *et al.* (eds), *Déliquance juvénile et développement socio-économique*, La Hague: Mouton.

Marx, K. and Engels, F. (1848), *Communist Manifesto*, pp. 23–31 in S. Hendel, (ed.) (1973), *The Soviet Crucible*, North Scituate, Mass.: Duxbury Press.

Massel, G. J. (1968), 'Law as an Instrument of Revolutionary Change in a Traditional Milieu – the Case of Soviet Central Asia', *Law and Society Review*, 2(2): 182–226.

Matalowska, A. (1981), 'Raport o narkomanii' (A Report on Drug-Addiction), *Polityka* (Warsaw), no. 31, 31 July: 8.

Mathiesen, T. (1974), *The Politics of Abolition*, Scandinavian Studies in Criminology (4), London: Martin Robertson; Oslo: Scandinvian University Books.

McAuley, A. (1977), 'The Distribution of Earnings and Incomes in the Soviet Union', *Soviet Studies*, 29(2), Apr.: 214–37.

McGrath, W. T. (eds), (1976), *Crime and Its Treatment in Canada* (2nd edn), Toronto: The Macmillan Co. of Canada.

'Meetings of the Presidium of the USSR Supreme Soviet' (1983), *Pravda*, 13 Jan.: 1–2, condensed in *CDSP*, 35(2), 9 Feb.: 13 and 24 ('Supreme Soviet Presidium Takes Action').

'Memorial by Polish Legal Scholars submitted on 30 Oct. 1980 to the Minister of Justice, Prof. Dr Jerzy Bafia on the Reform of Prevailing Polish Criminal Law and Policy' (1981) *Review of Socialist Law*, 7(3): 425–6.

Merton, R. K. (1938), 'Social Structure and Anomie', *American Sociological Review*, 3(5), Oct.: 672–82.

Mietkowski, A. (1982), 'Spisane beda czyny . . .' ('These Deeds Will Be Written Down . . .'), *Kontakt* (Paris), nos 3 and 4, July–Sept.: 29–33.

Mikusiński, W. J. (1981), 'Po prostu zwolniono z pracy' (It Was Simply a Dismissal from Work), *Solidarność* (Warsaw), no. 36, 4 Dec.: 10.

Milotworska, K. (1982), *Orzel Bialy* (London), no 1367/XLII, Dec.: 34–5.

'Moda rodem z Zachodu' (1984), (A Fashion from the West), *Express Wieczorny* (Warsaw), 27–9 Apr.: 3.

Mońko, M. (1981), 'Blad' (Mistake), *Solidarność* (Warsaw), no. 2, 10 Apr.: 2–3.

Montfort, H. (1966), *Le Massacre de Katyn: Crime Russe ou Crime Allemand?*, Paris: La Table Ronde.

Mościskier, A. (1976), 'Delinquency in Poland and Processes of Industrialization and Urbanization', *The Polish Sociological Bulletin*, no. 1.

—— (1978a), 'Rozwój ekonomiczny, uprzemyslowienie i urbanizacja a przestepczość (Economic Development, Industrialization, Urbanization and Crime), pp. 125–42 in J. Jasiński (ed.), *Zagadnienia Nieprzystosowania Spolecznego i Przestepczości w Polsce*, Wroclaw: Ossolineum.

—— (1978b), 'Przestepczość w Procesie Szybkich Zmian Spoleczynych' (Crime and the Processes of Rapid Social Change), pp. 143–63 in J. Jasiński (ed.), *Zagadnienia Nieprzystosowania Spolecznego i Przestepczości w Polsce*, Wroclaw: Ossolineum.

—— and Szelhaus, St. (1976), 'Przestepczość mlodzieży' (Juvenile Delinquency), pp. 487–511 in A. Podgórecki (ed.), *Zagadnienia Patologii Spolecznej*, Warsaw: PWN (Polish Scientific Publishers).

Moszyński, P. (1980), 'Budujemy nowy dom' (We Construct a New House), *Polityka*, (Warsaw), 24(42), 18 Nov.: 5.

Mozolowski, A. (1983), 'List otwarty do dr Z' (Open Letter to Doctor Z), *Polityka*, 27(50), 10 Dec.: 7.

Mungham, G. and Pearson G., (eds) (1976), *Working Class Youth Culture*, London: Routledge & Kegan Paul.

'Narada w Warszawie' (1984), (A Meeting in Warsaw), *Zycie Warszawy*, 27 Jan.: 2.

'Nasi okupanci' (1982), (Our Occupants), *Solidarność. Biuletyn Informacyjny*, no. 43, 17 Nov.: 13–14, Paris: Solidarité Pologne Publications.

'Nastolatki juź takźe' (1984), (Teenagers as well), *Zycie Warszawy*, 24–5 Mar.: 8.

Naumowicz, Z. (1970), 'Niektóre zagadnienia dotyczace przestepczości gospodarczej' (Selected Problems Related to Economic Crime), pp. 5–32 in *Prawnicy, Socjologowie i Psychologowie o Przestepczości i jej Zwalczaniu*, Warsaw: Prokuratura Generalna.

Neznansky, F. (1979), 'New Information on Soviet Criminal Statistics' (An Insider's Report). Paper presented to the Annual Meeting of the American Society of Criminology in 1979.

'Normalizacja' (1982) (Normalization), *Solidarność. Biuletyn Informacyjny*, no. 49, 24 Dec.: Paris: Solidarité Pologne Publications.

Novaya Konstitucija i Aktualnye Voprosy Borby s Priestupnostiju. (1979), (New Constitution and Timely Issues of the Struggle Against Crime), The Academy of Sciences of the Georgian Soviet Socialist Republic.

Nove, A. (1975), 'Y a-t-il une classe dirigeante en URSS?', *Revue d'Études Comparatives Est-Ouest*, 6(4), Dec.: 5–29, Paris: Editions du Centre National de la Recherche Scientifique.

Nove, A. (1978), *An Economic History of the USSR*, Harmondsworth, Middlesex: Penguin Books (Pelican Books).

'Nowa forma represji' (1983), *Kontakt* (Paris), no. 5, May: 64.

Nowakowska, E. (1982), 'Sześć kucharek nad dziurawym kotlem' (Six Cooks Over a Kettle Full of Holes), *Polityka* (Warsaw), 26(15), 29 May: 1, 4–10.

'Nowe oblicze spekulacji' (1982), (New Face of Speculation), *Zycie Warszawy*, 3 Nov.: 2.

'O przewozie miesa' (1983) (About Transporting of Meat), *Zycie Warszawy*, 23 Dec.

'Obraz Tygodnia' (1983) (Week Review),*Tygodnik Powszechny* (Cracow), no. 21, 22 May: 1.

'Obraz tygodnia' (1984) (Week review), *Tygodnik Powszechny* (Cracow), no. 16, 15 Apr.: 1.

'Oddajmy sprawiedliwość sedziom' (1983) (Let's Be Fair to Judges), *Solidarność: Biuletyn Informacyjny* (Paris), no. 59, 13 Apr.: 12–13.

Ogórek, M. (1982), 'Szczelny szlam' (Tight slime), *Polityka* (Warsaw), 26(15), 29 May: 5.

O'Hearn, D. (1980) 'The Consumer Second Economy: Size and Effects', *Soviet Studies*, 32(1): 218–34.

Olszewska, B. W. (1981), 'Raport o milicji' (Report on the police), *Polityka* (Warsaw), 25(32), 8 Aug.: 3–9.

Olszewski, J. (1981), 'Akcje kontrolne nie ustaja: Spekulacja nie może sie oplacać' (Control Operations Continue: Speculation Cannot Pay), *Trybuna Ludu* (Warsaw), 15–16 Aug.

'Opracowania i Ekspertyzy' (1981), (Surveys and Reports), *AS: Biuletyn Pism Zwiazkowych i Zakladowych*, 3–6 Dec.: 404, Warsaw: Agencja Prasowa Solidarność.

Oseka, J. (1981), 'Z czym na dywanik' (What Should be Scrutinized), *Polityka* 25(8), 18 Nov.: 6.

Ostroumov, S. S. and Chugunov, V. E. (1965), 'Study of the Criminal Personality from the Materials of Criminological Research', *Sovetskoye Gosudarstvo i Pravo*, no. 9, reprinted in *The Soviet Review*, 7(2), Summer 1966: 13–21.

Pashukanis, E. B. (1978), *Law and Marxism: a General Theory*, London: Ink Links.

Pashukanis, E. B. (1980), *Pashukanis: Selected Writings on Marxism and Law*, New York: Academic Press.

Pawelczyńska, A. (1979), *Values and Violence in Auschwitz: a Sociological Analysis*, Berkeley: University of California Press.

Pawelko, W. (1971), *Zapobieganie Przestepstwom Gospodarczym* (Economic Crime Prevention), Warsaw: PWN (Polish Scientific Publishers).

Pelc, J. (1981), 'Karmić sikorki . . .' (To Feed Coaltits . . .), *Solidarność* (Warsaw), no. 8, 22 May: 8–9.

The Penal Code of the Polish People's Republic (1973) The American Series of Foreign Penal Codes edited by G. O. W. Mueller, South Hackensack, N.J.: Fred B. Rothman & Co.; London: Sweet & Maxwell.

Piotrowski, A. (1976), 'Niektóre psychospoleczne determinanty przyjmowania przez mlodziez środków odurzajacych w latach 1963–1973' (Several Psychosocial Factors Conducive to Teenage Use of Hallucinogenic Substances) in M. Jarosz (ed.), *Wybrane Zagadnienia Patologii Rodziny*, Warsaw.

Piotrowski, M. (1984), 'Trzy śmierci Elżbiety' (Three Deaths of Elizabeth), *Tu i Teraz* (Warsaw), 3(2), 11 Jan.: 4.

'Plenarne obrady Sejmu PRL' (1982), (Plenary Session of the Polish Diet), *Trybuna Ludu* (Warsaw), 35(255), 27 Oct.: 3.

Pleńska, D. (1980), 'La criminalité féminine en Pologne', *Canadian Journal of Criminology*, 22(4): 464–75.

Podemski, St. (1981a), 'Nim zmienimy kodeksy' (Before We Change the Codes), *Polityka* (Warsaw), 15(14), 4 Apr.: 6.

—— (1981b), 'Amnestia bez schematów' (About Amnesty Unconventionally), *Polityka* (Warsaw), 15(21), 23 May: 3.

—— (1981c), 'Pakty i fakty' (Pacts and Facts), *Polityka* (Warsaw), 15(32), 8 Aug.: 6–7.

—— (1982a), "Czternaście lat watpliwości" (Fourteen years of doubt), *Polityka* (Warsaw), 26(16), 5 June: 6.

—— (1982b), 'Grzywna czy areszt?' (A Fine or Arrest?), *Polityka* (Warsaw), 26(16), 5 June: 5.

—— (1984a), 'Plama na rejestrze' (A Stain on the Register), *Polityka* (Warsaw), 28(1), 7 Jan.: 14.

—— (1984b), 'Sad o wolności wyznania' (The Court About Religious Freedom), *Polityka* (Warsaw), 28(7), 18 Feb.: 7.

Podgórecki, A. (1966) *Prestiż Prawa* (The Prestige of the Law), Warsaw: KiW.

—— (1969), 'Attitudes to the Workers' Courts', pp. 142–9 in V. Aubert (ed.), *Sociology of Law*, Penguin Books.

—— (1971), *Zarys Socjologii Prawa* (An Outline of Sociology of Law), Warsaw: PWN (Polish Scientific Publishers).

—— (1973), *Diagnostyczny Obraz Niektórych Trudnych Problemów Społeczeństwa Polskiego oraz Refleksje Socjotechniczne* (Diagnostic Picture of Some Difficult Problems of Polish Society and Sociotechnical Recommendations), University of Warsaw, 1973.

—— (1974), *Law and Society*, London: Routledge & Kegan Paul.

—— (1979), 'Tertiary Social Control', pp. 194–204 in A. Podgórecki and M. Łoś, *Multi-Dimensional Sociology*, London: Routledge & Kegan Paul.

——, Kurczewski, J., Kwaśniewski, J. and Łoś, M. (1971), *Poglady Społeczeństwa Polskiego na Moralność i Prawo* (Attitudes of Polish Society towards Law and Morality), Warszawa: KiW.

Poland Today: the State of the Republic (1981), compiled by the "Experience and the Future", Discussion Group, Armonk, N.Y.: M.E. Sharpe, Inc.

Polityka, an official Polish weekly magazine.

'Pollution Grows in Eastern Europe' (1982), *The New York Times*, 12 Sept.

Pomorski, St. (1977), 'Criminal Law Protection for Socialist Property in the USSR', pp. 223–58 in D. B. Barry, G. Ginsburgs and P. B. Maggs (eds), *Soviet Law after Stalin*, (Part I: *The Citizen and the State in Contemporary Soviet Law*), Leyden: A. W. Sijthoff.

—— (1978), 'Crimes Against the Central Planner: "Ochkovtiratelstwo"', pp.

291–317 in D. D. Barry, G. Ginsburgs and P. B. Maggs (eds), (Part II: *Social Engineering Through Law*, Alpen ann den Rijn: Sijthoff & Noordhoff.

—— (1981), 'Communists and their Criminal Law: Reflections on Igor Andrejew's "Outline of the Criminal Law of Socialist States"', *Review of Socialist Law*, 7(1): 7–34.

—— (1983), 'La corruption de functionnaires devant les tribunaux soviétiques', *Revue d'études comparatives est-ouest*, 14(1): 5–22.

Poprzeczko, J. (1984), 'Ratujmy Kraków' (Let's Save Cracow), *Polityka* (Warsaw), 28(7), 18 Feb.: 8.

'Porachunki mlodzieżowych gangów w Krakowie'. (1984), (Skirmishes of youth gangs in Cracow), *Zycie Warszawy*, 7 Mar.: 6.

Porowski, M. (1980), 'Prawne podstawy funkcjonowania administracji penitencjarnej i ochrona praw podmiotowych skazanego' (Legal basis of the functioning of the correctional administration and protection of convict's rights), pp. 57–78 in *Nowe Tendencje w Postepowaniu z Mlodzieża Spolecznie Nieprzystosowana*, Warsaw: Wydawnictwo Uniwersytetu Warszawskiego (Prace IPSiR, vol. 5).

'Posiedzenie Sejmu PRL' (1980), (A Meeting of the Polish Diet), *Zycie Warszawy*, 22–3 Nov.: 4.

'Posiedzenie Sejmu Polskiej Rzeczypospolitej Ludowej' (1983), (A Meeting of the Polish Diet), *Zycie Warszawy*, 6 Dec.: 2–3.

Powell, D. E. (1971), 'Alcoholism in the USSR', *Survey*, 16(1): 123–37.

Prestupnost' i Industrializatsiya (1974), (Crime and Industrialization), Stockholm: Scandinavian Research Council for Criminology.

Prisoners of Conscience in the USSR: Their Treatment and Conditions (1975), An Amnesty International Report, London: Amnesty International Publications.

Prisoners of Conscience in the USSR: Their Treatment and Conditions (1980), An Amnesty International Report, London: Quartermaine House Ltd.

Prologue to Gdańsk (1980), *A Report on Human Rights by the Polish Helsinki Watch Committee*, London: Information Centre for Polish Affairs.

Pruski, M. and Zukowski, Z. (1983), 'Skorpion' (Scorpion), *Polityka* (Warsaw), 27(41), 8 Oct.: 11.

'Przestrzeganie prawa publicznego i porzadku' (1984), (Conformity with the Public Law and Order), *Zycie Warszawy*, 15 Mar.: 1.

'Przyjmowali lapówki za zagraniczne kontakty handlowe' (1983) (They Accepted Bribes for Foreign Trade Contacts), *Zycie Warszawy*, 27 Oct.: 6.

Ptaczek, J. (1981), 'Raz jeszcze o odpowiedzialności' (Once more about responsibility), *Orzel Bialy* – Na Antenie (London), no. 202/1348, June: 22–4.

'Public Opinion and Law-Enforcement Agencies: The Prevention Service's Tasks' (1980), *Zarya Vostoka*, 14 Mar.: 4, condensed in *CDSP*, 32(17), 28 May: 16 ('"Parasites" Termed Major Factor in Georgian Crime Rates').

Pyrkh, I. (1982), 'The Ring of Crystal Was Heard From Afar: the Dyatkovo Plant Takes a Carefree Attitude Towards the Theft of Valuable Articles', *Sovetskaya Rossia*, 14 Mar.: 6, condensed in *CDSP*, 34(12), 21 Apr.: 16 ('Million-Rouble Pilferage Feeds Brisk Market in Crystalware').

Raina, P. (1978), *Political Opposition in Poland 1954–1977*, London: Poets and Painters Press.

Reddaway, P. (1973), *The Forced Labour Camps in the USSR Today: an Unrecognized Example of Modern Inhumanity*, Brussels.

'Rehabilitate the Man!'. (1983), *Nedelya*, 24–30 Jan.: 6, condensed in *CDSP*, 35(4), 23 Feb.: 1.

Reich, W. (1983), 'The World of Soviet Psychiatry', *The New York Times Magazine*, 30 Jan.: 20–6 and 50.

Reid, S. T. (1976), *Crime and Criminology*, Hindsdale, Ill.: The Dryden Press.

Rekunkov, A. (1982), 'The Citizen, Society and the Law: Dictated by the Norms of the Law', *Pravda*, 27 Apr.: 3, condensed in *CDSP*, 34(17), 26 May: 1–3 ('Top Prosecutor Hits Officials' Corruption').

Report to the Congress on Forced Labour in the USSR. Issued on 9 Feb., 1983 by the European Public Affairs Office, US Department of State.

La Repression en Pologne depuis 13 Décembre 1981 (1982), Brussels: Bureau de Coordination de NSZZ, "Solidarność" à l'Étranger.

Resich, Z. (1973), *Nauka o Organach Ochrony Prawnej* (On Agencies of Legal Protection), Warszawa: PWN (Polish Scientific Publishers).

Resolution of the Presidium of the Supreme Soviet of the RSFSR of 7 Aug., 1975, reprinted in L. Lipson and V. Chalidze (eds), (1977) *Papers on Soviet Law* (no. 1), New York: Institute on Socialist Law, pp. 198–9.

Reszke, I. (1978), 'Kulturowe i biopsychiczne unwarunkowania feminizacji zawodów' (Cultural and Bio-Psychological Factors in Feminization of Certain Occupations), *Studia Socjologiczne* (Warsaw), no. 3: 151–81.

Rimlinger, G. V. (1971), *Welfare Policy and Industrialization in Europe, America and Russia*, New York: John Wiley.

Rocznik Statystyczny (1980), (Statistical Yearbook), Warsaw: GUS (The Main Statistical Office).

Rogala, J. (1980), 'Rola niepowodzeń szkolnych w powstawaniu toksykomanii mlodzieżowej' (The Role of School Failure in Teenage Toxicomania), pp. 79–94 in *Przejawy Dewiacji Spolecznej i Postepowanie z Dewiantami*, Warsaw: Wydawnictwa Uniwersytetu Warszawskiego (IPSiR, vol. 6).

Roman, P. M. and Gebert, P. J. (1979), 'Alcohol Abuse in the US and USSR: Divergence and Convergence in Policy and Ideology', *Social Psychiatry*, 14: 207–16.

'Rośnie liczba wytwórców narkotyków' (1984), (The Number of Producers of Narcotics is Growing), *Zycie Warszawy*, 26 Mar.: 4.

'Różne' (1983), (Varia), *Biuletyn Informacyjny*, no. 72, 5 Apr., Committee in Support of Solidarity (New York).

'Rożwiazanie Patronatu' (1983), (Dissolution of Patronat), *Biuletyn Informacyjny* (reprinted from Polish underground press), no. 51, 19 Jan.: 9–10, Solidarité Pologne Publications (Paris).

Ruane, K. (1982), *The Polish Challenge*, London: British Broadcasting Corporation.

Rudenko, R. (1979/1980), 'The Citizen and the Law: With Full Severity', *Pravda*, 19 Dec., 1979: 3, condensed in *CDSP*, 31(51), 16 Jan.: 6 ('The Law on the USSR Prosecutor's Office. Rudenko Cites Need to Eliminate Laxity').

Rudnicki, St. (1981), 'Jacy sa sedziowie?' (What Judges Are Like?), *Solidarność* (Warsaw), no. 25, 18 Sept.: 13.

Rusche, G. and Kirchheimer, O. (1968; first published in 1939), *Punishment and Social Structure*, New York: Russel & Russel.

Ryashchenko, G. (1980), 'Before the Law: Housing for a Bribe', *Izvestia*, 26 Jan.: 6, condensed in *CDSP*, 32(4), 27 Feb.: 21 ('State and Law').

Rybicki, M. (1972), 'Les juridictions sociales en Pologne', *Droit Polonais Contemporain*, no. 17–18: 19–29.

Rzeczpospolita (1983), an official Polish weekly magazine established after the imposition of the state of war, no. 69.

Rzepliński, A. and Kutylowski, A. (1981), 'Opinie na temat lapownictwa jako przestepstwa i zjawiska spolecznego' (Views on Bribery as a Crime and Social Phenomenon), pp. 142–56 in B. Holyst (ed.), *Opinia Publiczna i Srodki Masowego Przekazu a Ujemne Zjawiska Spoleczne*, Warsaw: Wydawnictwo Prawnicze.

Sadikov, I. (1983), 'Problems and Opinions: Why Producers of Shoddy Goods Feel No Shame', *Pravda*, 25 Feb.: 3, condensed in *CDSP*, 35(8), 23 Mar.: 23–4.

Sakharov, A. (1975), 'Introduction' in H. E. Salisbury (ed.), *Sakharov Speaks*, London: Collins/Fontana.

Samokhin, N. (1975), 'The Story of a Trial: in the Presence of Witnesses', *Literaturnaya Gazeta*, no. 46, 12 Nov.: 12, condensed in *CDSP*, 27(47), 17 Dec.: 7–8 ('Writer Murdered by Young Hooligans').

Schapiro, L. (1977), *The Government and Politics of the Soviet Union* (6th edn), London: Hutchinson.

Schwartz, Ch. A. (1979), 'Corruption and Political Development in the USSR', *Comparative Politics*, 11(4): 425–43.

Schwendinger, H. and Shwendinger, J. (1979), 'Delinquency and Social Reform: A Radical Perspective', pp. 245–87 in La Mar I. Empey (ed.), *Juvenile Justice: the Progressive Legacy and Current Reform*, Charlottesville: University Press of Virginia.

'Sedziowie odchodza: Spory w polityce karnej: Nowy minister – stare klopoty', (1983), (Judges Leave: Quarrels on Penal Policy: New Minister – Old Troubles), *Zycie Warszawy*, 20 Dec.: 5.

'Sedziowie pod terrorem (1982), (Terrorized Judges), *Kontakt* (Paris), Apr.: 37.

Segal, B. M. (1977), 'Soviet Studies on the Effects of Hashish', Radio Liberty Research, no. 142/77, 10 June.

Sellin, J. T. (1976), *Slavery and the Penal System*, New York: Elsevier.

Serov, I. (1980), 'Who is outside the gate?', *Pravda*, 3 May: 2, condensed in *CDSP*, 32(18), 4 June: 17–8 ('Preventive Measures Urged to Keep the "Temporarily Unemployed" from Becoming Criminals').

Sharakhin, V. and Ivanov, K. (1975), 'Questions of Soviet Law: on the Effect of Justice', *Izvestia*, 26 July: 5, reprinted in *CDSP*, 27(30), 20 Aug.: 10 ('Simpler Handling of Petty Crimes Would Benefit Law Enforcement').

Sharlet, R. (1978), 'Legal Policy under Khrushchev and Brezhnev: Continuity and Change', pp. 319–30 in D. D. Barry, G. Grinsburgs and P. B. Maggs (eds), *Soviet Law after Stalin*, (Part II. *Social Engineering Through Law*), Alphen aan der Rijn: Sijthoff & Noordhoff.

Sharlet, R. (1979), 'The Communist Party and the Administration of Justice in the USSR', pp. 321–92 in D. B. Barry, F. J. M. Feldbrugge, G. Ginsburgs and P. B. Maggs (eds), *Soviet Law after Stalin*, (Part III. *Soviet Institutions and the Administration of Law*), Alphen aan den Rijn: Sijthoff & Noordhoff.

Shchekochikhin, Y. (1982/1983), 'Mercy. About "Risky Children" and the Risk of Experiment', *Literaturnaya Gazeta*, 10 Nov. 1982: 10, condensed in *CDSP*, 35(9), 30 Mar.: 16 ('Kursk Rehabilitation Gamble Pays Off').

Shelley, L. I. (1980a), 'Crime and Deliquency in the Soviet Union', pp. 208–26 in

J. Pankhurst and M. P. Sacks (eds), *Contemporary Soviet Society*, New York: Praeger Publishers.

——(1980b), 'Geography of Soviet Criminality', *American Sociological Review*, 45(1), Feb.: 111–22.

——(1981), 'Urbanization and Crime: the Soviet Case in Cross-Cultural Perspective', pp. 141–152 in L. I. Shelley (ed.), *Readings in Comparative Criminology*, Carbondale: Southern Illinois University Press.

Shenfield, S. (1982), 'Pripiski: False Statistical Reporting in Soviet-Type Economies'. Paper presented to Conference on Corruption, Birmingham, June 1982 (organized by Centre for Russian and East European Studies).

Shifrin, A. (1982), *The First Guidebook to Prisons and Concentration Camps of the Soviet Union*, Toronto, New York: Bantam Books.

Shliapochnikov, A. S. (1934), 'Tovarishcheskie sudy' (Comrades' courts) in N. V. Krylenko (ed.), *Sovetskaja ugolovnaia repressiia*, Moscow: Sov. Zokonodatelstvo.

Shtromas, A. (1977), 'Crime, Law and Penal Practice in the USSR', *Review of Socialist Law*, 3(3): 297–324.

Sidorczuk, B. (1981), 'A gdzie sa kobiety?' (And Where Are Women?), *Kobieta i Zycie* (Warsaw), no. 24, 14 June: 3, 15.

'Siedemdziesiat cztery-osobowa grupa przestepcza spekulowala w Legnicy' (1984) (A Criminal Group of 74 Persons Speculated in Legnica), *Zycie Warszawy*, 10 Jan.: 6.

Sieriebriakova, V. A. and Syrov, A. P. (1982), 'Kriminologiczeskije aspekty izuczenia sfery byta' (Criminological Aspects of the Analysis of Social Reality), *Sovetskoe Gosudarstvo i Pravo*, no. 5: 112–15.

Simes, D. K. (1975), 'The Soviet Parallel Market, *Survey*, 21(3): 345–55.

Simis, K. (1979), 'The Machinery of Corruption in the Soviet Union', *Survey*, 24(4): 35–55.

Simis, K. (1981), 'Death Penalty under Socialism', *Russia: a Quarterly Review of Contemporary Issues*, 1.

Simis, K. M. (1982), *USSR: the Corrupt Society*, New York: Simon & Schuster.

Skalski, E. (1980), 'O winie i karze' (On guilt and punishment), *Polityka*, (Warsaw), 24(50), 13 Dec.: 1 and 7.

Skupiński, J. (1982), 'Przeciw przymusowi pracy' (Against the Coercion to Work), *Polityka* (Warsaw), 26(19), 26 June: 3.

Smart, C. (1977a), *Women, Crime and Criminology*, London: Routledge & Kegan Paul.

Smart, C. (1977b), 'Criminological Theory: Its Ideology and Implications Concerning Women', *British Journal of Sociology*, 28(1), Mar.: 89–100.

Smirnov, V. (1982), 'Face to Face with the Law: The Dump Truck Vanished', *Izvestia*, 5 Jan.: 6, condensed in *CDSP*, 34(1), 3 Feb.: 18–19, ('State and Law').

Smith, H. (1976) *The Russians*, New York: Ballantine Books.

Smith, G. B. (1979), 'Procuratorial Campaigns Against Crime', pp. 143–67, in D. B. Barry, F. J. M. Feldbrugge, G. Ginsburgs and P. B. Maggs (eds), *Soviet Law after Stalin*, (Part III. *Soviet Institutions and the Administration of Law*), Alphen aan de Rijn: Sijthoff and Noordhoff.

Smith, G. B. (1980), 'Socialist Legality and Legal Policy in the Soviet Union', pp.

109–41 in G. B. Smith (ed.), *Public Policy and Administration in the Soviet Union*, New York: Praeger Publishers.

Smożewska-Wójcikiewicz, M. (1984), 'Spowiedź' (Confession), *Tu i Teraz* (Warsaw), 3(13), 28 Mar.: 5.

'"Social parasites" Face Soviet Labour Camps' (1983) *Globe and Mail* (Toronto), 20 Jan.

Sokolowska, M. (1982), 'Health as an Issue in the Workers' Campaign', pp. 91–105 in *Sisyphus, Sociological Studies*, (vol. III: *Crises and Conflicts: the Case of Poland 1980–81*), Warsaw: PWN (Polish Scientific Publishers).

Solidarność, a Polish weekly review published between Apr. and Dec. 1981 under the auspices of the Solidarity Union (censored).

Solomon, P. H. (1974), 'Soviet Criminology – Its Demise and Rebirth 1928–1963', pp. 571–93 in R. Hood (ed.), *Crime, Criminology and Public Policy*, London: Heinemann.

—— (1978), *Soviet Criminologists and Criminal Policy*, London: The Macmillan Press.

—— (1981–82), 'Criminalization and Decriminalization in Soviet Criminal Policy, 1917–1941'; *Law and Society Review*, 16(1): 9–43.

Soltysiński, St. (1981), 'Bezpartyjni a partia' (Non-Members and the Party), *Polityka* (Warsaw), 25(9), 28 Feb.: 3.

Solzhenitsyn, A. (1974), *The Gulag Archipelago*, vol. I, Great Britain: Collins/Harvill Press and Fontana.

Solzhenitsyn, A. (1976), *The Gulag Archipelago*, Vol. II, Great Britain: Collins/Harvill Press and Fontana.

Soroka, J. (1981), 'Bunt w Kamińsku' (Rebellion in Kaminsk), *Solidarność* (Warsaw), no. 34, 20 Nov.: 5 and 14.

'Sovetskoye Gosudarstvo i Pravo Round-Table' (1980/1981), *Sovetskoye Gosudarstvo i Pravo*, no. 12, Dec. 1980: 112–38, condensed in *CDSP*, 33(6), 11 Mar.: 1–6 ('Alcohol Abuse in the USSR: a Symposium').

'Soviet Women Spend More Time Lining up than with Their Kids' (1983), *The Citizen* (Ottawa), 16 Apr.

'Spekulacja nadal groźna' (1984), (Speculation Still Dangerous), *Zycie Warszawy*, 21–2 Jan.: 6.

Spotowski, A. (1981), 'Przestepstwa naduzycia sluzbowego' (Abuses of Office), *Solidarność* (Warsaw), no. 9, 29 May: 10.

'Sprawa Patronatu' (1981), *Biuletyn Informacyjny*, no. 6, 21 Apr.: 42–4, Information Centre for Polish Affairs (UK).

Staats, S. J. (1972), 'Corruption in the Soviet System', *Problems of Communism*, 21(1), Jan.–Feb.: 40–7.

'Stan wojenny w oczach dzieci' (1983), (The State of War in Children's Eyes), *Kontakt* (Paris), no. 3 and 4, Mar.–Apr.: 28–9.

Starczak-Kozlowska, K. (1982), 'Zycie w galopie' (Life in a Gallop), *Fakty*, 24(39): 4–5.

Starr, S. F. (1981), 'Prehistory of a Counterculture, 1945–56'. Paper presented to the Annual Meeting of the American Association for Advancement of Slavic Studies in Asilomar.

Starukhin, A. and Khalin, A. (1979), 'The Citizen Society and the Law: It's Time to Exercise Authority', *Pravda*, 3 Aug.: 3, condensed in *CDSP*, 31(13), 29 Aug.: 11–12 ('Fight Against Crime Found Wanting in Chita').

'Statute of the Labour Colonies for Minors of the USSR Ministry for the Protection of Public Order' (1868–9), *Vedomosti Verkhovnogo Soveta SSSR*, no. 23, Item 189, 1968. Reprinted in *The Soviet Review*, 10(1), Spring 1969: 53–62.

Stead, D. G. and Sterling, J. S. (1982), 'Legal Change: the Case from Vagrancy to Parasite Laws in the Soviet Union'. Paper presented at the Annual Meeting of the Law and Society Association, Toronto, June 1982.

Steinbergowa, A. (1977), *Widziane z Ławy Obrończej* (Seen from the Defence Bench), Paris: Instytut Literacki.

Stern, M. (with A. Stern) (1980), *Sex in the USSR*, New York, N.Y.: The New York Times Co.

Steven, S. (1982), *The Poles*, New York: Macmillan Publ. Co. Inc.

Strogovich, M. S. (1977), 'On the Rights of the Individual in Soviet Criminal Procedure', *The Soviet Review*, 18.

Strzelecka, J. (1981a), 'Sedziowie' (Judges), *Solidarność* (Warsaw), no. 11, 12 June.

Strzelecka, J. (1981b), 'Prawa wieźniow' (Prisoners' Rights), *Solidarność* (Warsaw), no. 26, 25 Sept.: 13.

Survey. (1982), 26(3) (Summer): *Poland Under Jaruzelski*, part I; 26(4) (Automn): *Poland Under Jaruzelski*, part II.

Swiecicki, A. (1977), *Alkohol: Zagadnienia Polityki Spolecznej* (Alcohol. Social Policy Issues), Warszawa: Spoleczny Komitet Przeciwalkoholowy.

'Syn zamordowal matke w Radomiu' (1984), (Son Murdered Mother in Radom), *Zycie Warszawy*, 23 Mar.: 6.

'Sytuacja w PZPR' (1983), (The Situation in the Polish United Workers' Party), *Kontakt* (Paris), no. 11, Nov.: 44–5.

Szelhaus, St. (1968), 'Kwestia skuteczności dlugoterminowych kar pozbawienia wolności' (The Question of Effectiveness of Long-term Imprisonment), *Państwo i Prawo*, 11.

Szerer, M. (1964), *Karanie a Humanism* (Punishment and Humanism), *Warszawa*.

—— (1979), 'Komisja do Badania Odpowiedzialności za Łamanie Praworzadności w Sadownictwie Wojskowym' (A Commission to Investigate the Responsibility for Violations of Legality in the Military Courts), *Zeszyty Historyczne*, 49: 71–160, Paris: Instytut Literacki.

—— (1981), 'Procesy przed najwyźszym sadem wojskowym', *Solidarność* (Warsaw), no. 36, 4 Dec., 1981: 12–13.

Szymanowski, T. (1976), *Powrotność do Przestepstwa po Wykonaniu Kary Pozbawienia Wolności* (Recidivism Following a Term in Prison), Warsaw: Wydawnictwo Prawnicze.

'Soviet Women Spend More Time Lining up than with Their Kids' (1983), *The Citizen* (Ottawa), 16 Apr.

'Spekulacja nadal groźna' (1984), (Speculation Still Dangerous), *Zycie Warszawy*, 21–2 Jan.: 6.

Spotowski, A. (1981), 'Przestepstwa naduzycia sluzbowego' (Abuses of Office), *Solidarność* (Warsaw), no. 9, 29 May: 10.

'Sprawa Patronatu' (1981), *Biuletyn Informacyjny*, no. 6, 21 Apr.: 42–4, Information Centre for Polish Affairs (UK).

Staats, S. J. (1972), 'Corruption in the Soviet System', *Problems of Communism*, 21(1), Jan.–Feb.: 40–7.

'Stan wojenny w oczach dzieci' (1983), (The State of War in Children's Eyes), *Kontakt* (Paris), no. 3 and 4, Mar.–Apr.: 28–9.

Starczak-Kozlowska, K. (1982), 'Zycie w galopie' (Life in a Gallop), *Fakty*, 24(39): 4–5.

Starr, S. F. (1981), 'Prehistory of a Counterculture, 1945–56'. Paper presented to the Annual Meeting of the American Association for Advancement of Slavic Studies in Asilomar.

Starukhin, A. and Khalin, A. (1979), 'The Citizen Society and the Law: It's Time to Exercise Authority', *Pravda*, 3 Aug.: 3, condensed in *CDSP*, 31(13), 29 Aug.: 11–12 ('Fight Against Crime Found Wanting in Chita').

'Statute of the Labour Colonies for Minors of the USSR Ministry for the Protection of Public Order' (1968–9), *Vedomosti Verkhovnogo Soveta SSSR*, no. 23, Item 189, 1968. Reprinted in *The Soviet Review*, 10(1), Spring 1969: 53–62.

Stead, D. G. and Sterling, J. S. (1982), 'Legal Change: the Case from Vagrancy to Parasite Laws in the Soviet Union'. Paper presented at the Annual Meeting of the Law and Society Association, Toronto, June 1982.

Steinbergowa, A. (1977), *Widziane z Ławy Obrończej* (Seen from the Defence Bench), Paris: Instytut Literacki.

Stern, M. (with A. Stern) (1980), *Sex in the USSR*, New York, N.Y.: The New York Times Co.

Steven, S. (1982), *The Poles*, New York: Macmillan Publ. Co. Inc.

Strogovich, M. S. (1977), 'On the Rights of the Individual in Soviet Criminal Procedure', *The Soviet Review*, 18.

Strzelecka, J. (1981a), 'Sedziowie' (Judges), *Solidarność* (Warsaw), no. 11, 12 June.

Tairov, L. (1979), 'Unity of Word and Deed', *Pravda*, 19 July: 2, excerpted in *CDSP*, 31(31), 29 Aug.: 9 ('Azerbaidzhan: the Shake-Ups Continue').

Tairova, N. (1979) 'The Citizen, Society and the Law: Comrades' Courts', *Pravda*, 10 Sept.: 3, condensed in *CDSP*, 31(36), 3 Oct.: 4 ('Comrades' Courts Called Ineffective').

Targonsky, A. (1977), *A Research Project on Legal Consciousness Carried Out by the All-Union Institute for the Study of the Causes of Crime*, (A Text in Russian with an English summary), Jerusalem: Hebrew University, Soviet Institutions Series, Paper no. 9.

Tarnawski, M. (1983), 'O zapobieganiu narkomanii slów kilka' (Several Words About Drug Abuse Prevention), *Tygodnik Powszechny* (Cracow), 37(44), 30 Oct.: 3.

'Teraz dopiero przyszla "Solidarność"' (1982), (Only Now Has "Solidarity" Arrived), *Kontakt* (Paris), Apr.: 16–19.

Timofeev, L. (1982), 'Black Market Technology in the USSR: or the Peasants' Art of Starving', *Telos*, no. 51, Spring: 5–21.

Timofeyeva, S. (1983), 'Man and the Service Sector: Just Where Are the Spare Parts?', *Pravda*, 26 Jan.: 3, condensed in *CDSP*, 35(4), 23 Feb.: 25–6.

T.O. (1981), 'Patronat', *Orzel Bialy* – Na Antenie (London) 206/1353, Oct.: 21–2.

Topiński, P. (1981), 'Ochrona środowiska – urok bilansu' (Protection of Environment – the Beauty of Appraisal), *Solidarność* (Warsaw), no. 14, 2 July: 11.

Treml, V. G. (1975), 'Alcohol in the USSR: a Fiscal Dilemma', *Soviet Studies*, 27: 161–77.

Treml, V. G. (1981), 'Alcohol Underground in the USSR'. Paper presented at the Annual Convention of AAASS, Asilomar, California.

Troyan, S. (1983a), 'Face to Face with the Law: Moral Degradation', *Izvestia*, 11 Jan.: 6, condensed in *CDSP*, 35(2), 9 Feb.: 19.

Troyan, S. (1983b), 'Face to Face with the Law: Collapse of a Firm', *Izvestia*, 24 Mar.: 6, condensed in *CDSP*, 35(12), 20 Apr.: 23 ('State and Law').

Tu i Teraz, an official Polish weekly magazine established after the imposition of the state of war.

Tuhan-Mirza-Baranowska, I. *et al.* (1971) *Przestepczość Nieletnich w Warszawie* (Juvenile Delinquency in Warsaw), Warsaw: Wydawnictwo Prawnicze.

Tverdokhlebov, A. (1972), 'Notes on Legislation in the Realm of Intensification of the Struggle Against Individuals Evading Socially Useful Labor and Leading an Anti-Social Parasitic Way of Life'. Report to the Moscow Human Rights Committee. Reprinted in L. Lipson and V. Chalidze (eds), *Papers on Soviet Law*, (no. 1), New York: Institute on Socialist Law, pp. 108–27.

'Two Soviets Executed for Taking Bribes' (1984), *The Citizen* (Ottawa), 14 Jan.: 14.

Tygodnik Powszechny, a Polish Catholic weekly review (censored).

Udachin, V. (1983a), 'A "Guardian of the Law" is Sentenced', *Sovetskaya Rossia*, 22 Mar.: 2, condensed in *CDSP*, 35(12), 20 Apr.: 5 ('Payoffs, Cover-Ups Rampant in Krasnodar').

Udachin, V. (1983b), 'Bribetakers Punished', *Sovetskaya Rossia*, 1 Apr.: 2, condensed in *CDSP*, 35(13), 27 Apr.: 18.

'Ujecie sprawców bestialskiego mordu w Gdyni' (1984), (Arrest of the perpetrators of a
brutal murder in Gdynia), *Zycie Warszawy*, 20 Mar.: 6.

'Ujecie sprawców wlamania i zabójstwa' (1984), (Arrest of Perpetrators of a Break-In and Homicide), *Zycie Warszawy*, 15 Mar.: 6.

'Ujeto morderce kobiet' (1983), (Arrest of a Murderer of Women), *Zycie Warszawy*, 27 Oct.: 6.

'Ukaranie nieuczciwego milicjanta' (1983), (Dishonest Policeman is Punished), *Zycie Warszawy*, 8 Nov.: 4.

'Ukrywanie towarów' (1983), (Hiding of Goods), *Zycie Warszawy*, 21 Nov.: 4.

Urban, G. (1979), 'A Conversation with Milovan Djilas', *Encounter*, Dec.: 10–42.

Urbanek, M. (1984), 'Ośrodki przystosowania spolecznego' (Social Adjustment Centres), *Tygodnik Powszechny* (Cracow), 38(12), 18 Mar.: 5.

URSS. Les prisonniers d'opinion (1980), Rapport d'Amnesty International, Paris: Éditions Mazarine.

Van den Berg, G. P. (1983), 'The Soviet Union and the Death Penalty', *Soviet Studies*, 35(2), Apr.: 154–74.

Van Voren, R. (1983), *Political Psychiatry in the USSR*, Bukovsky Paper no. 1, Amsterdam: Bukovsky Foundation.

Victims of Crime (1983), Canadian Urban Victimization Survey, Bulletin 1, Ottawa: Solicitor General of Canada.

'Victims of war' (1983), *Committee in Support of Solidarity Reports* (New York), no. 13, 5 Apr.: 13–14.

Volgyes, I. and Peters, J. G. (1978), 'Social Deviance in Hungary: the Case of Prostitution', pp. 35–63 in I. Volgyes (ed.), *Social Deviance in Eastern Europe*, Boulder, Colorado: Westview Press.

Voronitsyn, S. (1974), 'The Problem of "Unmotivated" Juvenile Delinquency', *Radio Liberty Dispatch*, 25 Feb.

Voslensky, M. (1980a), *La nomenklatura: Les privilégiés en URSS*, Pierre Belfond. Le libre de Poche.

Voslensky, M. (1980b), 'URSS: une caste de trois millions de privilégiés', (interview by Kosta Christitch), *Le Point*, no. 417, 15 Sept.: 50–5.

Walczak, K. (1984), 'NIK o ochronie środowiska' (The Superior Chamber of Control on Environmental Protection), Zycie Warszawy, 14–16 Jan.: 6.

Wald, I., Kulisiewicz, T., Morawski, J. and Boguslawski, A. (1981), *Raport o Problemach Polityki w Zakresie Alkoholu*, Zespól Ekspertów przy Stalej Komisji Rady Ministrów do Spraw Walki z Alkoholizmem, Warsaw.

Waligóra, B. (1970), 'Psychologiczne problemy wykonania kary pozbawienia wolności' (Psychological Problems of Deprivation of Liberty), pp. 202–12 in *Prawnicy, Socjologowie i Psychologowie o Przestepczości i Jej Zwalczaniu*, Warsaw: Prokuratura Generalna.

Wasilewski, J. (1970), Wplyw wyników badań socjologicznych na podejmowanie decyzji ustawodawczych (The Impact of Sociological Findings on the Legislative Decision-Making), Unpublished MA thesis, University of Warsaw, Faculty of Social Sciences.

'We accuse' (1982), *Committee in Support of Solidarity* (New York), Jan.: 13: 1.

'Wegiel i krew' (1983), (Coal and blood), *Solidarność: Biuletyn Informacyjny* (Paris), no. 60, 27 Apr.: 6–7.

Weschler, L. (1982), *Solidarity: Poland in the Season of Its Passion*, New York: Simon & Schuster.

Weschler, L. (1983), 'A Reporter at Large (Poland. Part II)', *New Yorker*, 18 Apr.: 52–123.

Wesolowska, M. (1981), 'Korzenie zla' (The Roots of Evil), *Polityka* (Warsaw), 25(18), 2 May: 5.

Wheatcroft, S. G. (1983), 'Towards a Thorough Analysis of Soviet Forced Labour Statistics', *Soviet Studies*, 35(2), Apr.: 223–37.

Who's Who. What's What: Lexykon Zwiazkowy. (1981), (Union Lexicon), Gdansk: BIPS.

Wieczorkowska-Bednarek, I. (1982), 'Zdrowie tych co pija' ('To the Health' of Those Who Drink), *Kobieta i Zycie* (Warsaw), no. 20, 18 Aug.: 5.

Wiezień (1981), A letter in the column 'Listy z Wiezienia' (Letters from Prison), *Solidarność* (Warsaw), no. 8, 22 May: 8.

Wiezień X. (1981), A Letter in the Column 'Listy z Wiezienia' (Letters from Prison) *Solidarność* (Warsaw), no. 8, 22 May: 9.

'Wieźniowie polityczni' (1982), (Political Prisoners), *Documenty*, no. 2, 30 Oct.: 48, Stockholm: Biuro Solidarności.

'Wilful disobedience by inmates now punishable by up to five years' further imprisonment' (1984), *Amnesty International Bulletin*, Canadian Section, 9(1): 18.

Wilk, E. (1984a), 'Aspiracje mlodych' (Youth's aspirations), *Zycie Warszawy*, 3 Feb.: 3 and 6.

Wilk, E. (1984b), 'Zajecia pozalekcyjne w szerokim wachlarzu' (A Broad Scope of Extra-Curriculum Activities), *Zycie Warszawy*, 13 Mar.: 3.

Wnuk-Lipiński, E. (1982), 'Dimorphism of Values and Social Schizophrenia. A Tentative Description', pp. 81–9 in *Sisyphus: Sociological Studies*, (Vol. III, *Crises and Conflicts: the Case of Poland 1980–81*), Warsaw: PWN (Polish Scientific Publishers).

Wódź, J. (1981), 'Opinia publiczna, środki masowego komunikowania a przestepstwo zgwalcenia' (Public Opinion, the Mass Media and the Crime of Rape), pp. 157–68 in B. Holyst (ed.), *Opinia Publiczna i Srodki Masowego Przekazu a Ujemne Zjawiska Spoleczne*, Warsaw: Wydawnictwo Prawnicze.

Wóycicka, I. 'Pod kreska' (Below the line), *Solidarność* (Warsaw), no. 4, 24 Apr.: 11.

Wróblewski, A. K. (1981), 'Wychodzi, ze nie starczy' (It Looks as if There Will Be a Shortage), *Polityka* (Warsaw), 25(15), 11 Apr.: 1 and 4.

Wróblewski, W. (1981), 'Warunki w Wiezieniach' (Conditions in Prisons), *Orzel Bialy – Na Antenie* (London), nos 203–4/1350–1, July–Aug.: 28–30.

Wróblewski, W. (1982), 'Psychiatria na uslugach policji' (Psychiatry Working for the Police), *Orzel Bialy* (London), no. 1367/XLII, Dec.: 32–4.

'Wydalenie ze sluzby w organach MO' (1983), 'Dismissal from the Police Force'), *Zycie Warszawy*, 3–4 Dec.: 2.

'Wykonanie wyroku śmierci na W. Krakosie' (1983), (Execution of W. Krakos), *Zycie Warszawy*, 15–16 Oct.: 2.

'Wykonano wyrok na "podlaskim wampirze"' (1983), (A 'Vampire' Executed), *Zycie Warszawy*, 15 Dec.: 4.

'Wyrok w procesie zabójcy olsztyńskiego taksówkarza' (1984), (Sentence in the Trial of the Murderer of a Taxi-Driver in Olsztyn), *Zycie Warszawy*, 23 Jan.: 2.

'Wyroki za usilowanie zabójstwa milicjanta' (1984), (Sentences for Attempted Murder of a Policeman), *Zycie Warszawy*, 11 Jan.: 6.

Yin, J. (1982), 'Popular Participation in the Administration of Soviet Justice'. Paper presented to the Annual Meeting of the Canadian Association of Slavists at the University of Ottawa, June 1982.

'Z Sejmu: O tych co sie nie ucza i nie pracuja' (1982), (From the Diet: on Those Who Neither Study nor Work), *Polityka* (Warsaw), 25(6), 27 Mar.: 2.

'Zabil matke i udusil syna: Makabryczne morderstwo w Pruszkowie' (1984), (Killed a Mother and Strangled Her Son: Gruesome Murder in Pruszków), *Zycie Warszawy*, 15 Mar.: 6.

'Zabójstwo taksówkarza w Nowym Dworze Gdańskim' (1983), (Murder of a Taxi-Driver in Nowy Dwór Gdański), *Zycie Warszawy*, 27 Dec.: 2.

Zadrzyńska, E. and Juńczyk, E. (1981), 'Nieba nie widać' (No Sight of the Sky), *Tygodnik Powszechny* (Cracow), no. 32, 9 Aug.: 1 and 4.

'Zagrozenie zycia i zdrowia w wielu zakladach' (1984), (Threat to Life and Health in Many Industrial Plants), *Zycie Warszawy*, 10–11 Mar.: 2.

Zalega, B. (1981), 'O nieprawdziwej odpowiedzi ministerstwa' (About a False Answer by a Ministry), *Solidarność* (Warsaw), no. 36, 4 Dec.: 10.

'Zarzadzenie Ministra Sprawiedliwości z dnia 25 stycznia 1974 w sprawie tymczasowego regulaminu wykonywania kary pozbawienia wolności (Decree by Minister of Justice of 25 Jan. 1974 on temporary regulations on deprivation of liberty), Dziennik Urzedowy Ministerstwa Sprawiedliwości, Warsaw, no. 2, 2 Mar. 1974: 1–11.

'Zarzadzenie Ministra Sprawiedliwości z dnia 19 maja 1981 w sprawie zmiany tymczasowego regulaminu wykonywania kary pozbawienia wolności'

(Decree by Minister of Justice of 19 May 1981 on changes in temporary regulations on deprivation of liberty), *Dziennik Urzedowy Ministerstwa Sprawiedliwości*, Warsaw, no. 2, 30 Apr. 1981: 3–6.

'Zarzuty prokuratora wobec mecenasa Wl. Sily-Nowickiego' (1984), (Changes Against Attorney Wl. Sila-Nowicki), *Zycie Warszawy*, 2 Mar.: 6.

Zawadzki, S. and Kubicki, L. (1972), 'L'élément populaire et le juge professionnel dans la procédure pénale en Pologne', *Droit Polonais Contemporain*, no. 17/18: 31242.

Zawodny, J. K. (1962), *Death in the Forest: the Story of the Katyń Forest Massacre*, University of Indiana Press.

Zbrodnia Katyńska w Swietle Dokumentów (1982), (Katyń Crime in Light of Documents), London: Gryf (the 10th edn).

'Zbrodnia na zamówienie. Wynajeci mordercy stana przed sadem' (1983), (Contracted Crime: Hired Murderers Will Answer Before the Court), *Zycie Warszawy*, 2 Dec.: 5.

Zeldes, I. (1981), *The Problems of Crime in the USSR*, Springfield, Ill.: Charles C. Thomas.

Zemtsov, I. (1975), 'Problems of Soviet Youth', Radio Liberty Research, no. 125, 21 Mar.

—— (1976), *La corruption en Union Soviétique*, Paris: Les Editeurs Réunis.

—— (1979), 'The Ruling Class in the USSR', *Crossroads*, no. 2, Winter.

Zenczykowski, T. (1983), *Dwa Komitety: 1920, 1944* (Two Committees: 1920, 1944), Paris: Spotkania Editions.

Zieliński, T. (1978), 'Ubezpieczenia spoleczne w systemie prawa PRL' (Social Insurance in the Legal System of the Polish People's Republic), *Państwo i Prawo* (Warsaw), no. 10, Oct.: 33–46.

Zmarzlik, J. (1981), 'Zycie codzienne skazanego' (Daily Life of a Convict), *Solidarność* (Warsaw), no. 8, 22 May: 8–9.

Zukowska, A. (1981), 'Nie wierze w przymus' (I Do Not Believe in Coercion), *Kobieta i Zycie* (Warsaw), no. 50, 13 Dec.: 5.

Zycie i Nowoczesność (1981), A Supplement to *Zycie Warszawy*, 16 Apr.

Zycie Literackie, an official Polish weekly magazine.

Zycie Warszawy, an official Polish nationwide daily newspaper, published in Warsaw.

Index